Psychology, Law, and the Wellbeing of Children

American Psychology-Law Society Series

Series Editor
Patricia A. Zapf

Editorial Board
Gail S. Goodman
Thomas Grisso
Craig Haney
Kirk Heilbrun
John Monahan
Marlene Moretti
Edward P. Mulvey
J. Don Read
N. Dickon Reppucci
Ronald Roesch
Gary L. Wells
Lawrence S. Wrightsman

Books in the Series

Trial Consulting
Amy J. Posey and Lawrence S. Wrightsman

Death by Design
Craig Haney

Psychological Injuries
William J. Koch, Kevin S. Douglas, Tonia L. Nicholls, and Melanie L. O'Neill

Emergency Department Treatment of the Psychiatric Patient
Susan Stefan

The Psychology of the Supreme Court
Lawrence S. Wrightsman

Proving the Unprovable
Christopher Slobogin

Adolescents, Media, and the Law
Roger J. R. Levesque

Oral Arguments Before the Supreme Court
Lawrence S. Wrightsman

God in the Courtroom
Brian H. Bornstein and Monica K. Miller

Expert Testimony on the Psychology of Eyewitness Identification
Edited by Brian L. Cutler

The Psychology of Judicial Decision-Making
Edited by David Klein and Gregory Mitchell

The Miranda Ruling: Its Past, Present, and Future
Lawrence S. Wrightsman and Mary L. Pitman

Juveniles at Risk: A Plea for Preventive Justice
Christopher Slobogin and Mark R. Fondacaro

The Ethics of Total Confinement
Bruce A. Arrigo, Heather Y. Bersot, and Brian G. Sellers

International Human Rights and Mental Disability Law
Michael L. Perlin

Using Social Science to Reduce Violent Offending
Edited by Joel Dvoskin, Jennifer L. Skeem, Raymond W. Novaco, and Kevin S. Douglas

Children Who Resist Postseparation Parental Contact
Barbara Jo Fidler, Nicholas Bala, and Michael A. Saini

Stress, Trauma, and Wellbeing in the Legal System
Edited by Monica K. Miller and Brian H. Bornstein

Psychology, Law, and the Wellbeing of Children
Edited by Monica K. Miller, Jared Chamberlain, and Twila Wingrove

Psychology, Law, and the Wellbeing of Children

Edited by

Monica K. Miller

Jared Chamberlain

Twila Wingrove

UNIVERSITY PRESS

Oxford University Press is a department of the University of Oxford.
It furthers the University's objective of excellence in research, scholarship,
and education by publishing worldwide.

Oxford   New York
Auckland   Cape Town   Dar es Salaam   Hong Kong   Karachi
Kuala Lumpur   Madrid   Melbourne   Mexico City   Nairobi
New Delhi   Shanghai   Taipei   Toronto

With offices in
Argentina   Austria   Brazil   Chile   Czech Republic   France   Greece
Guatemala   Hungary   Italy   Japan   Poland   Portugal   Singapore
South Korea   Switzerland   Thailand   Turkey   Ukraine   Vietnam

Oxford is a registered trademark of Oxford University Press
in the UK and certain other countries.

Published in the United States of America by
Oxford University Press
198 Madison Avenue, New York, NY 10016

© Oxford University Press 2014

All rights reserved. No part of this publication may be reproduced, stored in a
retrieval system, or transmitted, in any form or by any means, without the prior
permission in writing of Oxford University Press, or as expressly permitted by law,
by license, or under terms agreed with the appropriate reproduction rights organization.
Inquiries concerning reproduction outside the scope of the above should be sent to the Rights
Department, Oxford University Press, at the address above.

You must not circulate this work in any other form
and you must impose this same condition on any acquirer.

Library of Congress Cataloging-in-Publication Data
Psychology, law, and the wellbeing of children / edited by Monica K. Miller, Jared C. Chamberlain,
Twila Wingrove.
   pages cm. — (American Psychology-Law Society series)
Includes index.
ISBN 978-0-19-993421-8
1. Children—Legal status, laws, etc.—United States.   2. Forensic child psychology.
I. Miller, Monica K., editor of compilation.   II. Chamberlain, Jared C.,
editor of compilation.   III. Wingrove, Twila, editor of compilation.
K639.P79 2014
342.08′772—dc23   2013028794

To my sister Brenda, who enhanced my childhood wellbeing in more ways than she will ever know.

—MM

To my brothers, Brandon, Cory, and Caleb, who sometimes challenged, but ultimately strengthened, my wellbeing.

—JC

To my grandparents, Andy and Lou, who provided me unconditional love and encouragement. If that isn't the foundation for wellbeing, I don't know what is.

—TW

Contents

Series Foreword ix
Acknowledgments xi
About the Editors xv
Contributors xvii

1 Psychology, Law, and the Wellbeing of Children: An Overview 1
 Monica K. Miller and Jared Chamberlain

2 Psychology, Law, and the Wellbeing of Children: A Developmental Perspective 13
 Twila Wingrove and Sarah J. Beal

Part I: Legal Actions Affecting the Wellbeing and Recognizing (or Ignoring) the Developmental Abilities of Juvenile Delinquents

3 Psycholegal Aspects of Juvenile Delinquency 33
 Cheryl D. Wills

4 Police Interviewing and Interrogation of Adolescent Suspects: Process and Outcomes 50
 Hayley M. D. Cleary and Sarah Vidal

5 Applying Sex Offender Registry Laws to Juvenile Offenders: Biases Against Stigmatized Youth   66
Jessica M. Salerno, Margaret Stevenson, Cynthia J. Najdowski, Tisha R. A. Wiley, Bette L. Bottoms, and Liana Peter-Hagene

6 Female Juvenile Offenders' Perceptions of Gender-Specific Programs   83
Monica K. Miller, Lacey Miller, and Angela D. Broadus

7 Balancing Legal, Ethical, and Clinical Considerations When Managing Suicidality in Research With Juvenile Justice–Involved Youth   103
Christy L. Giallella, Naomi E. S. Goldstein, and David DeMatteo

Part II: Legal Actions Affecting the Wellbeing of Children Experiencing Parental Divorce

8 Hearing the Voice of the Child in Divorce   121
Robin H. Ballard, Brittany N. Rudd, Amy G. Applegate, and Amy Holtzworth-Munroe

9 Establishing Child Support and Visitation Enforcement Offices: Promoting Fairness, Compliance, and Children's Wellbeing   138
Monica K. Miller and Jon Maskaly

10 Parental Alienation and the Best Interests of the Child   155
R. Brian Howe and Katherine Covell

Part III: Legal Actions Affecting the Wellbeing of Children

11 The Search for Therapeutic Solutions to Maternal Incarceration: Promoting the Wellbeing of Children   173
Monica K. Miller and Lacey Miller

12 Immigrant Parents' Perceptions of the "Best Interests of the Child"   192
Qingwen Xu

13 Assessment of Mock Jurors' Attributions and Decisions in Child Abuse Cases: Protecting the Wellbeing of Obese Children   210
Jenny Reichert and Monica K. Miller

14 A Preliminary Analysis of Public Commentary Supporting and Opposing Mandatory HPV Vaccination: Implications for Policy   234
Lorie L. Sicafuse and Monica K. Miller

15 The Law and Child Wellbeing: Where Are We and Where Do We Go From Here?   255
Twila Wingrove and Jennifer L. Jarrett

Index   269

Series Foreword

This book series is sponsored by the American Psychology-Law Society (APLS). APLS is an interdisciplinary organizations devoted to scholarship, practice, and public service in psychology and law. Its goals include advancing the contributions of psychology to the understanding of law and legal institutions through basic and applied research; promoting the education of psychologists in matters of law and the education of legal personnel in matters of psychology; and informing the psychological and legal communities and the general public of current research, educational, and service activities in the field of psychology and law. APLS membership includes psychologists from the academic, research, and clinical practice communities as well as members of the legal community. Research and practice is represented in both the civil and criminal legal arenas. APLS has chosen Oxford University Press as a strategic partner because of its commitment to scholarship, quality, and the international dissemination of ideas. These strengths will help APLS reach its goal of educating the psychology and legal professions and the general public about important developments in psychology and law. The focus of the book series reflects the diversity of the field of psychology and law, as we will publish books on a broad range of topics.

In the latest book in the series, *Psychology, Law, and the Wellbeing of Children*, Monica Miller, Jared Chamberlain, and Twila Wingrove have compiled a series of chapters, each presenting research and psycholegal analysis of various legal actions that affect the wellbeing of children and adolescents involved with the legal system. The book is divided into three parts: In the first part, various legal actions that affect the wellbeing of juveniles involved with the legal system are presented; the second part examines issues relevant to children experiencing parental divorce; and the final part examines legal actions that affect the wellbeing of children. Each of the chapters presents a synthesis of the empirical literature and a psycholegal analysis of the most relevant issues regarding the wellbeing of children and adolescents. Both positive and negative aspects of wellbeing are included to provide a broad perspective on wellbeing in the legal system. The result of this approach is a broad perspective with unique insights into how the legal system can be changed to promote the wellbeing of children and adolescents and those who are involved with these populations as service providers.

Miller, Chamberlain, and Wingrove begin by providing an introduction to the organization of the book and the themes that run throughout as well as a developmental perspective to provide relevant background for the reader. In Part I, issues relevant to juvenile delinquents are discussed, including police interviewing and interrogation, sex offender registry laws, gender-specific programming, and issues related to suicidality. In Part II, legal actions affecting the wellbeing of children involved in parental divorce are presented, including hearing the voice of the child in divorce, child support and visitation issues, and parental alienation concerns. Part III presents issues relevant to the wellbeing of children, including maternal incarceration, best interests of the child, child abuse and the special issue of childhood obesity, and mandatory HPV vaccination. Finally, the editors present a conclusory chapter that reiterates the themes throughout the book and discusses strategies for moving forward.

Psychology, Law, and the Wellbeing of Children presents a comprehensive and detailed analysis of issues most relevant to improving the experiences of juveniles and children who participate within the legal system at various levels and in various roles. Practitioners, scholars, and researchers will undoubtedly find that this book has the potential to help to shape the future of interactions with the legal system.

Patricia A. Zapf
Series Editor

Acknowledgments

Every morning, I'm welcomed into the new day by wagging tails and pleas for a morning hike in the Sierra Mountain foothills that rest right outside my door. My furry friends are the bastions of my wellbeing, and hiking promotes wellbeing in all of us. During these walks, I continuously monitor the environment for threats such as coyotes and rattlesnakes, largely as a protective measure for my dogs who are unaware of such threats. While on one such hike, I started thinking about the way the law promotes or hinders wellbeing of groups like children (and my dogs!) who are not fully capable of being their own advocates or protecting their wellbeing (or sometimes even knowing what is best for their wellbeing). The nexus of psychology and law is the perfect place to begin an investigation of children's wellbeing. "Psychology" can define and measure wellbeing, while the "law" can promote or hinder wellbeing through legal actions, policies, and processes.

This book sprung from these thoughts. Of course, the topic of "psychology, law, and the wellbeing of children" is quite broad, and it would be difficult for any one person to cover the entire topic with adequate attention and expertise. Thus, I realized quickly that the book would be an edited volume. I'm confident the authors have supplied the necessary attention and applied their expertise to make this a good read for anyone interested in these topics.

After formulating a rough idea for the book, I recruited two able editors I knew could provide their own expertise and skills. When Jared arrived at the University of Nevada, Reno as my graduate student, I'm not sure whether he knew his path would lead him to studying the wellbeing of children. As he initially intended, our first works dealt with jury decision making. But it wasn't long before he was authoring articles concerning how laws and legal actions affect children of gay parents. And so he got sucked into the world of psychology, law, and the wellbeing of children. Twila and I met—dare I say it—nearly 15 years ago. We both developed our passion for using social science and justice principles to study children's wellbeing while working as graduate students at the Center for Children, Families, and the Law in Lincoln, Nebraska. The Center was elemental in developing our interests in this area, and we are grateful for the advising and opportunities that cultivated our interests in children's wellbeing. Back in the day, who knew that someday we'd be putting together a complete volume of such topics!

The three of us put our heads together and came up with the plan for the book you're holding right now. Despite the thousands of miles and three time zones between us, we were able to make it work. As I expected, it was a delightful experience that I would repeat again. Working on this book gave us an excuse to stay in touch, bounce ideas off one another, and strengthen and build friendships.

We are very fortunate that the American Psychology-Law Society book series and Oxford University Press were interested in publishing the book. I'd previously had great experiences publishing with both and was confident this would be a great match. Jared, Twila, and I are honored to be part of the APLS and Oxford teams.

As with any project of this magnitude, we could not have done it alone. There are lots of people who made this possible. For most of the period during which the book was being edited, I (Monica) was on sabbatical leave from the University of Nevada, Reno. I am deeply grateful for the time away from teaching and day-to-day professorial responsibilities, which enabled me to concentrate on this project. For a good part of the fall, I was at the International Institute for Sociology and Law in Oñati, Spain. I am grateful for the use of their incredible library, professional and personal support, and a quiet and beautiful place to work. I'd also like to thank the UNR College of Liberal Arts Scholarly and Creative Activities Grant Program for funding that enabled me to stay in Spain and work on this project (and others).

The reviewers of the book prospectus were very helpful in providing thoughtful and encouraging feedback even before we began the book itself. We also thank all the chapter authors who provided their insights, were unusually responsive to feedback, and put up with all our edits to make the individual chapters fit together as a cohesive book. The chapter authors are really what make this book such a success! A special thanks goes to Patty Zapf, editor of the American Psychology-Law Society book series. Without her patience and valuable input, this book would not have been possible. And of course Sarah Harrington, Andrea Zekus, and everyone else at Oxford University Press deserve a great big "thank you" for making the publishing process relatively painless.

Both before and during the production of this book, there were many who provided support, whether it was moral support when the work piled up, cheerleading support for celebrating our milestones, or scholarly support when we needed some feedback. We are especially grateful for our friends and family who are always there for us—during this project and beyond. Monica would like to thank Bart Lydon for his unwavering love, support, and laughter; and all her colleagues at UNR and beyond who have provided encouragement along the way. Jared would like to thank all his colleagues at the Arizona School of Professional Psychology for their scholarly help, his wife Jaclyn for her love and support, and the Phoenix heat for keeping him indoors (and focused on editing). Twila would like to thank her colleagues in the "junior faculty wing" at Appalachian State University—Lisa Emery, J. P. Jameson, and Will Canu—for listening patiently, offering sound advice, informal support, and, when all else failed, an impromptu happy hour.

Brian Bornstein also deserves a special "thanks" for putting the idea of "wellbeing in the legal system" in my head by hiring me (Monica) as a graduate student assistant to work on his grant studying juror stress (and we won't even mention how many years ago *that* was!)

Along the way, our family, friends, and significant others lent support by asking, "How's the book coming along?", offering a neck rub, humoring us as we described the ins and outs of editing a book, and patiently tolerating our absences. Our friends and family (even the furry, four-legged ones!) also gave us good reason to take breaks from working so we could enjoy the world around us. They contributed to this book more than they can imagine. Celebrating our accomplishments would mean little if they were not here to share the moment with us. In the spirit of the book's theme, we thank all of these people for everything they do to enhance our wellbeing.

About the Editors

Monica K. Miller, J.D., Ph.D., is an associate professor with a split appointment between the Criminal Justice Department and the Interdisciplinary Ph.D. Program in Social Psychology. She is the director of the Criminal Justice Department's graduate program. She is also an adjunct faculty member at the Grant Sawyer Center for Justice Studies and a faculty associate for the Women's Studies Program. Her interests involve the application of psychological theories and justice principles to laws and policies. Specifically, she is interested in the role of religion in the legal system; how the law regulates sexual behavior, pregnancy, and family issues; jury decision making; and community sentiment and public policy.

Jared Chamberlain, Ph.D., is an assistant professor at the Arizona School of Professional Psychology (ASPP) at Argosy University, Phoenix. As a social psychologist with research interests in legal and policy issues, he has published articles concerning celebrity influences in the legal system, stress among the judiciary, and the legal rights and responsibilities of gay parents. Dr. Chamberlain also works part-time as a trial consultant in the Phoenix area.

Twila Wingrove, J.D., Ph.D., is an assistant professor in the Department of Psychology at Appalachian State University. Dr. Wingrove is a legal psychologist with interests in children's involvement in the legal system. She has published articles regarding juvenile adjudicative competence, child protection, and procedural justice theory as it applies to children and the law.

Contributors

Amy G. Applegate, J.D.
Indiana University Maurer School of Law

Robin H. Ballard, Ph.D.
Ryther Child Center in Seattle, Washington

Sarah J. Beal, Ph.D.
Cincinnati Children's Hospital and Medical Center

Bette L. Bottoms, Ph.D.
University of Illinois at Chicago

Angela D. Broadus, Ph.D.
University of Nevada, Reno

Jared Chamberlain, Ph.D.
Arizona School of Professional Psychology at Argosy University, Phoenix

Hayley M. D. Cleary, MPP, Ph.D.
Virginia Commonwealth University

Katherine Covell, Ph.D.
Cape Breton University, Canada

David DeMatteo, J.D., Ph.D.
Drexel University

Christy L. Giallella, M.S.
Drexel University

Naomi E. S. Goldstein, Ph.D.
Drexel University

Amy Holtzworth-Munroe, Ph.D.
Indiana University–Bloomington

R. Brian Howe, Ph.D.
Cape Breton University, Canada

Jennifer L. Jarrett, M.A.
Appalachian State University

Jon Maskaly, M.A.
East Carolina University

Lacey Miller, M.A.
University of Nevada, Reno

Monica K. Miller, J.D., Ph.D.
University of Nevada, Reno

Cynthia J. Najdowski, Ph.D.
University at Albany–SUNY

Liana Peter-Hagene, M.A.
University of Illinois at Chicago

Jenny Reichert, Ph.D. (ABD)
University of Nevada, Reno

Brittany N. Rudd, B.A.
Indiana University–Bloomington

Jessica M. Salerno, Ph.D.
Arizona State University

Lorie L. Sicafuse, Ph.D. (ABD)
University of Nevada, Reno

Margaret Stevenson, Ph.D.
University of Evansville

Sarah Vidal, MPP
Georgetown University

Tisha R. A. Wiley, Ph.D.
National Institute on Drug Abuse

Cheryl D. Wills, M.D.
Western Reserve University
University Hospitals of Cleveland

Twila Wingrove, J.D., Ph.D.
Appalachian State University

Qingwen Xu, Ph.D.
Tulane University

Psychology, Law, and the Wellbeing of Children

1

Psychology, Law, and the Wellbeing of Children: An Overview

Monica K. Miller and Jared Chamberlain

"Psychology, law, and the wellbeing of children." What does that mean? When thinking of these terms, together and separately, there are many images that might come to mind. A child experiencing confusion and anxiety as he is being interviewed by police; a child feeling sad and invisible as his parents divorce; an immigrant child struggling to adapt to a new culture while being pressured by her parents to maintain the native culture; a child struggling to cope with separation from his mother while she is incarcerated; a juvenile delinquent coping with the mental illness that underlies his behavior. Any of these images—and countless others—may come to mind. All are topics that were selected for this book because they are at the nexus of law, psychology, and the wellbeing of children.

The present volume reviews legal developments and social science research concerning legal actions that affect the wellbeing of children. Thus, defining these terms establishes an important foundation for the rest of the book.

What Is Psychology?

Psychology is broadly defined as the study of human behavior, cognition, and affect. Two subdisciplines within the field—developmental psychology and social psychology—will be explored and utilized throughout this volume. A basic discussion of developmental psychology—which focuses on physical and psychological change throughout the life span—is essential in understanding many of the topics contained in this book. Thus, Chapter 2 introduces the elements of developmental psychology that are germane to the study of law and children's wellbeing. Other chapters further this goal. Chapter 3 traces the history of the juvenile justice system and discusses how the structure and procedures of the system have (or have not) been based on consideration of juveniles' developmental capacities; the chapter also focuses more specifically on the developmental needs of female and mentally ill juvenile delinquents. Chapter 4 addresses juveniles' maturity and capacity to understand their rights during police interrogations. Chapter 5 addresses how the developmental maturity of the child plays a role in whether and how much voice a child should have in his living situation after his parents' divorce. These chapters highlight how children's maturity and development can interact with legal procedures to affect children's wellbeing.

Several areas within the realm of social psychology—defined as the study of how people think, feel, and act in social contexts—will also be addressed, including gender, culture, mental health, and attitudes. For instance, Chapters 3 and 6 discuss the special gender-related rehabilitative needs of female juveniles, and Chapter 11 discusses how meeting the needs of incarcerated mothers can benefit their children. Chapter 12 describes the cultural differences that might make immigrant parents the targets of a child protection investigation. Chapters 10 and 11 discuss how interactions with the law can affect children's mental health, including anxiety, depression, and self-esteem, and Chapter 3 discusses how mental health issues often underlie juvenile delinquency. Finally, several chapters address how attitudes toward legal issues are important: Chapter 14 discusses the importance of community sentiment in shaping legislation toward mandatory HPV vaccinations. Chapter 5 discusses how prejudice or biased attitudes against juveniles (e.g., based on race, sexual orientation, socioeconomic status) can lead to harsher penalties. As these examples highlight, the psychological perspectives contained within this book are numerous, as are the psychological effects children can experience because of their interactions with the law.

What Is Law?

The second definition critical to the foundation of this book is the term "law." In this book, we define law broadly to encompass laws, policies, and actions of a wide range of legal actors. For instance, the chapters address legislation (Chapters 5 and 14), the United Nations Convention on the Rights of the Child (Chapters 9 and 10), and a range of policies (Chapters 8 and 9). The book also focuses on the actions or decisions of child protection workers (Chapter 12), guardians ad litem (Chapter 8), judges (Chapters 8, 10, and 12), jurors (Chapter 13), police (Chapter 4), and the public (Chapter 14). Finally, the book focuses on legal institutions such as juvenile detention centers (Chapters 3 and 6), prisons (Chapter 11), child protection services (Chapter 12), and courts (Chapters 8, 9, and 10). This broad definition of "law" illustrates the difficulty in finding an area of the legal system that does not have potential to affect children's wellbeing.

What Is Wellbeing?

The final core definition involves the book's approach to wellbeing. There is a diversity of measures and definitions of wellbeing, a diversity of steps the law has taken to protect children's wellbeing, and a diversity of ways the law can affect children's wellbeing for better or worse. The term "wellbeing" is rather elusive; it is also quite inclusive. It generally refers to the state of one's mental or physical health (e.g., Miller & Bornstein, 2013). Wellbeing threats can range from minor inconveniences to devastating losses or injuries. In this book, authors use the definitions and measures of "wellbeing" most commonly used in their particular subfield. For instance, Chapter 11 reviews research indicating that children of imprisoned mothers are susceptible to anxiety, depression, school dropout, and violence. Some chapters address physical health aspects of wellbeing. For instance, Chapter 14 addresses child wellbeing as related to vaccinations that prevent HPV and cervical cancer, Chapters 3 and 7 discuss children's risks of suicide, and Chapter 13 addresses childhood obesity as a threat to wellbeing. Wellbeing can also be measured by quality and quantity of the child's relationships. Chapter 10 discusses how loss of a relationship with a parent due to parental alienation can affect a child's ability to trust others and develop future relationships. Similarly, Chapter 9 discusses how a child custody office could promote parent–child relationships. Wellbeing can also be measured by children's treatment within the legal system. Children's wellbeing can be harmed if they are labeled as a sex offender (Chapter 5) or give up due process rights (Chapter 4). In contrast, children's wellbeing can benefit if the children have a say in their living situation after parental divorce (Chapter 8) or receive appropriate rehabilitation (Chapter 3 and 6).

In addition to these psychology-based definitions of wellbeing, there is also a legal definition related to children's wellbeing; it is typically referred to as the "best interests of the child" standard and is used in making many legal decisions. For instance, Chapters 9 and 10 focus on the best interests of the child to have a healthy relationship with both parents. Similarly, Chapter 8 notes that the best interests might involve giving children a voice in custody decisions, while Chapter 4 discusses the best interests of juveniles who are being questioned by police.

In sum, the definitions, causes, and measures of wellbeing are quite varied. This will become evident as the reader explores each chapter in this volume.

Should the Legal System Address the Wellbeing of Children?

Should legal actors—judges, jurors, lawmakers, and policymakers—and legal institutions address issues related to the wellbeing of children? This is a normative question, with legitimate "no" and "yes" answers. On one hand, there are reasons the answer should be "no." First, perhaps wellbeing concerns are not within the range of responsibilities of legal actors. Strictly speaking, legal actors are supposed to uphold the law and interpret the Constitution—they are not counselors, nor are they social scientists. Thus, considerations about a child's wellbeing may only serve to confound and disrupt the legal process. Second, given the often strenuous nature of the legal profession, legal actors may not have the time and cognitive resources to address issues related to children's wellbeing. For instance, a judge determining a child custody case might not have the time to examine and apply current research about the best interests of the child. Finally, legal actors may not be qualified to assume the role of counselor or social scientist. For instance, a legislator may not have the research acumen to fully and accurately interpret social science research that may inform decisions. In short, proponents of this perspective would argue that the legal system is designed to address legal issues—not psychological ones.

On the other hand, there are many reasons the answer to this question should be "yes." First, it may be unconstitutional to ignore developmental differences in juveniles. For instance, Justice Kennedy cited research supporting developmental differences between juveniles and adults in *Roper v. Simmons* (2005). Thus, the Supreme Court has established a precedent for utilizing research in determining the wellbeing of children as a legal consideration. Second, if people have negative impressions of the legal system resulting from perceived injustice, they may lose faith in the system: They may fail to report crimes, fail to follow the laws, fail to vote, refuse to serve on a jury, and have reduced feelings that the system has "legitimacy" (Tyler, 2006). Taken further, those who feel that the legal system is unfair may decide not to work for the legal system or government as a whole. Therefore, it is important to consider fairness and wellbeing because doing so will encourage citizens to invest in the legal system. Third, threats to wellbeing have personal, societal, and legal consequences that can be both immediate and long term. For instance, a failure to consider wellbeing could lead to a child being separated from one parent. In the short term, this might lead to attachment and relationship issues and these maladaptive processes *could* later manifest into divorce, domestic violence, and child abuse. A failure to consider a child's wellbeing in the legal process may also be connected to a greater risk of crime, missed days of work, alcoholism, and even suicide. These have obvious negative implications for the individuals directly impacted, but society as a whole may pay a large price for neglecting the wellbeing of children in both fiscal (increased taxes) and legal (increased crime) terms.

Therapeutic jurisprudence, the study of law as a therapeutic agent (Wexler, 1995), suggests that legal actors should aim to maximize positive and minimize negative outcomes for those affected—children in this case. From this perspective, legal actors can and should consider therapeutic outcomes to promote the wellbeing of those impacted by the legal system (see Sicafuse

& Bornstein, 2013). For these reasons, and others beyond the scope of this chapter, it is important that the legal system protect and promote the wellbeing of children. Although this has become a recent imperative among scholars, judges, and lawmakers, the legal system has sometimes failed to consider children's wellbeing, as will be discussed in the next section.

Children in the Legal System: Historical and Current Approaches

In the early history of the United States, the special needs of juveniles were rarely considered as policymakers were constructing laws, policies, and legal procedures. Through the years, the courts have shifted between rehabilitative and retributive approaches (see Chapter 3 for a detailed history of the juvenile courts). Similarly, the understanding of children's psychological development has shifted over time. At one time, juveniles were treated under the English Common Law Rule of Sevens: Offenders under 7 years were not culpable, offenders over 14 were culpable for all purposes, and offenders between 7 and 14 were culpable only if the prosecutor showed sufficient evidence of maturity. In the 1820s, courts started sending juveniles to Houses of Refuge and other "rehabilitation" homes, sometimes for indeterminate periods of time. The early 1900s saw the rise of juvenile courts, which were primarily designed to protect abused and neglected children and to rehabilitate delinquents. Juvenile courts treated juveniles in a way that was less criminalized (e.g., by using different terms than the adult criminal courts). In the 1960s, the Supreme Court started granting juveniles due process rights such as the right to notice of hearings, the right to remain silent, and the right to confront witnesses (e.g., *In re Gault*, 1967; *Kent v. US*, 1966). Indeterminate sentences were declared unconstitutional. Such rulings protected juveniles' rights and recognized their need for special treatment.

Eventually, however, the use of waivers became popular; this led to juveniles being tried in adult court and receiving adult punishments, including prison and the death penalty. That is, until *Roper v. Simmons* (2005), when the Supreme Court ruled that juveniles cannot receive the death penalty. Judges in this case and others have recognized that juveniles' development and cognitive capacities are different from adults' in ways that make them less culpable (e.g., they have less impulse control and ability to understand long-term consequences of behavior). This reasoning was reflected in *Miller v. Alabama* (2012), when the Court determined that youth has to be considered as a mitigating factor before a juvenile can be sentenced to life without parole. Such cases protect juvenile offenders by making them ineligible for the most severe punishments—or at least requiring the sentencer to consider their youth before delivering an extreme punishment. Courts have also tackled issues of police procedures involving juveniles; for instance, *J.D.B. v. North Carolina* (2011) required police to consider the offender's age when making decisions related to interrogating and holding juveniles in custody (see Chapters 3 and 4 for the history of court cases involving juvenile offenders' rights). Importantly, many of these cases have increasingly recognized the role of psychology in determining the capacities of juveniles.

Children who are not accused of crime but are nevertheless involved in the legal system have also received special treatment designed to promote their wellbeing. For instance, juvenile victims can testify behind screens or on closed-circuit TV (Rush, Quas, & McAuliff, 2013) and juveniles are sometimes asked their opinions about their living situations when their parents divorce (Chapter 8, this volume). Lawmakers have required vaccinations to protect children's health (Chapter 14), and prosecutors have sought to prosecute or terminate the parental rights of parents who allowed their children to become obese (Chapter 13). Prisons have adopted programs that allow incarcerated mothers to maintain and improve their relationships with their children (Chapter 11). Thus, the steps the legal system has taken to protect children's wellbeing are many and varied.

Some of the chapters in this book detail the history of the law and psychology as they relate to children's wellbeing in certain domains (e.g., juvenile offenders, divorce). While there are many situations in which children can become involved in the legal system, this book focuses on a few that have received a great amount of attention from lawmakers and researchers in recent years. The topics selected for this book are among the most current and hotly debated topics in psychology and law as pertaining to children. For instance, Chapter 8 discusses an innovative new approach to allowing children to voice their opinions during their parents' divorce; Chapter 5 discusses newly adopted or proposed laws against "sexting," which have implications for juvenile offenders; Chapter 14 discusses laws that are proposed or recently adopted which require children to receive HPV vaccinations; and Chapter 6 discusses gender-specific programming that is gaining popularity in many juvenile detention centers. As a whole, the book presents a wide variety of legal actions that have implications for psychology and the wellbeing of children.

Recurring Themes

The book has several themes that run through multiple chapters. First, many chapters address the relationship between sentiment and the law. The sentiment of the general public (Chapters 5 and 14), parents (Chapter 12), child welfare workers (Chapter 12), jurors (Chapter 13), and guardians ad litem (Chapter 8) are all explored in this book. Such sentiment may vary by culture (Chapter 12), individual traits (Chapter 5 and 13), and beliefs/motivations (Chapter 5 and 14) of the decision maker. Each of these chapters suggests that laws should be consistent with sentiment.

Second, several chapters discuss how children's developmental abilities and limitations can affect their wellbeing when they become involved in the legal system. This starts with an introduction to a developmental perspective on children's wellbeing (Chapter 2) and includes discussions and data about children's capacities to be interviewed (Chapters 4 and 8), make major life decisions (Chapter 8), and benefit from specifically tailored treatments (Chapter 6). These chapters provide new (Chapters 4 and 6) and existing (Chapter 8) empirical data to understand how to account for children's developmental perspectives in various legal contexts (see also Chapter 3 for discussion of whether the legal system considers children's development).

A third common theme among chapters is the "best interests of the child" standard the legal system often uses when making decisions about children. Perceptions of this standard may vary by culture (see Chapter 12), children may not be competent to understand their own best interests (see Chapter 8), and legal actors make potentially faulty assumptions about what is in the children's best interests (Chapters 9 and 10). These chapters highlight the importance of the best interests standard as a mechanism challenging judges and lawmakers to consider how laws, policies, and decisions will impact a child's wellbeing, despite the fact that perceptions of "best interests" can be inconsistent across different perspectives and based on faulty information.

An additional theme among chapters is that most deal with ethical considerations (Chapter 7) and justice principles, including legitimacy (Chapters 9, 10, 11, and 14), therapeutic jurisprudence (Chapter 6 and 11), procedural justice (Chapters 4, 9, and 14), and distributive justice (Chapter 9). These chapters underscore the importance of considering how the law is perceived and impacts children and their families; they also argue for legal actors to consider wellbeing when making legal decisions.

A final common theme among all chapters is that each offers suggestions for policies, procedures, and laws. Specific recommendations are made for legal processes that impact female juvenile offenders (Chapter 3), policies surrounding police interrogation of adolescents (Chapter 4), procedures for determining suicide risk in child participants (Chapter 7), and measures to address parental alienation (Chapter 10), to name a few. Most chapters (Chapter 4, 5, 6, 7, 11, 12, 13, and 14) also make suggestions for researchers. For instance, these chapters highlight the need for future research to investigate factors that impact community sentiment about child sex registries (Chapter 5), whether programs for incarcerated mothers are effective (Chapter 11), and a more holistic understanding of cultural differences in perceptions of the best interests standard (Chapter 12). A more specific overview of the parts and chapters within this book is provided in the next section.

Overview of Chapters

The book contains three parts. Each part tackles a major area of law that has psychological underpinnings that can affect the wellbeing of children.

Part I: Juvenile Delinquents

The first part of the book focuses on how laws, policies, and legal procedures affect the wellbeing of juvenile delinquents by addressing (or ignoring) the developmental, mental health, and gender-specific needs that some juveniles face. The part begins with a general chapter by Wills (Chapter 3) on how the law considers the developmental abilities and needs of children who are involved with the juvenile justice system. After a brief discussion of the processes and procedures of the juvenile justice system, the chapter overviews the developmental and mental health issues juvenile delinquents often face. This provides a foundation for the entire part. The chapter focuses on special populations (e.g., females and juveniles with mental health issues) and legal issues that are currently being debated (e.g., waivers to adult court). Using case studies, the chapter illustrates the challenges that the juvenile justice system faces in addressing the needs of those it serves, while still protecting the community. Policy recommendations are offered which would meet both of these justice goals.

The second chapter in this part (Chapter 4) continues the theme of addressing the needs of juvenile offenders and addresses a specific aspect of the legal process: interrogations. This chapter is an original research article that is unique because previous observational interrogation research has typically focused on interrogations of *adults*. The study analyzes interrogations from across the country and provides detailed descriptive data about juvenile interrogation procedures, participants, and outcomes. Results have implications for the legal system (e.g., due process concerns) and for the protection of juvenile suspects (e.g., developmentally based vulnerabilities such as the tendency to comply with authorities might play a large role in adolescents' interrogation decision making). Recommendations for policy and practice are offered to protect juveniles while still allowing the police to investigate.

Chapter 5 addresses the issue of juveniles who are accused of sex offenses ranging from sexting to having sex with one's girlfriend/boyfriend to forcible rape. The chapter summarizes recently enacted laws and describes studies investigating the public sentiment surrounding these laws. Psychological literature suggests the application of these laws to juvenile offenders may be based on erroneous assumptions about juvenile behavior and decision making and that the motives for supporting such laws may lead to bias against groups of juveniles that are already stigmatized. Policy recommendations offer possible solutions to these issues.

Chapter 6 is original research that investigates the perceptions of female juveniles who completed a gender-specific rehabilitation program. Such programs are gaining popularity across the country. Gender-specific programming is thought to be beneficial because it addresses the needs and experiences that are unique to juvenile females. Gender provides differing social contexts for males and females; specifically, the experiences (e.g., sexual abuse), development, and underlying causes of delinquency are different for males and females. Thus, programs that address these specific needs are thought to be more helpful than those that do not. Interviews indicate that the graduates of the program perceived the program to be generally helpful, including the gender-specific elements of the program. The results lead to policy recommendations for development of programs that meet the gender-specific developmental needs and thus promote wellbeing of juveniles.

The final chapter in this part (Chapter 7) reviews the legal, ethical, and clinical considerations that researchers face when a juvenile delinquent whom they are studying reports suicidal ideations or intent. This is particularly an issue in some of the research discussed in this part of the book, but it may also come into play in other situations. Potential conflicts among these areas (legal, ethical, clinical) are discussed, and recommendations for researchers are presented.

As a whole, Part I discusses a variety of ways in which juveniles' needs are being addressed—or should be addressed—when juveniles come into contact with the legal system. Programs and procedures such as those discussed in this part should be developed and studied, as they have the potential to help protect juveniles' wellbeing.

Part II: Divorce

Part II discusses several ways the courts can protect children whose parents are divorcing: giving them a voice as to their wishes (e.g., which parent to live with), ensuring that both parents get to spend time with the child, and protecting them from parental alienation. This part begins with a chapter (Chapter 8) that generally discusses the wellbeing of children whose parents are divorcing. Then, it discusses the benefits and risks associated with allowing children to have a say in which parent they want to live with after the parents' divorce. It concludes with recommendations for policy and procedure, which are based on those used in Australian courts but not yet common in the United States.

The second chapter (Chapter 9) in this part discusses an innovative solution to protecting the wellbeing of children experiencing parental divorce. By establishing a "Child Support and Visitation Enforcement Office," courts can ensure that children are able to spend time with both parents. Much research indicates that, in most cases, children's best interests are served when they are able to have continued contact with the noncustodial parent. While there are penalties for noncompliance with child support orders, there are often no similar penalties for noncompliance with visitation orders (e.g., the custodial parent can prevent the noncustodial parent from seeing the child). The chapter demonstrates how such an office can promote justice and also be economically feasible.

The final chapter in this part (Chapter 10) furthers the discussion of the child's best interests by discussing the controversial issue of parental alienation and its possible effects on children. The chapter offers policy suggestions that the legal system can adopt in order to address this phenomenon and promote the wellbeing of children.

In all, Part II provides three separate but related chapters that all address how the legal system can protect the wellbeing of children whose parents are divorcing or divorced. The programs and policy suggestions discussed are all relatively new and innovative. Researchers and legal actors interested in these topics are at the forefront of current movements to address the wellbeing of children in such situations.

Part III: General Legal Actions

Part III discusses how a variety of legal actions have affected the health and wellbeing of children. Several current issues are discussed here, including children whose parents are prison inmates, children who are legally required to receive an HPV vaccination, children who are obese, and children involved in the child welfare system. All of these hotly debated topics have recently been issues discussed in both legal and psychological circles. The variety of topics discussed here highlights the breadth of social issues and legal actions that either intentionally or inadvertently affect children's health and wellbeing.

The first chapter in this part (Chapter 11) discusses recent efforts to address the wellbeing of children who have mothers who are in prison. This psycholegal analysis provides a discussion of the pros and cons of legal solutions to this issue. For instance, in-prison day cares that allow inmates to have contact with their children protect the parent–child bond but place the child in a foreign environment. Policy recommendations are offered based on research, theory, and justice principles.

The second chapter in Part III (Chapter 12) discusses the wellbeing of another at-risk population: children involved in the child welfare system. Focus group methodology was used to investigate the various meanings that immigrant parents give to the term "best interests of the child." Results indicate that a one-size-fits-all approach to child welfare may not reflect the cultural practices of various ethnic groups. Policy recommendations are made based on findings of this study.

Chapter 13 is another study that addresses the wellbeing of children whose parents are accused of abuse or neglect. Recently, parents of obese children have been charged with child abuse or neglect. Because such prosecutions are very new, it is important to study relevant community sentiment. Two studies utilized a mock-jury paradigm to investigate how attributions, individual differences, and extra-legal factors (e.g., mother's weight) affected verdicts in a case in which a mother is charged with child abuse for allowing her child to become morbidly obese. A third study further investigated participants' thoughts about this issue. Results have implications for the community support of such prosecutions and laws designed to protect the health of children.

The following chapter (Chapter 14) continues the theme of community sentiment toward laws protecting the health of children. This chapter presents results of a content analysis of commentary which supports or opposes mandatory human papilloma virus (HPV) vaccination for children. Recently, 23 states have considered or adopted these controversial laws; lawmakers may consider the community's sentiment in deciding whether to support the laws and thus it is important to understand this sentiment. The study identifies several themes in the commentary, including morality, emotion, cognitive biases, and justice principles. Results have implications for lawmakers and policy concerning the wellbeing of children.

In sum, Part III discusses various legal actions taken by lawmakers, courts, child welfare professionals, and prisons that affect the wellbeing of children. Many of these actions are so new that they cannot yet be fully analyzed; however, the analyses here provide preliminary insight as to the possible effects of and community sentiment toward such actions. Future research is needed to determine the best ways to protect children in such circumstances.

Conclusion

In recent decades, there is much debate as to how the legal system does or should handle juveniles who come into contact with the legal system as offenders (Chapters 3 through 7). Similarly, laws and procedures have been enacted to address the health and wellbeing of children whose parents are divorcing (Chapters 8, 9, and 10) or are in prison (Chapter 11). Further, legal actions have been adopted to protect the health of children and society in general (e.g., HPV vaccination laws [Chapter 14] and child welfare laws [Chapters 12 and 13]). Research in this domain often involves studying legal actors (Chapter 4), parents (Chapter 12), community members (Chapters 5 and 14), and juveniles (Chapter 3, 4, and 7). Such research often poses ethical, legal, and clinical dilemmas (Chapter 7). This book investigates a broad variety of these legal actions, demonstrating how they affect the wellbeing of children—for better or worse.

The American legal system has come a long way in protecting and promoting the wellbeing of children. The chapters here identify ways in which the system can continue to do so; for instance, by adopting the policy recommendations in these chapters. Additionally, education of legal actors is necessary to develop laws, policies, and procedures that protect children while still upholding the law. Although the legal system has addressed wellbeing in many areas, there are many areas that have not been addressed. As the world changes, new situations arise that threaten or promote the wellbeing of children. New technology brings new ways for children to offend and be victimized. New psychological findings arise which indicate that wellbeing is threatened. New programs are developed to protect children. Thus, the legal system must continue to adapt in order to promote and protect the wellbeing of children.

Research has revealed that juveniles' decision making, behavior, and cognitions are different from those of adults. The legal system has adapted through the years to protect the wellbeing of society's youngest members and still continues to morph today. In creating this book, we hope to encourage legal actors to consider the impact their actions have on children's wellbeing. We also hope to encourage researchers to continue studying how these legal actions affect the well-being of children. Together, legal actors and social scientists can better address the special needs of children involved in the legal system.

References

In re Gault, 387 US 1 (1967).
J.D.B. v. North Carolina, 131 S. Ct. 2394 (2011).
Kent v. US, 383 US 541 (1966).
Miller v. Alabama, 567 US 10-9646 (2012).
Miller, M. K., & Bornstein, B. L. (2013). *Stress, Trauma, and Wellbeing in the Legal System*. New York: Oxford University Press.
Roper v. Simmons, 543 US 551 (2005).
Rush, E., Quas, J. A., & McAuliff, B. D. (2013). Stress, trauma, and wellbeing in the legal system: Where do we go from here? In M. K. Miller & B. H. Bornstein (Eds.), *Stress, trauma, and wellbeing in the legal system* (pp. 89–121). New York, NY: Oxford University Press.
Sicafuse, L. L., & Bornstein, B. H. (2013). Using the law to enhance wellbeing: Applying therapeutic jurisprudence in the courtroom. In M. K. Miller & B. H. Bornstein (Eds.), *Stress, trauma, and wellbeing in the legal system* (pp. 15–41). New York, NY: Oxford University Press.
Tyler, T. R. (2006). Psychologyical perspectives on legitimacy and legitimation. *Annual Review of Psychology, 57*, 375–400.
Wexler, D. B. (1995). Reflections on the scope of therapeutic jurisprudence. *Psychology, Public Policy, and Law, 1*, 220–236.

2

Psychology, Law, and the Wellbeing of Children: A Developmental Perspective

Twila Wingrove and Sarah J. Beal

Put simply, developmental psychology is the study of how people change over time. Of course, any developmental psychologist will be quick to qualify that definition. Developmentalists attempt to identify and understand *meaningful* change, which is change that extends over a period of time (i.e., going from happy to sad to happy would not be an example of development), is directed or regulated from within a person (in contrast to something external that forces change in an individual), is progressive (i.e., systematic and leading to a goal or outcome), and results in qualitative shifts (i.e., a novel state of being; Moshman, 2005). Importantly, this qualitative shift (e.g., sexual maturation from prepubertal to pubertal) may encompass gradual, continuous underlying processes, but for change to be meaningful, the individual should have an altered state of being after the change, and this altered state should not be transient.

Typically, developmental researchers narrow their field of study by focusing on specific age groups and by focusing on specific subdomains. There are four age groups that are relevant to the topics of this book: infancy (roughly 0–2 years), early childhood (roughly 2–5 years), middle childhood (5–11 roughly years), and adolescence (roughly 12–19 years). While terminology may vary, developmental researchers typically study development in one or more of the following subdomains: physical, cognitive, and social/emotional development.

There is no way to comprehensively cover all relevant research with regard to child and adolescent development within a single chapter; rather, our intention is to provide a brief summary of the bodies of developmental psychology literature to provide a foundation for readers who are unfamiliar with child and adolescent development. In this chapter we provide a summary of physical and cognitive development and elaborate on three aspects of social/emotional development; specifically, identity development, relationships with parents, and relationships with peers. Our summary highlights major changes from infancy through adolescence.

In the course of each summary, we will also connect the information to relevant chapters within this book. Before embarking on that summary, we begin with a section summarizing the major influences on development: biology and environment.

Influences on Development

When considering the impact of the legal system on children's wellbeing, it is particularly important to recognize the dual contributions of biology and environment on development. We all understand that physical development is the outcome of an interaction of nature (i.e., biological influences, including our inherited genetic material) and nurture (i.e., environmental influences). The environment can be defined broadly, to include virtually any external force on development, including parenting, physical resources, schooling, peers, and others.

Developmental researchers study the influence of biology on multiple levels. Some researchers study physiology and the impact of physiology on psycho-social outcomes. For example, many resources are devoted to understanding brain development and associations with youth's affect, behavior, and cognition. Steinberg's (2008) research on the relationship between development in the prefrontal cortex and decision-making abilities during adolescence and early adulthood fits into this line of inquiry. Not all of these researchers focus solely on the brain. For example, researchers also investigate how physical changes (e.g., puberty) and hormonal changes (e.g., cortisol reactivity) influence behavior and development. Importantly, stressful experiences can alter these processes (for a reveiw, see Tarullo & Gunnar, 2006).

Of course, the role of biology also includes genetics. Understanding of the role of genetic influences on development has come a long way, but this knowledge remains incomplete and continues to evolve. Even where researchers have identified a gene or genes involved in the development of a particular outcome, this does not mean that they necessarily understand the process of how the gene gets translated into the outcome. In genetic terms, the identified gene(s) is referred to as a "genotype," while the expression of that genotype is referred to as a "phenotype." Development of the phenotype is clearly directly related to the genotype, but there is room for environmental influence. For example, there is variability in how susceptible individuals are to stressful environments, which alters activation of the hypothalamic-pituitary-adrenal axis (which is responsible for mounting a hormonal stress response) and this variability appears to be related to specific genotypes (Ellis & Boyce, 2011).

Understanding the gene–environment interaction has been the subject of developmental research since the field emerged, but the framework of this discussion has shifted. Historically, emphasis was placed on dissecting how much of any particular trait was due to genetic versus environmental factors. This kind of work was frequently done using kinship studies or investigating twins reared apart; the result was the creation of heritability estimates. Today, developmentalists recognize that point of view as overly simplistic. Genetic and environmental influences are not wholly independent forces that can be separated and assigned pure numerical values.

Modern geneticists and developmentalists recognize that genetics and environment mutually influence each other, as well as the developmental outcomes of interest. For example, researchers in the field of epigenetics have demonstrated that our environment can directly influence how our genes are expressed. Identical twins—born with the exact same genetic material—grow more and more different as they age (Fraga et al., 2005). The reason for these differences is that the environment itself exerts a direct influence on our genome, turning certain genes on and off.

In addition to the field of epigenetics, developmentalists also focus their resources on understanding the underlying process of development, meaning that they seek to understand the patterns of gene–environment interactions. Without going into too much detail, a number of patterns of interaction exist and they differentially explain certain categories of developmental outcomes. For example, certain universal physical milestones, like learning to walk, are best explained as manifesting from a process called "canalization," meaning that they are so robust that they appear inevitable unless some major environmental or genetic intervention occurs.

Environmental influences can also be understood as occurring at multiple levels. Bronfenbrenner's (1992) ecological systems theory is useful for understanding environmental influences. It posits that development is influenced by levels of systems: microsystem (environments the child has direct contact with; e.g., family, school, day care), mesosystem (interactions between microsystems), exosystem (larger social networks that indirectly affect the child; e.g., parent's work environment), and the macrosystem (the largest system of influence; e.g., culture, ethnicity, laws, and policies). The final system in Bronfenbrenner's theory is the chronosystem, which acknowledges the influence of the passage of time.

Taken together, the research reviewed thus far should demonstrate that no developmental outcome is the result of purely environmental or purely genetic influences. The consequence of this proposition for the legal system is that no legal intervention can exert complete control over developmental outcomes. However, the legal system can leverage the strength and quality of environmental influences in a number of ways. For example, juvenile delinquency laws actively alter adolescents' microsystems. Whether they do so in a way that promotes or hinders wellbeing is debated in the media and studied by researchers; it is also at the heart of how policies are implemented within a particular jurisdiction or by individual legal authorities.

Importantly, the legal system has the opportunity to intervene with regard to the environment during periods of physiological, emotional, and cognitive stress. Many of the chapters in this book identify periods of stress and discuss specific legal interventions that occur during these times (e.g., when children are removed from the home, when children's parents divorce, or when youth are interrogated). From a psychological perspective, stress is often a mechanism for creating turning points in the trajectory of development (Moffitt, Caspi, Harrington, & Milne, 2002; Sampson & Laub, 1993), which further illustrates the need to ensure that legal interventions take development into account, rather than using the same policies and practices across all developmental settings. By ensuring that policies and practices account for development and potential epigenetic influences to create the ideal environment for children, the legal system may be a key player in ensuring the best outcome for the youth it serves.

Development in Childhood and Adolescence: An Overview

In order to understand what "wellbeing" is and how the legal system can impact it, it is important to understand the multidimensionality of children's development. As discussed in the introductory chapter of this book, wellbeing is not merely physical health or emotional health. In developmental terms, child and adolescent wellbeing requires nurturance in all domains of development. Thus, to understand the legal system's effects on wellbeing, one must understand the basics of these different domains of development. This section is devoted to briefly describing child and adolescent development within these major domains: physical, cognitive, and social/emotional. An additional goal of this section is to provide examples of how the legal system can and does impact each of these domains of development.

Before providing this primer on youth development, it is important to acknowledge two caveats. First, in discussing each of these domains separately, it might be easy to think of them as independent systems. That is most certainly not the case. Physical development influences cognitive development (e.g., brain changes lead to changes in cognition); cognitive development influences emotional development (e.g., as ability to take other people's perspectives develops, so does empathy); and so on. Second, one must always take a life course perspective when considering how legal interventions will impact youth. This means that the impact of a legal intervention will vary depending on when in a person's life it occurs (Elder & Shanahan, 2006).

Physical Development

Physical development refers to the biological changes that occur throughout life. In childhood, physical development is primarily associated with growth—increased coordination, strength, and size, for example. The rate of physical growth varies depending on both the age of the child and the particular body system of interest. In general, children experience the most rapid periods of physical development in infancy and adolescence (Rogol, Clark, & Roemmich, 2000). Growth in the body does not occur evenly and simultaneously (Sun & Jensen, 1994). Prenatally, heads grow faster than bodies. At birth, infants' heads represent roughly one-fourth of their total body length, but that reduces to one-fifth by the end of infancy (Centers for Disease Control and Prevention [CDC], 2011). Children also tend to grow from the center of their bodies outward. Prenatally, the chest and trunk are among the first to develop (Sun & Jensen, 1994). During infancy and childhood, the arms and legs grow a little faster than the hands and feet. Importantly, these patterns of growth correspond with patterns of motor development. Infants develop motor control of their heads first, generally develop control of their arms and upper body before their lower body, and develop gross motor skills (e.g., voluntary control of posture and balance) before honing fine motor skills (e.g., finger control; Smitsman, 2004).

Rapid growth during the first 5 years of life creates a sensitive period for physical development (Johnson, 2004). Understanding how physical development unfolds is essential for ensuring appropriate environments and identifying opportunities for intervention, as well as for recognizing key periods of vulnerability. For example, a child who enters the child welfare system at the age of 2 would, assuming a case progresses from removal to permanency in a 24-month period, be expected to be mastering gross and developing fine motor skills during her time in foster care. Recognizing movement-related issues and securing physical or occupational therapy during this time may be appropriate for some youth, but it may be overlooked by the legal professionals who have the opportunity to order the provision of such services.

In adolescence, physical development includes pubertal changes, with related activation of the hypothalamic-pituitary-gonadal axis, leading to the secretion of estrogen or testosterone, maturation of reproductive organs, and the development of primary and secondary sexual characteristics (Dorn & Biro, 2011; Susman & Rogol, 2004). Importantly, these changes unfold over an extended period of time, and both when puberty occurs for an individual (i.e., timing) and how long an individual moves through the stages of puberty (i.e., tempo) vary. Puberty presents another sensitive period in development. Onset of mental health issues, especially internalizing disorders, is associated with puberty (Angold, Costello, & Worthman, 1998), and adolescents' experiences in their environment appear to have a profound influence on the structure and function of the brain during this time (Blakemore, Burnett, & Dahl, 2010). Importantly, pubertal changes appear to be related to both genetic coding and environmental experiences, resulting in differences in the timing and tempo of pubertal development for youth depending on stress exposure and genetic makeup, for example (Belsky, 2012).

The two sensitive periods for brain development occur in early childhood and adolescence. In both cases, development and reorganization of neural pathways, through synaptogenesis and synaptic pruning, is shaped by both genetics and the environment (Blakemore & Choudhury, 2006). What results, for both children and adolescents, is a better functioning and more adaptive system. This aids in motor development and control, enhances cognitive capacities, and helps the individual function in his or her environment more efficiently. However, deprivation of the environment or substances or toxins introduced to the brain may be especially problematic if it occurs during these periods (Chambers, Taylor, & Potenza, 2004).

Several chapters of this book speak to policies that directly impact physical wellbeing (Chapters 7, 11, 13, and 14). Chapter 13 tackles the issue of childhood obesity and whether it should be seen as a form of child maltreatment. It is not our role in this chapter to evaluate the public policy debate surrounding this issue. However, when considering child obesity, it is important to keep in mind evidence from the developmental literature. First, it is clear that childhood obesity is an epidemic (Ebbeling, Pawlak, & Ludwig, 2002) and that obesity, especially long term, can have serious implications for health, cognition, and social/emotional functioning. Second, the causes of obesity are as complicated as disentangling the causes of any developmental outcome. Obesity is not equally distributed across childhood, with higher rates of obesity in adolescence than childhood (National Center for Health Statistics, 2012). This would indicate the importance of targeting obesity at specific periods in the life course. Researchers have found that obesity is amenable to early intervention (Foster et al., 2008); both school-based and family-based interventions have shown some promise, but real physical changes are often mild (Ebbeling et al., 2002).

Another chapter that touches on policies that directly affect physical development is Chapter 14, which discusses new policies to promote use of human papilloma virus (HPV) vaccines. HPV vaccines could protect adolescent and adult wellbeing by preventing cancer, but the authors acknowledge and evaluate how these potential benefits balance against the rights of parents to make decisions about their children's medical care and potentially negative community sentiment about government-mandated vaccines.

Because physical, cognitive, and emotional development are so intertwined, legal policies and programs discussed in this book could also indirectly affect physical wellbeing. For one example, any involvement with the legal system is likely going to be characterized by high stress for children. In addition, interaction with the legal system almost always *increases* stress. Stress is a physiological state, and chronic stress can lead to long-term negative health consequences (Johnston-Brooks, Lewis, Evans, & Whalen, 1998). However, to the extent that the legal system can (1) reduce stress exuded on children and their families, and (2) put policies in to support children and families during these periods of stress, there is an immense opportunity to capitalize on developmental sensitivities or readiness for positive change. Leveraging this developmental readiness would likely create a better outcome for children, in part because of children's sensitivity and vulnerability when the legal system is involved in their lives (Graber & Brooks-Gunn, 1999). This may be especially true for physical development (Stratakis, Gold, & Chrousos, 1995), but it is also true for cognitive and social/emotional development.

Cognitive Development

In brief, cognitive development is how information (physical, auditory, perception, etc.) is organized, processed, and used, and, more important, how those processes *change in meaningful ways* across development. In infancy, cognitive development begins with visual and auditory perception—infants observe the world around them, process what is routine or expected in their environment, and organize this information to form rules about how they expect the world to behave (Bremner, 2004). The notion that infants learn about how to process information through interaction with the environment is the founding principle of Piaget's first stage of cognitive development: the sensorimotor period (Piaget, 2000). Piaget argued that, from birth to approximately age 2 years, children are creating mental representations and cognitive structures that organize what they are learning. This process is reflected in behaviors that are commonly observed in infants and toddlers: learning about the properties of objects by putting them in their mouths, where they discover how the object feels, tastes, and smells; dropping objects on the floor to learn about what objects retain their shape (e.g., a ball) and what objects do not (e.g., applesauce). It is worth noting that, during this period, children are gaining the foundation for an understanding of cause and effect—that when I drop something off the edge of my high chair, it falls; children are also beginning to learn how their behaviors impact people around them, when there has been enough consistency to establish a pattern.

Children move from learning about and organizing the world around them through direct interaction to the use of mental representation (Piaget, 2000). Referred to as the preoperational stage, children from ages 2 to 7 years develop mental representations, which means that they can imagine an object, rather than having to see the object in front of them (Flavell, Miller, & Miller, 2002). This is critical for the emergence of imaginary play, and it is stimulated by interactions with peers and adults. One limitation to this process is that children can imagine an action (e.g., they do not have to drop peas off the edge of a high-chair, they can imagine what would happen if they did so) but cannot mentally manipulate that image. This is reflected in the play children engage in, which is often scripted and follows a clear pattern that likely mirrors what they have observed. This notion of learning about the world via observation and using it to develop scripts for play and interacting with others may be reflected in the behavior problems commonly observed in preschoolers exposed to domestic violence (Jonson-Reid, 1998), for example.

By ages 7–11 years, children are gaining the ability to manipulate mental representations, during a stage termed "concrete operations" (Piaget, 2000). Mental rotations and reversed images (e.g., mentally reversing observed actions) can be used to inform the conclusions children come to, which allows for more advanced thinking and reasoning than in previous periods. During this period, children are able to solve story problems in math classes and reason about cause and effect in a more sophisticated manner. However, the ability to think abstractly—to reason based on premises that are not grounded in the world around them—is difficult for children before age 11 or 12 years (Moshman, 2005). When this ability develops, where adolescents can consider objects or events that are not based on their own experiences or environments, individuals can also use that information to inform reasoning and decision making.

While Piaget's theory ended with formal operational reasoning, advances in research have pointed to important developmental processes occurring throughout adolescence and well into early adulthood. These processes have a profound impact on adolescent cognitive processes and decision making. As a result of neurological development occurring from puberty to the mid- to late-twenties (Blakemore et al., 2010), adolescents first experience advancements in reward processing (Steinberg, 2008). Consequently, adolescents are motivated to engage in behaviors that offer immediate positive gain and, especially in emotionally charged situations (positive or negative), often fail to recognize long-term consequences of their actions. Thus, adolescents, especially when they are with their peers, are at increased risk of engaging in poor decision making and risky behaviors (e.g., reckless driving; Steinberg, 2011). Simultaneously, development of sophisticated and adult-like reasoning abilities continues, such that, when adolescents are not emotionally charged (often called cool cognition), their reasoning and decision-making abilities match that of adults (Steinberg et al., 2008). For this reason, adolescents can do very well in school, for example, but make poor decisions with their friends. It is not until the end of the third decade of life that two processes—reward processing and cognitive control—have both matured to the point that there is balance in reasoning ability (Chein, Albert, O'Brien, Uckert, & Steinberg, 2011).

Cognitive development is especially relevant in the context of child custody (see Chapters 8 and 10) and juvenile delinquency (see Chapters 3 and 4). In the custody context, children's cognitive maturity should factor into the expectations that parents and the courts have for the child's understanding of the process and their level of participation in the process. As noted in Chapter 8, courts have some freedom to take children's wishes into account, sometimes with the caveat that they should first consider the child's maturity and understanding. This places a burden on the court (or information gatherers for the court, like attorneys and evaluators) to speak directly to the child's level of cognitive sophistication when making recommendations to the court about the child's level of participation in the proceedings. Likewise, parents' understanding of their child's cognitive maturity should determine how parents go about explaining the divorce and custody process to their children.

Similarly, recognition of cognitive capacity is important for the legal system's processing of juveniles in the legal system, either as juveniles or adults. As both Chapters 3 and 4 acknowledge, the Supreme Court recently held that police need to consider a juvenile's age when deciding whether a child is in custody and *Miranda* rights should be read (*J.D.B. v. North Carolina*, 2011). Importantly, from a developmental perspective, age may be a weak indicator when determining the cognitive capacities of adolescents. In general, everyone develops at a different pace; this is especially true for time periods of rapid change, like adolescence. Most research measuring adolescents' legal abilities suggests that teenagers in the 14–16 year age range are especially varied in their understanding of the legal process (e.g., Grisso et al., 2003). In addition, participating in interrogation, deciding whether to make a plea bargain, and actively participating in a legal defense are all incredibly weighty decisions that require sophisticated reasoning and they are likely to be happening under emotional and stressful conditions. As described earlier, these are exactly the kind of conditions in which adolescents experience the most impairment in their reasoning abilities. Importantly, this variability not only occurs across adolescents (i.e., some adolescents being more advanced than others) but also *within* adolescents. In other words, an adolescent may display good judgment and decision making in one context, but poor judgment and decision making in another. Often (as discussed previously) this is due to an interaction between cognitive development and emotional development.

Social and Emotional Development

Social and emotional development is a wide subdomain in developmental psychology that includes the study of such topics as moral development, the development of emotional understanding and maturity, and the development of self-esteem and self-concept. In this section, we identify three subtopics that are particularly relevant to the study of children's wellbeing in the legal system and the issues raised in this book. The first two topics are the two major sources of influence on children's social and emotional development: parents and peers. In the third section, we take a slight change in subject and focus not on influences on social and emotional development but rather on the developing individual. Specifically, the third topic is identity development, which is the process by which children and adolescents develop a self-concept about their distinctive characteristics, group affiliations, and individuality. In short, it is how individuals come to define who they are and what they value. Importantly, identity development directly stems from individuals' interactions with their environment, including relationships with parents and peers.

Parent–Child Relationships. Arguably, parent–child relationships are the foundation for building healthy relationships throughout life, serving as a model for relationship development. Erikson (1980) argued that infants who are shown appropriate love and caretaking develop the capacity for basic trust (or mistrust in the absence of appropriate caretaking). In this way, infancy is critical for establishing patterns that carry forward into future relationships. The quality of the infant–parent relationship is often measured in terms of "attachment," which refers to a strong bond between parent (and other caretakers) and the infant (Ainsworth, 2010; Bowlby, 1980). Parent–child attachment can either be "secure" or "insecure." Secure attachments are present when infants use their parents as a base for exploring environments. Infants with secure attachments react negatively when a parent is absent and actively seek contact with the parent when they return. Infants with insecure attachments do not follow this pattern, and either act indifferent, angry, or resistant when the parent is in the room or returns from an absence.

Importantly, attachment security is linked to later emotional development, including development of social competence (Englund, Kuo, Puig, & Collins, 2011), empathy (Hutman & Dapretto, 2009), and even antisocial or delinquent behavior (Kochanska & Kim, 2012). However, there is a crucial caveat—the quality of the parent–child relationship in infancy is only a strong predictor of later adjustment when that quality is maintained throughout childhood (Thompson, 2000). In contrast, children who experience secure parent–child attachment in infancy but then face decreases in parenting quality or frequent changes in caregivers do not exhibit the same long-term benefits of secure attachment. Further, the impact of parenting quality on attachment is modified by genetics (Bakermans-Kranenburg & Van Ijzendoorn, 2007), speaking to the importance of genetics and the environment in shaping child development.

Disruption of caregiving is inevitable during divorce (see Clarke-Stewart & Brentano, 2006 for a review of the consequences of divorce on children). The immediate consequences of divorce are high parental stress, a decrease in income for the custodial parent, and a reduced frequency of contact with the noncustodial parent. These changes negatively affect children immediately after divorce. While most children do recover within a couple years, research still finds that many children of divorce never quite catch up with their peers on a number of factors, including academic achievement, self-esteem, and social competence (Lansford, 2009). The negative consequences of divorce, especially in the short term, are why the legal system must prioritize protecting children's wellbeing during the divorce proceedings. The authors of Chapters 8–10 make some suggestions for how court practices and public policies could accomplish this goal.

Given these findings about the long-term implications of attachment, most developmentalists agree that secure infant attachment is important to set the stage for a positive long-term parent–child relationship. Secure attachment is associated with effective parenting, and when it continues into childhood and adolescence, that supports wellbeing. When characterizing parenting in childhood, developmentalists generally agree that the most effective parents are authoritative, which means that they express warmth and affection to their children but also exhibit a degree of sensitivity to their children's maturity level that allows them to require age-appropriate behaviors, enforce those behaviors with age-appropriate punishments, and allow an age-appropriate level of autonomy or freedom of choice (Baumrind, 2013).

Importantly, while authoritative parenting is associated with positive child outcomes, there are cultural variations. For example, some Chinese parents express more control and less warmth, and so long as it is not extreme, their children still experience positive benefits (Chen, Wu, Chen, Wang, & Cen, 2001). These findings of cultural variations in effective parenting are highly relevant to child protection decision-making. As the author of Chapter 12 notes, immigrant parents might behave in ways that seem inconsistent with what we expect from "good parents" in the United States, but they are not actually harmful to their children. This cultural mismatch between American child protection workers and parents could lead to legal intervention when it is not necessary. Even when intervention is necessary, the cultural mismatch could still interfere with successful implementation of services.

In adolescence, a healthy parent–child relationship is associated with gradual increases in child autonomy and decreases in parental monitoring. Importantly, some amount of delinquency becomes normative during adolescence (Moffitt, 1993), but some adolescents embark on a path of serious, repetitive delinquency that will continue into early adulthood. Serious, repetitive delinquency is associated with a family environment that is inconsistent with the indicators mentioned earlier. In other words, juveniles in families with low warmth, high conflict, and inconsistent discipline are at greatest risk of becoming repeat offenders.

Peers. Peer interaction is important for socialization and development. Peers stimulate cognition, expose us to new ideas and environments, and provide companionship (Eckerman & Peterman, 2004). As children recognize differences between self and other, interaction with peers becomes intentional, and by 16 months, children begin coordinating action with one another, especially if the peer is familiar. Children sit side by side and engage in ritual-like behavior, such as tapping blocks on the floor. By the age of 2 years, they become more interactive. Children coordinate actions in play and imitate behavior. Before children turn 3 years old, they are proficient at coordinating play and engaging with same-aged peers to accomplish mutual goals, using both verbal and nonverbal communication. Through these processes, children are learning important social skills, including turn-taking behavior, partnering with others to accomplish a goal, sharing, and peer reliance. Children are also learning problem-solving skills, especially when there is conflict during play. While these experiences can be difficult, development of self-regulation, more efficient coordination of behavior, and resolving conflict all stem from those experiences (Shonkoff & Phillips, 2000).

By preschool, attachment to and preference for particular peers develops, and friendship relationships emerge. In middle childhood, one or two close friendships develop. This pattern of relationships has a different dynamic than having a broader peer group. There is evidence to suggest that, in childhood and adolescence, those more intense relationships are extremely important for providing companionship (Brown, 2004). Same-gendered friend dyad or triads often merge in adolescence, creating larger, mixed-gender friendship groups. Importantly, disruption of peer relationships can be an unintended consequence of interaction with the legal system—divorce and maltreatment can both result in a change in the child's living situation, and while children are in foster care, for example, participating in birthday parties or sleepovers can be challenging or impossible because of limitations in where youth can be left without the supervision of a caseworker or foster caregiver. All of these dynamics can contribute to atypical experiences with peers.

Throughout childhood and adolescence, the impact of peers is important. However, as children get older, more time is typically spent with peers than with family or adults, resulting in a greater impact of peers in adolescence (Brown, 2004). There is some evidence that the influence of peers in adolescence moves beyond a simple desire to be liked or accepted. Peer relationships also seem to stimulate the pathway in the brain most sensitive to reward, influencing adolescent judgment and decision-making. For example, the presence of peers leads to more impulsive decisions in situations like risky driving and substance use, where adolescents perceive immediate benefits as more rewarding and simultaneously downplay long-term consequences (Chein et al., 2011). In this way, peers have a profound impact on adolescent behavior and development. This may be especially important to consider within the context of juvenile offending and recidivism (Monahan, Steinberg, & Cauffman, 2009). For example, rehabilitation programs that directly address the role of peers and social environment may be especially effective at reducing the risk of recidivism. One promising approach to juvenile rehabilitation—gender-specific programming—is discussed in Chapter 6.

Identity Development

If cognition is how information *in general* is organized, processed, and used (Flavell et al., 2002), then identity would be how information *about the self* is organized, processed, and used (Harter, 2006). As such, cognitive development and identity development are close companions. Identity development begins the first 2 years of life. Two processes occur simultaneously during this period: Infants are establishing trust in the world around them (Erikson, 1980) and are becoming aware that they are distinct from the people and things in their environment (Damon & Hart, 1982). The establishment of trust (described earlier) is translated into a central tenant of identity in early childhood—that the child is either an independent being who is valued by the world around her or an independent being who is not valued by the world around her (van den Boom, 2004). It is with this basic premise that children enter the world and continue interacting with it, gaining more information about self as they go. Unfortunately, the parental conflicts associated with divorce can sometimes lead parents to communicate negative messages to their children about parental trust and love (see Chapter 11).

After age 2, children's sense of identity orients toward describing their self. Identity includes their name and other physical features of self, including age, hair and eye color, and gender (Damon & Hart, 1982; Harter, 2006). Children are classifying the world around them, and likewise, classify themselves into particular categories. As a result, gender and ethnicity are often salient components in identity during this period. Other aspects of identity include the awareness of personal preferences, including activities, foods, colors, and toys children like or do not like. How children describe themselves reflects this (e.g., I am smart, I am fast) and often reflects how they hear themselves described by the people around them. Later in childhood, and somewhat concurrent with concrete operations, identity begins to include comparisons between self and other (Flavell et al., 2002). At this stage, children use classifications to make distinctions between who they are and who people around them are. Membership to groups of people also become important for identity—especially in the areas of family or peer membership (Harter, 2006). Children are also able to reflect on internal states as part of their sense of self, and may include those in their self-description.

By adolescence, individuals recognize that identity transcends personal preferences, appearance, or activities—and identity becomes more about internal qualities (Damon & Hart, 1982). During this time, there is also a growing awareness that internal qualities are not always consistent, which creates some difficulty with identity integration (Harter, 2006). For example, an adolescent might describe herself as a happy, fun-loving person, but then recognize that when she is at home, she can be grouchy or depressed. It is not until late adolescence that there is some reconciliation of these conflicting self-experiences (Harter, 2012). It is also during adolescence that individuals develop the ability to consider their current identity as a factor in considering future identities (e.g., I could be a doctor; Nurmi, 2004). In this way, adolescents' identities are influential in preparing them for an important developmental transition: the transition to adulthood. This process appears to begin with consideration of a present identity and how it may impact future identity in one domain at a time (e.g., education) but eventually moves to considering multiple future identity states simultaneously (e.g., education, occupation, and parenting)—laying the groundwork for an integrated sense of self across the life span (Crockett & Beal, 2012).

The implications of legal involvement on identity development are profound. Monitoring implicit and explicit messages provided to children (e.g., addressing offending and recidivism) without having messages internalized as a defining aspect of self (e.g., a criminal, danger to society) is challenging and has the potential for a lifelong impact.

Conclusion

For children and adolescents, "wellbeing" is a state of being healthy: physically, cognitively, socially, and emotionally. The emergence of wellbeing requires biological and environmental influences that support normative development. For many children and adolescents, the legal system becomes a major environmental influence. Changes to legal practice, even seemingly minor ones, can either promote or hinder wellbeing. Similarly, policies that impact children can create avenues for a smooth trajectory toward healthy adulthood or place barriers along that path. For these reasons, legal actors and policy-makers must be educated about developmental factors that are relevant to any youth-related policies and practices. Furthermore, experts in child and adolescent development have the duty to be the educators. Together, educators and lawmakers can work together to promote wellbeing for children who interact with the legal system.

References

Ainsworth, M. (2010). Security and attachment. In R. Volpe (Ed.), *The secure child: Timeless lessons in parenting and childhood education* (pp. 43–53). Charlotte, NC: Information Age Publishing.

Angold, A., Costello, E. J., & Worthman, C. (1998). Puberty and depression: The roles of age, pubertal status, and pubertal timing. *Psychological Medicine, 28,* 10. doi: 10.1017/S003329179700593X.

Bakermans-Kranenburg, M. J., & Van Ijzendoorn, M. H. (2007). Research Review: Genetic vulnerability or differential susceptibility in child development: The case of attachment. *Journal of Child Psychology and Psychiatry, 48*(12), 1160–1173.

Baumrind, D. (2013). Authoritative parenting revisited: History and current status. In R. E. Larzelere, A. Morris, & A. W. Harrist (Eds.), *Authoritative parenting: Synthesizing nurturance and discipline for optimal child development* (pp. 11–34). Washington, DC: American Psychological Association.

Belsky, J. (2012). The development of human reproductive strategies: Progress and prospects. *Current Directions in Psychological Science, 21*(5), 310–316. doi: 10.1177/0963721412453588.

Blakemore, S. J., Burnett, S., & Dahl, R. E. (2010). The role of puberty in the developing adolescent brain. *Human Brain Mapping, 31*(6), 926–933. doi: 10.1002/hbm.21052.

Blakemore, S. J., & Choudhury, S. (2006). Development of the adolescent brain: Implications for executive function and social cognition. *Journal of Child Psychology and Psychiatry, 47*(3-4), 296–312. doi: 10.1111/j.1469-7610.2006.01611.x.

Bowlby, J. (1980). *Attachment and loss.* New York, NY: Basic Books.

Bremner, J. G. (2004). Cognitive development: Knowledge of the physical world. In G. Bremner & A. Fogel (Eds.), *Blackwell handbook of infant development.* Malden, MA: Blackwell. doi: 10.1111/b.9780631212355.2004.x.

Bronfenbrenner, U. (1992). Ecological systems theory. In R. Vasta (Ed.), *Six theories of child development: Revised formulations and current issues* (pp. 187–249). London, UK: Jessica Kingsley Publishers.

Brown, B. B. (2004). Adolescents' relationships with peers. In R. M. Lerner & L. Steinberg (Eds.), *Handbook of adolescent psychology* (2nd ed., pp. 363–394). Hoboken, NJ: Wiley.

Centers for Disease Control and Prevention. (2011). CDC growth charts. Retrieved August 6, 2013, from http://www.cdc.gov/growthcharts/cdc_charts.htm.

Chambers, R. A., Taylor, J. R., & Potenza, M. N. (2004). Developmental neurocircuitry of motivation in adolescence: A critical period of addiction vulnerability. *American Journal of Psychiatry, 160*(6), 12.

Chein, J., Albert, D., O'Brien, L., Uckert, K., & Steinberg, L. (2011). Peers increase adolescent risk taking by enhancing activity in the brain's reward circuitry. *Developmental Science, 14*(2), F1–F10.

Chen, X., Wu, H., Chen, H., Wang, L., & Cen, G. (2001). Parenting practices and aggressive behavior in Chinese children. *Parenting: Science and Practice, 1*(3), 159–184. doi:10.1207/S15327922PAR0103_01.

Clarke-Stewart, A., & Brentano, C. (2006). *Divorce: Causes and consequences.* New Haven, CT: Yale University Press.

Crockett, L. J., & Beal, S. J. (2012). The life course in the making: Gender and development of adolescents' expected timing of adult role transitions. *Developmental Psychology, 48*(6), 1727–1738. doi: 10.1037/a0027538.

Damon, W., & Hart, D. (1982). The development of self-understanding from infancy through adolescence. *Child Development, 53*(4), 24. doi: 10.2307/1129122.

Dorn, L. D., & Biro, F. M. (2011). Puberty and its measurement: A decade in review. *Journal of Research on Adolescence, 21*(1), 180–195. doi: 10.1111/j.1532-7795.2010.00722.x.

Ebbeling, C. B., Pawlak, D. B., & Ludwig, D. S. (2002). Childhood obesity: Public-health crisis, common sense cure. *The Lancet, 360*(9331), 473–482.

Eckerman, C. O., & Peterman, K. (2004). Peers and infant social/communicative development. In G. Bremner & A. Fogel (Eds.), *Blackwell handbook of infant development.* Malden, MA: Blackwell.

Elder, G. H., & Shanahan, M. J. (2006). The life course and human development. In Damon, William and Lerner, Richard M. (Eds.), *Handbook of Child Psychology*(pp. 665–715). Hoboken, NJ: Wiley Publishing.

Ellis, B. J., & Boyce, W. T. (2011). Differential susceptibility to the environment: Toward an understanding of sensitivity to developmental experiences and context. *Development and Psychopathology, 23*(1), 1–5. doi: 10.1017/S095457941000060X.

Englund, M. M., Kuo, S., Puig, J., & Collins, W. (2011). Early roots of adult competence: The significance of close relationships from infancy to early adulthood. *International Journal of Behavioral Development, 35*(6), 490–496. doi:10.1177/0165025411422994.

Erikson, E. H. (1980). *Identity and the life cycle.* New York, NY: Norton.

Flavell, J. H., Miller, P. H., & Miller, S. A. (2002). *Cognitive development* (4th ed.). Upper Saddle River, NJ: Prentice-Hall.

Foster, G. D., Sherman, S., Borradaile, K. E., Grundy, K. M., Vander Veur, S. S., Nachmani, ... Shults, J. (2008). A policy-based school intervention to prevent overweight and obesity. *Pediatrics, 121* (4), 794–802. doi: 10.1542/peds.2007-1365.

Fraga, M. F., Ballestar, E., Paz, M. F., Ropero, S., Setien, F., Ballestar, M. L.,... Esteller, M. (2005). Epigenetic differences arise during the lifetime of monozygotic twins. *Proceedings of the National Academy of Sciences USA, 102*(30), 10604–10609. doi: 10.1073/pnas.0500398102.

Graber, J. A., & Brooks-Gunn, J. (1999). Transitions and turning points: Navigating the passage from childhood through adolescence. *Developmental Psychology, 32*(4), 9.

Grisso, T., Steinberg, L., Woolard, J., Cauffman, E., Scott, E., Graham, S.,... Schwartz, R. (2003). Juveniles' competence to stand trial: A comparison of adolescents' and adults' capacities as trial defendants. *Law and Human Behavior, 27*(4), 333–363. doi:10.1023/A:1024065015717.

Harter, S. (2006). The self. In N. Eisenberg, W. Damon, & R. Lerner (Eds.), *Handbook of child psychology* (Vol. 3, pp. 505–570). Hoboken, NJ: Wiley.

Harter, S. (2012). *The construction of the self: Developmental and sociocultural foundations* (2nd ed.). New York, NY: Guilford Press.

Hutman, T., & Dapretto, M. (2009). The emergence of empathy during infancy. *Cognition, Brain, Behavior: An Interdisciplinary Journal, 13*(4), 367–390.

J.D.B. v. North Carolina, 131 S. Ct. 2394 (2011).

Johnson, M. H. (2004). Functional brain development during infancy. In G. Bremner & A. Fogel (Eds.), *Blackwell handbook of infant development* (pp. 169–190). Malden, MA: Blackwell.

Johnston-Brooks, C. H., Lewis, M. A., Evans, G. W., & Whalen, C. K. (1998). Chronic stress and illness in children: The role of allostatic load. *Psychosomatic Medicine, 60*(5), 597–603.

Jonson-Reid, M. (1998). Youth violence and exposure to violence in childhood. *Aggression and Violent Behavior, 3*(2), 159–179.

Kochanska, G., & Kim, S. (2012). Toward a new understanding of legacy of early attachments for future antisocial trajectories: Evidence from two longitudinal studies. *Development and Psychopathology, 24*(3), 783–806. doi:10.1017/S0954579412000375.

Lansford, J. E. (2009). Parental divorce and children's adjustment. *Perspectives on Psychological Science, 4*(2), 140–152. doi:10.1111/j.1745-6924.2009.01114.x

Moffitt, T. E. (1993). Adolescence-limited and life-course-persistent antisocial behavior: A developmental taxonomy. *Psychological Review, 100*(4), 674–701. doi:10.1037/0033-295X.100.4.674.

Moffitt, T. E., Caspi, A., Harrington, H., & Milne, B. J. (2002). Males on the life-course-persistent and adolescence-limited antisocial pathways: Follow-up at age 26 years. *Development and Psychopathology, 14*(1), 179–207. doi:10.1017/S0954579402001104.

Monahan, K. C., Steinberg, L., & Cauffman, E. (2009). Affiliation with antisocial peers, susceptibility to peer influence, and antisocial behavior during the transition to adulthood. *Developmental Psychology, 45*(6), 1520–1530. doi: 10.1037/a0017417.

Moshman, D. (2005). *Adolescent psychological development: Rationality, morality, and identity* (2nd ed.). Mahwah, NJ: Erlbaum.

National Center for Health Statistics. (2012). *Prevalence of Obesity in the United States, 2009-2010*. NCHS Data Brief, 82, 1-7. Retrieved online August 6, 2013. http://www.cdc.gov/nchs/data/databriefs/db82.pdf

Nurmi, J. E. (2004). Socialization and self development: Channeling, selection, adjustment, and reflection. In R. Lerner & L. Steinberg (Eds.), *Handbook of adolescent psychology* (2nd ed., pp. 85–124). Hoboken, NJ: Wiley.

Piaget, J. (2000). Piaget's theory. In K. Lee (Ed.), *Childhood cognitive development: The essential readings* (pp. 33–47). Malden, MA: Blackwell.

Rogol, A. D., Clark, P. A., & Roemmich, J. N. (2000). Growth and pubertal development in children and adolescents: Effects of diet and physical activity. *American Journal of Clinical Nutrition, 72*(2), 521s–528s.

Sampson, R. J., & Laub, J. H. (1994). Urban poverty and the family context of delinquency: A new look at structure and process in a classic study. *Child Development, 65,* 523–540.

Shonkoff, J. P., & Phillips, D. A. (2000). *From neurons to neighborhoods: The science of early childhood development*. Washington, DC: National Academy Press.

Smitsman, A. W. (2004). Action in infancy—perspectives, concepts, and challenges: The development of reaching and grasping. In G. Bremner & A. Fogel (Eds.), *Blackwell handbook of infant development*. Malden, MA: Blackwell.

Steinberg, L. (2008). A social neuroscience perspective on adolescent risk-taking. *Developmental Review, 28*(1), 78–106. doi: 10.1016/j.dr.2007.08.002.

Steinberg, L. (2011). Adolescents' risky driving in context. *Journal of Adolescent Health, 49*(6), 557–558. doi: 10.1016/j.jadohealth.2011.10.001.

Steinberg, L., Albert, D., Cauffman, E., Banich, M., Graham, S., & Woolard, J. (2008). Age differences in sensation seeking and impulsivity as indexed by behavior and self-report: Evidence for a dual systems model. *Developmental Psychology, 44*(6), 1764–1778. doi: 10.1037/a0012955.

Stratakis, C. A., Gold, P. W., & Chrousos, G. P. (1995). Neuroendocrinology of stress: Implications for growth and development. *Hormone Research in Paediatrics, 43*(4), 162–167. doi: 10.1159/000184269.

Sun, H., & Jensen, R. (1994). Body segment growth during infancy. *Journal of Biomechanics, 27*(3), 265–275. doi: 10.1016/0021-9290(94)90003-5.

Susman, E. J., & Rogol, A. (2004). Puberty and psychological development. In R. M. Lerner & L. Steinberg (Eds.), *Handbook of adolescent psychology* (2nd ed., pp. 15–44). Hoboken, NJ: Wiley.

Tarullo, A. R., & Gunnar, M. R. (2006). Child maltreatment and the developing HPA axis. *Hormones and behavior, 50*(4), 632–639. doi: 10.1016/j.yhbeh.2006.06.010.

Thompson, R. A. (2000). The legacy of early attachments. *Child Development, 71*(1), 145–152. doi:10.1111/1467-8624.00128.

van den Boom, D. (2004). First attachments: Theory and research. In G. Bremner & A. Fogel (Eds.), *Blackwell handbook of infant development* (pp. 296–325). Malden, MA: Blackwell.

Part I

LEGAL ACTIONS AFFECTING THE WELLBEING
AND RECOGNIZING (OR IGNORING)
THE DEVELOPMENTAL ABILITIES OF
JUVENILE DELINQUENTS

3

Psycholegal Aspects of Juvenile Delinquency

Cheryl D. Wills

In the past century, the US Supreme Court has afforded juvenile offenders increased legal protection while legislators have increased the likelihood that violent juvenile offenders will be prosecuted as adults (Feld, 1993; Mears, Hay, Gertz, & Mancini, 2007). This chapter will argue that the government needs to facilitate individualized rehabilitation for juveniles, including treatment of mental disorders, in an effort to positively shift the developmental trajectory of each youth while fostering skills that are conducive to healthful coping, self-control, decision making, and problem solving. Strengths-based multidisciplinary interventions that are gender and offense specific might improve each youth's wellbeing and reduce the likelihood of recidivism (Koller & Svoboda, 2002; Saleebey, 1996). Nonetheless, legal and practice reforms have not led to improved rehabilitations efforts.

The US Supreme Court recently determined that youth is a mitigating factor in legal proceedings involving juveniles (e.g., *Miller v. Alabama*, 2012). The Court has granted juveniles greater protections than adults with regard to capital sentencing (*Roper v. Simmons*, 2005) and life without parole for both homicide (*Miller v. Alabama*, 2012) and nonhomicide (*Graham v. Florida*, 2010) offenses. The Court also held, in *J.D.B. v. North Carolina* (2011), that police officers must consider a youth's age before informing the youth of the right to remain silent and placing the youth in custody. Adolescent emotional development is a dynamic process. A youth who is socially immature, has experienced neglect or trauma, or has an untreated mental disorder might, with appropriate intervention, be more amenable to change than a mature adult. The Court underscores the importance of considering the emotional wellbeing of justice-involved youths who may be receptive to rehabilitation. Although it might seem that the US Supreme Court recently has begun to focus on the wellbeing of youths by shielding them from the most punitive legal outcomes, the history of the US juvenile justice system illuminates the extent to which the Court and legislators have been responsive to the developmental needs of youths.

This chapter will examine the history, mission, and structure of the US juvenile justice system and how it affects the wellbeing of youth offenders. Through the use of case study examples, the needs of special populations, such as youths with mental disorders and female offenders, will be introduced to illustrate key concepts.[1]

The Evolution of the US Juvenile Justice System

The evolution of the juvenile justice system in the United States reflects an ever-shifting balance between two goals: rehabilitation and retribution. While initially the court represented a rehabilitative model, courts in the past 100 years have shifted juvenile court policies increasingly toward punishment and the promotion of public safety, often at the cost of truly rehabilitative outcomes.

The Origins of the Juvenile Court

The question of when juveniles are sufficiently mature enough to be held legally accountable as adults has been a contentious one. In the early to mid 19th century, juvenile accountability for criminal offenses was determined by the English Common Law Rule of Sevens (Streib, 1987). Youths older than 14 years were tried and sentenced as adults; some were subjected to capital punishment (Brumberg, 2003). Youths younger than 7 years were not accountable for criminal offenses, and youths between ages 7 and 14 years were in a gray zone for culpability; they were deemed criminally responsible if the prosecutor presented sufficient persuasive evidence to the court.

By the mid to late 19th century, social reform advocates began to attribute disruptive youth behavior to poverty and inadequate adult supervision. Activists supported implementation of the English Common law philosophy of *parens patriae*, which authorized the state to function as a parent by providing supervision and guidance for all children within its boundaries (Platt, 1977). By 1825, the Society for the Reformation of Delinquents opened the first of several Houses of Refuge that provided youths with shelter, meals, supervision, and structure. As the number of juveniles involved with courts grew, some jurisdictions began to separate youths from adult offenders.

In 1899, the Illinois Legislature enacted the Juvenile Court Act, which formalized the distinction between juvenile delinquents (who disregarded

---

[1] Case examples are based on years of clinical experience but are not based on any particular person or case.

the law) and dependent youths who had not committed criminal offenses but needed additional supervision due to abuse, neglect, or incorrigible behavior. The Act authorized formation of special courts and a probation system for juveniles between 7 and 16 years old. Juvenile courts used a less intimidating protocol for hearings, which included noncriminalized language. For example, juveniles did not plead guilty or not guilty to crimes or charges; they admitted or denied engaging in offensive behavior (Mack, 1909). The Illinois Juvenile Court Act also required child guidance teams, comprised of developmental and social services professionals, to conduct social assessments and to inform judges about each youth's history and rehabilitative needs. The multidisciplinary assessment model continues to be used in some mental health centers and juvenile courts today.

The juvenile justice movement that spread throughout the United States was ambitious, but legislators lacked sufficient resources for proper program implementation and maintenance. In the early 20th century, Houses of Refuge were replaced by juvenile training or reform schools that were not subjected to judicial or governmental oversight. By the mid 20th century, the juvenile justice system's mission had shifted from rehabilitation to retribution, restraint, and punishment. Although training schools did not have standardized programs and staff credentialing, juvenile court judges routinely gave delinquent minors indeterminate commitments with infrequent judicial progress reviews. School administrators determined when each youth was fit to return home, while adult offenders received finite sentences for the same offenses (*In re Gault*, 1967).

Increased Legal Protections in the Face of an Increasingly Punitive Juvenile System

A legal shift toward protecting the safety and rights of minors occurred in the 1960s. The legislative movement to shield children from abusive caretakers took hold after the publication of *The Battered Child Syndrome* (Kempe, Silverman, Steele, Droegemueller, & Silver, 1962). Soon after, the US Supreme Court addressed legal safeguards for youths in the juvenile justice system in a series of Court decisions. In 1966, Justice Fortas, speaking for the majority of the Court in *Kent v. US*, stated, "There may be grounds for concern that the child receives the worst of both worlds: that he gets neither the protections accorded to adults nor the solicitous care and regenerative treatment postulated for children" (p. 566). The *Kent* Court held that prior to transferring a youth's case from juvenile to criminal court, the youth has a right to a hearing in juvenile court and to meaningful representation from an attorney who has access to the evidence that would be used by the court to determine whether the waiver is valid. Also, the waiver order must be accompanied by a statement of the reasons for the transfer. The following year, the Court decided that during delinquency hearings, juveniles must be afforded the right to counsel, the right to timely notification of the allegation(s) or charge(s), the right to protection against self-incrimination, and the right to confront witnesses (*In re Gault*, 1967).

The Court continued to extend the legal protections associated with criminal court defendants to juveniles through the 1970s. Specifically, in 1970, the US Supreme Court held that, like in criminal court hearings, the legal standard for delinquency adjudication is beyond a reasonable doubt (*In re Winship*, 1970). The following year, the Court decided that, although juveniles do not have a constitutional right to a jury trial, a state may provide one if it chooses to do so (*McKeiver v. PA*, 1971). The US Supreme Court also determined that juvenile courts cannot violate the US Constitution's Double Jeopardy Clause by transferring a youth's case to criminal court after the youth has been adjudicated delinquent in juvenile court (*Breed v. Jones*, 1975; *Swisher v. Brady*, 1978).

In recent years, the US Supreme Court has taken up a renewed movement in limiting judicial power, but in a slightly different form. Rather than focusing on due process, the Supreme Court has limited the sanctions available to juvenile defendants, holding that no one under the age of 18 can receive the death penalty (*Roper v. Simmons*, 2005) or automatically receive life without parole without individualized consideration of the defendant's youth (*Miller v. Alabama*, 2012). The *Miller* ruling does not guarantee parole for juveniles who commit homicides. Rather, the offender must first convince the jury that he or she does not merit a life sentence and convince the parole board that she or he has been rehabilitated. The language of these recent cases has reflected an acknowledgment that juveniles, as a group, are less culpable for their actions than adults, and therefore, should not be as subject to the harshest of criminal sanctions. Nonetheless, mental health professionals remain concerned that the Court has not focused enough on the original rehabilitative goal of the juvenile justice system (Henggeler & Schoenwald, 2011).

Focus on Rehabilitation

Since the 1960s, the US Supreme Court has set limits on the use of judicial power in juvenile courts and increased juveniles' legal protections; however, it is important to note that these changes have revolved around the increasingly punitive nature of the juvenile court, with little attention being paid to the historical goal of rehabilitation. While the juvenile court's effort to meet the developmental and rehabilitation needs of each offender must be balanced carefully against community safety, the result of this balance is that youths who have engaged in dangerous offenses, lacked sufficient parental supervision and support, or have failed to comply with community-based rehabilitation have been placed in inadequate residential programs under court supervision.

The mental health community has clearly demonstrated that structure, supportive guidance, education, and other interventions can positively affect a youth's maturation (Burke, Loeber, & Birmaher, 2002; Fabiano et al., 2009), but these are unfortunately characteristics that many facilities and treatment programs lack. In fact, in some cases, failure to provide rehabilitation services to juvenile offenders has resulted in youths receiving additional legal complaints or charges (based on events that occurred in juvenile detention and corrections facilities) that are processed in criminal court (Peterson & Wills, 2010; Wills, 2009). In such cases, at the end of the residential commitment, youths may be transported from a juvenile corrections or detention facility to an adult jail or prison cell. This unfortunate situation illuminates the need for access to improved therapeutic interventions for all juvenile offenders.

The policy struggle with the balance between punitive and rehabilitative goals has been apparent in public policy and constitutional debates since the inception of the juvenile court. This balance is also apparent at the case-processing level, which is the subject of the next section.

How Juveniles Are Processed

In the past 20 years, psychiatrists, psychologists, and the legal community have paid significant attention to changes in how and where juveniles are processed. In particular, two issues related to the processing of juvenile cases have been the subject of considerable scholarship: transfer of juveniles to criminal court and juveniles' competency to be adjudicated or stand trial. This section will provide a brief overview of traditional juvenile processing and then review the literature specifically related to these two processes.

Traditional Juvenile Court Processing

States vary with regard to the age at which a person may be adjudicated in juvenile court rather than tried in criminal court, with the typical cutoff being between 16 and 18 years. When retained in juvenile court, youths may be processed via delinquency or dependency protocols based on the reasons the youth has entered the system. If youths have engaged in criminal behavior, then they are processed as delinquents. In contrast, dependent youths have not engaged in criminal behavior but still require court intervention, because they did not submit to the reasonable supervision of their caretakers. Truancy, curfew violations, underage drinking, sexual promiscuity, and/or running away from home are common behaviors, called "status offenses," that may result in a youth having to appear in court as a dependent.

In many ways, the roots of the original juvenile court of the early 1900s still exists in how juveniles are processed today, both in terms of language and the wider availability of processing options available in juvenile court when compared to criminal court. In terms of language, a minor does not make a "plea" but admits or denies an allegation. A juvenile is not "tried" but is "adjudicated." And a juvenile is not "sentenced" but receives a "disposition."

In terms of processing variability, juveniles may be formally processed, as described earlier, meaning that they go through an adjudication hearing and a disposition hearing (sometimes combined), in which they receive a sanction. Sanctions may range from a warning, unsupervised probation or supervised probation, or placement in a facility for a period of months or years (akin to a sentence). Probationers must submit to caretaker supervision, attend school or work, avoid conflict, abstain from substance use, and follow other court requirements. In some cases, the court may require the youth to live with a particular caretaker or foster parent in an effort to foster rehabilitation.

Juveniles may avoid formal processing, however, in two ways. They may be informally processed, avoiding adjudication or trial altogether, or they may be transferred and tried in criminal court. Informal processing occurs when a juvenile court may, at its discretion, refer the youth's case to another program in lieu of adjudication. Informal processing, including case diversion, can be a cost-effective way to address problematic youth behaviors while deferring a youth's involvement in the justice system. Diversion programs may provide structure and guidance, instill leadership skills, and/or offer alternative strategies for coping in an effort to reduce the youth's risk for reoffending. Youths may be referred to mental health, mentoring, or athletic programs, community service organizations, and so on. Some diversion programs, such as youth courts (also called "teen" or "peer courts"), require youths to admit to the alleged behavior before they are referred to the program. Youth courts have disposition or sentencing requirements (e.g., restitution, community service, anger management classes, or apology letters) that are decided by an ad hoc judge, with input from a peer jury. Youths may be invited back or required to serve as youth jurors, prosecutors, defense attorneys, or bailiffs as part of their sentencing. A youth who fails to complete a diversion program can be referred back to juvenile court for formal processing.

Transfer of Juvenile Cases to Criminal Court

In some cases, juveniles may be selected for formal processing in the adult criminal court. Transfer mechanisms vary from state to state, but they typically depend on some combination of the age of the juvenile, the severity of the alleged offense, and factors related to the individual (Grisso, 2010). The topic of juvenile transfer has received increased attention in the mental health community because of the large increase in the volume of transfers that has occurred since the 1980s. A spike in community violence in the 1980s resulted in codification of more punitive sanctions for juvenile offenders at the expense of therapeutic programming (Feld, 1993). Public perception that youths could not be rehabilitated in the juvenile justice system resulted in legislators enacting "tough on crime" laws, including automatic transfer of the most violent juvenile offenses to criminal courts.

Most states have a combination of judicial, prosecutorial, and legislative mechanisms in place to control whether a juvenile will be adjudicated in juvenile court or tried in criminal court. Juvenile court judges had full discretion in all waiver cases for much of the 20th century, but the process was arbitrary due to the absence of procedural requirements. In *Kent* (1966), the Court introduced eight criteria for courts to use when determining whether to waive juvenile cases to adult court. Mental health professionals who conduct youth waiver evaluations typically consider three of these criteria: severity of alleged offense/community safety, youth maturity, and rehabilitation potential (Grisso, 2010). These evaluations are used by mental health professionals to inform the court about a youth's mental health, trauma and treatment history, intellectual limitations, and other salient clinical matters.

In addition to refining discretion in judicial waiver cases, reforms have shifted the judicial power to select which cases to waive for classes of violent offenses to legislative and prosecutorial mechanisms. Legislative waivers mandate automatic transfer for certain kinds of allegations, often specifying a minimum age as well. Prosecutorial waivers permit the district attorney to use subjective criteria, including specific details about the alleged offense, community safety, and previous offenses to determine whether a juvenile's case will be processed in juvenile or criminal court (Feld, 1993; Griffin, Addie, Adams, & Firestine, 2011; Grisso 2010). The increased use of prosecutorial and legislative waivers means that mental health professionals have less of a role in individual cases, because they are not called for evaluations.

At least partially as a result of these reforms, between 1983 and 1998, the number of juveniles in adult jails increased 3.6 fold (Austin, Johnson, & Gregoriou, 2000). In some jurisdictions, youths as young as 10 years old could have their cases transferred to criminal court. In legislative and some prosecutorial waiver cases, a youth's mental health history, rehabilitation potential, and maturity may not be used to mitigate culpability; the information may not be tendered in court until the sentencing stage. These concerns were cited by the *Miller* Court when it declared automatic life without parole unconstitutional for juveniles (*Miller v. Alabama*, 2012). Despite the stated concern, the US Supreme Court has thus far declined to hear cases regarding the constitutionality of these types of waivers.

Given that waiver mechanisms have become so common, researchers have focused considerable resources on evaluating the effectiveness of waiver in both reducing future crime and promoting juvenile wellbeing. Juveniles whose cases are transferred to the criminal justice system complete suicide at higher rates than their peers who remain in the juvenile justice system (Flaherty, 1980; for more on this topic, see Chapter 7 of this volume). Youths in the criminal justice system also have higher rates of more acute mental health disorders, as evidenced by "substantial distress or treatment needs," than their peers in juvenile corrections facilities and adults in the criminal justice system (Murrie, Henderson, Vincent, Rockett, & Mundt, 2009). Research also suggests that in the criminal justice system, youths are three times more likely to suffer from major depressive disorder than incarcerated adults (Washburn et al., 2008). Further examination of the association between untreated acute mental disorder and violent juvenile offenders is warranted.

It is difficult to track the legal outcomes of cases that are waived to criminal court. According to the US Department of Justice, in 2007, 21 states transferred 14,000 cases from juvenile court to criminal court (Griffin et al., 2011). Even fewer states reported this information publicly, and still fewer reported demographic information, types of offenses, and sentencing outcomes (Griffin et al., 2011). Although juvenile offending has diminished in recent years, the upward spike in punitive dispositions for juvenile offenders persists. Yet when researchers control for the severity of the offense and the number of past offenses, juveniles whose cases are transferred to criminal court have higher rates of recidivism and are arrested sooner after they are released to the community (Myers, 2001, 2003). This latter trend may exist for myriad reasons, including the following characteristics of the criminal justice system: (a) the system is not designed to provide developmentally informed rehabilitation for juveniles; (b) it emphasizes punishment, deterrence, and restraint instead of rehabilitation; (c) youths in prison experience reduced family support and involvement relative to youths in juvenile detention and corrections facilities; (d) juveniles are exposed to and may learn negative behavior from seasoned adult offenders; (e) juveniles in prison are physically and sexually victimized at higher rates (Redding, 2003); and (f) youths have fewer employment and education opportunities upon release due to having a criminal record.

In summary, the rates of juveniles being tried in criminal court have increased over the past two decades, despite the fact that researchers have found little evidence that transfer reduces recidivism but significant evidence that youths processed in criminal court have more serious mental health concerns. An additional concern that psychiatrists and psychologists have recently noted is whether juveniles have the legal abilities required to understand and engage in their defenses, as discussed next.

Competency to Be Adjudicated in Juvenile Court or Stand Trial in Criminal Court

In the United States, defendants are presumed to be capable of proceeding with adjudication, even when they are affected by serious mental conditions that can impede their efforts to advocate for themselves in court, such as psychosis, intellectual disorder (formerly mild mental retardation) or autistic spectrum disorder (*Dusky v. US*, 1960). When mental impairment appears evident, the court or an attorney can request a mental health evaluation to determine the youth's ability to proceed with adjudication. In 1960, the US Supreme Court held that a criminal defendant is incompetent to stand trial if a severe mental disease or defect renders the person incapable of engaging in reasonable and rational consultation with his or her attorney or of having a "rational as well as factual understanding of the proceedings against him" (*Dusky v. US*, 1960, p. 402).

The Supreme Court has not explicitly extended this constitutional right to juveniles adjudicated in juvenile court; therefore, the issue of whether juveniles cannot be adjudicated if incompetent is left up to states to decide. Many states still remain silent on the issue. Only a few states have wholly accepted and extended the adult standard to juveniles in juvenile court. For those states that have yet to decide or have decided to extend some form of this competency right to juvenile court, a larger issue is what legal standard should apply.

The National Youth Screening & Assessment Project attempted to address the issue of juvenile competency by publishing a guide for lawmakers and other stakeholders seeking to develop or revise juvenile competence-to-stand-trial legislation (Larson & Grisso, 2011). The document is informed by developmental psychology, describes adjudicative competence, and explains how mental disorders and child development can affect a juvenile's ability to assist his or her attorney with a defense and understand legal proceedings.

Although severe impairment from a mental disorder is generally accepted as a legally permissible reason for adjudicative incompetence in juveniles, most states have not directly addressed how courts should weigh developmental immaturity. This creates a challenge for defense attorneys who estimate that 10% of juveniles lack adjudicative capacity due to immaturity (Viljoen, McLachlan, Wingrove, & Penner, 2010). Defense attorneys request adjudicative competency evaluations in about half of the suspected cases (Viljoen et al., 2010).

Juveniles who are adjudicated incompetent to proceed with adjudication may be ordered to participate in a competency restoration program that includes mental health treatment and/or legal education. Although the restoration process may help youths with severe mental impairment achieve stability and progress through the legal system, it also can obfuscate treatment and/or rehabilitation goals, especially when the youth's mental disorder is not likely to improve substantially. In such cases, developing an individualized rehabilitation plan for the youth, under court supervision, may modify the youth's behavior so that the youth will be able to function safely and appropriately in the community. A mental health evaluation can inform the court about individualized rehabilitation planning for the youth. Therapeutic interventions may include educational support; mental health treatment, including anger management and behavior modification programs, caretaker coaching, family therapy, and intensive case management; other medical services; home detention monitoring using GPS technology; residential placement; and respite care services.

Special Topics in Juvenile Justice: Mental Health and Gender

Controversies such as transferring juvenile cases to the criminal justice system are not new to the juvenile justice system. In recent years, the system's approach to challenging matters, both longstanding and recent, has been informed by evolving research, law, policy, and technology. This section will examine two topics (e.g., mental illness and gender) in juvenile justice that have implications for the wellbeing of children.

Mentally Ill Youths

Adolescence is a time of physiological, social, and emotional transition, which can be challenging. The fifth edition of *The Diagnostic and Statistical Manual of Mental Disorders* (*DSM-5*; APA, 2013) suggests that the prevalence of serious mental disorders begins to increase during adolescence and those mental disorders of childhood, such as attention-deficit/hyperactivity disorder (ADHD), may persist into adolescence and adulthood (APA, 2013). Research suggests that youths in juvenile detention and adult corrections facilities are more likely to suffer from psychosis than their peers in the community (Fazel, Doll, & Långström, 2008). Youths who have experienced physical emotional and/or sexual trauma and its psychological manifestations are disproportionately represented in the juvenile justice system (Abram et al., 2004). Legal problems sometimes bring previously undiagnosed mental disorders to the attention of families, youths, and the court.

Competent mental health assessment, diagnosis, and treatment are needed to contain the adverse effects of mental disorders on adolescent development. Youths with mental disorders respond better to caretaker supervision and other therapeutic interventions when mental health stabilization and rehabilitation are top priorities. This occurs because youths who receive effective treatment suffer less social, interpersonal, and behavioral impairment from their mental disorders (APA, in press). A collaborative relationship among the mental health provider, youth, and caretaker(s) is conducive to successful mental health rehabilitation. When the alliance is compromised, the youth may regress psychologically and behaviorally, as in the case that follows.

Justin, a 15-year-old youth, was adjudicated delinquent for assault and possession of marijuana based on events that occurred in school. His father informed the court that Justin has "severe" ADHD and refuses to cooperate with treatment that helps him concentrate, follow directions, and make better choices. When he stopped taking medication, his behavior became unmanageable at home and in school, where he earned poor grades, argued with teachers, walked out of class, ran through halls, and injured a peer during a fight. The court ordered Justin to complete a residential drug rehabilitation program, from which he was expelled for fighting.

The court sought consultation from a forensic child and adolescent psychiatrist who recommended mental health treatment, including medication management, social skills and anger management therapies, intensive mental health case management, and a high level of structure for Justin. The psychiatrist recommended that Justin enroll in a drug rehabilitation program as soon as his mental health stabilized. The judge ordered Justin to comply with the recommendations. As soon as Justin resumed mental health treatment, his behavior and grades improved and he was able to complete a drug rehabilitation program.

In Justin's case, the court reinforced the importance of mental health and addictive disorders treatment as key components of his rehabilitation. When Justin complied, his academic performance, behavior, and progress in the drug rehabilitation program were no longer problematic. When juveniles with mental illness receive and adhere to mental health treatment, they likely will have less impairment due to their mental disorders, be more receptive to therapeutic interventions, and be more cognizant of appropriate boundaries. Access to mental health treatment can be a barrier to youth rehabilitation. Budgetary restrictions and a shortage of child psychiatrists, especially those with forensic interests or training, create barriers to mental health care for justice-involved youths.

Today, just as one century ago, families and communities lack sufficient resources to provide comprehensive rehabilitative programming for youths. Although now more is known about mental health interventions, some youths with mental disorders continue to experience substantial impairment. The solution is multidisciplinary. Juvenile justice, education, recreation, and mental health care professionals have to collaborate with community leaders and families to craft interventions that are conducive to prosocial and healthful behaviors for at-risk youths.

In some cases, caretaker, youth, and/or systemic resistance may prevent a youth from receiving mental health care even when it is available. This increases the risk of adverse consequences, including suicide (Farand, Chagnon, Renaud, & Rivard, 2004). Juvenile justice professionals should be trained to identify signs of mental disorders in youths and to refer them for mental health services. Caretakers also should be held accountable for obtaining mental health services for youths who require them. Court-centered interventions for youths with serious mental disorders include youth mental health court and youth drug court programs, which support motivated youths as they receive community-based rehabilitative interventions, instead of incarceration or other residential treatment.

Female Delinquents in the Juvenile Justice System

Gender-informed rehabilitation of youths in the juvenile justice system is important because females mature and respond to stressors differently than males. Although most juvenile offender research focuses on males, the female offender population is growing at a faster rate. In 2009, approximately 1,504,100 juvenile delinquency cases were processed by the courts (Puzzanchera, Adams, & Hockenberry, 2012). Between 1985 and 2009, the representation of female offenders in juvenile delinquency cases grew from 19% to 28%. The 3% annual growth rate of female offender cases during that time period was three times that of male offenders (Puzzanchera et al., 2012). There is a need for more evidence-based rehabilitative interventions for female youth offenders. See Chapter 6 of this volume for a study of gender-specific programming for female juvenile delinquents.

Incarcerated females have gynecological and other health care needs that increase their rehabilitation costs. They have higher rates of sexual trauma and are more likely than males to require mental health services for depression, posttraumatic stress disorder, nonsuicidal self-injurious behavior (APA, 2013), and suicide attempts (Giaconia et al., 1995; Leeb, Lewis, & Zolotor, 2010; McCabe, Lansing, Garland, & Hough, 2002).

Female offenders are more challenging to work with in residential settings and they may respond differently to adversity and threats (Wills, 2003). Females tend to engage in indirect or relational aggression more than males, whose disruptive behavior tends to be more externalized and physical (Kroneman, Loeber, Hipwell, & Koot, 2009). Generally speaking, training manuals for staff at detention centers, jails, and prisons are designed to equip staff to work with offenders who engage in direct aggression. Also, the diagnostic criteria for conduct disorder emphasize externalizing behaviors and tend to capture more males than females (Cote et al., 2001).

The gender bias inherent in conduct disorder has compelled some researchers to suggest gender-specific diagnostic criteria for conduct disorder so that larger groups of females can be studied (Cote et al., 2001). Although this proposal may ultimately lead to effective gender-specific rehabilitative programming for female juvenile offenders, females could be subjected to more punitive treatment since the juvenile justice system and others tend to view the antisocial behavior criteria for conduct disorder unfavorably (Jones & Cauffman, 2008; Rockett, Murrie, & Boccaccini, 2007). At times, antisocial behavior in females can be indicative of treatable emotional problems. The following case example illustrates this concept.

Fifteen-year-old Sarah was referred to the youth mental health team after she received several disciplinary write-ups in the juvenile corrections facility for aggression toward staff and peers and for nonsuicidal self-injurious behavior. During her early childhood, Sarah repeatedly witnessed violence and hid in a closet for her protection. When she was 12 years old, she was sent to live with her maternal aunt, who declined mental health services for Sarah on several occasions.

During the clinical interview, Sarah described nightmares, flashbacks, and other symptoms that were consistent with posttraumatic stress disorder. Therapy helped Sarah identify situations that triggered intrusive recollections of her past trauma, including yelling, being restrained, and being locked in small spaces. The mental health team reviewed Sarah's situation with the residential unit supervisor. They modified Sarah's rehabilitation program so that she would not be physically restrained or locked in her room if she agreed to go to the calm-down room when directed to do so. Sarah also was excused from the trauma victims' group therapy program because her self-injurious behavior consistently occurred after this group met; hearing her peers' stories retraumatized and destabilized Sarah. Her quarterly court report indicated that her behavior had improved significantly. The judge praised her for her progress and decided not to add time to her commitment for her past aggression toward staff as long as she continued to rehabilitate herself.

A healthy collaboration between supervisory staff and mental health professionals made Sarah's comprehensive mental health assessment and treatment possible. The clinician's awareness of how trauma can affect young females and the facility's commitment to individualized rehabilitation made it possible for Sarah to be excused from the trauma victims' group. Candidates for the trauma group should be screened prior to being invited to participate in the group. Research is needed to identify cost-effective interventions for female juvenile offenders. Education on gender-related issues discussed earlier is also essential if mental health professionals and facilities are to best address the special needs of female juveniles.

Summary and Future Directions

During the past century, the US juvenile justice system has struggled to find a balance among holding youth offenders accountable, rehabilitating them, and maintaining community safety. When legislators have favored accountability and community safety, rehabilitation of youth offenders often has been overlooked. In the mid 1960s, the US Supreme Court began to formalize procedural protections for juveniles in court. Recent US Supreme Court decisions have illuminated the need for courts to consider mental health and maturity during legal decisions involving youths, as they may be more amenable to rehabilitation than adult offenders.

Therapeutic interventions are essential to improving the wellbeing of justice-involved youths. Rehabilitation programs should be multidisciplinary, foster emotional stability, encourage prosocial behavior, and illuminate the capacity of each youth to effect positive change in his or her life and community. Research may identify effective practices to incorporate into therapeutic interventions for juveniles. Programs should address basic needs (educational, medical, nutritional, social) as well as concerns that are specific to individual youths, such as type of offense, gender, trauma and victimization history, culture, physical disability, intellectual limitations, mental disorders, and addictive behavior, including substance use and gambling.

One specific area that deserves additional study is the rehabilitation of juveniles involved in stalking and sex offenses, including an examination of the role of technology in youth sexual offending and victimization. Youth involvement in cyberstalking, identity theft, cyber bullying, and sexting has become more common due to facility, perceived anonymity, and access to electronic devices (Mitchell, Finkelhor, Jones, & Wolak, 2012; Sacco, Argudin, Maguire, & Tallon, 2010). Technological innovation has outpaced the implementation of laws and policies that govern it. The influence of technology on juvenile offending will increase in the 21st century.

In addition, some groups of high-risk juvenile offenders need special attention from researchers. First, youths whose offensive behavior begins prior to adolescence need effective remediation; they have a higher rate of recidivism than those whose offending begins during adolescence. Second, juveniles in the adult criminal justice system need effective interventions since, relative to youths in the juvenile justice system, they have committed more violent offenses and are more vulnerable to victimization, mental disability, and completed suicide. Third, studies are needed to find effective ways to identify and rehabilitate juveniles who may lack adjudicative competency. These groups need safe, developmentally informed, individualized, evidence-informed rehabilitation.

In sum, community-based rehabilitation will continue to prove valuable if it reduces recidivism, community violence, and the population of youths in residential juvenile justice settings. Research into early intervention programs for at-risk youths is needed to identify models that reduce these youths' risk for future offending. Special attention should be paid to certain groups, like females and mentally ill youth, as they have special needs that should be addressed. Improving the quality of and access to effective therapeutic youth programs should be a top priority in the 21st century.

References

Abram, K. M., Teplin, L. A., Charles, D. R., Longworth, S. L., McClelland, G. M., & Dulcan, M. K. (2004). Posttraumatic stress disorder and trauma in youth in juvenile detention. *Archives of General Psychiatry, 61*(4), 403–410. doi: 10.1001/archpsyc.61.4.403.

American Psychiatric Association. (2013). *Diagnostic and statistical manual of mental disorders* (5th ed.). Washington, DC: Author.

Austin, J., Johnson, K. D., & Gregoriou, M. (2000). *Juveniles in adult prisons and jails: A national assessment.* Washington, DC: US Department of Justice.

Breed v. Jones, 421 U.S. 519 (1975).

Brumberg, J. J. (2003). *Kansas Charley: The story of a 19th-century boy murderer.* New York, NY: Viking Press.

Burke, J. D., Loeber, R., & Birmaher, B. (2002). Oppositional defiant disorder and conduct disorder: A review of the past 10 years, part II. *Journal of the American Academy of Child and Adolescent Psychiatry, 41,* 1275–1293. doi: 10.1097/00004583-200211000-00009.

Cote, S., Zoccolillo, M., Tremblay, R. E., Nagin, D., & Vitaro, F. (2001). Predicting girls' conduct disorder in adolescence from childhood trajectories of disruptive behaviors. *Journal of the American Academy of Child and Adolescent Psychiatry, 40,* 678–684. doi: 10.1097/00004583-200106000-00013.

Dusky v. United States, 362 U.S. 402 (1960).

Fabiano, G. A., Pelham, W. E., Jr., Coles, E. K., Gnagy, E. M., Chronis-Tuscano, A., & O'Connor, B. C. (2009). A meta-analysis of behavioral treatments for attention-deficit/hyperactivity disorder. *Clinical Psychology Review, 29*(2), 129–140. doi: 10.1016/j.cpr.2008.11.001.

Farand, L., Chagnon, F., Renaud, J., & Rivard, M. (2004). Completed suicides among Quebec adolescents involved with juvenile justice and child welfare services. *Suicide and Life Threatening Behavior, 34*(1), 2–35. doi:10.1521/suli.34.1.24.27774.

Fazel, S., Doll, H., & Långström, N. (2008). Mental disorders among adolescents in juvenile detention and correctional facilities: A systematic review and metaregression analysis of 25 surveys. *Journal of the American Academy of Child and Adolescent Psychiatry, 47*(9), 1010–1019. doi: 10.1097/CHI.0b013e31817eecf3.

Feld, B. C. (1993). Criminalizing the American juvenile court. *Crime and Justice, 17*, 197–280.

Flaherty, M. G. (1980). *An assessment of the national incidence of juvenile suicide in adult jails, lockups and juvenile detention centers.* Urbana-Champaign: University of Illinois Press.

Giaconia, R. M., Reinherz, H. Z., Silverman, A. B., Pakiz, B., Abbie, K., & Cohen, E. (1995). Traumas and posttraumatic stress disorder in a community population of older adolescents. *Journal of the American Academy of Child and Adolescent Psychiatry, 34*(10), 1369–1380. doi: 10.1097/00004583-199510000-00023.

Graham v. Florida, 130 S. Ct. 2011 (2010).

Griffin, P., Addie, S., Adams, B., & Firestine, K. (2011). *Trying juveniles as adults: An analysis of state transfer laws and reporting.* US Department of Justice. Retrieved July 2013, from https://www.ncjrs.gov/pdffiles1/ojjdp/232434.pdf.

Grisso, T. (2010). Clinicians' transfer evaluations: How well can they assist judicial discretion? *Louisiana Law Review, 71*, 157–189.

Henggeler, S., & Schoenwald, S. J. (2011). Evidence-based interventions for juvenile offenders and juvenile justice policies that support them. *Social Policy Report, 25*, 1–20.

In re Gault, 387 U.S. 1 (1967).

In re Winship, 397 U.S. 385 (1970).

J.D.B. v. North Carolina, 131 S. Ct. 2394 (2011).

Jones, S., & Cauffman, E. (2008). Juvenile psychopathy and judicial decision making: An empirical analysis of an ethical dilemma. *Behavioral Sciences and the Law, 26*, 151–165. doi: 10.1002/bsl.792.

Kempe, C., Silverman, F. N., Steele, B. F., Droegemueller, W., & Silver, H. K. (1962). The battered-child syndrome. *Journal of the American Medical Association, 181*(1), 17–24.

Kent v. U.S., 383 U.S. 541 (1966).

Koller, J. R., & Svoboda, S. K. (2002). The application of a strengths-based mental health approach in schools. *Childhood Education, 78*, 291–294. doi: 10.1080/00094056.2002.10522744.

Kroneman, L. M., Loeber, R, Hipwell, A. E., & Koot, H. M. (2009). Girls' disruptive behavior and its relationship to family functioning: A review. *Journal of Child and Family Studies, 18*, 259–273. doi: 10.1007/s10826-008-9226-x.

Larson, K. A., Grisso, T., & National Youth Screening & Assessment Project. (2011). *Developing statutes for competence to stand trial in juvenile delinquency proceedings: A guide for lawmakers.* Retrieved July 2013, from http://works.bepress.com/thomas_grisso/106.

Leeb, R. T., Lewis, T., & Zolotor, A. J. (2010). A review of physical and mental health consequences of child abuse and neglect and implications for practice. *American Journal of Lifestyle Medicine, 5*, 454–468. doi: 10.1177/1559827611410266.

Mack, J. S. (1909). The juvenile court. *Harvard Law Review, 23*, 104–122.

McCabe, K. M., Lansing, A. E., Garland, A., & Hough, R. (2002). Gender differences in psychopathology, functional impairment, and familial risk factors among adjudicated delinquents. *Journal of the American Academy of Child and Adolescent Psychiatry, 41*(7), 860–867. doi: 10.1097/00004583-200207000-00020.

McKeiver v. Pennsylvania, 403 U. S. 528 (1971).

Mears, D. P., Hay C., Gertz, M, & Mancini, C. (2007). Public opinion and the foundation of the juvenile court. *Criminology, 45*, 223–257. doi: 10.1111/j.1745-9125.2007.00077.x.

Miller v. Alabama, 132 S. Ct. 2455 (2012).

Mitchell, K. J., Finkelhor, D., Jones, L. M., Wolak. J. (2012) Prevalence and characteristics of youth sexting: A national study. *Pediatrics, 129*(1), 13–20. doi: 10.1542/peds.2011-1730.

Murrie, D.C., Henderson, C.E., Vincent, G.M., Rockett, R. L., & Mundt, C. (2009). Psychiatric symptoms among juveniles incarcerated in adult prison. *Psychiatric Services, 60*, 1092–1097. doi: 10.1176/appi.ps.60.8.1092.

Myers, D. L. (2001). *Excluding violent youths from juvenile court: The effectiveness of legislative waiver*. New York, NY: LFB Scholarly.

Myers, D. L. (2003). The recidivism of violent youths in juvenile and adult court: A consideration of selection bias. *Youth Violence and Juvenile Justice, 1*, 79–101. doi: 10.1177/1541204002238365.

Peterson, B., & Wills C.D. (2010) Ohio River Valley Juvenile Corrections Facility site visit: Behavioral health report. November 16-17, 2010. *SK. v. Stickrath* Stipulation Agreement, 2:04-CV-1206.

Platt, A. M. (1977). *The child savers: The invention of delinquency*. Chicago, IL: University of Chicago Press.

Puzzanchera, C., Adams, B., & Hockenberry, S. (2012). *Juvenile court statistics 2009*. National Center for Juvenile Justice. Retrieved July 2013, from http://www.ojjdp.gov/pubs/239114.pdf.

Redding, R. E. (2003). The effects of adjudicating and sentencing juveniles as adults: Research and policy implications *Youth Violence and Juvenile Justice, 1*, 128–155. doi: 10.1177/1541204002250875.

Rockett, J. L., Murrie, D. C., & Boccaccini, M. T. (2007). Diagnostic labeling in juvenile justice settings: Do psychopathy and conduct disorder findings influence clinicians? *Psychological Services, 4*, 107–122. doi: 10.1037/1541-1559.4.2.107.

Roper v. Simmons, 543 U.S. 551 (2005).

Sacco, D., Argudin, R., Maguire, J. & Tallon, K. (2010). *Sexting: Youth practices and legal implications* [Berkman Center Research Pub. No. 2010-8]. Retrieved July 2013, from Social Science Research Network: http://dx.doi.org/10.2139/ssrn.1661343.

Saleebey, D. (1996). The strengths perspective in social work practice: Extensions and cautions. *Social Work, 41*, 296–305. doi:10.1093/sw/41.6.683-a.

Streib, V. L. (1987). *Death penalty for juveniles*. Bloomington: Indiana University Press.

Swisher v. Brady, 438 U.S. 204 (1978).

Viljoen, J. L., McLachlan, K., Wingrove, T., & Penner, E. (2010). Defense attorneys' concerns about the competence of adolescent defendants. *Behavioral Sciences and the Law, 28*, 630–646. doi: 10.1002/bsl.954.

Washburn, J., Teplin, L., Voss, L., Simon, C., Abram, K., & McClelland, G. (2008). Psychiatric disorders among detained youths: A comparison of youths processed in juvenile court and adult criminal court. *Psychiatric Services, 59*, 965–973. doi: 10.1176/appi.ps.59.9.965.

Wills, C. D. (2003, August). *Rehabilitating traumatized youth in Louisiana and beyond*. Paper presented at the annual meeting of the Judicial Council of the National Bar Association, New Orleans, LA.

Wills, C. D. (2009). Ohio River Valley Juvenile Corrections Facility site visit: Behavioral health report: February 11-12, 2009. *SK. v. Stickrath* Stipulation Agreement, 2:04-CV-1206.

4

Police Interviewing and Interrogation of Adolescent Suspects: Process and Outcomes

Hayley M. D. Cleary and Sarah Vidal

Police interviewing is at the forefront of psycholegal research, especially in the past 20 years. Driven by high-profile false confession cases such as Michael Crowe and the Central Park Jogger suspects (Kassin, 2008), the media increasingly focused on police interaction with citizens, and researchers (e.g., Leo, 1996; Kassin et al., 2007) have studied these interactions and their potentially momentous justice implications. Interrogation research is significant and timely because it crosses multiple disciplines: Legal professionals care about the practice implications of evolving case law and legislative decisions, social scientists care about the social implications of false convictions and unjust imprisonment, clinicians care about preserving the rights of mentally ill suspects, and developmentalists care about child and adolescent vulnerabilities that may impact the course and outcome of police interrogations of youth.

Recent Supreme Court cases suggest that police interrogation is, and will continue to be, a hotly contested social and legal issue. In 2004, the Supreme Court issued a controversial opinion in *Yarborough v. Alvarado* that declared that police do not have to consider age when determining whether a suspect is in police custody for the purposes of *Miranda*. The circumstances of 17-year-old Alvarado's interaction with police raised a host of concerns about adolescents' capacities to make informed judgments about their own legal best interests. The case, in conjunction with *Roper v. Simmons* (2005), which outlawed the juvenile death penalty, and several cases that struck down several aspects of mandatory life without parole for juveniles (*Graham v. Florida*, 2010; *Jackson v. Hobbs*, 2012; *Miller v. Alabama*, 2012), demonstrated that the

Supreme Court will indeed tackle questions regarding juvenile defendants' decision-making abilities and will even consider developmental psychological research in its opinions. Perhaps most significant among recent Supreme Court decisions is the opinion in *J.D.B. v. North Carolina* (2011), which reversed the Court's position in *Alvarado* and decreed that police must indeed consider age in custody determinations. Such a drastic change after just 7 years demonstrates the need, perhaps now more than ever, for interrogation research to keep pace with evolving legal standards pertaining to juvenile suspects and defendants. It is clear that these difficult questions will remain in the public limelight, and it is critical that psycholegal research continues to assist the courts in untangling them.

Despite the potentially grave consequences that interrogations can have for juveniles, we know surprisingly little about this unique context. While empirical interest in police interrogation has proliferated in recent years, most research examines the interrogation-related capacities that suspects bring into the interrogation room; social science lacks even basic descriptive information about the interrogation setting and its participants. Though theory-driven research on components of the interrogation process is important, research that eschews presumptions about this context to actually document real interrogations is critical for framing future research. Moreover, most existing interrogation research examines adult suspects only. Given the myriad of developmentally based vulnerabilities youth exhibit via laboratory and self-report methods (e.g., poor comprehension of *Miranda* rights, Grisso et al., 2003; susceptibility to false confessions, Redlich & Goodman, 2003), interrogation research that adopts a developmental framework is imperative.

Why Study Interrogation?

There are numerous legal and procedural incentives to understanding the interrogation process. First, police hold tremendous influence over the fate of criminal and delinquency cases. Officers may arrest, detain, or release individuals based (among other things) on the information acquired during questioning. Police decide whom to question about a crime as well as where, when, and how to conduct questioning in order to obtain accurate and complete information. Second, research demonstrates that confession evidence is extremely powerful (Drizin & Leo, 2004). Drizin and Leo (2004) characterized confession evidence as "inherently prejudicial and highly damaging to a defendant, even if it is the product of coercive interrogation, even if it is supported by no other evidence, and even if it is ultimately proven false beyond any reasonable doubt" (p. 959). Laboratory studies reveal that confession evidence affects mock jurors' verdicts more than eyewitness and character testimony (Kassin & Neumann, 1997), regardless of whether the confession is perceived as voluntary or coerced (Kassin & Sukel, 1997).

Third, interrogation is a legal context that may be especially susceptible to due process violations or other procedural justice concerns, even inadvertently. Due to the "innate secrecy of such proceedings" (*Miranda v. Arizona*, 1966, p. 532), the Supreme Court has historically acknowledged the impossibility of transparency in police interrogations and has accordingly imposed restrictions on police behavior and interrogation procedures. For example, police are not allowed to make explicit threats or promises (*Bram v. United States*, 1897), and physical force has long been prohibited (*Brown v. Mississippi*, 1936). Though the incidence of such behaviors cannot be determined, the frequency of overt police misconduct is likely low relative to the potential due process violations that are more relevant to routine interrogation procedures that are ill defined in case law and policy. For example, if research demonstrates that youth disproportionately perceive the interrogation process itself as coercive or unjust, that police treat adolescent suspects differently from adults, or that police (inadvertently) use interview strategies that unduly coerce *Miranda* waivers, then these elements of routine police interrogation could affect due process for exponentially more youth in the justice system than overt police misconduct likely would.

Why Study Juveniles Separately?

Developmental traits that differentiate youth from adults intellectually, psychosocially, and emotionally as a matter of normative developmental patterns are well documented. These developmental differences suggest that juveniles may experience the interrogation process differently than adults, which may put them at a greater risk of engaging in behaviors or decision making (e.g., false confessions) that jeopardize their wellbeing via serious psychological, legal, and social consequences. It is well known, for example, that adolescents are less risk-averse than adults. When making choices about risks, adolescents orient more toward opportunities for gains than toward protection against losses (Gardner & Herman, 1990). Adolescents are more present-oriented than adults (Steinberg & Scott, 2003); they accord more weight to the short-term consequences of decisions (both risks and rewards) and are more likely to discount the future (Gardner & Herman, 1990; Reyna & Farley, 2006). Compared to adults, adolescents in the interrogation room may be disproportionately influenced by differential risk perceptions and foreshortened time perspective, particularly with regard to *Miranda* waiver and confession. They may comply with interrogators' requests to whatever extent necessary for them to be released, even to their legal detriment. Grisso (1981) empirically demonstrated this tendency when he asked a delinquent youth sample to describe the consequences of waiving one's right to silence when questioned by police. The consequence mentioned most frequently was the police's immediate response (i.e., police will let youth "go home" if they talk). Today's juvenile suspects likely find themselves in an unfamiliar environment in which short-term benefits (e.g., getting to "go home") appear extremely appealing, even if they result in poor decisions (e.g., waiving *Miranda* rights, confession) that disserve the youth's long-term legal best interest.

An additional distinguishing feature of adolescence involves a greater propensity compared to adults to comply with requests from authority figures. Though data are limited, several studies report age-based differences in interrogation-related compliance. In a recent large-scale study with both incarcerated and community populations, youth aged 15 years and younger were more likely to comply with requests from police and attorneys in a vignette than older adolescents and young adults (Grisso et al., 2003). When presented with a specific interrogation scenario including options to (a) confess to the offense, (b) deny the offense, or (c) refuse to talk, nearly 60% of youth in the youngest age category (11–13 years) chose confession as the "best choice," compared to only 20% of young adults (18–24 years; Grisso et al., 2003). Results did not vary across ethnicity, gender, or detained/community status. Redlich and Goodman (2003) employed the famed *alt-key paradigm* (Kassin & Kiechel, 1996) in which all participants were accused of incorrectly pressing the alt-key and causing a computer to crash; half were presented with "false evidence" of their guilt (a computer printout showing all keys pressed). The authors reported that compliance rates for signing an (untrue) confession statement decreased with age and were as high as 78% for 12- to 13-year-olds (Redlich & Goodman, 2003).

Taken together, these vulnerabilities experienced by even typically developing youth suggest that youthful suspects' wellbeing may be jeopardized in the interrogation room to a greater extent than adults by virtue of their developmental status alone. Given that developmentally based vulnerabilities such as foreshortened time perspective and compliance with authority are presumably transient characteristics of adolescence, it seems inherently unjust to "penalize" youth for behaviors and decisions that may be driven by developmental status alone. More and better data about juvenile behavior and decision making during interrogation would greatly inform the public discourse in research, law, and policy pertaining to police interviewing of youth.

Characteristics of Juvenile Interrogations

Despite increasing empirical attention to this issue, we still know remarkably little about what actually occurs when police question suspects (Feld, 2006a). Leo (1996) noted, "law professors, lawyers, and law students have created a formidable law review literature that focuses almost entirely on the doctrinal and ethical aspects of interrogation and confession case law, rather than on the routine activities of legal actors and institutions" (p. 267). Social science has been equally remiss in studying routine police interrogations. Though we have learned a great deal about interrogation-related capacities as well as interrogation decision making in laboratory settings, we lack fundamental descriptive data about routine police questioning of adults *or* juveniles. In the four decades since the *Miranda* decision was handed down, only a handful of studies in the United States have employed observational methods to document *actual* interrogations and even fewer are contemporary.

Leo (1996) observed 122 live interrogations and 60 videotaped interrogations for his descriptive study of adult suspects in several California police departments. His analysis reported key descriptive variables about the interrogation context and its participants: race, class, gender, prior record, *Miranda* waiver/invocation, and interrogation length and outcome, among others. He reported that 69% of interrogations were conducted by a single detective and 31% by two detectives together. Interrogating officers were primarily White (69% of primary detectives and 65% of secondary detectives; Leo, 1996). The typical suspect was a young, Black, working-class male accused of a person crime (81% of cases) or property crime (19%). More than three-fourths of the suspects in his samples waived their *Miranda* rights and agreed to speak with police. Notably, he also recorded the frequency and type of interrogation techniques detectives used to elicit confessions.

Leo's (1996) study greatly advanced the interrogation literature because it employed observational methods to illuminate what has traditionally been a highly veiled social context. His work correctly underscores the need to examine *routine* police procedures—as opposed to "leading cases...which are unrepresentative of the larger universe of court cases and thus may depict atypical police practices as the norm" (p. 267)—in order to better understand everyday interrogation practices. Despite its considerable contribution to the field, the study raises concerns about observer bias because the interrogators were aware of the researcher's presence, though the author addresses this with care (Leo, 1996). A second disadvantage is that, by observing interrogations contemporaneously, the researcher gets only a single pass at coding an extensive array of variables. Interrogations are rarely unambiguous in every respect, and making extemporaneous judgments about highly complex social interactions is challenging. Nonetheless, Leo's groundbreaking (1996) work begs replication in other jurisdictions.

Feld's (2006a) observational study identified 66 juvenile cases from the pool of all juvenile cases in one Minnesota jurisdiction during a 7-year period that contained either videotaped interrogations or interrogation transcripts. His sample included 16- to 18-year-old felony suspects, just over half of which (52%) were accused of person crimes. In addition to many of the variables Leo (1996) examined, this study also coded interrogators' strategies to predispose youth to waive *Miranda* as well as youths' positive or negative responses to interrogation. Like Leo's (1996) sample, most of these suspects were minority males whom Feld (2006a) characterized as a "criminally sophisticated group of delinquents" due to the substantial proportion with prior felony arrests or juvenile court referrals (p. 69). Eighty percent of juvenile suspects waived their *Miranda* rights and consented to police questioning. Most (88%) were arrested prior to questioning and nearly all (95%) interrogations occurred in a custodial physical setting (e.g., detention center or police station). A much larger follow-up study (N = 307; Feld, 2013) reported similar findings using a wider range of Minnesota jurisdictions.

To date, Feld's (2006a, 2013) studies of juvenile felony cases provide the only existing data drawn from actual juvenile interrogations. Their sampling strategies attenuate selection bias by drawing a comprehensive or complete sample from a single jurisdiction or state over a substantial time period. However, in any given jurisdiction, a host of variables (measured or unmeasured) may be particular to that community, including suspect demographic characteristics, youth orientation toward law enforcement, police attitudes, law enforcement interviewer training, and state or local juvenile justice policies. Moreover, much of Feld's (2006b) extensive reporting on youth attitudes, demeanor, and behavior during interrogation is drawn from interviewer notes accompanying interrogation transcripts. Given that police officers are not neutral parties in the interrogation context and that police (and humans in general) are notoriously inaccurate at detecting deception (Vrij, 2008), researchers should take care when generalizing from these results. Feld's (2006a, 2006b, 2013) studies are a substantial step forward in the empirical study of juvenile interrogations; much more research is needed to examine whether its conclusions hold true in other jurisdictions using other methods.

The Present Study

Though we have learned a great deal about the capacities and goals that both youth and police *bring into* the interrogation room, social science lacks even basic descriptive data about the interrogation context itself. It is imperative that we first answer some of the fundamental questions about what transpires when police question youth. Observational data are by far the best feasible option for addressing these fundamental questions. The present exploratory study aimed to document actual behavior and decision making in police interrogations of youth suspects. Access to juvenile records is an enormous barrier to this type of research, and Feld's (2006a, 2013) reports are the only existing observational studies of this kind. The present study replicates key elements of those works and also expands upon the number and type of variables measured. It is also the first observational study of juvenile interrogation to employ a diverse multijurisdictional sample of electronically recorded juvenile interrogations. While these descriptive pilot data are only exploratory in nature, it is hoped that they will begin to shed light on the actual processes and outcomes that occur during juvenile interrogations.

Specifically, we were guided by the following research goals—(a) document the individual factors that characterize interrogation participants (e.g., youthful suspects, law enforcement officials) and (b) describe the context into which routine police interrogation of youthful suspects takes place.

Method

Recruitment

Though electronic recording of police interrogations has not been mandated at the national level, numerous states, jurisdictions, and local police departments do record interviews in accordance with state legislative mandate, state Supreme Court decision, or voluntary department policy. At the time data collection was initiated, eight states[1] had enacted legislation requiring police departments to record custodial interrogations, and another six states[2] received recording mandates from state supreme court decisions (NACDL, 2009). Additionally, criminal defense attorney and mandatory recording advocate Thomas Sullivan (2004) identified 238 individual law enforcement agencies in 38 states that record interrogations, most of which do so voluntarily. Using publicly available contact information from the agencies' Web sites, we established a list of every police department in the mandatory recording states as well as the Sullivan report (2004) agencies ($n = 3,230$). The first recruitment phase consisted of letters via postal mail informing these agencies of the study and requesting voluntary participation.

The initial response rate was extremely low (less than 1%), so a second recruitment phase was initiated. This effort consisted of follow-up phone calls to select agencies in the list. Our goals were fourfold: (1) reintroduce the project, (2) establish direct contact by having phone conversations with an actual staff member, (3) provide additional information about the study and answer questions, and (4) assist interested departments in overcoming practical barriers to participation (e.g., obtaining the appropriate permissions, receiving regular reminders, etc.). Agencies appeared in the list ordered alphabetically by state; every third state was selected for follow-up phone calls (approximately 700 agencies in total).

Participants

Nineteen police agencies and one county prosecutor's office contributed a total of 85 electronically recorded interrogations to the project. Data came from agencies in all four US Census Bureau geographic regions: Northeast (two agencies), South (twelve), Midwest (one), and West (five; US Census Bureau, 2012). More than half of participating agencies ($n = 11$) came from small communities with fewer than 50,000 residents. All other descriptive statistics are reported below for the electronic recordings, not the police agencies, because the recordings are the units of analysis. The eligibility criteria

---

[1] Illinois, Maine, Maryland, Nebraska, New Mexico, North Carolina, Wisconsin, and the District of Columbia.
[2] Alaska, Massachusetts, Minnesota, New Hampshire, Wisconsin, and New Jersey.

for submitted recordings were as follows: (a) adjudication of the case is closed and no appeals are pending regarding the charge discussed on the recording, (b) the interview is relative to a felony or other serious charge, (c) the interview is with a suspect or person of interest (i.e., not a victim or witness), and (d) the interviewee is a juvenile (defined here as under age 18).

Coding Procedures

This was the first juvenile interrogation study to code data using digital video coding software. We employed the Observer XT (Noldus Information Technology, 2009), a software program designed for coding and analyzing observational data. Though commonly used for infant/child behavior research or animal behavior research, Observer was applied to the present study because of its significant advantages over traditional observational methods. Observer allows researchers to create a digital coding scheme that "maps onto" precise moments in the video recording. For complex behaviors and/or variables that require multiple coders for reliability purposes, Observer can combine all coders' files into a single master file containing all variable codes. The program also enables easy pause and playback to ensure coding accuracy and completeness.

Two coders were trained by the project director on the coding scheme using publicly available interrogation videos as training materials. Reliability analyses were executed by hand using a confusion matrix that compares each coder's log to the reliability coder's (the project director's) log. Cohen's kappa (Cohen, 1960) between each coder and the project director was calculated (a) for each recording and (b) for the training recordings overall. Each coder's overall kappa value was required to meet the 0.7 level, an acceptable standard given the data's exploratory nature and Cohen's kappa's general conservativeness as a measure of intercoder reliability (Hsu & Field, 2003). Both coders achieved the required kappa value after one round of training.

To ensure continued reliability throughout data collection, every fourth interview was double coded for reliability purposes (14 interviews or approximately 25% of the total sample). Due to the small number of behaviors assigned to each coder, behaviors were collapsed across all 14 reliability recordings and a single overall kappa (Cohen, 1960) was calculated for each coder. Intercoder reliability ratings for coder 1 (kappa = .77) and coder 2 (kappa = .87) met the required threshold.

Results

Eighty-five interrogations were submitted to the study. Two interrogations were excluded because the discs contained only audio files, 16 due to technological difficulties, and 10 because the interviewee was 18 years or older, yielding a final $N = 57$ interviews. Two juveniles were interviewed simultaneously during one interrogation, so demographic data are reported for 58 juvenile interviewees.

Individual Factors

Results showed a pattern of individual characteristics consistent with previous reports of justice-involved youth (e.g., Feld, 2006a). Fifty-two of the 58 juvenile interviewees (90%) were male. The average age was approximately 15 and a half years old ($M = 15.44$, $SD = 1.14$) for the 41 juvenile interviewees for which age could be determined. The youngest interviewees were 13 years old (two youth) and the oldest were 17 (eight youth). Of the 58 juvenile interviewees, 41.4% were White, 41.4% were Black, and 5.2% were Latino/a. Race could not be reasonably determined for seven interviewees (12.1%).[3]

We also coded as much information as possible about the juvenile's custody status at the time of the interview. Of the 35 (60%) interrogations for which custody status could be determined, 16 juveniles had just been arrested, 18 were present voluntarily, and 1 was brought to the interrogation room from detention. As expected, most (93%) of the interrogations involved serious and/or violent offenses; 41 juveniles were interrogated in regard to person crimes and 12 in regard to property crimes.

Law enforcement officials' involvement in interrogations occurred in several forms. All interrogations involved at minimum one primary interrogator (PI, a term created for this study; $n = 57$). The PI was operationalized as the officer who conducted the majority of questioning or otherwise acted as the "lead" investigator. Most of the primary interrogators were White males (84%). The remaining interviews involved a Black male PI (one recording), White female PI (four recordings), and four PIs (one female, three male) whose race could not be determined. Secondary interrogators (SIs), as defined in this study, were police officers who participate in an interrogation by asking questions but were involved to a lesser degree than PIs. Secondary interrogators were present in 21 interrogations (36.8%). As with PIs, the majority (71.4%) of SIs were White males. Three SIs were White females and two were males of an undetermined race. Finally, noninterviewing officers (NIOs) were defined as police officers who were present for some or all of an interrogation but did not participate in questioning. For example, they may enter the room to handcuff the juvenile suspect, deliver paperwork to the PI, or supervise the juvenile suspect when the PI leaves the room. NIOs were present in five of the 57 interrogations (8.8%). Four NIOs were White males and one was a White female.

---

[3] We acknowledge the challenges of determining race/ethnicity based on visual observation and the biases inherent within such judgments. Although skin color is not necessarily an indicator of racial identity, we use this proxy because self-report data are not available. In effort to be as conservative as possible, we defaulted to the "cannot be determined" code whenever race/ethnicity (as represented by skin color) was even remotely in question.

In addition to juvenile suspects and police officers, the most common party present in our sample was a parent (12 interrogations, or 21.1%). Eight of these were mothers and four were fathers. A second parent (the father, in all cases) was present in three interrogations (5.3%).[4] Three recordings, all from the same police department, contained an Interested Adult—a White female who worked for social services. Finally, one recording contained an adult relative and another two contained a representative from the district attorney's office. An attorney was not present on behalf of the juvenile in any of the 57 interrogations.

Contextual Factors

Two-thirds of our interrogations with known interview dates ($n = 25$) occurred within the last 5 years. Over half our sample of interrogations (36 cases, or 63.2%) took place at the police station. Location could not be determined for 20 cases, and the remaining one interrogation occurred in the office of the school resource officer at the youth's school.

Given the considerable speculation in the media and literature about extended interrogations as a risk factor for false confessions, we were very interested in documenting the length of the interviews we received. We also recorded whether the juvenile suspect was physically restrained, as restraints may also contribute to the perceived coercion a suspect may experience. The median time of interrogation was 46 minutes ($M = 65.6$ minutes, $SD = 59.0$ minutes), though the range of interrogation lengths was quite extensive. The shortest interrogation lasted only 6 minutes and the longest was 4 hours and 48 minutes. Overall, 68% percent of interrogations concluded in less than 1 hour and 84% in less than 2 hours. Nine juvenile suspects (15.5%) were physically restrained in handcuffs or leg shackles during the interrogation.

Perhaps our most important aspect of this research concerned how juvenile interrogations are resolved. Results indicated that interrogation outcomes were varied. In our sample of 58 juvenile suspects, 21 youth (36.2%) fully confessed to the offense in question. Eighteen youth (31.0%) made incriminating admissions (i.e., they admitted only partial involvement in the offense or admitted to some charges but not others). Another 15 juvenile suspects (25.8%) denied culpability completely. Finally, four youths' interrogations (6.9%) were not resolved, either because the suspect invoked his *Miranda* rights or because the recording ended before the interview concluded.

Cross-tabular analyses comparing interrogation duration (split at the median duration of 46 minutes) with interrogation outcome indicate no meaningful overall relationship between these variables. Juvenile suspects who fully confessed to their interrogators were distributed equally among shorter and longer interrogations (10 confessors from interrogations shorter than 46

---

[4] When two parents were present, the parent who spoke most frequently was designated the primary parent.

minutes; 11 confessors from interrogations longer than 46 minutes). Juvenile suspects who denied the allegations were approximately equally distributed (6 from shorter interrogations; 8 from longer interrogations). However, twice as many ($n = 12$) juvenile suspects made incriminating admissions in shorter interrogations than youth in longer interrogations ($n = 6$). Chi-squared analyses were not conducted due to small cell sizes.

Discussion

The goal of this exploratory study was to provide fundamental descriptive data about the participants and context of routine police interrogation of juvenile suspects. Our data paint a portrait of White or Black middle-adolescent males accused of serious person or property crimes, including murder, sexual assault, robbery, and arson. These youth are typically questioned by one or two White male interrogators in a session lasting about an hour on average, though the range of interview durations is quite extensive.

Individual Factors

Consistent with previous reports of justice-involved youth (e.g., Feld, 2006a; Grisso, 1981), our sample was predominantly male. The racial distribution of our sample somewhat differed from Feld's (2006a) sample, probably due to population differences in the cities from which the tapes originated. Given minority groups' well-known overrepresentation in all facets of the justice system (Piquero, 2008), our sample contained more White youth and fewer Latino/a youth than a truly representative sample may have contained. The mean age (15.4 years) and range (13–17 years) of our juvenile suspects suggest that older youth may be more likely to find themselves in the interrogation room. Whether this is because older youth commit more serious crimes or because police interrogate older and younger youth at different rates is unknown. In 2008, the FBI's annual Uniform Crime Report attributed 11.9% of all arrests for violent crimes to 15- to 17-year-olds compared to 4.3% of arrests for youth under 15 (Federal Bureau of Investigation, 2009). Feld (2006a), whose study had access to all case records from the sample jurisdiction, noted that charges in his interrogation cases were more serious than the jurisdiction's typical juvenile felony cases. Over 90% of our sample was interrogated in connection to a person crime or serious property crime, and only nine of the 58 juvenile suspects were known to be under age 15 at the time of the interrogation.

Nearly a third of the youth in our study were not officially under arrest, meaning that legally they were free to decline or discontinue questioning and leave. It remains unclear why noncustodial youth would consent to questioning and even confess to crimes. Perhaps the youth do not fully understand their right to decline police questioning when not in custody. This speaks to the widespread confusion regarding the definition of police custody. If a police officer visits a youth's home and politely asks him to answer a few questions at the police station, the youth may comply because he does not fully understand that he has a choice. His "choice" may be further confounded if parents encourage his compliance or themselves do not understand that compliance is not compulsory (see Woolard, Cleary, Harvell, & Chen, 2008). Second, it is likely that the youth do not yet possess the wherewithal, due to transient developmental features, to assert themselves when asked to consent to questioning. Though research on interrogation-specific compliance is limited, vignette methods as well as laboratory deception paradigms have demonstrated age-based differences in propensity to comply with authority figures, including legal authorities; these developmental propensities were reported for both community and justice-involved youth (Grisso et al., 2003; Redlich & Goodman, 2003). Finally, it could be the case that the youth deliberately change their minds in favor of confession during the course of police interrogation. This possibility pertains to the foreshortened time perspective and inability to anticipate future consequences that typifies developmentally normative youth. Grisso's (1981) study and numerous case studies of juvenile false confessors (e.g., Drizin & Colgan, 2004) demonstrate that these developmental tendencies do manifest in police interrogations specifically. It is possible that youth believed they could "explain away" the situation by making police understand why they committed the act in question.

Like the two previous observational interrogation studies (Feld, 2006a; Leo, 1996), we found that most primary and secondary interrogators were White males. These data are consistent with national data from the Bureau of Justice Statistics (Hickman & Reaves, 2006), reporting that approximately 88% of sworn officers are male, 76% are White, and 21% are Black or Latino/a. More than a third of our recordings involved a secondary interrogator, either concurrently or sequentially. Interested adults, adult relatives, and prosecutors were less frequently present but also did occasionally appear in the recordings. Perhaps most important, none of the interrogations in our sample contained a defense attorney present on the juvenile suspect's behalf. Though attorney presence is not required, this nonetheless suggests the widespread occurrence that juvenile suspects are making interrogation decisions without the knowledge or advice of counsel.

Unlike Feld's (2006a) sample, in which a parent was present in only one of 66 interrogations, over one-fifth of our sample involved at least one parent, usually a mother. The difference is likely due to state and local policy variations requiring or permitting parental presence in minors' interrogations. Our finding differs from Feld's (2006a) report and suggests that parental presence may be more common than previously thought. Addressing the question of whether parents are at least in the interrogation room is a critical first step in addressing the broader question of how parents are involved and whether their involvement serves or deserves the youth's legal best interest. For example, while parents may possess some basic justice system comprehension, they do not necessarily have adequate knowledge to successfully navigate the intricacies of the juvenile justice system (Woolard et al., 2008).

Contextual Factors

Not surprisingly, most of our electronically recorded interrogations took place at a police station, while one occurred at the youth's school and the location of the remaining was undetermined. Though we cannot infer that most interrogations generally occur at a police station because the proportion of interrogations conducted off-site and off-camera is unknown, these data do allow us to observe the cadence of juvenile interrogations that take place in a controlled environment. Our goal was to report observable process characteristics that may impact juvenile suspects' subjective experiences in this context.

This study is the first to report data on juvenile interrogation length. Our findings are relatively consistent with what little previous research exists on adult interrogation lengths; Leo (1996) reported that 71% of his adult sample concluded in under 1 hour and 92% in under 2 hours, though he did not report median or mean interrogation length. Other studies on adult interrogations estimated mean interrogation lengths of about 30 minutes to 1.5 hours (e.g., Kassin et al., 2007). Additional observational studies drawing different samples would shed more light on how juvenile interrogation lengths compare to those of adult suspects, but our data suggest the durations are somewhat similar. More research is needed to understand whether or how interrogation duration impacts the legal and psychological wellbeing of children who are questioned by police. It is possible, for example, that a youthful suspect may perceive a 1-hour questioning period as more stressful and more coercive than an adult suspect and may be more likely to comply with interrogative requests as a result.

Our study grouped interrogation outcomes into four categories based primarily on existing literature: full confession, incriminating admission, denial, and no resolution. Our confession rates (37%) were higher than those in the only existing observational study of juvenile interrogations (17% confessions; Feld, 2006b), while our incriminating admission (31%) and denial rates (24%) were somewhat lower (53% and 30%, respectively). Variations in outcome distribution between our study and Feld's (2006b) may be due partially to our inclusion of a *no resolution* category and partially to both studies' small sample sizes. Replicating these studies with the same methods but using larger samples would likely stabilize these percentages somewhat. For now, we may cautiously conclude that youths' interrogation decision making in context is quite variable.

Limitations

The present study employed a nonprobability sample that may limit the generalizability of study results. It was impossible to randomly select potential participants from a known universe of agencies that record interviews because no such universe exists. Even for states that require electronic recording at a statewide level, recording policies may not be universally observed because of technological limitations or insufficient resources. Given the lack of an existing population from which to sample, as well as the aforementioned numerous barriers to participation, we solicited participation using every avenue available.

By attempting to increase sample size, we subjected the sample to selection bias in several ways. First, our database recruitment strategy targeted states and jurisdictions that were presumed to follow electronic recording procedures resulting from case law or legislation. Aside from the voluntarily recording agencies listed in the Sullivan report, our database recruitment strategy would not have captured other jurisdictions nationwide that may also voluntarily record interviews. Second, among the agencies we contacted, those that chose to participate may differ in important ways (both measurable and immeasurable) from the agencies that declined. For example, participating agencies may have more human resources to devote to identifying and submitting interview recordings or may be more positively oriented toward research. Finally, selection bias may also exist at the interview level. The number of interviews received from a single agency ranged from 1 to 15; it is unlikely that these figures represent a department's entire collection of interview recordings. We do not know what decision criteria were applied to these selections, and it is possible that chosen interviews differ from those not chosen.

Conclusion

The data presented here comprise the first ever observational study of juvenile interrogations to be derived entirely from electronic recordings. This pilot study draws data from jurisdictions in multiple locations across the nation and is the first to employ digital coding technology to obtain precise and thorough measurements of observed behaviors. We believe the present study's principal asset is its descriptive approach to an understudied phenomenon. Juvenile interrogation is at once a legal, social, and developmental context in which suspects likely experience a range of emotions under a variety of circumstances. Juvenile suspects are in a critical stage of development, "when identity formation is at its peak and the development of human and social capital sets the stage for later life opportunities" (Schubert, Mulvey, Loughran, & Losoya, 2012, p. 72). The decisions suspects make—to confess, to cooperate, to resist, even to speak at all—may very well have lasting consequences that extend far beyond the span of that single conversation. Researchers, policymakers, attorneys, parents, and all other stakeholders with an interest in child wellbeing should collaborate to develop empirically driven solutions that serve public safety interests while accommodating youths' transient, developmentally based vulnerabilities that may unduly influence behavior and decision making in the interrogation context.

References

Bram v. United States, 168 US 532 (1897).
Brown v. Mississippi, 297 US 278 (1936).
Cohen, J. (1960). A coefficient of agreement for nominal scales. *Educational and Psychological Measurement, 20*, 37–46. doi: 10.1177/001316446002000104
Drizin, S. A., & Colgan, B. A. (2004). Tales from the juvenile confessions front. In G. D. Lassiter (Ed.), *Interrogations, confessions, and entrapment* (pp. 127–162). New York, NY: Kluwer.
Drizin, S. A., & Leo, R. A. (2004). The problem of false confessions in the post-DNA world. *North Carolina Law Review, 82*, 891–1007.
Federal Bureau of Investigation. (2009). *Crime in the United States, 2008:Table 39, Arrests by age, 2008.* Retrieved from http://www2.fbi.gov/ucr/cius2009/data/table_36.html.
Feld, B. C. (2013). *Kids, cops, and confessions: Inside the interrogation room.* New York: NYU Press.
Feld, B. C. (2006a). Juveniles' competence to exercise *Miranda* rights: An empirical study of policy and practice. *Minnesota Law Review, 91*, 26–100.
Feld, B. C. (2006b). Police interrogation of juveniles: An empirical study of policy and practice. *Journal of Criminal Law and Criminology, 97*(1), 219–316.
Gardner, W., & Herman, J. (1990). Adolescents' AIDS risk taking: A rational choice perspective. *New Directions for Child Development, 50*, 17–34. doi: 10.1002/cd.23219905004.
Graham v. Florida, 130 S. Ct. 2011 (2010).
Grisso, T. (1981). *Juveniles' waiver of rights: Legal and psychological competence.* New York, NY: Plenum.
Grisso, T., Steinberg, L., Woolard, J., Cauffman, E., Scott, E. S., Graham, S., ... Schwartz, R. (2003). Juveniles' competence to stand trial: A comparison of adolescents' and adults' capacities as trial defendants. *Law and Human Behavior, 27*, 333–363. doi: 10.1023/A:1024065015717.
Hickman, M. J., & Reaves, B. A. (2006). *Local police departments, 2003.* Washington, DC: Bureau of Justice Statistics, US Department of Justice.
Hsu, L. M., & Field, R. (2003). Inter-rater agreement measures: Comments on Kappa[n], Cohen's Kappa, Scott's Pi, and Aickin's Alpha. *Understanding Statistics: Statistical Issues in Psychology, Education and the Social Sciences, 2*, 205–219.
Jackson v. Hobbs, 567 US 10-9647 (2012).
J.D.B. v. North Carolina, 131 S. Ct. 2394 (2011).
Kassin, S. M. (2008). False confessions: Causes, consequences, and implications for reform. *Current Directions in Psychological Science, 17* (4), 249–253. doi: 10.1111/j.1467-8721.2008.00584.x.
Kassin, S. M., & Kiechel, K. L. (1996). The social psychology of false confessions: Compliance, internalization, and confabulation. *Psychological Science, 7*, 125–128. doi: 10.1111/j.1467-9280.1996.tb00344.x.
Kassin, S. M., Leo, R. A., Meissner, C. A., Richman, K. D., Colwell, L. H., Leach, A. M., & LaFon, D. (2007). Police interviewing and interrogation: A self-report survey of police practices and beliefs. *Law and Human Behavior, 31*, 381–400. doi: 10.1007/s10979-006-9073-5.
Kassin, S. M., & Neumann, K. (1997). On the power of confession evidence: An experimental test of the "fundamental difference" hypothesis. *Law and Human Behavior, 21*, 469–484. doi: 10.1023/A:1024871622490.

Kassin, S. M., & Sukel, H. (1997). Coerced confessions and the jury: An experimental test of the "harmless error" rule. *Law and Human Behavior, 21*, 27–46. doi: 10.1023/A:1024814009769.

Leo, R. A. (1996). Inside the interrogation room. *Journal of Criminal Law and Criminology, 86*(2), 266–303.

Miller v. Alabama, 567 US 10-9646 (2012).

Miranda v. Arizona, 384 US 436 (1966).

National Association of Criminal Defense Lawyers. (2009). *Mandatory electronic recording of interrogations resources page*. Retrieved from http://www.nacdl.org/criminal-defense/recording-interrogations/.

Noldus Information Technology. (2009). The Observer XT 8.0, The Netherlands.

Piquero, A. R. (2008). Disproportionate minority contact. *The Future of Children, 18*(2), 59–79. doi: 10.1353/foc.0.0013.

Redlich, A. D., & Goodman, G. S. (2003). Taking responsibility for an act not committed: The influence of age and suggestibility. *Law and Human Behavior, 27*, 141–156. doi: 10.1023/A:1022543012851.

Reyna, V. F., & Farley, F. (2006). Risk and rationality in adolescent decision making: mplications for theory, practice, and public policy. *Psychological Science in the Public Interest, 7*(1), 1–44. doi: 10.1111/j. 1529-1006.2006.00026.x.

Roper v. Simmons, 543 US 551 (2005).

Schubert, C., Mulvey, E., Loughran, T., & Losoya, S. (2012). Perceptions of institutional experience and community outcomes for serious adolescent offenders. *Criminal Justice and Behavior, 39*, 71–93. doi: 10.1177/0093854811426710.

Steinberg, L., & Scott, E. S. (2003). Less guilty by reason of adolescence: Developmental immaturity, diminished responsibility, and the juvenile death penalty. *American Psychologist, 58*(12), 1009–1018. doi: 10.1037/0003-066X.58.12.1009.

Sullivan, T. P. (2004). *Police experiences with recording custodial interrogations*. Chicago, IL: Center on Wrongful Convictions.

US Census Bureau, Population Division (2012). Retrieved from http://www.census.gov/econ/census07/www/geography/regions_and_divisions.html.

Vrij, A. (2008). *Detecting lies and deceit: Pitfalls and opportunities* (2nd ed.). New York, NY: Wiley.

Woolard, J. L., Cleary, H. M. D., Harvell, S. A. S., & Chen, R. (2008). Examining adolescents' and their parents' conceptual and practical knowledge of police interrogation: A family dyad approach. *Journal of Youth and Adolescence, 37*, 685–698. doi: 10.1007/s10964-008-9288-5.

Yarborough v. Alvarado, 541 US 652 (2004).

5

Applying Sex Offender Registry Laws to Juvenile Offenders: Biases Against Stigmatized Youth

Jessica M. Salerno, Margaret Stevenson, Cynthia J. Najdowski, Tisha R. A. Wiley, Bette L. Bottoms, and Liana Peter-Hagene

The emotion and urgency surrounding society's need to protect children from dangerous sex offenders has led to policies that require sex offenders to register with police and on public online registries. These laws were created to help parents better protect their children from sex offenders who live in their community and have recently been extended to include juvenile offenders (Sex Offender Registration and Notification Act [SORNA], 2006). The question addressed in this chapter is: Considering that these laws were designed for adult offenders, is their application to juveniles appropriate, necessary, and supported by public sentiment? Psychology has a role to play in addressing these issues. For example, research suggests that the application of registry laws to juvenile offenders might have inadvertent negative consequences for the wellbeing of those who are registered—including juveniles whose cases fit the letter, but not the spirit, of these laws (e.g., juveniles registered for mooning schoolmates or having sex within committed peer relationships; Trivits & Reppucci, 2002).

As will be reviewed, research provides strong support for applying registry laws to juveniles in the abstract, but more mixed reactions for applying registry laws to specific, less severe, consensual cases. This ambiguity surrounding when registry laws should be enforced against juveniles might provide a context in which biases against stigmatized classes of offenders or victims can be expressed through support for juvenile registration policies.

This chapter reviews current sex offender registration laws and policies and discusses research addressing the psychological issues surrounding the application of these laws to juveniles, including (a) psychological research that speaks to assumptions underlying these laws, (b) public sentiment toward these laws, (c) offender and victim factors that might drive biases in public support for these laws, and (d) underlying psychological motivation for supporting these laws (i.e., punitive versus utilitarian goals). Finally, the chapter draws from the reviewed research and presents implications for juvenile sex offender policy.

Sex Offender Registration Laws

In an effort to prevent child sexual abuse and facilitate the apprehension of repeat sex offenders, the federal government passed the Jacob Wetterling Crimes Against Children and Sexually Violent Offender Registration Act (1994). This federal law required all sex offenders to register personal information (e.g., name, address, photograph, etc.) with the police. Two years later "Megan's Law" (1996) was passed, requiring states to establish procedures to inform community members about sex offenders living in their community. Both acts were passed in reaction to public outrage about sex crimes against children. For example, Megan's Law was passed after 7-year-old Megan Kanka was raped and murdered by a previously convicted sex offender in her neighborhood. The public was outraged that they were unaware of the dangerous offender in their community and believed that being aware of the offender would have helped Megan's parents protect her. Thus, it is easy to understand why the public supported the implementation of these laws.

Support for these laws becomes more complicated in cases in which the *offenders* are children as well. Sexual activity between juveniles meets the legal definition of a sex offense in many states—even when both parties are underage and the activity is consensual (James, 2009).[1] Juveniles who record their technically illegal sex acts through videotaping or sexting (e.g., texting a photograph) are also particularly vulnerable to prosecution (e.g., Eraker, 2010; Lithwick, 2009). In 2006, federal legislation was expanded with the Sex Offender Registration and Notification Act (SORNA, 1996). This policy, part of the Adam Walsh Act, requires all states to participate in a federal national online registry. This federal registry includes juvenile sex offenders who are either (a) convicted in adult criminal court or (b) at least 14 years old and adjudicated delinquent in juvenile court for sex offenses involving aggravating circumstances (e.g., use of force, threat of serious violence).

---

[1] We use the term "consensual" while acknowledging the social, moral, and psychological difficulties of defining the age at which adolescents are capable of giving consent to sexual activity; also while acknowledging that they may not be *legally* able to consent.

Individual states are allowed, however, to set harsher standards. In other words, states can include more offenders than the guidelines require; as long as they meet the *minimum* guidelines and participate in the federal registry, the state is considered compliant with the Adam Walsh Act. For example, currently registered juveniles who committed minor crimes, such as a 12-year-old who mooned a class of 5- to 6-year-old classmates in Texas or a mildly mentally retarded 17-year-old who grabbed an 18-year-old's buttocks in Nebraska (Trivits & Reppucci, 2002) could be registered under these guidelines. Thus, not all juveniles on the registry fit the highly publicized dangerous and violent sex offender profile that inspired these laws (Human Rights Watch, 2007).

According to the latest review of juvenile registration laws across the United States (Salerno, Stevenson et al., 2010), a majority of states ($n = 33$) require juveniles to register as sex offenders under some circumstances. In fact, in many of those states ($n = 26$), juvenile registration is automatic and mandatory. Juveniles as young as 8 years old can be placed on sex offender registries (e.g., in Montana). Only four states explicitly prohibit the registration of juveniles under age 14 (Indiana, Ohio, Oklahoma, South Dakota). Further, in most states, registration extends long after adolescence (22 states require registration for at least 10 years, and several require registration for life), often with no opportunity for discretion, appeal, or petition. Other states' laws reflect greater recognition of the developmental differences between juvenile and adult offenders by taking juveniles' ages into account when deciding registration duration (e.g., limiting the duration of registration until the juvenile is 18 or 21 years old) or by allowing juveniles to petition for removal from the registry after 3 to 5 years. The type of offenses for which a juvenile is required to register also varies across states. In some states, registration is required only in cases that involve threats, the use of force, or incapacitation. In at least 19 other states, however, juveniles adjudicated guilty of nonforceful offenses can be required to register. Information about juvenile sex offenders is publicly available via online databases in many states (Salerno, Stevenson et al., 2010).

Although all states are federally mandated to comply with the Adam Walsh Act or risk losing 10% of their federal funding for law enforcement activities (42 U.S.C. §16911; Caldwell, Ziemke, & Vitacco, 2008), 35 states missed the deadline of July 2011 for implementing these guidelines into their sex offender registration programs. As of the writing of this chapter, only 15 states have substantially implemented these guidelines according to the Office of Sex Offender Sentencing, Monitoring, Apprehending, Registering, and Tracking (SMART; US Department of Justice [DOJ], 2012). In fact, the DOJ has specifically cited resistance to public disclosure of juvenile sex offenders' information as "one of the largest impediments to SORNA implementation" (US Department of Justice, 2010), and states, such as Nebraska, Ohio, and Vermont, have modified or passed new legislation to limit punishment for juveniles who commit less severe sex crimes (e.g., ensuring lesser punishment for teenagers who engage in sexting as compared to adults charged with child pornography).

Assumptions Underlying the Application of Sex Offender Registration Laws to Juveniles

The rationale behind registration laws is intuitive and reflects good intentions—alerting police and community members of dangerous sex offenders in order to protect children. Given that a goal of registration laws was to reduce sex offender recidivism (for review, see Welchans, 2005), extending these laws to juvenile offenders reflects two major unsupported assumptions about juvenile sex offenders: First, that juvenile and adult sex offenders are similar in their amenability to treatment and their recidivism, and, second, that sex offender registries are effective in reducing recidivism. Regarding the first assumption, research reveals that not only are juvenile sex offenders amenable to treatment (for reviews, see Chaffin, 2008; Trivits & Reppucci, 2002), but that juveniles respond to different treatments than adults. Treatments that typically work for nonviolent juvenile offenders reduce the likelihood that juvenile sex offenders will recidivate, but treatments typically used to treat adult sex offenders do not (St. Amand, Bard, & Silovsky, 2008). In other words, juvenile sex offenders appear to be more similar to juveniles who commit nonsexual crimes than they are to adult sex offenders in terms of rehabilitation potential. Further, the recidivism rate is lower for juvenile offenders compared to adult sex offenders. Only 5%–15% of juvenile sex offenders reoffend, compared to 20%–40% of adult sex offenders (for reviews, see Chaffin, 2008; Salerno, Stevenson et al., 2010; Trivits & Reppucci, 2002). Juvenile sex offenders may be no more likely to commit future sexual crimes than are juveniles who commit nonsexual offenses (Caldwell, 2007; Caldwell et al., 2008; Carpentier, Silovsky, & Chaffin, 2006; Zimring, Piquero, & Jennings, 2007). Thus, the argument that sex offender registries are equally necessary for juvenile and adult sex offenders is based on flawed assumptions that contradict a central tenet of our juvenile justice system: the idea that juveniles are a special group who can and should be rehabilitated.

Regarding the second assumption, there is little evidence that registration reduces sex offender recidivism in general (Adkins, Huff, & Stageberg, 2000; Letourneau & Armstrong, 2008; Sandler, Freeman, & Socia, 2008). Letourneau and Armstrong (2008) matched 111 registered and nonregistered juvenile sex offenders on case and demographic characteristics (e.g., crime severity, prior offenses, age, race) and found no differences in recidivism rates between the registered and nonregistered juveniles—even after more than 4 years. Further, time-series analyses do not indicate that registration implementation has had an impact on offender recidivism. For example, the enactment of sex offender registration in New York State did not appear to reduce sex offense rates among either first-time or previously convicted adult sex offenders (Sandler et al., 2008). The implementation of public sex offender registration requirements was associated with a significant decrease in rape rates in only 3 of 10 states, and a significant *increase* in rape rates in 1 state (Vasquez, Maddan, & Walker, 2008).

The assumption that these laws reduce sex offenses is based, at least in part, on the belief that would-be juvenile sex offenders are deterred by the risk of registration. Stevenson, Najdowski, and Wiley (2013) investigated whether registration policies deter juveniles from committing sex offenses. Nearly three out of five of their sample of young adults were unaware that juveniles can be registered as sex offenders. Further, even after participants were informed of the fact that juveniles can be registered, many still held inaccurate beliefs about the types of sex offenses that can warrant registration (e.g., consensual sex with a minor) and what registration means. For example, a majority of participants were unaware that registered juvenile sex offenders can have their information made publicly available on the Internet or can remain on the registry as adults or even for the rest of their lives. Further, the less the young adult participants knew about juvenile registration policies, the more likely they were to report having engaged in behaviors that could have warranted registration when they were younger than 18 years old. These findings suggest that recent policies do little to deter youth from sexual behavior that puts them at risk of registration. Even if juveniles are aware of the legal consequences, these policies still might not be an effective deterrent. In a study of high school students, Strassberg and colleagues (2012) found that 20% had sexted a nude photograph of themselves and, of those sexters, one-third did so despite being aware of the legal consequences.

Public registries might not only be ineffective in reducing recidivism; they might also have unintended negative consequences on offenders' lives. For example, in extreme cases, registered offenders have been targeted through the registry and killed by vigilantes, and others have committed suicide after being required to register (Human Rights Watch, 2007). Beyond these extreme cases, there are less severe, yet pervasive negative consequences resulting from registration that could theoretically affect offenders' rehabilitation potential and lead to *increased* recidivism. Substantial percentages of registered sex offenders also report that discovery of their registration status has led to serious consequences, such as job loss, being forced out of a place to live, harassment by neighbors, physical assault, and property damage (Levenson, Brannon, Fortney, & Baker, 2007; Levenson & Cotter, 2005; Tewksbury, 2005). The majority of registered sex offenders experience isolation, loss of close relationships, shame, embarrassment, hopelessness, and stress (Levenson et al., 2007; Levenson & Cotter, 2005; Tewksbury, 2005; Tewksbury & Lees, 2006).

Although these studies focus on adult offenders, interviews with parents of juveniles on the registry for consensual sexual activity suggest that juveniles are likely to have similar experiences (Conmartin, Kernsmith, & Miles, 2010). Psychologists have argued that these factors might have the iatrogenic effect of leading to *increased* recidivism (Letourneau & Miner, 2005) because juvenile delinquency is more likely to occur when "individuals' bonds to society are attenuated" (Sampson & Laub, 2005, p. 15), the chance of which might be increased by registration laws. Thus, the argument that sex offender registries will reduce juvenile offender recidivism is based on a potentially flawed assumption that these registries are effective.

Public Support for Sex Offender Registration Laws

As reviewed earlier, empirical research has demonstrated that juvenile (versus adult) sex offenders recidivate less and other research has *failed* to demonstrate that registry laws decrease sexual offenses. Even so, the assumption that there is high public support for these laws might deter politicians and policymakers from modifying the laws. The public is, in fact, strongly in favor of policies that require *adult* sex offenders to register and notify community members about neighborhood adult sex offenders (Caputo & Brodsky, 2004; Proctor, Badzinski, & Johnson, 2002; Redlich, 2001). For example, Levenson, Brannon, Fortney, and Baker (2007) found that 76% of community members surveyed believed that all adult sex offenders should be subject to community notification, and Phillips (1998) found that 80% of survey respondents believed that community notification laws were very important. This research suggests that a political platform built on being "tough on sex crimes" would be more popular with the public than a platform that could be perceived as prioritizing concerns about offenders over potential victims (Chaffin, 2008). The question remains, however, as to whether public support for the registry extends to *juvenile* sex offenders—especially juveniles who engaged in less severe, consensual sexual activity with peers. If not, policymakers might feel more free to base their decision to support juvenile registry laws on social scientific evidence about the laws' actual effectiveness (or lack thereof), rather than on the unsupported belief that the policies are effective at deterring recidivism and protecting the community.

The original philosophy of the juvenile justice system was rehabilitative (for review, see Reppucci, Michel, & Kostelnik, 2009; see also Chapter 3 of this volume), reflecting actual developmental differences that tend to render juvenile offenders less legally culpable than adult offenders (e.g., Cauffman & Steinberg, 2000). Following a shift toward increased punitiveness toward juvenile offenders in the 1990s (Levesque, 1996), public attitudes might now be shifting back toward treating juveniles more leniently than adult offenders (Scott, Reppucci, Antonishak, & DeGennaro, 2006). This might not be the case for juvenile *sex* offenders, however. There are few studies that have assessed public support for sex offender registration for juveniles. One such study demonstrated that 86% of respondents agreed that a juvenile under the age of 18 who forced someone to have sex should be required to register, but the juvenile was perceived as less worthy of registration than adults who sexually abused children (Kernsmith, Craun, & Foster, 2009). This study's focus on a very severe juvenile sex offense and the confounding of age and offense limits our ability to draw conclusions about how the public reacts to registration for juveniles who commit less severe offenses based on consensual sexual activity among peers.

Other research has assessed support for sex offender registration for juveniles more directly. For example, one study demonstrated that family law attorneys support registry laws less for juveniles than for adults, but that prosecutors and laypeople support juvenile and adult sex offender registration equally in the abstract—even though they perceive juveniles as generally less threatening than adults (Study 1; Salerno, Najdowski et al., 2010). The public's support for juvenile registration laws might be an artifact, however, of how they are typically asked about these laws and might not apply to all types of cases. Participants in this study were asked about applying sex offender registration laws to juvenile offenders in the abstract, without being given a specific case example. Laypeople are less supportive of registry laws, however, when they envision less severe cases—either spontaneously on their own, or when they are asked to think of a less severe case (Salerno, Najdowski et al., 2010). Thus, community members support registration much less for juveniles who commit less severe (e.g., consensual sex between same-aged peers) as opposed to severe sex offenses (e.g., violent rape). Thus, mandatory registry laws that include all sex offenses committed by juveniles regardless of severity are not in line with public sentiment. For example, Stevenson and colleagues (2009) found that most community members did not support public online registration for a 15-year-old boy in a case involving mutually desired oral sex with an underaged girl (which can be legally defined as statutory rape).

Thus, although there is strong support for adult sex offender registration, support for juvenile registration is ambiguous. For adult offenders, the appropriateness of registration is relatively unambiguous—these are the type of cases for which the registry was designed. For *juveniles* who engage in less severe offenses (e.g., sexual activity with their peers), however, the basis for judgments about whether registration is appropriate is more ambiguous. For example, consider a 16-year-old juvenile sentenced to lifelong registration for having sex with a minor within a committed relationship (Human Rights Watch, 2007), or two teenagers texting each other naked photographs of themselves (*A.H. v. State of Florida*, 2007). They have technically committed sex offenses, but they do not represent the prototypical dangerous offenders for which registries were created. Because of the ambiguity surrounding the application of sex offender registration laws to juveniles in these types of cases, the public's support for these laws might be particularly vulnerable to biases against juveniles from stigmatized groups.

Juvenile Offender and Victim Factors

Although blatant prejudice has declined, certain situations can elicit subtle prejudice against stigmatized groups, especially in ambiguous situations (Dovidio & Gaertner, 2004). For example, people exhibit less helping behavior toward

African Americans when the appropriateness of helping is more ambiguous and less obvious as compared to when it would be normatively inappropriate not to help (e.g., Frey & Gaertner, 1986). That is, people usually adhere to normative egalitarian standards when situations clearly dictate them, but when situations are more ambiguous and standards are less clear, biases tend to emerge. The ambiguity generally surrounding whether sex offender registration should be applied to juveniles might set the stage for biases to influence judgments in these cases. Specifically, juveniles might be at greater risk of being required to register when they belong to stigmatized groups compared to nonstigmatized groups, and conversely they might be at lesser risk of being required to register when their victims are from stigmatized as compared to nonstigmatized groups. In fact, research has shown that juveniles accused of nonsexual crimes are perceived differently depending on factors such as the juvenile's race or history of experiencing abuse (for review, see Stevenson, Najdowski, Bottoms, & Haegerich, 2009). This section reviews a set of recent studies which each identify a stigmatized characteristic of offenders and victims (i.e., race, socioeconomic status, abuse history, sexual orientation) that can influence public support for applying sex offender registration policies to juvenile sex offenders.

Race

Legal decision-making research has revealed evidence of a racial bias against African American offenders, such that African American adults (see Sweeney & Haney, 1992, for review) and juveniles (e.g., Bridges & Steen, 1998; Stevenson & Bottoms, 2009) are sometimes perceived more negatively and treated more harshly than their White counterparts. This seems to be true particularly when Black defendants are accused of sexual crimes against White victims (e.g., Bottoms, Davis, & Epstein, 2004; Klein & Creech, 1982). Stevenson and colleagues (2009) tested whether race has similar effects on public support for juvenile sex offender registration. Community member participants read a vignette describing a 15-year-old boy who received "consensual" oral sex from a girl of the same age. The race of the boy and girl were manipulated by describing them as African American or Caucasian and by using race-consistent names (i.e., Tyrone or Jacob for the boy and Shaniqua or Elizabeth for the girl). Participants were marginally more supportive of registration when the defendant and victim were different races (i.e., a Black defendant with a White victim or a White defendant with a Black victim) than when they were the same race. These results suggest that public support for registration in the context of sex crimes described as consensual might be affected by racial biases directed, not just at the offender, but at interracial relationships. Specifically, the authors theorized that in the context of an ambiguously serious sex crime (i.e., described as consensual sex), some participants might perceive it as a crime, whereas other participants might view it as normative adolescent activity. Yet because interracial relationships are still perceived as more deviant and less normative than same-race relationships (e.g., Ross,

2005), it is likely that participants perceived the sex crime as more like a true crime when it was interracial than when the adolescents were the same race. In other words, these results might reflect lingering societal disapproval of interracial relationships.

Socioeconomic Status

Public perceptions of criminal offenders are also influenced by offenders' socioeconomic status (SES). For instance, participants in a study of mock jurors' perceptions of a juvenile charged with robbery and murder were more likely to convict when the juvenile was described as coming from a low- versus middle/high-SES background (Farnum & Stevenson, 2013). To test whether such a bias would also emerge in cases involving juvenile sex offenders, Sorenson Farnum, Stevenson, and Skinner (2011) presented participants with a vignette describing a 15-year-old boy convicted of forcibly raping a 15-year-old girl. The SES of both the boy offender and girl victim were varied from low SES to middle SES. Participants' support for requiring the boy to register as a sex offender was not affected by his SES, but participants were more supportive of registration as an outcome when the girl victim was described as coming from a low-SES background (i.e., her family made $19,000 annually) as compared to a middle-SES background (i.e., her family made $65,000 annually). Participants made more uncontrollable attributions for a defendant's behavior (e.g., "he couldn't help himself") and expressed less desire for retribution when he raped a middle-SES girl than a low-SES girl, and in turn, supported registration less.

History of Abuse

Because approximately one-third of juvenile sex offenders have themselves been sexually abused (for review, see Worling, 1995), researchers have examined how juvenile sex offenders' own abuse histories affect public support for registration (Stevenson et al., 2013, unpublished manuscript). In these studies, community members approximated that 65% of juvenile sex offenders have been sexually abused as children, which is nearly identical to community members' estimates for adult sex offenders (Levenson et al., 2007), but more than twice as high as actual prevalence rates (31%; Worling, 1995). Many participants also, in turn, assumed that experiencing sexual abuse is a precursor for sex offending. When asked about juvenile sex offenders in the abstract (i.e., when they are asked about juvenile offenders in general, without being given a specific case to think about), the extent to which participants believed that sexual abuse leads to sexual offending was associated with reduced support for registering juvenile sex offenders. When asked about juvenile sex offenders in specific cases, however, the effect of juveniles' own histories of abuse on participants' registration support depended on the type of sexual offense committed. Consistent with how participants responded to abstract cases, juvenile sex offenders' own abuse experiences had a mitigating effect on registration support in cases involving more severe offenses (e.g., forced rape), but an *aggravating* effect in cases involving *less* severe offenses (e.g., statutory rape). These results are consistent with prior research showing that people who are asked about sex offenders in the abstract tend to imagine offenders who commit heinous crimes (Salerno, Najdowski et al., 2010). In the context of more severe offenses, a juvenile's history of abuse might elicit sympathy and reduce registration support, but in the context of less severe offenses, a juvenile's history of abuse might make otherwise normative sexual behavior seem sexually deviant and increase registration support. This would conflict with laws mandating that a history of abuse be used as a mitigating factor in juvenile cases (e.g., Juvenile Court Act, 1987).

Sexual Orientation

The ambiguity surrounding the application of sex offender laws to juveniles might also lead to the manifestation of anti-gay biases in judgments about juveniles engaging in consensual sexual activity with their peers. Salerno, Murphy, and Bottoms (2012) tested whether people would support harsher registry punishments for gay versus straight juveniles who engaged in consensual sex with a minor (i.e., a peer) and engaged in sexting behavior with an underaged peer. For adult offenders, participants showed no sexual orientation bias, recommending similarly high rates of registration for straight as gay adults. In the more ambiguous context of juvenile offenders, however, participants were significantly more likely to support harsher registry laws when the juvenile engaged in gay versus straight consensual oral sex with a minor. Researchers conceptually replicated this finding in a second study, finding that when a boy sent a sexting message, participants were significantly more likely to support harsher punishments when he was gay versus straight. This anti-gay bias did not, however, replicate for girl offenders: When a girl sent a sexting message, participants were marginally *less* likely to support harsher punishments when she was gay versus straight.

Summary

Research indicates that public support for juvenile sex offender registration can be influenced by characteristics of the offender, victim, or a combination of the two. This raises the question of whether registration requirements are applied fairly in actual cases. The public's subjective biases against stigmatized offenders and victims might be more likely to manifest in more ambiguous cases involving juveniles engaging in less severe, consensual sexual activity, compared to less ambiguous cases involving adult offenders. The one study that included an adult offender control group indicated that biases emerged only for juvenile sex offenders, not for less ambiguous adult offender cases (Salerno et al., 2012). It is also noteworthy that the public is not a singular entity but rather composed of individuals who vary along a multitude of factors, which might influence registry support. For example, Stevenson and colleagues (2009) found that White women supported registration more than White men when the juvenile sex offender's victim was portrayed as White (and thus similar to perceivers' race), but this effect did not emerge when the victim was portrayed as Black. Thus, future research could explore how citizens' characteristics shape their support for juvenile registration.

Psychological Motivations Driving Support for Juvenile Sex Offender Registration

A final question relevant to the topic at hand is: What motives drive public support for juvenile sex offender registration policy? A series of studies identified psychological mediators that explain, in part, why the public supports juvenile registration. Specifically, Salerno, Najdowski et al. (2010) found that community members who read about more severe offenses (compared to less severe offenses) perceived the offender as more of a threat and reported feeling more moral outrage toward the offender, which both in turn increased support for registering the juvenile. In other words, both utilitarian concerns for protecting society (perceived threat) as well as retributive desires to punish the offender (moral outrage) emerged as significant mechanisms explaining how the public's reactions to juveniles influenced their support for registration.

Two additional studies uncovered evidence that biases associated with race and sexual orientation are typically driven by retributive desires for punishment (e.g., moral outrage), rather than utilitarian desires to protect society. Specifically, as described earlier, Salerno and colleagues (2012) found that participants supported registration more for a low-severity crime (i.e., consensual sex) when the two juveniles were the same gender than when they were of the opposite gender. This anti-gay bias was driven by moral outrage toward the offender, such that they were more morally outraged at a gay versus straight offender, which in turn led them to be more likely to support harsher registry laws. Similarly, Stevenson et al. (2009) found that greater registration support for interracial juvenile sex crimes (compared to same-race sex crimes) was significantly mediated by a retributive desire to punish the offender. Neither the anti-gay bias nor the bias against interracial relationships was driven by a utilitarian desire to protect society, however. Biases against gay youth and interracial sexual activity appear to be driven by a desire to punish the offender rather than protect society—a goal that is antithetical to the stated legislative purpose of registration policy.

Policy Implications

Research regarding the psychological issues surrounding the application of sex offender registration policies to juveniles whose offenses do not fit the spirit of these laws is timely and important. The media has reported countless news stories sparking debate about whether a given case involving consensual sexual activity among teenagers is an appropriate application of these laws. For example, many reports debate the appropriateness of prosecuting teenagers for sexting (e.g., Hoffman, 2011; Klepper, 2011). Despite the fact that sexting behavior is common among minors (Strassberg et al., 2012), it meets the legal criteria of child pornography and leads to prosecution and registration of juveniles as sex offenders in many states (e.g., *A.H. v. State of Florida*, 2007; for review, see Eraker, 2010). Although questioning the application of sex offender laws to juveniles is not a popular thing to do, it is important to do so because this issue influences many adolescents in this country—particularly those from stigmatized groups.

This review of the literature reveals several important points relevant to public policy regarding juvenile sex offender registration. First, in many states, registration for juvenile sex offenders is mandatory and judges may not exercise discretion based on offense severity (Salerno, Stevenson et al., 2010). Our data suggest that sentencing juveniles to sex offender registration for less severe offenses is not in line with public sentiment. Thus, laws that do not allow judges discretion might prevent them from delivering judgments that are in line with public sentiment (e.g., not sentencing teenagers to registration when they commit less severe offenses). Second, although it seems like a significant step in the right direction to allow judges more discretion, it is worth noting that our data suggest that support for applying sex offender registration laws to juveniles can be biased against stigmatized offenders and victims. Thus, granting judges discretion might place juveniles who belong to stigmatized groups at greater risk of being registered than other juveniles—even if they commit the same offense. Third, one of the purposes of the sex offender registry is to deter potential offenders from committing crimes for which they might be registered. Our data suggest that most young adults are either unaware of or hold incorrect beliefs about the possibility of juvenile sex offender registration and that the less aware they were, the more likely they were to have committed registration-worthy offenses when they were minors. Thus, efforts made to deter juvenile offenders through policy might be futile unless coupled with efforts to educate juveniles about these policies.

Since SORNA became a law in 2006, a number of public commentators, advocates, and academics have identified problems associated with the application of its guidelines to juvenile sex offenders. Although additional legislation has not been enacted, administrative guidelines have addressed some of the more problematic provisions. For example, the Department of Justice's Supplemental Guidelines, released in 2011, explicitly (a) provided jurisdictions with the discretion to determine whether a juvenile sex offender's information need be publicly disclosed, (b) clarified the intent of the law to require registration only for juveniles who commit the most serious kinds of offenses, and (c) indicated that there is no requirement to register juveniles for lesser offenses wherein the criminality depends on the age of the victim

(Supplemental Guidelines for Sex Offender Registration and Notification, 2011). As of the writing of this chapter, SORNA is being considered for reauthorization (Adam Walsh Reauthorization Act of 2012). Assuming that SORNA is reauthorized, it is important to keep in mind that, although SORNA sets *minimum* guidelines for states, states are free to enact harsher rules. In other words, states are free to be more inclusive of juveniles in their guidelines; as long as they meet the minimum requirements of SORNA, they are considered compliant. The history of SORNA illustrates that policy can be influenced both legislatively and administratively. For advocates who wish to influence the policy process, it will be important to observe how individual states enact this law and to be proactive in providing lawmakers with information about how to apply registration laws to juveniles in developmentally appropriate ways.

Conclusion

The need to protect children from dangerous sex offenders has led to policies that require juvenile sex offenders to register on public online registries. It is important to determine the implications of these laws for the wellbeing of child victims but also for the wellbeing of juvenile offenders on these registries. A review of current sex offender registration policies and psychological literature calls into question whether the application of these laws to juvenile offenders actually improves the wellbeing of children by protecting them from dangerous, repeat sex offenders. Specifically, research does not support the assumptions inherent in these laws: that juvenile sex offenders' amenability to treatment and recidivism rates are similar to adult sex offenders', and that sex offender registries effectively reduce sex offenses. Furthermore, applying sex offender registration laws to juveniles who commit less severe, consensual offenses might be detrimental to the wellbeing of these juvenile offenders. Not only is registering juveniles for these types of crimes not in line with public sentiment, it leads to negative consequences that could increase juveniles' likelihood of recidivating. Finally, the ambiguity surrounding the application of these laws to juveniles who commit less severe, consensual offenses can lead to biases against youth who belong to stigmatized groups. These issues are important for policy makers to consider when assessing the implications of juvenile registration laws for the wellbeing of children—both potential victims and offenders.

Author's Note

The views and opinions expressed in this report are those of the authors and should not be construed to represent the views of NIDA or any of the sponsoring organizations, agencies, or the US government.

References

A. H. v. Florida, 949 So. 2d 234 (Fla. 1st Dist. 2007).
Adam Walsh Act, 42 U.S.C.A. § 16911 et seq. (West, 2006).
Adam Walsh Reauthorization Act of 2012, H. R. 3796, 112th Cong. (2012).
Adkins, G., Huff, D., & Stageberg, P. (2000). *The Iowa sex offender registry and recidivism.* Des Moines: Iowa Department of Human Rights.
Bottoms, B. L., Davis, S., & Epstein, M. A. (2004). Race and jurors' decisions in child sexual abuse cases. *Journal of Applied Social Psychology, 34,* 1–33. doi: 10.1111/j.1559-1816.2004.tb02535.x.
Bridges, G. S., & Steen, S. (1998). Racial disparities in official assessments of juvenile offenders: Attributional stereotypes as mediating mechanisms. *American Sociological Review, 63*(4), 554–570. doi:10.2307/2657267.
Caldwell, M. F. (2007). Sexual offense adjudication and sexual recidivism among juvenile offenders. *Sex Abuse, 19,* 107–113. doi: 10.1007/s11194-007-9042-7.
Caldwell, M. F., Ziemke, M. H., & Vitacco, M. J. (2008). An examination of the sex offender registration and notification act as applied to juveniles: Evaluating the ability to predict sexual recidivism. *Psychology, Public Policy, and Law, 89,* 89–114. doi: 10.1037/a0013241.
Caputo, A. A., & Brodsky, S. L. (2004). Citizen coping with community notification of released sex offenders. *Behavioral Sciences and the Law, 22,* 239–252. doi: 10.1002/bsl.566.
Carpentier, M., Silovsky, J. F., & Chaffin, M. (2006). Randomized trial of treatment for children with sexual behavior problems: Ten-year follow-up. *Journal of Consulting and Clinical Psychology, 74,* 482–388. doi: 10.1037/0022-006X.74.3.482.
Cauffman, E., & Steinberg, L. (2000). (Im)maturity of judgment in adolescence: Why adolescents may be less culpable than adults. *Behavioral Sciences and the Law, 18,* 741–760. doi: 10.1002/bsl.416.
Chaffin, M. (2008). Our minds are made up—Don't confuse us with the facts: Commentary on policies concerning children with sexual behavior problems and juvenile sex offenders. *Child Maltreatment, 13,* 110–121. doi: 10.1177/1077559508314510.
Conmartin, E. B., Kernsmith, P. D., & Miles, B. W. (2010). Family experiences of young adult sex offender registration. *Journal of Child Sexual Abuse, 19,* 204–225. doi:10.1080/10538711003627207.
US Department of Justice, Office of Justice Programs, Office of Sex Offender Sentencing, Monitoring, Apprehending, Registering, and Tracking. (2012). *Sorna.* Retrieved July 2013, from http://www.ojp.gov/smart/sorna.htm.
Department of Justice, Office of the Attorney General (2010). *Supplemental Guidelines for Sex Offender Registration and Notification.* Federal Register 75 (93), 27362–27366. Retrieved July 2013, from http://www.gpo.gov/fdsys/pkg/FR-2010-05-14/html/2010-11665.htm.
Dovidio, J. F., & Gaertner, S. L. (2004). Aversive racism. In M. P. Zanna (Ed.), *Advances in experimental social psychology* (Vol. 36, pp. 1–51). San Diego, CA: Academic Press.
Eraker, E. C. (2010). Stemming sexting: Sensible legal approaches to teenagers' exchange of self-produced pornography. *Berkeley Technology Law Journal, 25,* 555–596.

Farnum, K. S., & Stevenson, M. C. (2013). Economically disadvantaged juvenile offenders tried in adult court are perceived as less able to understand their actions, but more guilty. *Psychology, Crime & Law*, (Epub ahead of print), 1–18. doi: 10.1080/1068316X.2013.793766.

Frey, D. L., & Gaertner, S. L. (1986). Helping and the avoidance of inappropriate interracial behavior: A strategy that perpetuates a nonprejudiced self-image. *Journal of Personality and Social Psychology, 50*, 1083–1090. doi: 10.1037/0022-3514.50.6.1083.

Hoffman, J. (2011). States struggle with minors' sexting. *New York Times*. Retrieved July 2013, from http://www.nytimes.com/2011/03/27/us/27sextinglaw.html?_r=0.

Jacob Wetterling Crimes against Children and Sexually Violent Offender Registration Act, 42 U.S.C. §14071 (West 2004).

James, S. (2009). Romeo and Juliet were sex offenders: An analysis of the age of consent and a call for reform. *University of Missouri-Kansas City Law Review, 78*, 241–262.

Juvenile Court Act. 705 Ill. Comp. Stat. § 405/5-805, 5-810, 5-130 (1987).

Kernsmith, P. D., Craun, S. W., & Foster, J. (2009). Public attitudes toward sexual offenders and sex offender registration. *Journal of Child Sexual Abuse, 18*, 290–301. doi:10.1080/10538710902901663.

Klein, K., & Creech, B. (1982). Race, rape, and bias: Distortion of prior odds and meaning changes. *Basic and Applied Social Psychology, 3*, 21–33. doi:10.1207/s15324834basp0301_2.

Klepper, D. (2011). Teen sexting penalties may be relaxed by states. *The Huffington Post*. Retrieved July 2013, from http://www.huffingtonpost.com/2011/06/13/teen-sexting-penalties_n_875783.html.

Letourneau, E. J., & Armstrong, K. S. (2008). Recidivism rates for registered and nonregistered juvenile sexual offenders. *Sexual Abuse, 20*, 393–408. doi:10.1177/1079063208324661.

Letourneau, E. J., & Miner, M. (2005). Juvenile sex offenders: A case against the legal and clinical status quo. *Sexual Abuse, 17*, 293–312. doi: 10.1007/s11194-005-5059-y.

Levenson, J., Brannon, Y., Fortney, T., & Baker, J. (2007). Public perceptions about sex offenders and community protection policies. *Analyses of Social Issues and Public Policy, 7*, 1–25. doi: 10.1111/j.1530-2415.2007.00119.x.

Levenson, J., & Cotter, L. (2005). The effect of Megan's law on sex offender reintegration. *Journal of Contemporary Criminal Justice, 21*, 49–66. doi:10.1177/1043986204271676.

Levesque, R. J. R. (1996). Is there still a place for violent youth in juvenile justice? *Aggression and Violent Behavior, 1*, 69–79. doi:10.1016/1359-1789(95)00006-2 6-2.

Lithwick, D. (2009, February 14). Teens, nude photos, and the law. *Newsweek*. Retrieved July 2013, from http://www.thedailybeast.com/newsweek/2009/02/13/teens-nude-photos-and-the-law.html

Human Rights Watch. (2007). *No easy answers: Sex offender laws in the US*. Retrieved July 2013, from http://www.hrw.org/en/reports/2007/09/11/no-easy-answers

Megan's Law, 42 U.S.C.A. § 13701 (West 1996).

Phillips, D. (1998). *Community notification as viewed by Washington's citizens*. Washington State Institute for Public Policy. Retrieved from July 2013, http://www.wsipp.wa.gov/rptfiles/CnSurvey.pdf.

Proctor, J. L., Badzinski, D. M., & Johnson, M. (2002). The impact of media on knowledge and perceptions of Megan's Law. *Criminal Justice Policy Review, 13*, 356–379. doi: 10.1177/088740302237804.

Redlich, A. D. (2001). Community notification: Perceptions of its effectiveness in preventing child sexual abuse. *Journal of Child Sexual Abuse, 10*, 91–116. doi:10.1300/J070v10n03_06.

Reppucci, N. D., Michel, J. L., & Kostelnik, J. O. (2009). Challenging juvenile transfer: Faulty assumptions and misguided policies. In B. L. Bottoms, C. J. Najdowski, & G. S. Goodman (Eds.), *Children as victims, witnesses, and offenders: Psychological science and the law* (pp. 295–312). New York, NY: Guilford Press.

Ross, W. (2005). The perceptions of college students about interracial relationships. *National Forum of Applied Educational Research Journal, 17E*(3), 1–16.

Salerno, J. M., Najdowski, C. N., Stevenson, M. C., Wiley, T. R. A., Bottoms, B. L., Pimentel, P. S., & Vaca, R. (2010). Psychological mechanisms underlying support for juvenile sex offender registry laws: Prototypes, moral outrage, and perceived threat. *Behavioral Sciences and the Law, 28*, 58–83. doi: 10.1002/bsl.921.

Salerno, J. M., Stevenson, M. C., Wiley, T. R. A., Najdowski, C. J., Bottoms, B. L., & Doran, R. A. (2010). Public attitudes toward applying sex offender registration laws to juvenile offenders. In J. M. Lampinen & K. Sexton-Radek (Eds.), *Protecting children from violence: Evidence based interventions* (pp. 193–218). New York, NY: Psychology Press.

Salerno, J. M., Murphy, M. C., & Bottoms, B. L. (2012, January). *Give the kid a break—but only if he's straight: Moral outrage drives biases in juvenile sex offender punishment decisions.* Poster presented at the Meeting of the Society for Personality and Social Psychology, San Diego, CA.

Sampson, R. J., & Laub, J. H. (2005). A life-course view of the development of crime. *Annals of the American Academy of Political and Social Science, 602*, 12–45. doi: 10.1177/0002716205280075.

Sandler, J. C., Freeman, N. J., & Socia, K. M. (2008). Does a watched pot boil? A time-series analysis of New York State's sex offender registration and notification law. *Psychology, Public Policy, and Law, 14*, 284–302. doi: 10.1037/a0013881.

Scott, S. S., Reppucci, N. D., Antonishak, J., & DeGennaro, J. T. (2006). Public attitudes about the culpability and punishment of young offenders. *Behavioral Sciences and the Law, 24*, 815–832. doi: 10.1002/bsl.727.

Sex Offender Registration and Notification Act, 42 U.S.C.A. § 16913 (West 2006).

Sorenson Farnum, K. M., Stevenson, M. C., & Skinner, A. L. (2011, March). *When does juvenile rape "make sense?": Victim socioeconomic status shapes perceptions of juvenile sex offenders.* Paper presented at the American Psychology Law Society Conference, Miami, FL.

St. Amand, A., Bard, D. B., & Silovsky, J. F. (2008). Meta-analysis of treatment for child sexual behavior problems: Practice elements and outcomes. *Child Maltreatment, 13*, 145–166. doi: 10.1177/1077559508315353.

Stevenson, M. C., & Bottoms, B. L. (2009). Race shapes perceptions of juvenile offenders in criminal court. *Journal of Applied Social Psychology, 39*, 1660–1689. doi: 10.1111/j.1559-1816.2009.00499.x.

Stevenson, M. C., Najdowski, C. J., Bottoms, B. L., & Haegerich, T. M. (2009). Understanding adults' perceptions of juvenile offenders. In B. L. Bottoms, G. S.

Goodman, & C. J. Najdowski (Eds.). *Child victims, child offenders: Psychology and law* (pp. 349–368). New York, NY: Guilford Press.

Stevenson, M. C., Najdowski, C. J., & Wiley, T. A. (2013). Young adults' understanding of juvenile sex offender registration laws. *Journal of Child Sexual Abuse, 22,* 103–118.

Strassberg, D. S., McKinnon, R. K., Sustaita, M. A., & Rullo, J. (2012). Sexting by high school students: An exploratory and descriptive study. *Archives of Sexual Behavior.* doi: 10.1007/s10508-012-9969-8

Supplemental Guidelines for Sex Offender Registration and Notification, 76 Fed. Reg. 1630 (2011).

Sweeney, L. T., & Haney, C. (1992). The influence of race on sentencing: A meta-analytic review of experimental studies. *Behavioral Sciences and the Law, 10,* 179–195. doi: 10.1002/bsl.2370100204.

Tewksbury, R. (2005). Collateral consequences of sex offender registration. *Journal of Contemporary Criminal Justice, 21,* 67–81. doi: 10.1177/1043986204271704.

Tewksbury, R., & Lees, M. (2006). Perceptions of sex offender registration: Collateral consequences and community experiences. *Sociological Spectrum, 26,* 309–334. doi: 10.1080/02732170500524246.

Trivits, L., & Reppucci, N. (2002). Application of Megan's Law to juveniles. *American Psychologist, 57,* 690–704. doi: 10.1037/0003-066X.57.9.690.

Vasquez, B. E., Maddan, S., & Walker, J. T. (2008). The influence of sex offender registration and notification laws in the United States. *Crime and Delinquency, 58,* 175–192. doi: 10.1177/0011128707311641.

Welchans, S. (2005). Megan's Law: Evaluations of sexual offender registries. *Criminal Justice Policy Review, 16,* 123–140. doi: 10.1177/0887403404265630.

Worling, J. (1995). Sexual abuse histories of adolescent male sex offenders: Differences on the basis of the age and gender of their victims. *Journal of Abnormal Psychology, 104,* 610–613. doi: 10.1037/0021-843X.104.4.610.

Zimring, F. E., Piquero, A. R., & Jennings, W. G. (2007). Sexual delinquency in Racine: Does early sex offending predict later sex offending in youth and young adulthood? *Criminology and Public Policy, 6,* 507–534. doi: 10.1111/j.1745-9133.2007.00451.x.

6

Female Juvenile Offenders' Perceptions of Gender-Specific Programs

Monica K. Miller, Lacey Miller, and Angela D. Broadus

Throughout US history, juvenile justice system programming has focused on various methods to deal with young offenders (Frabutt, DiLuca, & Graves, 2008), including efforts to decrease crime, keep juveniles safe, and reform youth into healthy, productive members of society (Humphrey, 2004; Sherman, 2005). Programs ranged from punitive "tough on crime" approaches to nurturing, rehabilitative approaches (US Department of Justice, 2007), and in accordance with the equal protection clause of the Fourteenth Amendment, were believed to be gender neutral. In the early 1990s, however, researchers recognized that use of a primarily male juvenile population in the development of the gender-neutral programming had contributed to the creation of programs that better served males than females. For instance, programs were more likely to focus on addressing the overt, aggressive behaviors common to male juvenile offenders than the more subtle, self-destructive behaviors common to female juvenile offenders. As a result, these male-based programs failed to reduce recidivism or address the wellbeing and needs of young female offenders (Morgan & Patton, 2002). Instead, female offenders, who were predominantly arrested for status offenses relating to their own physical and sexual abuse, were revictimized by incarceration rather than helped to cope with the underlying issues (Humphrey, 2004). Researchers and advocates suggested that, if gender-specific programming was designed to meet the unique needs of females, they would be more successful than the traditional male-based model of juvenile incarceration and rehabilitation (Sherman, 2005).

This advocacy for gender-specific programming coincided theoretically with the restorative justice (RJ; Sherman & Strang, 2013) and therapeutic jurisprudence (TJ; Wexler & Winick, 2003) rehabilitative movements. These movements suggested that recidivism and harm could be reduced through recognition of an interdependence between the offender, the victim, and the community, and through a better focus on the wellbeing of the offender. In the following sections, we examine the need for gender-specific juvenile justice programming based on RJ and TJ principals and through the foundations of social context theory. We also present a qualitative study of female juveniles' perceptions about one gender-specific program in Reno, Nevada. Program graduates indicated whether they recognized the programming as gender specific and believed that it was helpful. Finally, the graduates considered how their experiences might have differed if they had been in a traditional, "gender-neutral" program.

Rationale for Gender-Specific Programming

When compared to males, arrests of female juveniles disproportionally result from noncriminal status offenses such as running away from home, drug use, and truancy (Humphrey, 2004), although violent criminal behavior has been increasing in recent years (see e.g., Martin, Martin, Dell, Davis, & Guerrieri, 2008). From 1985 to 2002, juvenile crime rates declined *overall*, but *female* offender rates increased significantly (Humphrey, 2004).

Research comparing male and female juveniles suggested that the etiology of delinquency might differ due to differences in underlying issues. Female juveniles were more likely than males to have experienced physical and sexual abuse (Martin et al., 2008) and to suffer from mental health disorders (Grande et al., 2012), childhood abuse, neglect, or substance abuse (Roe-Sepowitz, 2009). Female offenders also were more likely than males to have had parental criminal involvement (Martin et al., 2008). Gender-specific programming with focus on the issues relevant to young females such as connectedness to family, community and education, treatment for emotional and physical trauma, and mental health issues could help females develop coping skills, resolve the underlying causes of delinquency, increase overall wellbeing, and stop the intergenerational cycle of offending (Morgan & Patton, 2002; Sherman, 2005). See Chapter 11, this volume, for discussion of gender differences in offending in adult females, and discussion of intergenerational offending.

Restorative Justice and Therapeutic Jurisprudence

Gender-specific programming incorporates principles of restorative justice (RJ) through holistic efforts to resolve the criminogenic factors underlying female delinquency. RJ focuses on humanely and effectively reducing crime and recidivism, while improving victim and societal recovery from criminal acts (Sherman & Strang, 2013). Unlike conventional forms of justice that view criminals as qualitatively different than victims, RJ suggests an interdependence between criminals, society, and victims of crime with four basic assumptions:

> [1] victims should be at the center rather than excluded from the process...[2] victims and offenders are not natural enemies...[3] victims are not primarily retributive in their view of justice, [and 4] prison is not necessarily the best way to prevent repeat crime. (Sherman & Strang, 2013, p. 12)

RJ strategies typically include remedies such as face-to-face mediation between victims and offenders, court-ordered financial restitution, and community service. These approaches tend to be more effective than conventional justice (CJ) strategies in reducing recidivism after juvenile violent and property crimes (Sherman & Strang, 2013). RJ principles are present in gender-specific programming because there is a focus on repairing harm (e.g., community service, education, improving relationships), which helps the females, their parents, and the community. While programs do not often involve the victim if the crime is directed at a person or entity specifically (e.g., shoplifting), they do involve victims if the victim is the community (e.g., graffiti), the family (e.g., running away), or the female herself (e.g., drug use).

Gender-specific programming also follows the principles of therapeutic jurisprudence (TJ) by focusing on the wellbeing of the offender (see also Chapters 9 and 11, this volume, for more on TJ). TJ relies on social science to identify the psychological and emotional impact that law, legal actors, and legal actions have on those involved (Sicafuse & Bornstein, 2013; Wexler & Winick, 2003). TJ recognizes that legal processes can have a therapeutic (or nontherapeutic) influence for those involved. For example, incarceration without the possibility of early release for a drug-related offense provides no motivation to reform behavior or address the risk factors that led to crime (Wexler, 2011). Alternatively, drug courts represent a therapeutic approach that addresses the needs of the offender and their social situation, environment, and relationships, with the end goal of positive change rather than (or in addition to) punishment (Wexler, 2011; Wexler & Winick, 1996). In the same vein, incarceration of female juvenile offenders for running away from home to avoid abuse provides no chance to acknowledge or ameliorate the underlying issue. Instead, gender-specific programming recognizes and addresses abuse and helps the offender develop more effective coping skills than running away from home.

Gender-specific programming for juveniles utilizes the findings of social science and psychology to highlight and address risk factors leading to female offending (TJ principles), while acknowledging society/victim/offender interdependence and helping the female offender to repair the harm and reconnect with society (RJ principles).

Social Context Theory

Social context theory (SCT) provides a social psychological rationale for the rehabilitative response associated with gender-specific programming. According to SCT, macrosocietal structures external to the individual (e.g., social class, religion, education, family, and government); microsocial processes (e.g., values, beliefs); and social realities (e.g., norms, laws) influence social behavior in a community (Earle & Earle, 1999). For example, beliefs about femininity and masculinity derived from macrostructures such as religion and family shape individual behavior by influencing beliefs about gender roles and establishing norms for behavior within that community. Social context also shapes the individual's response to community expectations regarding gender, relationships, and behavior (Burke, Joseph, Pasick, & Barker, 2009; Earle & Earle, 1999; Pasick & Burke, 2008). As such, gender serves as part of the social context and shapes the way that individuals see and react to their social environment.

Gender-specific juvenile programs use social psychological concepts to encourage change in female offenders' behavior. First, offenders are encouraged to form bonds with others within the macrosocietal context of a program "community" that focuses on gender issues and needs. From this community, the offenders learn the attitudes and values central to the community (social processes) and learn acceptable ways of behaving (norms, laws, and rules). By incorporating the social identity of the community into their own identity, the offenders become more likely to conform and adopt more positive behavior.

Overview of the Study

While a gender-specific approach to juvenile rehabilitation seems plausible, few such programs have been adopted, much less evaluated. In addition, very few studies have investigated *offender perceptions* of gender-specific programs. The current research is a first step in filling this gap through assessment of female juveniles' perceptions of a gender-specific program in Reno, Nevada. Females who graduated from the program completed interviews assessing whether they recognized the programming as gender specific, believed it was helpful to them, and thought their experience would have differed if they had been involved in non-gender-specific programming. The study also assessed participants' perceived developments in relationships, health, education, and self-improvement (the three foci of the program). Although this study did not directly assess the *effectiveness* of the program, it did assess whether female juvenile offenders *perceived* that the gender-specific programming had a positive impact.

This study examined three research questions: (1) Do the respondents remember gender-specific programming? (2) Do respondents think the gender-specific programming was helpful? and (3) How do respondents feel their experience and success may have been different if they would have been in a non-gender-specific program?

The Charles M. McGee Center, a 24-bed center for adolescent programs in Reno, Nevada, offers a 3- to 6-month gender-specific residential program for young females, aged 13–17 years, called the "Girls' Program." The Center began in 1992 as part of the Children's Cabinet campus, a private and publicly funded program in Washoe County. The Girl's Program, one of the truancy reduction and detention alternatives programs, is supervised and managed by the Prevention and Early Intervention Division of the Washoe County Department of Juvenile Services. The program is housed in the department's status offense shelter, off site from the detention facility. Juvenile female offenders who have committed status (e.g., running away from home) or criminal offenses can volunteer for the program or be court ordered to attend.

Upon intake, residents receive psychological and substance abuse evaluations, and individual or family counseling. Facility staff work with residents to develop case plans addressing educational and credit needs due to course failures or truancy (Washoe County Department of Juvenile Services, 2008). Residents live in a homestyle environment where they help with chores, receive education, and attend various classes and counseling.

The Girls' Program focuses on family reunification and strengthening relationships at home, in school, and within the community. Specifically, the program addresses the needs of young women by creating positive relationships, role modeling, and facilitating family rehabilitation (Washoe County Department of Juvenile Services, 2008). Residents also learn skills by participating in classes such as Family Wellness, Resolving Anger Peacefully, Aggression Replacement Training, Thinking for a Change, and Girls Circle "to make better decisions that can positively impact their present and future lives" (Washoe County, Nevada, 2009). While some of the classes and programs are gender specific (e.g., Girls Circle and Girl Scouts), others, although not designed as gender specific, are considered so because only females are involved and they focus on the needs of the females.

Parents are encouraged to participate in classes and sessions (Charles M. McGee Center for Adolescent Programs, 2008). The program also works closely with a community nonprofit agency to provide individual and family counseling, and community service groups, in order to regain connectedness with the family and community (Washoe County, Nevada, 2009). Because this program and the classes are exclusive to young women, they are instilled with a sense of empowerment and are taught to express themselves with others who are like them.

Methods

Participants

Sixteen females in the McGee Center Girls' Program graduated during the 6-month study period and thus qualified to be participants. Eleven graduates volunteered to participate in the study, and five declined or initially agreed but did not follow through. Of these (aged 14–17 years; M = 15.4; Mdn = 16), six were Latina (54.6%) and five were White. Participants ranged in level of juvenile justice involvement. Four had been assigned to prevention/early intervention status. Either these had no legal referral but the family had sought help for issues they were having, or they had been referred to the Washoe County Department of Juvenile Services for a status offense. Two were on informal status as for a status or misdemeanor offense. One was pending court for a misdemeanor offense, and four were on open probation status for a delinquent offense. The respondents varied in their levels of education, family background, and traumatic experiences.

Instruments and Procedures

Participants were recruited through an information sheet and parental permission form. These forms explained the objectives of the study. After obtaining parental consent and participant assent for the interview, participants were informed that they could refuse to answer any question and/or stop the interview at any time.

The primary researcher, also an employee within the program, conducted all interviews at the McGee Center 2 weeks after the participant graduated from the program, and at the parents' discretion. All were completed within a 6-month period. The 30-minute interviews were recorded by audiocassette, transcribed to a computer file, and printed to a paper copy. Respondents chose a "code name" in order to maintain anonymity. Respondents first answered four questions (see Table 6.1) that broadly inquired about their experiences in the program and how the program may have been helpful with their relationships, health, education, or other aspects of their lives. These questions determined whether respondents would offer unsolicited information about gender-specific programming. The next eight questions asked participants their perceptions of gender-specific programs. The final six questions asked whether participants thought their experiences would have been different if they had been in a non-gender-specific program. Additional probes were utilized as needed for further elaboration or clarification. The methodology and instrumentation were approved by the university's Institutional Review Board.

Analysis

Content analysis of participants' responses to interview questions occurred in phases. Initially, responses were separated into comments, defined as a "remark...made as an expression of opinion" (Neufeldt & Guralnik, 1988, p. 280) regarding a particular topic or thought. Comment size ranged from one-word to several sentences. Next, researchers grouped similar comments

Table 6.1 Participant Interview Items

1. Can you tell me what parts, if any, of your experience at the McGee Center helped you with your relationships with your family?
2. Can you tell me what parts, if any, of your experience at the McGee Center helped you with your own personal health?
3. Can you tell me what parts, if any, of your experience at the McGee Center helped you with your education?
4. Can you tell me if there are any parts of your experience at the McGee Center that helped you with anything else?
5. What was it like for you to be in a program involving only girls?
6. What are issues that you face specific to being a girl?
7. Do you remember any parts of the program that were specific to being a girl?
8. Was the "Thinking for a Change" class helpful to you? If so, how?
9. Was the "ACT" class helpful to you? If so, how?
10. Was "Girls Circle" helpful to you? If so, how?
11. Was participating in Girl Scouts helpful to you? If so, how?
12. Was participating in group counseling helpful to you? If so, how?
13. How do you think your experience would have been different if you were in a program that was not specifically for girls?
14. If you weren't in a program with only girls, in what ways would it be different?
15. Are there positive aspects of being in a program for girls only?
16. Are there negative aspects of being in a program for girls only?
17. If you had classes with boys, how might your participation be different?
18. Would having boys in the program have impacted your success? If so, how?

together and categorized them according to the relevant research question: (1) Do the respondents remember gender-specific programming? (2) Do respondents think gender-specific programming is helpful in areas of health, relationships, and education? (3) How do respondents feel their experience and success may have varied in a non-gender-specific program? A comment could be coded in multiple categories, for example, if a participant said that being in a gender-specific program helped her learn a lot about her personal health that she could not learn if there were males in the program, then this comment would fit under both "personal health" and "experience would differ if in a non-gender-specific program" categories.

With each research question, subcategories emerged. Informal inter-rater reliability of the thematic categorizations addressed reliability of categorization. No precise calculations of agreement were calculated because initial agreement was nearly perfect, as categorization was not particularly subjective. Interview questions corresponded with research questions and categories, and nearly all responses fit neatly into the question and category they were assigned to address. For instance, question 13 asked, "How do you think your experience would have been different if you were in a program that was not specifically for girls?" and was designed to address the research question "How do respondents feel their experience and success may have varied in a non-gender-specific program?" Nearly all responses were relevant to this interview question and research question and thus were easily categorized. Further, responses were quite clear; for example, if a participant said, "My experience would have been different if…" it was categorized under the subcategory "differences." Thus, categorizing was not considered a major issue for the study because it was not particularly subjective. The primary researcher initiated the categorization process; the secondary researcher served as a check on categorization procedures randomly throughout the data collection and analysis phase. Discussions then took place as necessary (which was infrequently) for the resolution of discrepancies in categorization.

Results

Analysis was based on three themes: remembered gender-specific programming, perceived helpfulness of gender-specific programming, and perceptions of whether a nongendered program would be different. These themes mirrored the research questions.

Research Question 1: Remembered and Recognized Gender-Specific Programming

The first four survey items provided data for the first research question regarding participants' unsolicited memory of gender-specific programming. Results indicated that most participants remembered the gender-specific programming before being specifically asked about it. Seven participants mentioned various aspects of the programming and six specifically praised the "Thinking for a Change" class (T4C; which is gender specific because only girls are enrolled and they discuss issues relevant to females) as having a positive impact upon them. For example,

> I am able to think about the situations that I'm in and how am I going to act to them. Like when my mom tells me "no, you can't go to this party,"…I am able to like think about it.…And to not get mad at her and to be able to talk it out…it helped me think about situations like I would get in trouble in.

Six participants also commented on other programs, including Planned Parenthood, Aggression Control Training (ACT), and Girls Circle. For instance,

> Counseling helped because some of the problems that we couldn't solve ourselves... Me and some of the other girls... go through the same problems with our parents... talking with some of the other girls [in group counseling]... helped me see things different.

Finally, four participants, without targeting a specific class or curriculum, commented that "hanging out with" or "living together" promoted group cohesiveness and improvements in relationships. These comments were significant, because even though no gender-specific class was mentioned, the act of residing together is part of gender-specific programming.

Research Question 2: Perceived Helpfulness of Gender-Specific Programming

Survey items 1–12 provided data for the second research question regarding perceived helpfulness of gender-specific programming. Most participants thought the program was helpful. Participants learned skills for improving relationships, health, and education, and reported self-improvement in creativity and attaining new experiences. Participants also discussed how each program addressed issues important to success and described aspects of the programs they disliked, found to be difficult, or believed were not helpful.

Areas of Improvement. Overall, most participants believed that they had improved in the main areas they were asked about: relationships, personal health, education, and other (e.g., self-improvement, creativity).

Relationships   All participants noticed at least some improvement in their relationships. Nine noted improvements in family relationships through better communication skills, re-earned trust, and increased positive feelings toward one another. One spoke about how her new communication skills helped her relationship with her mother:

> [W]ith me and my mom, like we bonded more, we're now getting along way better than we used to....we talk about our feelings.

Nine participants also mentioned improved relationships with girls in particular. Many seemed surprised that they were able to bond with and develop friendships with girls they did not know or who came from different backgrounds. For example,

> I learned a lot about... how other girls are....I learned there's a lot of different type of girls....before I would just be like, oh you're a jerk, I don't like you... [Now] I put it into consideration... that's just their personality.

Finally, five participants reported improved relationships and communication with people in general. For example, one said she was "learning to get along with people that you necessarily don't know...to just to communicate better and...[have] more tolerance."

Health Nine participants identified improvement in personal health while in the Girls' Program. The area of improvement most often cited related to drug or alcohol use. Six participants commented that they remained sober and drug free during the program, even during school, work, and home visits. One said,

> It made me think differently...I used to make mistakes a lot. It made me think...differently about alcohol...I used to drink like nonstop.... And I still have problems...when I see it I want it. But I kind of just like stay away from it.

Four indicated they learned about their bodies, got more exercise, or ate better. Three reported that program staff addressed medical issues, including prescription eyeglasses, vaccinations, and regulating medications. For example, "Before I came in here, I used to basically not take my medicines...But since I've been here, I have been obligated to."

Education All participants mentioned education-related improvements. Seven caught up with or got ahead on school credits. One took her GED, and three reported improved study habits, better grades, and an overall improved outlook on education. One noted,

> I went to school and stuff but I just didn't do anything, just kind of slept the whole time [I had] pretty much like all F's except for English. Yeah, I actually learned a lot while being here. I just brought my grades up.

Other Improvements Throughout the interviews, 27 comments noted improvements not addressed specifically in the interview questions. All of the participants mentioned self-improvements such as being able to better control emotions, focusing on themselves and their needs, and achieving better self-image. Others remarked that they developed abilities or experienced new things. All participants believed they had improved emotionally, for example, being able to control anger, cope with stressful situations, or think about consequences before reacting to a situation. One said, "[I learned] to stop and think before reacting...I use to always just react and freak out and start yelling and breaking things."

Eight participants described improving personal wellbeing such as being in tune with themselves, feeling accomplished, learning manners, working on trust issues, being able to unwind, and learning to adapt to rules and structure. As one stated, "the girl's program helped me be more like in tune with myself, my feminine side."

Three participants realized they liked not having to worry about their looks (e.g., wearing makeup, getting dressed up) because they felt safe among other females. One stated,

> The positive thing is that we can be ourselves, instead of being all dressed up.... if we did something embarrassing it's alright because we're with like our own gender... being with girls can give you a lot of strength.

Eight enjoyed the creative and bonding aspects of the program, while three were pleased with the new experience of participating in community service. As one remembered,

> Doing the makeup together... the slumber party... My mom never let me go to none... It was fun... to stay up with a bunch of girls.

Participant Perceptions about Specific Programs. In survey items 8–12, participants responded to questions about the program in general and about specific curricula. The majority of participants commented positively about the Thinking for Change program (10 participants), Girls Circle (10 participants), Girl Scouts (8 participants), and Aggression Control Training (ACT; 7 participants). Perceptions were mixed about group counseling, with six participants making negative and five making positive remarks. Finally, three participants commented positively about Planned Parenthood, although this program was not included in the questionnaire. Specific participants' comments are shown below.

Girls' Program in General   Seven participants expressed negative remarks about the Girls' Program in general. These participants reported there was a lot of drama among the females, including difficulties getting along with one another and gossiping. As an example, one stated, "The drama that goes on... girls are catty, like they're not very nice. There's just a lot of drama that happens with girls, like there's a lot of like hierarchy and things like that."

In addition, one of the respondents commented that even though there were things that she did like about the program (e.g., she got ahead in school), it did not really help her because "things went back to the same at home" when she returned after having graduated.

Thinking for Change   Ten stated the *Thinking for a Change* program was helpful, while one stated that the class was "just common sense" and not helpful. In general, participants indicated that this class helped them to think about their actions and consequences, control anger, and develop communication skills. For example,

> Thinking for a Change...now I am able to think about the situations that I'm in and how am I going to act...to not get mad...and to be able to talk it out.

Girls Circle   Girls Circle was described as a fun time to unwind and talk, learn about others, and do "some cool stuff," although one participant indicated that this program was not particularly helpful because she spent group time looking at magazines. Comments supporting helpfulness included:

> [Girls Circle is] just our time...where we can talk, we can say anything we want......you can just be yourself...I like it.

and

> In the McGee Center...there is so much stress and drama going on; it was just a place to unwind and relax and just forget about everything.

Girl Scouts   Eight participants mentioned Girl Scouts as helpful, using descriptors such as "fun, creative, a place to get close to other girls, and even become more self-aware." Three participants did not believe this program was particularly helpful.

Aggression Control Training   Seven participants asserted that the aggression control training (ACT) taught them to recognize and control anger, to think first, and to discuss issues without acting inappropriately. For example, "It teaches me to like calm down when I'm mad and think about consequences and...bring me down from being angry." Two participants, however, did not believe the class was helpful, and two did not participate in ACT. One stated,

> I think [ACT] is just retarded...when you're going to do something...you're not going to be "Oh, what's my cues? What's my reducers?"...You just do it, I don't even think that's helping me.

Group Counseling   Five participants described group counseling as a helpful program in which participants could work out problems, express themselves, and feel trust. One said,

> [We] solve a lot of our problems there...we can talk about it...I would always wait until...girls counseling and just talk...and they...help us out a lot...every girl...give[s] their opinion and then you see an adult's opinion, the counselors.

Six described group counseling as a negative experience used primarily for arguing and complaining about each other, the staff, or other aspects of the program (e.g., food, privileges).

> [Group counseling] kind of irritated me...people would be calling each other out, and like complaining...it is a waste of time...I just think that people should get over it because it's in the past...[they complain about] staff here, and the food or "oh, I don't get to do this, and I don't get to wear this."

Planned Parenthood   Three participants described Planned Parenthood as helpful in areas of health and relationships, although the interview questions did not ask about the program.

> Planned Parenthood...was a good program...[It taught us] to use protection and have a healthy lifestyle. If you're going to go out and do stuff...make sure that you're protected. And even the relationships with boys.

Research Question 3: If the Program Had Not Been Gender Specific

Survey items 13–18 provided data for the third research question: How do respondents feel their experience and success would have been different if they would have been in non-gender-specific programming? Themes that emerged included how the program would have been different, what problems might have occurred, whether inclusion of males might have improved the program, and whether their success would have differed if males were included.

Program Differences. Four participants indicated that inclusion of males into the program would have resulted in stricter rules, with staff more watchful of participant interactions. Three believed that staff would have treated males differently than females. One stated, "I think it would be different...we're not even allowed to be near...each other at all and if there were guys...[staff] would watch us even more."

Negative Aspects of Non-Gender-Specific Programming. Nine participants mentioned potential issues associated with including males in the program. These included distractions because, for example, girls might talk or flirt with the males. One young woman said, "It could have been distracting.... you'd be like paying attention to [males]." Six added that inclusion of males in the classes and discussions would make the females feel uncomfortable, embarrassed, or awkward. "[It would be] different...I would feel like awkward...I'm just not used to doing things...while being around a guy...But with girls it's different. Even if I don't know them I'm still comfortable." Three claimed that males would have caused problems because they "are annoying" or "try to be someone they are not." Finally, one participant added that there would have been increased drama among the females if males were present.

Positive Aspects of Non-Gender-Specific Programming. Seven participants reported that they would have had a better experience if males had been included. These asserted that they get along better with males, that males are more "chill and mellow" and easier to cope with than females, or that they may have gained from male insight. For example,

[I] might have learned stuff from both sides. And... probably would have been a lot easier to have some guys to talk to. Like learn stuff about the guys.

Influencing Success. The last question of the interview asked whether including males in the program would have influenced their success. Six participants assumed that males would not have influenced their success in the Girls' Program. One stated,

I don't think [males] would have [changed things]. I would have [graduated] anyway.

Four believed that they would not have been *as* successful, or they would have graduated but experienced difficulty. One commented that she would not have graduated at all if males were present, "[I]f there were boys in the program... I'd probably not be right here... because I'd be getting in a lot more trouble. I think it is easier to go along without guys."

Discussion

In order to assess the effectiveness of gender-specific programs for juvenile females, it is a beneficial first step to determine how participants perceive this type of programming. One gender-specific program for female juveniles is the McGee Center in Reno, Nevada. Female juveniles convicted of status or criminal offenses may volunteer for the program or be court-ordered to attend.

Residents participate in a variety of classes designed to help them with anger management, communication skills, relationship building, self-esteem, and self-efficacy.

Female juveniles in the Girls' Program generally perceived gender-specific programming as having had a positive impact and as having improved specific aspects of their lives. They described how particular programming and classes were helpful to them and identified what differences there might have been in the program and their progress if the program had included males. Most participants talked about the gender-specific aspects of the program even before being asked about them, and identified particular classes and program practices that helped them improve relationships, personal health, education, and other personal skills. Participants also reported increased community connectedness and a greater willingness to get along with others. Finally, participants indicated that the programming influenced their intentions to make better choices and avoid future offending (e.g., drug use, fighting, running away from home).

Though most participants stated that including males in the program would not have affected their success, several added that it might have made them struggle. Many also preferred a female-only program, believing that males would have been distracting, annoying, or could have increased drama. A few participants believed that including males might have improved their learning and participation because they could relate better to males, believed males to be calmer and less dramatic than females, and believed that a male perspective might have increased understanding of certain situations they faced as young females.

Last, not all responses to the program were positive. Some participants reported that drama was a barrier. One indicated that neither the classes nor the programming was helpful. Another stated that the program did not work because it did not change her home environment, and a few mentioned that even though gender-specific programs might work best for some, it was not essential to their success. These results have implications for programming and theory.

Implications for Using Justice Approaches in Programming

Placement of offenders in a community-based, rehabilitative program holds the offender accountable by "serving time," protects the community from the offender's behavior, and provides a space to address the issues that led to the offending behavior (Bazemore & Day, 1996; Wexler & Winick, 1996). However, research supports that criminogenic issues may differ across gender and that gender-specific programs might be more therapeutic for females than a program based on a traditional male model. This study supported that gender-specific programming could be an important tool in the rehabilitation of female offenders, because it addressed female criminal behavior using restorative justice and therapeutic jurisprudence approaches.

Gender-specific programming provides restorative justice through inclusion of the community in the rehabilitative process. Community involvement (e.g., through community service or community-based programs) in the offender rehabilitation process helps to restore community members' sense of safety and security and repair the offender/community relationship. For example, the McGee Center program works with a community nonprofit agency to provide individual and family counseling, and community service groups, in order to regain connectedness with the family and community (Washoe County, Nevada, 2009). The community also benefits from participants' more normative and positive behavior. Participants in this study indicated that the program helped them understand their parents' perspectives and improved relationships with parents. Through gender-specific programming, participants also reduced or stopped drug use, communicated intentions for sobriety, and succeeded in school. The community benefitted through deterrence of future offenses and improvement in offenders' ability to handle anger issues without aggression. Thus, by repairing the harm to the parents, victims, and community, the principles of restorative justice are upheld (Bazemore & Day, 1996).

Gender-specific programming also uses a therapeutic jurisprudence approach; programming addresses the wellbeing of female offenders with rehabilitation rather than punishment alone. Punitive approaches used in traditional juvenile programs have been less effective with female offenders (Sherman, 2005). Females are less likely to reoffend if rehabilitation addresses underlying criminogenic issues and helps them form positive connections with individuals or programs (Sherman, 2005). In the current study, participants perceived that the program focused on female issues and their best interests. Participants learned about their own bodies and skills to protect themselves. They participated in crafts, talked about female issues, and bonded with other females. Some formed bonds with the instructors and counselors that helped them feel comfortable dealing with their issues. Finally, participants perceived their placement in the gender-specific program as fair and just, thus increasing perceptions of the juvenile justice professionals and system as legitimate (Tyler, 2006). Because of this perception of legitimacy, female juvenile offenders should be more likely to comply with parental rules and expectations, societal standards, and the law (Tyler, 2006).

Implications for Theory

This study supported the use of social context theory (Earle & Earle, 1999) in the development of gender-specific programming. Gender-specific programming addressed the behaviors of young females by changing their social context, attitudes, and norms (Burke et al., 2009). Through programmatic shaping of the environmental structure, their day-to-day experiences influenced their overall behaviors (Pasick & Burke, 2008). Also, in an environment where their needs and relationships were valued, participants adjusted their behaviors to conform to the community's norms. Importantly, by recognizing that gender is part of one's social context, the program was able to address needs that are specific to the female juveniles.

Changing the females' social context contributed to positive changes in their lives. Relationships built while in the program and the changes perceived in the relationships outside of the program affected the choices participants made. Several participants indicated that they gained a better understanding of the consequences of their past choices and intended to make better choices in the future. Some addressed personal issues through counseling and group discussions that dealt with underlying reasons for behaviors such as running away or drug/alcohol use. Participants learned to cope with their emotions in a more effective manner. Some participant comments suggest that these accomplishments were possible, at least in part, because of the context of gender-specific programming and the female-only program.

Through similar education and relationship development, gender-specific programming could reduce female reoffending. Because experiences mold attitudes and beliefs, positive perceptions of gender-specific programming should yield positive behaviors (Burke et al., 2009). As such, the use of social context theory may lead to the meaningful development of gender-specific programs as a means to combat female juvenile offending.

Limitations

The study is not without its limitations. First, the sample consisted of females aged 14–17 years who had committed relatively minor crimes or status offenses and who graduated from one program in Nevada. This specific and small sample size (which prevents true analysis) is a sizable limitation. This leads to concerns with generalizability and ecological validity (Gay, Mills, & Airasian, 2006), because the study results might not be generalizable to females who are younger, committed serious offenses, attended different programs, attended the program in a different city, or did not graduate.

Another limitation was response bias associated with participant self-reports (Gay et al., 2006). Participants might have exaggerated or fabricated responses due to a desire to seem "rehabilitated." They might have also responded to please the interviewer (a staff member of the program). Despite these limitations, this study is useful because it supports that gender-specific programming might have a perceived positive impact. Future studies can address these limitations by using different populations, programs, participants, and procedures. In addition, future research might incorporate quantitative and mixed methods and analysis.

Conclusion

In recent years, there has been an increase in delinquency for young females (Humphrey, 2004; Morgan & Patton, 2002; Sherman, 2005). Causes of female delinquency include abuse, neglect, disconnectedness, and lack of positive relationships. Such findings have led to recent increases in trauma-sensitive (Ariga et al., 2008) and gender-specific programs designed for female offenders. These programs must be evidence based and prevent recidivism (Frabutt et al., 2008). Programming must focus on the female's issues and address the multilevel needs such as education, health care, and counseling (Biden, 2003). Successful programs also must enlist staff trained in the specific needs of young females and include meaningful gender-focused assessment tools (Biden, 2003).

The current study found that most participants perceived that gender-specific programs have positive effects. As such, policymakers should fund such programs and juvenile detention centers should adopt evidence-based programs based on theory and justice principles. When these female juvenile offenders perceived that their issues were recognized and when they were able to form meaningful relationships and feel accomplished (in school, in being able to get along), then they were able to make positive changes that could ultimately lead to reduced recidivism. Further research is needed to determine how gender-specific programming can increase protective factors and decrease risk factors. Ultimately, this will help protect the community and protect the wellbeing of female juveniles.

References

Acoca, L. (1999). Investing in girls: A 21st century strategy. *Juvenile Justice, 6*, 3–13.

Ariga, M., Uehara, T., Takeuchi, K., Inshige, Y., Nakano, R., & Mikuni, M. (2008). Trauma exposure and post traumatic stress disorder in delinquent female adolescents. *Journal of Child Psychology and Psychiatry, 49*, 79–87. doi:10.1111/j.1469-7610.2007.01817.

Bazemore, G., & Day, S. E. (1996). Restoring the balance: Juvenile and community justice. *Juvenile Justice, 3*, 3–14.

Biden, J. R. (2003). Children, crime and consequences: Juvenile justice in America—What about the girls? The role of the federal government in addressing the rise in female juvenile offenders. *Stanford Law and Policy Review, 14*, 29–45.

Burke, N. J., Joseph, G., Pasick, R. J., & Barker, J. C. (2009). Theorizing social context: Rethinking behavioral theory. *Health Education and Behavior, 36*, 55–70. doi: 10.1177/1090198109335338.

Charles M. McGee Center for Adolescent Programs. (2008). *Girls' program*. Reno, NV: Washoe County Department of Juvenile Services.

Earle, L., & Earle, T. (1999). Social context theory. *South Pacific Journal of Psychology, 11*(2), 1–12.

Frabutt, J. M., DiLuca, K. L., & Graves, K. N. (2008). Symposium on youth and the law: Panel: Lost innocence: Hope and punishment in the juvenile justice system: Envisioning a juvenile justice system that supports positive youth development. *Notre Dame Journal of Law, Ethics and Public Policy, 22*, 107–125.

Gay, L. R., Mills, G. E., & Airasian, P. (2006). *Educational research: Competencies for analysis and applications*. Upper Saddle River, NJ: Pearson Education.

Grande, T. L., Hallman, J., Rutledge, B., Caldwell, K., Upton, B., Underwood, L. A., ...Rehfuss, M. (2012). Examining mental health symptoms in male and female incarcerated juveniles. *Behavioral Sciences and the Law, 30*, 365–369. doi: 10.1002/bsl.2011.

Humphrey, A. (2004). The criminalization of survival attempts: Locking up female runaways and other status offenders. *Hastings Women's Law Journal, 15*, 165–184.

Martin, D., Martin, M., Dell, R., Davis, C., & Guerrieri, C. (2008). Profile of incarcerated juveniles: Comparison of male and female offenders. *Adolescence, 43*, 607–622.

Morgan, M., & Patton, P. (2002). Gender-responsive programming in the justice system: Oregon's guidelines for effective programming for girls. *Federal Probation, 66*, 57–65.

Neufeldt, V., & Guralnik, D. (Eds.). (1988). *Webster's new world dictionary* (3rd college ed.). Cleveland, OH & New York, NY: Simon and Schuster.

Pasick, R. J., & Burke, N. J. (2008). A critical review of theory in breast cancer screening promotion across cultures. *Annual Review of Public Health, 29*, 351–368. doi: 10.1146/annurev.publhealth.29.020907.143420.

Roe-Sepowitz, D. E. (2009). Comparing male and female juveniles charged with homicide. *Journal of Interpersonal Violence, 24*(4), 601–617. doi: 10.1177/0886260508317201.

Sherman, F. T. (2005). *Detention reform and girls: Challenges and solutions: A project of the Annie E. Casey Foundation: 13 pathways to juvenile detention reform*. Baltimore, MD: The Annie E. Casey Foundation.

Sherman, L. W., & Strang, H. (2013). Restorative justice: The evidence. *The Smith Institute*. Retrieved from http://www.smith-institute.org.uk/file/RestorativeJusticeTheEvidenceFullreport.pdf.

Sicafuse, L. L., & Bornstein, B. H. (2013). Using the law to enhance wellbeing: Applying therapeutic jurisprudence in the courtroom. In M. K. Miller & B. H. Bornstein (Eds.), *Stress, trauma, and wellbeing in the legal system* (pp. 15–41). New York, NY: Oxford University Press.

Tyler, T. R. (2006). Psychological perspectives on legitimacy and legitimation. *Annual Review of Psychology, 57*, 376–394. doi: 10.1146/annurev.psych.57.102904.190038.

US Department of Justice. (2007, December 3). *Fundamental concepts of restorative justice*. Retrieved July 2013, http://www.ojp.usdoj.gov/nij/topics/courts/restorative-justice/fundamental-concepts.htm.

Washoe County, Nevada. (2009). *McGee Center Girls' Program*. Wexler, D. B. (2011). The relevance of therapeutic jurisprudence and its literature. *Federal Sentencing Reporter, 23*(4), 278–279.

Wexler, D. B., & Winick, B. J. (1996). *Law in a therapeutic key: Developments in therapeutic jurisprudence*. Durham, NC: Carolina Academic Press.

Wexler, D. B., & Winick, B. J. (2003). Putting therapeutic jurisprudence to work. *ABA Journal, 89*, 54–57.

7

Balancing Legal, Ethical, and Clinical Considerations When Managing Suicidality in Research With Juvenile Justice–Involved Youth

Christy L. Giallella, Naomi E. S. Goldstein, and David DeMatteo

Researchers who work with delinquent youth often face legal, ethical, and clinical decision-making challenges. Frequently, researchers may encounter situations in which they must decide how to manage indications of suicidality[1] among participants. Suicide is a major public health problem in the general population and federal agencies have responded to increasing concerns by launching joint initiatives to support suicide reduction research, practice, and policies (Insel, 2010). The Centers for Disease Control and Prevention (CDC, 2010) reported that more than 34,000 people commit suicide each year, with elevated rates among adolescents. Furthermore, youth in the juvenile justice system are four to five times more likely to commit suicide than their nonoffending peers (Farand, Chagnon, Renaud, & Rivard, 2004; Hayes, 2005; see

---

[1] The term *suicidality* will be used throughout this chapter to describe the broad category of suicidal thoughts, feelings, and behaviors. Although there has been extensive debate about the distinction between suicide and self-injurious behaviors, a thorough discussion of this issue is beyond the scope of this chapter. In this chapter, "suicidality" will refer broadly to suicidal ideation, self-injurious acts, and suicidal behaviors. For additional information, discussion, and definitions of these constructs, see Linehan (2000); Muehlenkamp and Gutierrez (2004); and Pearson, Stanley, King, and Fisher (2001).

also Chapter 3 in this volume for more on suicide by juveniles in the legal system).

Among adolescents and young adults aged 15–24 years, suicide accounts for more than 12% of annual deaths and represents the third leading cause of death (CDC, 2009). For each completed suicide, there are approximately 100 to 200 suicide attempts within this age group (CDC, 2009). Delinquent youth are at elevated risk for suicide, with higher rates of suicidal ideation and attempts than their nondelinquent counterparts (Gallagher & Dobrin, 2006; Ruffolo & Savas, 2004). Given the salience of the problem, juvenile justice researchers must be equipped with appropriate mechanisms for managing participants who express suicidal thoughts. Researchers must consider how their responses to participants' suicidal thoughts, feelings, and behaviors will affect the wellbeing of the youth and align with legal and ethical requirements, as well as with research protocols.

At times, legal, ethical, and clinical guidelines conflict, and researchers must make difficult decisions about how to proceed. They must consider and balance legal requirements, ethical guidelines, clinical concerns, relationships with participants and juvenile justice staff, participants' rights as research subjects, research protocols, and the wellbeing of youth. The legal, ethical, and clinical expectations and requirements might differ based on the researcher's role (e.g., assessor, therapist) and the laws and guidelines that govern the field in which he or she conducts research (e.g., psychology, social work, criminal justice). Further, researchers have specific roles and responsibilities that make their management of and responses to suicidality different from other professionals (e.g., clinicians, probation officers, corrections officers) who interact with delinquent youth. Researchers often have limited contact with youth, and research protocols outline the types and breadth of interactions with participants that are permitted. The quantity and quality of data collected are prescribed prior to commencing the study, and information about suicidality might not be elicited in the context of the research study. In research in which suicidality is not the focus of the research, researchers' ability to gather information on and respond to suicidality among participants is limited. This chapter discusses considerations relevant to social science researchers who conduct clinically oriented research[2] with juvenile offenders across multiple

---

[2] Although nonclinicians conduct research with juvenile offenders, this discussion focuses on clinical research. Clinical researchers tend to interact with youth; are trained to identify and respond to suicidality; and may have legal, ethical, or clinical responsibilities to manage suicidality among their participants. Although the discussion may be useful to nonclinical researchers, there may be differences in responsibilities related to variability in training and professional background (i.e., nonclinical researchers may not have the relevant clinical training). Clinical research refers to research that is conducted by clinically trained professionals (e.g., psychologists, social workers) and that involves face-to-face interactions with youth (e.g., assessment-based studies, treatment outcome research).

fields of study. This chapter will review the legal, ethical, and clinical considerations that typically should be considered when youth indicate suicidality. Potential inconsistencies among the areas considered will be discussed, and recommendations for decision making will be presented. Although many of the issues raised will apply to all youth, this chapter highlights the challenges that are specific and unique to working with youth involved with the juvenile justice system. For example, these youth often present with common factors that increase their risk of suicidality (e.g., trauma histories, mental health problems), they may be placed out of their homes with varying levels of social support and available resources, and there are additional protections needed when conducting research with children. The recommendations presented here will help protect the wellbeing of youth in the legal system by providing researchers with an overview of relevant legal, ethical, and clinical considerations.

Determining Suicide Risk

Researchers who work with juvenile offenders must be equipped to handle participants' suicidality. Initially, researchers must be able to determine what constitutes risk for suicidality. The recommended approach to assessing suicide risk is based on an evaluation of the presence of established risk factors (Simon, 2002). This review of risk factors provides information to help researchers determine whether there is a problem that needs to be considered and managed in a way that meets the legal, ethical, and clinical considerations discussed later in this chapter.

Beyond statistics indicating that incarcerated and detained youth are at heightened risk for suicidality relative to youth in the general population (Gallagher & Dobrin, 2006; Ruffolo & Savas, 2004), there are some characteristics among juvenile justice youth that place them at greater risk for suicide. More specifically, past suicide attempts tend to predict future suicidal behavior (Hayes, 2005); one study of detained juveniles revealed that 1 in 10 of these youth had suicide attempt histories (Abram et al., 2008), and another study found that 1 in 3 had such histories (Robertson & Husain, 2001). Additionally, psychiatric diagnoses (Abram et al., 2008) and trauma histories (Blaauw, Winkel, & Kerkhof, 2001) are associated with increased risk for suicidality, and youth involved with the juvenile justice system present with elevated rates of mental health disorders (Teplin, Abram, McClelland, Dulcan, & Mericle, 2002) and traumatic experiences (Abram et al., 2004). Among delinquent youth, major depression and generalized anxiety disorder significantly predicted recent suicide attempts after accounting for comorbidity among diagnoses (Abram et al., 2008). Substance use also appears to be positively related to suicidality among juvenile detainees, and this risk factor likely interacts with the complex mental health and traumatic histories of these youth (Chapman & Ford, 2008). In fact, relationships have been found between trauma histories and substance use among juvenile offenders (Chapman & Ford, 2008), and approximately 1 out of 3 juvenile detainees display comorbid mental health and substance abuse disorders (Robertson, Dill, Husain, & Undesser, 2004). These frequently co-occurring risk factors may interact to increase the risk of suicide among these youth. For instance, substance use increases impulsivity in both the short and long term (de Wit, 2008), which could exacerbate other mental health symptoms and negative emotional states, thereby increasing youths' likelihood of acting on suicidal thoughts.

Demographic characteristics also are associated with heightened risk of suicidality. Paralleling suicide trends in the general population, suicide risk has been associated with gender and ethnicity among juvenile justice–involved youth. Specifically, female juvenile offenders, non-Hispanic White youth, and Hispanic female youth appear to be at increased risk for suicidality (Abram et al., 2008; Cauffman, 2004).

Important factors related to youths' confinement also might affect suicide risk. A national study of completed suicides that occurred in juvenile justice placements demonstrated that nearly half of the youth who completed suicide were relegated to room confinement or isolation at the time, suggesting that seclusion and isolation might increase risk (Hayes, 2009). It is unclear whether this risk is due to lack of supervision, opportunity, stress, or other factors. However, this startling statistic indicates that suicide risk is particularly elevated during this time, warranting attention and concern. Additionally, in contrast to findings from studies with adult inmates, Hayes (2009) found no difference in suicide rate by length of time in placement; suicide was just as likely to occur toward the beginning of a youth's stay as later in placement.

In addition to the identified factors associated with increased risk for suicidality, youth also present with protective factors, which decrease their risk. Connectedness to parents/guardians and schools, presence of caring adults, and emotional wellbeing have been identified as protective factors among adolescents and appear to decrease suicide risk (Borowsky, Ireland, & Resnick, 2001; Eisenberg, Ackard, & Resnick, 2007). Although research has identified characteristics that are broadly associated with increased or decreased suicide risk among juvenile justice–involved youth, each youth presents with his or her own unique combination of risk and protective factors. Researchers who work with juvenile offenders face the challenge of understanding the individual youth's risk for suicide.

Clinically, the standard of care for suicide risk assessment requires thoroughly considering and evaluating the interactions between risk and protective factors (Simon, 2002). However, the aim and design of a research study affect the amount of contact that the researcher has with the youth and, consequently, the amount of risk-relevant information that the researcher collects. Further limiting the quantity of information obtained, researchers who have limited contact with participants likely have little opportunity to establish meaningful rapport, and youth who do not develop senses of trust and allegiance might withhold relevant information (Packman, O'Connor Pennuto,

Bongar, & Orthwein, 2004). Additionally, unless researchers are specifically assessing for depression and anxiety, these internalizing disorders might not be readily identified in youth. Thus, there are many factors that make it difficult for researchers to identify a juvenile's risk of suicidality.

Legal Considerations

In addition to facing challenges involved with assessing risk, researchers must make difficult decisions regarding their responses to youth who appear to be at risk for suicide. Ultimately, researchers' management of suicidality among their participants must align with legal requirements.

Social science researchers who conduct studies with juvenile offenders must meet federal regulations for human subjects research. Institutional Review Boards (IRBs) were developed to oversee studies involving human subjects and to ensure that they comply with legal requirements (Protection of Human Subjects, 2005). Federal regulations (i.e., 45 CFR 46) indicate that all institutions that conduct human subjects research must form IRBs for the purpose of enforcing federal policies and protecting participants. Although all studies involving human participants are subject to oversight and monitoring, the National Institutes of Health (NIH) recommends that Data Safety and Monitoring Boards (DSMBs) oversee studies of greater risk, size, or complexity. Typically, Phase III clinical trials are required to form DSMBs (NIH, 1998). These committees of experts are intended to monitor participant safety and data integrity (NIH, 1998), and because suicidal ideation and behaviors directly impact participants' safety and wellbeing, DSMBs are often tasked with reviewing incidents involving participants' suicidality.

Although there are no specific federal regulations that govern the management of participants' suicidality, the Code of Federal Regulations does indicate that researchers must report unanticipated problems or risks to participants to research oversight agencies (e.g., IRBs). In this vein, a participant's suicide and, at times, suicidal thoughts or behaviors would constitute a serious adverse event, which, in turn, would require the submission of a report to agencies that oversee the research (Pearson, Stanley, King, & Fisher, 2001). In addition to the obvious impact on a youth participant's wellbeing, suicidal actions could threaten the completion of a research study, and researchers often worry about the occurrence of adverse events. Adverse events can influence the risk level of the study, particularly if an IRB finds that participation in the study influenced or caused the adverse event. For example, if an IRB believes that study procedures caused or exacerbated a participant's suicidal behaviors, the risk level of the study could increase and, subsequently, the researcher's ability to complete the study as designed could be threatened. In line with the obligation to protect human subjects under federal regulations, an IRB could require that study procedures be altered to minimize risk or that the study be terminated.

Other than general regulations governing risk and adverse events, there is little legal guidance on the management of research participants' disclosures of suicidal ideation or plans. In fact, to our knowledge, no legislation or case law has addressed the issue within the context of research. However, this issue has been raised in other contexts, and these legal precedents can provide some guidance to researchers.

Some case law exists that addresses a mental health professional's potential responsibility to foresee or predict the risk of suicide. In *O'Sullivan v. Presbyterian Hospital in City of New York at Columbia Presbyterian Medical Center* (1995), a New York appellate court considered a psychiatrist's liability in the suicide of one of his patients. The court held that the psychiatrist did not perform a competent assessment and committed multiple failures in assessment and treatment. Importantly, though, the court acknowledged that liability might not be imposed "for honest errors in medical judgment" (*O'Sullivan v. Presbyterian Hospital in City of New York at Columbia Presbyterian Medical Center*, 1995, p. 103). Mental health professionals are not expected to be able to predict suicide; they are expected to conduct adequate assessments regarding suicide risk (Packman et al., 2004).

Although this legal precedent might help researchers understand their potential responsibility to conduct an adequate suicide risk assessment, the relationship between *psychiatrists* and their patients differs from the relationship between *researchers* and their participants. The different roles could, subsequently, create a difference in responsibility and liability. It also is important to note that *O'Sullivan* was decided in a New York court, so it is not binding in other jurisdictions. Additionally, researchers often face constraints related to the research project and research methodology that can limit their opportunities to detect suicide risk and affect their abilities to conduct suicide risk assessments. Including a comprehensive suicide risk evaluation in a research assessment battery may be unduly burdensome to researchers and to participants and might not be relevant to the research question or study goals.

Other cases addressed the potential responsibility to provide appropriate treatment and supervision to suicidal clients in hospital settings. *Vistica v. Presbyterian Hospital* (1967) and *Meier v. Ross General Hospital* (1968) were wrongful death actions involving the suicide of patients confined to psychiatric hospitals; in each case, the California Supreme Court found that the hospital had a duty of care to protect individuals from their own actions. It is possible that the heightened duty that appears to exist within psychiatric hospitals could apply to mental health activities within residential juvenile justice facilities. However, even investigators conducting clinical research in juvenile justice placements have access to different information and play different roles than do psychiatrists who are responsible for the care of inpatients, further complicating the application of this case law to researchers. *Bellah v. Greenson* (1978), a case decided by a California appellate court, extended the duty of care to outpatient psychiatrists. In that case, though, the court denied the extension of *Tarasoff v. Regents of University of California* (1976), which held that a therapist had a duty to protect identifiable third parties from harm and that the duty might involve breaching confidentiality and disclosing personal information. Instead, in *Bellah*, the court noted that the scope of the duty imposed on those responsible for the patient's care would differ depending on the setting.

In addition to the differences in responsibility by setting, case law has addressed differences in responsibility based on the role of the treating individual. In *Nally v. Grace Community Church of the Valley* (1988), the California Supreme Court addressed whether to impose a duty on "nontherapist counselors (i.e., persons other than licensed psychotherapists who counsel others concerning their emotional and spiritual problems)" (*Nally v. Grace Community Church of the Valley*, 1988, p. 283). The duty considered in this case involved a referral of individuals at risk for suicide to licensed mental health professionals. The *Nally* court held that a duty to prevent suicide, or a more general duty of care, would not be extended to nontherapist counselors. It remains unclear whether juvenile justice researchers would be considered "nontherapist counselors," particularly in the case of clinical research by licensed mental health professionals.

Notably, case law does not directly address researchers' responsibilities when working with suicidal youth or specify any duties imposed on researchers. However, a potential duty of care might rest on the nature of the relationship between the researcher and the participant, the setting of the research study, the researcher's qualifications and training, and the nature of the research project (e.g., therapeutic intervention, academic intervention, assessment-based study, archival record review).

Ethical Considerations

Researchers also must meet ethical standards when conducting research with youth involved with the juvenile justice system. Research ethics, following the principle of beneficence, indicate that researchers who work with human subjects attempt to minimize harm (NIH, 1979). This general, guiding principle drives researchers to conduct studies with the wellbeing of their participants in mind. Situations involving suicidality inherently involve the wellbeing of youth participants, and suicidal behaviors represent harmful actions that researchers should seek to prevent in efforts to minimize harm.

Juvenile justice researchers also must meet specific ethical standards reflected in their respective fields' (e.g., psychology, social work, criminal justice) ethics codes. However, relevant ethics codes often are vague and do not provide direct guidance for managing suicidality in research. For example, the Code of Ethics of the National Association of Social Workers (NASW, 1996, Standard 5.02(j)) states that social workers who conduct research "should protect participants from unwarranted physical or mental distress, harm, danger or deprivation." The NASW Code of Ethics (1996) does not specify that indications of suicidality obligate researchers to take action nor what would constitute appropriate or required actions in such situations. That is, there are no clear ethical guidelines that dictate the specifics of a researcher's responsibility in situations involving youth participants' suicidality.

A conflict arises between requirements to maintain participants' confidentiality and ethical requirements to protect participants from harm. Attempts to minimize harm might require a breach of confidentiality. However, although researchers are generally required to maintain participants' confidentiality, many ethics codes also contain provisions that allow for the breaching of confidentiality to protect clients from harm (e.g., ACA, 2005; APA, 2002; NASW, 1996). For example, the American Psychological Association's (APA) Ethical Principles of Psychologists and Code of Conduct (2002) indicates that psychologists may disclose confidential information without consent to "protect the client/patient, psychologist, or others from harm" (APA, 2002, Standard 4.05(b)). Additionally, courts tend to uphold clinicians' decisions to breach confidentiality in certain situations (e.g., suicidality; Baerger, 2001), minimizing the potential conflict between ethics and law. Although the scope of a researcher's legal and ethical obligations is unclear, he or she may decide, in some situations, that a participant's risk warrants a breach of confidentiality to protect the participant from harm. When making this determination, researchers also must consider to whom they would disclose the information. Again, this population involves added considerations because the availability and appropriateness of resources vary. For instance, juveniles in placement tend to have access to additional resources and supervision options; juveniles in the community are more likely to be under the supervision of their parents, guardians, or foster parents. In most research contexts, parents/guardians would, legally, have access to the information provided by their children, so confidentiality would not be a barrier when deciding whether to disclose suicidal intentions to parents/guardians in an effort to keep the youth safe.

Researchers may struggle to balance youth participants' wellbeing, ethical requirements to minimize harm, and obligations to maintain confidentiality when responding to participants' suicidality in the context of juvenile justice research. Although ethical guidelines require researchers to minimize harm, the guidelines are vague and do not specify mechanisms by which harm can be minimized and participants protected. The guidelines also do not delineate how to decide whether harm reaches a sufficient threshold to breach confidentiality or initiate alternative mechanisms of protection. A researcher must apply these principles, without the existence of firm rules, to the unique experience of each juvenile justice participant in the study.

Clinical Considerations

Researchers' responses to suicidality among their participants directly impact the wellbeing of youth participants. Researchers are responsible for minimizing harm among their participants (NIH, 1979), and they should strive to avoid negative outcomes associated with suicidality and encourage positive outcomes. Although researchers must meet legal and ethical requirements when determining how to respond to indications of suicidality, they also must consider how their responses will impact participants clinically (e.g., mental health symptoms, level of distress, wellbeing).

The process of managing indications of suicidality has the potential to be stressful and upsetting to juveniles. Researchers have varying levels of involvement with youth, depending on the goals and design of the research project, and youth may be particularly uncomfortable with researchers with whom they only interact one time. Conversely, researchers conducting treatment outcome studies may have extensive contact with youth and may be in better positions to manage suicidality because they have developed stronger, more trusting relationships and have acquired more information about the youth. Regardless of the type of research project, however, the process might invoke painful or upsetting feelings among youth. Additionally, if researchers do not handle the situation with care, their responses to suicidality may alienate the youth, cause resentment toward the researcher, negatively affect the youth's mental health, and, potentially, even exacerbate suicidal ideation.

When evaluating potential responses to suicidality, researchers also should consider the consequences of their decisions on youths' wellbeing. For example, youths' intentions may differ with self-injurious and suicidal behaviors; self-injury without the intent to die may reflect a desire to release pain, control feelings, or gain attention (Muehlenkamp & Gutierrez, 2004), in contrast to behaviors with suicidal intent. Researchers' responses to self-injurious behaviors are likely to have different effects on the youths' wellbeing depending on the intentions behind the behaviors. However, many researchers do not have sufficient information to accurately determine the function of the harmful behavior, further complicating the decision-making process involved in responding to suicidality.

Researchers also should consider the unique aspects of working with juvenile justice–involved populations. The resources available for managing suicidality among this population vary depending on the setting in which the research is conducted. For example, a project conducted in a residential juvenile justice facility is likely to have staff (e.g., corrections, mental health) available 24 hours per day. In contrast, if research is conducted in community-based programs, youth may have little oversight and social support during their hours at home. Facilities and day programs typically have established crisis response teams or structured processes for managing suicidality, and these protective mechanisms may be triggered or accessed by researchers. Community-based programs, on the other hand, might not have extensive or available supports, and researchers might consider relying on parents or guardians to protect the youth from harm. Such consideration, though, requires reflection about parent/guardian capacities to provide protection for youth in this population. Parents or guardians of juvenile justice–involved youth might be inaccessible or inappropriate supports due to practical difficulties in contacting parents/guardians; parental absence and low levels of parental supervision, monitoring, and involvement (Demuth & Brown, 2004); parent criminality and violence (Alltucker, Bullis, Close, & Yovanoff, 2006); and low levels of emotional support from parents (Henry, Tolan, & Gorman-Smith, 2001). For these reasons, researchers' response options could be limited because parental involvement may, at times, negatively affect the youths' wellbeing.

Juvenile offenders represent a population at increased risk for suicide, and researchers who work with these youth must be prepared to respond to indications of suicidality. It is intended that this review will provide researchers with a resource for understanding the issues that must be considered when developing study protocols and conducting research with juvenile offenders. Researchers are then charged with the challenge and responsibility of balancing the legal, ethical, and clinical considerations when responding to suicidality among their participants.

Recommendations

The following recommendations are provided to assist researchers in meeting the challenge of effectually responding to indications of suicidality among their juvenile participants. These recommendations can be useful when conceptualizing studies, developing protocols, and executing research with juvenile offenders. Recommendations include strategies for developing procedures based on legal, ethical, and clinical knowledge; determining suicide risk among participants; and intervening as needed. The importance of documentation also is discussed.

Developing Policies and Procedures Based on Legal, Ethical, and Clinical Knowledge

Researchers must understand the legal and ethical requirements that govern their responsibilities in situations in which participants might be dangers to themselves. Because researchers may serve multiple roles and work in different states or settings, they must thoroughly review and understand jurisdiction-specific policies. For example, the case law discussed earlier would only apply to the jurisdictions in which the decisions were held, so they might not apply to all researchers. Additionally, the juvenile justice agency or organization with which the researcher works also might have policies that must be learned and followed. The challenges discussed earlier highlight the need for researchers to develop procedures that are based on a combination of legal mandates, professional ethical standards, and the policies of the juvenile justice agencies with which they work. To become better informed, prior to beginning the study, researchers should consult with colleagues, legal and ethical texts, and/or their organizations' IRB or legal counsel to develop procedures that meet appropriate standards. Researchers also could consult civil commitment statutes in their states as additional resources. All states have statutes that allow for the involuntary commitment of individuals dangerous to themselves (e.g., Mental Health Procedures Act, 1976; see Melton, Petrila, Poythress, & Slobogin, 2007). These statutes address an individual's danger and/or need for treatment and outline the situations in which treatment can be court ordered.

In addition to understanding the ethical and legal guidelines that govern their roles, researchers should be knowledgeable about the clinical aspects of suicidality in juvenile offenders. Researchers who conduct intervention or other clinical research that involves more extensive contact with youth should have experience or training in the management of suicidality and be able to recognize population-specific suicide risk factors.

Determining Suicide Risk and Developing Risk Management Protocols

As reviewed earlier, an assessment of established risk factors represents the clinical standard for determining suicide risk. However, most research studies will not gather sufficient information to reliably make this determination. It would be unreasonable and inappropriate to suggest that researchers fully assess suicide risk during all interactions with participants; this suggestion would likely add undue burden, stray from the goals of most research studies, intrude on participants' privacy, and substantively alter the role of the researcher. Instead, the information presented earlier should be considered in the context of the information that is already being gathered for a particular study. The legal, ethical, and clinical guidelines discussed earlier can serve to help researchers determine whether they should consider taking action or intervening with a participant who indicates some level of suicidality.

In addition to developing a thorough understanding of the standards that govern their work, researchers must decide how to manage suicide risk among their participants. Pearson and colleagues (2001) suggested that researchers estimate the frequency of suicidal behavior in their sample, and decisions about the nature and extent of risk management should be commensurate with the expected frequency of suicidal behavior. To determine the expected suicide risk in specific samples of juvenile offenders, researchers can review the relevant literature and consult with the juvenile justice agencies with which they work. It also might be helpful to communicate this information to IRBs and DSMBs so that policies can be appropriately tailored to the specific sample. Researchers also should base their risk management decisions on the type of research they conduct and the nature and extent of interaction with participants. In particular, intervention studies with frequent interactions with participants about sensitive topics would require different risk management procedures than short-term, assessment-based studies that do not elicit these types of information.

Procedures for managing suicide risk should be developed prior to beginning a research study. Researchers should develop operationalized criteria that would trigger various actions. This way, all members of the research team who interact with youth can be trained to assess and respond to suicide risk in a consistent way. Researchers should use the consent and assent processes to describe to participants the actions that might be taken if participants display suicidal ideations or behaviors. For example, situations that would require a participant's removal from the study should be described in consent and assent forms. Limits to confidentiality should also be fully explained in consent and assent forms, and researchers should take care to ensure that youth and their families understand the situations that would necessitate breaches of confidentiality and the consequences of such disclosures.

Intervening to Reduce Risk

The level of clinical intervention by the researcher will vary depending on the nature of the researcher's role and his or her involvement with the youth. To facilitate positive outcomes associated with reporting self-injurious intentions, a researcher could involve the youth in the reporting and protection process. For instance, if appropriate, a researcher might wish to include the participant in making written or oral reports of self-injurious intent and/or safety planning with juvenile justice staff, parents/guardians, or hospital staff. This approach might prevent resentment of the researchers by the youth, maintain the quality of the youth's relationship with the researchers in a clinical trial, improve the participant's perceptions of the accuracy and extent of reported information, decrease concerns about liability associated with disclosing information, and decrease the likelihood of the participant withdrawing from the study. These procedures could be included in study protocols to demonstrate attempts to minimize risk and commitment to participants' wellbeing.

There are a variety of intervention options available to researchers as they decide how to manage indications of suicidality among juvenile participants. Due to the time-limited nature of research studies, investigators may decide that it is clinically beneficial to refer a youth participant to juvenile justice staff for evaluation and intervention. Many juvenile justice agencies have mental health staff available that can serve as useful resources for assessing and managing potential harm, and youth might have existing therapeutic relationships with these staff members. Researchers also could consider involving youth participants' family members in the monitoring and treatment of suicide risk. For youth participants who present with high, imminent risk, researchers could choose to seek hospitalization to protect participants. Decisions about how to respond to suicidal youth should be based on a combination of risk level, available resources, and the researcher's role.

After deciding how to best protect a youth's safety, researchers should then consider how the protective actions impact the youth's participation in the study and the quality of the data. As specified in consent/assent documents, the researchers might choose to exclude youth from continued participation in the research. The researchers also might choose to exclude participants from data analysis if the integrity of the research protocol or data collection process was compromised because of actions taken to protect the youth from harm.

Documentation

The earlier sections review possible response options for researchers who are faced with the decision of when and how to respond to indications of suicidality. No single action or set of actions is appropriate to manage all situations with indications of suicidality. However, across all such situations, researchers should document indications of suicidality, the researchers' consideration of responses, and actions taken. More specifically, documentation should include descriptions of relevant interactions with suicidal youth, any consultations with colleagues or other professionals, professional judgments, reasoning for judgments, and courses of action (Packman et al., 2004). Documentation has been described as the "most important risk management technique" (Packman et al., 2004, p. 708) in situations involving suicidal patients, and failure to keep accurate records has been noted as a failure that could produce potential liability (Bongar, Maris, Berman, & Litman, 1998; Packman et al., 2004).

Conclusion

The Office of Human Research Protections (OHRP) and IRBs provide information to investigators about how to design and conduct research with human subjects; however, research with juvenile offenders often involves situations that do not neatly align with established rules. As a group, juvenile offenders are at heightened risk for suicide (Gallagher & Dobrin, 2006; Ruffolo & Savas, 2004) and researchers must be prepared to respond to participants' suicidality. Researchers must balance legal, ethical, and clinical considerations when addressing suicidality in juvenile justice youth; further, guidelines are often unclear and, at times, in conflict with one another.

Although case law and ethics codes (e.g., Ethical Principles of Psychologists and Code of Conduct; APA, 2002) provide guidance in the management of suicidality, researchers' responsibilities do not necessarily parallel requirements and guidelines established for mental health professionals. Researchers come from different training backgrounds, are regulated by different agencies, and engage in different types of activities than clinicians. These differences suggest that researchers might have different responsibilities in terms of suicide risk assessment and intervention, and the depth of these responsibilities remains unclear. Case law and ethical standards do not specifically address researchers' requirements when youth disclose suicidal thoughts or intentions.

Adding another layer of complexity, in addition to all of the possible conflicts between legal, ethical, and clinical guidelines, researchers must follow study protocols. Importantly, researchers' roles and goals differ from those of other mental health professionals, and, in addition to prioritizing the wellbeing of their participants, they must consider the execution of research protocols. The practicality of executing a research project and limiting the types and quantity of information collected from participants places additional constraints on the assessment and management of suicide risk among juvenile justice–involved youth. Researchers are charged with the difficult task of balancing legal, ethical, and research responsibilities while considering how responses to suicidality may impact youths' wellbeing.

References

Abram, K. M., Choe, J. Y., Washburn, J. J., Teplin, L. A., King, D. C., & Dulcan, M. K. (2008). Suicidal ideation and behaviors among youths in juvenile detention. *Journal of the American Academy of Child and Adolescent Psychiatry, 47*(3), 291–300. doi: 10.1097/CHI0b013e318160bce.

Abram, K. M., Teplin, L. A., Charles, D. R., Longworth, S. L., McClelland, G. M., & Dulcan, M. K. (2004). Posttraumatic stress disorder and trauma in youth in juvenile detention. *Archives of General Psychiatry, 61*, 403–411.

Alltucker, K. W., Bullis, M., Close, D., & Yovanoff, P. (2006). Different pathways to juvenile delinquency: Characteristics of early and late starters in a sample of previously incarcerated youth. *Journal of Child and Family Studies, 15*(4), 475–488. doi: 10.1007/s10826-006-9032-2.

American Counseling Association. (2005). *ACA code of ethics*. Retrieved August 2013, from http://www.counseling.org/Resources/aca-code-of-ethics.pdf.

American Psychological Association. (2002). Ethical principles of psychologists and code of conduct. *American Psychologist, 57*, 1060–1073. doi: 10.1037/0003-066X.57.12.1060.

Baerger, D.R. (2001). Risk management with the suicidal patient: Lessons from case law. *Professional Psychology: Research and Practice, 32* (4), 359–366. doi: 10.1037/0735-7028.32.4.359.

Bellah v. Greenson, 81 Cal. App. 3d 614 (1978).

Blaauw, E., Winkel, F.W., & Kerkhof, A.D. (2001). Bullying and suicidal behavior in jails. *Criminal Justice and Behavior, 28*(3), 279–299. doi: 10.1177/0093854801028003002.

Bongar, B., Maris, R. W., Berman, A. L., & Litman, R. E. (1998). Outpatient standards of care and the suicidal patient. In B. Bongar, A. L. Berman, R. W. Maris, M. M. Silverman, E. A. Harris, & W. L. Packman (Eds.), *Risk management with suicidal patients* (pp. 4–33). New York, NY: Guilford Press.

Borowsky, I. W., Ireland, M., & Resnick, M. D. (2001). Adolescent suicide attempts: Risks and protectors. *Pediatrics, 107*(3), 485–493. doi: 10.1542/peds.107.3.485.

Cauffman, E. (2004). A statewide screening of mental health symptoms among juvenile offenders in detention. *Journal of the American Academy of Child and Adolescent Psychiatry, 43*, 430–439. doi: 10.1097/00004583-200404000-00009.

Centers for Disease Control and Prevention, National Center for Injury Prevention and Control. (2009). *Suicide: Facts at a glance*. Retrieved July 2013, from http://cdc.gov/violenceprevention/pdf/Suicide-DataSheet-a.pdf.

Centers for Disease Control and Prevention, National Center for Injury Prevention and Control. (2010). *Understanding suicide: Fact sheet*. Retrieved July 2013, from http://cdc.gov/violenceprevention/pdf/Suicide-FactSheet-a.pdf.

Chapman, J. F., & Ford, J. D. (2008). Relationships between suicide risk, traumatic experiences, and substance use among juvenile detainees. *Archives of Suicide Research, 12*(1), 50–61. doi: 10.1080/13811110701800830.

de Wit, H. (2008). Impulsivity as a determinant and consequence of drug use: A review of underlying processes. *Addiction Biology, 14*(1), 22–31. doi: 10.1111/j.1369-1600.2008.00129.x.

Demuth, S., & Brown, S. L. (2004). Family structure, family processes, and adolescent delinquency: The significance of parental absence versus parental gender. *Journal of Research in Crime and Delinquency, 41*(1), 58–81. doi: 10.1177/0022427803256236.

Eisenberg, M. E., Ackard, D. M., & Resnick, M. D. (2007). Protective factors and suicide risk in adolescents with a history of sexual abuse. *Journal of Pediatrics, 151*(5), 482–487. doi: 10.1016/j.jpeds.2007.04.033.

Farand, L., Chagnon, F., Renaud, J., & Rivard, M. (2004). Completed suicides among Quebec adolescents involved with juvenile justice and child welfare services. *Suicide and Life-Threatening Behavior, 34*, 24–35. doi: 10.1521/suli.34.1.24.27774.

Gallagher, C. A., & Dobrin, A. (2006). Deaths in juvenile justice residential facilities. *Journal of Adolescent Health, 38*, 662–668. doi: 10.1016/j.jadohealth.2005.01.002.

Hayes, L. M. (2005). Juvenile suicide in confinement in the US: Results from a national survey. *Journal of Crisis Intervention and Suicide Prevention, 26*(3), 146–148. doi: 10.1027/0227-5910.26.3.146.

Hayes, L. M. (2009). Juvenile suicide in confinement: Findings from the first national survey. *Suicide and Life-Threatening Behavior, 39*(4), 353–363.

Henry, D. B., Tolan, P. H., & Gorman-Smith, D. (2001). Longitudinal family and peer group effects on violence and nonviolent delinquency. *Journal of Clinical Child Psychology, 30*(2), 172–186. doi: 10.1207/S15374424JCCP3002_5.

Insel, T. (2010). *The under-recognized public health crisis of suicide*. Retrieved July 2013, from National Institute of Mental Health website http://www.nimh.nih.gov/about/director/2010/the-under-recognized-public-health-crisis-of-suicide.shtml.

Linehan, M. M. (2000). Behavioral treatments of suicidal behaviors: Definitional obfuscation and treatment outcomes. In R. W. Maris, S. S. Cannetto, J. L. McIntosh, & M. M. Silverman (Eds.), *Review of suicidology* (pp. 84–111). New York, NY: Guilford Press.

Meier v. Ross General Hospital, 445 P.2d 519 (Cal. 1968).

Melton, G. B., Petrila, J., Pythress, N. G., & Slobogin, C. (2007). *Psychological evaluations for the courts: A handbook for mental health professionals and lawyers* (3rd ed.). New York: Guilford Press.

Mental Health Procedures Act, Pa. Stat. Ann. tit. 50, § 7301(a) (1976).

Muehlenkamp, J. J., & Gutierrez, P. M. (2004). An investigation of differences between self-injurious behavior and suicide attempts in a sample of adolescents. *Suicide and Life-Threatening Behavior, 34*(1), 12–23. doi: 10.1521/suli.34.1.12.27769.

Nally v. Grace Community Church of the Valley, 763 P.2d 948 (Cal. 1988).

National Association of Social Workers. (1996). *Code of ethics of the National Association of Social Workers.* Retrieved July 2013, from http://www.socialworkers.org/pubs/code/code.asp.

National Institutes of Health. (1998). *NIH policy for data safety and monitoring.* Retrieved July 2013, from http://grants.nih.gov/grants/guide/notice-files/not98-084.html.

National Institutes of Health, Office of Human Subjects Research. (1979). *The Belmont report: Ethical principles and guidelines for the protection of human subjects of research.* Retrieved August 2013, from http://www.hhs.gov/ohrp/humansubjects/guidance/belmont.html.

O'Sullivan v. Presbyterian Hospital in City of New York at Columbia Presbyterian Medical Center, 634 N.Y.S.2d 101 (New York App. Div. 1995).

Packman, W. L., O'Connor Pennuto, T., Bongar, B., & Orthwein, J. (2004). Legal issues of professional negligence in suicide cases. *Behavioral Sciences and the Law, 22*, 697–713. doi: 10.1002/bsl.613.

Pearson, J. L., Stanley, B., King, C., & Fisher, C. (2001). *Issues to consider in intervention research with persons at high risk for suicidality.* Retrieved July 2013, from National Institute of Mental Health website http://www.nimh.nih.gov/health/topics/suicide-prevention/issues-to-consider-in-intervention-research-with-persons-at-high-risk-for-suicidality.shtml.

Protection of Human Subjects, 45 C.F.R. § 46 (2005).

Robertson, A. A., Dill, P. L., Husain, J., & Undesser, C. (2004). Prevalence of mental illness and substance abuse disorders among incarcerated juvenile offenders in Mississippi. *Child Psychiatry and Human Development, 35*(1), 55–74. doi: 10.1023/B:CHUD.0000039320.40382.91.

Robertson, A., & Husain, J. (2001). *Prevalence of mental illness and substance abuse disorders among incarcerated juvenile offenders.* Retrieved July 2013, from National Center for Mental Health and Juvenile Justice website http://www.ncmhjj.com/resource_kit/pdfs/Special%20Issues/References/PrevMISA.pdf.

Ruffolo, M. C., & Savas, S. A. (2004). Mental health issues in juvenile justice residential placements: A multi-method agency evaluation. *Residential Treatment for Children and Youth, 22*(1), 19–32. doi: 10.1300/J007v22n01_02.

Simon, R. I. (2002). Suicide risk assessment: What is the standard of care? *Journal of the American Academy of Psychiatry and the Law, 30* (3), 340–344.

Tarasoff v. Regents of University of California, 551 P.2d 334 (Cal. 1976).

Teplin, L. A., Abram, K. M., McClelland, G. M., Dulcan, M. K., & Mericle, A. A. (2002). Psychiatric disorders in youth in juvenile detention. *Archives in General Psychiatry, 59*, 1133–1143.

Vistica v. Presbyterian Hospital, 432 P.2d 193 (Cal. 1967).

Part II

LEGAL ACTIONS AFFECTING THE WELLBEING OF CHILDREN EXPERIENCING PARENTAL DIVORCE

8

Hearing the Voice of the Child in Divorce

Robin H. Ballard, Brittany N. Rudd, Amy G. Applegate, and Amy Holtzworth-Munroe

Many children in the Western world experience the divorce or separation of their parents.[1] Unfortunately, such children are at risk for negative consequences, including psychological and behavioral problems and difficulties in school and interpersonal relationships (e.g., Amato, 2010). Child adjustment after parental divorce is determined by multiple factors, such as levels of conflict between parents, competent parenting from both parents, maintenance of important relationships, and economic security (for review, see Kelly & Emery, 2003). Family law professionals, researchers, and policymakers are all interested in mitigating the potentially harmful effects that divorce can exert on children. The chapter will outline the legal history of the child's role in divorce, examine the controversies that arise from hearing from children during divorce proceedings, and present research on what children have expressed they wished they could contribute to the divorce process, as well as the empirical evidence relevant to children's voices in divorce proceedings and capacity to participate. The chapter will also discuss issues about interviewing

---

[1] In this chapter, we are concerned with children whose parents are married and divorcing, children whose parents had a relationship but were never married and are dissolving their relationship, and children of parents who may not have had an ongoing relationship but must resolve issues of child custody and parenting time. Despite this broad scope, we will usually refer, more narrowly, to "divorce." This is, in part, a convenience. But it also reflects the state of the field, as the majority of research has examined divorce, not other types of custody decisions.

children properly, considering the professionals and others who interview children during the divorce process. This chapter will end with a discussion of, and recommendations for, procedures for interviewing children in divorce proceedings.

A Brief Legal History of the Child's Role in Divorce

Children whose parents divorce have been treated in different ways historically. Early on, children were viewed as "property" of the father. Later, children were viewed as benefiting primarily from a strong relationship with a mother, especially in their "tender years." More recently, family law has operated under the "best interest of the child" standard (Crossman, Powell, Principe, & Ceci, 2002; Moloney, 2008).

The Uniform Marriage and Divorce Act (UMDA), Section 402 (1979), which has become the framework for custody laws in the United States, provides that "The court shall determine custody in accordance with the best interest of the child" and lists relevant factors for determining best interest. These factors include wishes of the parents; wishes of the child; the relationships between the parents, children, siblings, and others affecting the child's best interest; adjustment to home, school, and community; and the mental and physical health of all parties. All states have adopted some form of the UMDA. As of the late 1990s, four states had even made the wishes of an adolescent the controlling factor in custody decisions (Nemechek, 1998). Thus, the law provides a basis for hearing the voice of the child in custody determinations.

Controversies Surrounding Hearing From Children During Divorce Proceedings

There remains much controversy surrounding whether children should be heard during divorce proceedings. This chapter presents both sides of the debate.

Benefits of Hearing From Children During Divorce Proceedings

There are many who believe that hearing from children can provide benefits during the divorce process (e.g., Cashmore, 2011; Cashmore & Parkinson, 2008). Warshak (2003) provides both an "enlightenment rationale" and an "empowerment rationale" for listening to children. The "enlightenment rationale" suggests that children have critical information that could impact decisions made for them. Children are the experts on their preferences; by listening to their opinions, those with the power to make decisions will be enlightened and make better decisions for them. The "empowerment rationale" is the idea that children directly benefit from contributing to the decision-making process. That is, they feel the respect that comes with having their opinions acknowledged, and they gain a greater sense of control over their lives.

Several possible mechanisms have been hypothesized regarding how hearing from children can lead to better decisions. For example, a study of child-inclusive mediation extracted three potential mechanisms from qualitative data, suggesting that hearing from the child may serve (1) as "a wake-up call" in which parents are confronted by how much the divorce is actually affecting their children; (2) to "level the playing field for fathers" by taking mothers out of a gatekeeping role; and (3) to increase the chances of parents reaching "developmentally correct arrangements" that focus on the needs of the child rather than getting a "fair share" for each parent (McIntosh, Wells, Smyth, & Long, 2008, p. 118). Others concur that hearing from children can provide a needed check on self-centered parental thinking (Simpson, 1989), offering parents a way to change their positions during negotiations without the feeling that they have "given in" to the other parent (Timms, 2003). Finally, hearing from children might prevent parents from losing sight of the children's needs, with the result that plans are made not for a child of that particular age, but for the unique needs of their particular child (Neale, 2002).

In terms of direct benefits (i.e., the empowerment rationale), most children report wanting to be heard during parental separation (Cashmore, 2011; Cashmore & Parkinson, 2008). As described later, this participation can range from informally expressing their opinions to the more formal option of talking directly to the presiding judge. Particularly if children have not had the opportunity to discuss the upheaval in their family life, being able to discuss the situation can be therapeutic (Simpson, 1989). The vast majority of children in an Australian study reported that talking to someone about the divorce or separation was helpful (McIntosh et al., 2008). There are also the potential direct benefits of being treated with respect, gaining competence through the experience of voicing an opinion, and being more accepting of decisions in which one has had a part (Smith, Taylor, & Tapp, 2003).

Risks of Hearing From Children During Divorce Proceedings

There are many who disagree with hearing from the child in the divorce process; such critics are concerned that it puts the child in an unnecessarily harmful situation. Researchers and legal professionals have worried that risks include putting children in the middle of their parents' dispute and forcing them to assume an adult role (Simpson, 1989). Emery (2003) has argued that rights and responsibilities are inextricable and that to recognize children's rights in a custody context means that they will assume some responsibility for the decisions. He has expressed concern that, rather than feeling empowered, some children may feel burdened.

Potentially undermining the enlightenment rationale, what children say they want may not actually be what they want or what is best for them (Warshak, 2003). For example, children might feel the need to side with a parent, and thus might advocate for less time with the other parent. Chapter 10 (this volume) discusses situations in which a parent alienates the child from the other parent, leading the child to inappropriately reject one parent. In another example, adolescents might enjoy living with the more permissive parent who less effectively monitors their activities. Thus, while children might have a preference, that preference may be counter to their actual best interest.

Finally, including the child as a legitimate, self-interested third party has the potential to complicate already difficult negotiations and decisions (Resetar & Emery, 2008). Including the minimum number of parties may simplify and facilitate the settlement process.

Empirical Evidence Relevant to Children's Voices in Divorce Proceedings

Some research is available to inform practitioners about children's desire and capacity to participate in the process of their parent's divorce. Furthermore, there is extensive research on methods for interviewing children, so a brief introduction to that topic is also provided.

Research on Children's Desire to Participate

Researchers have asked children what they wanted during a divorce or separation, generally relying on retrospective reports from older children. Children report the importance of open communication and the feeling of being treated with respect, while also understanding the need to have parents remain the decision makers (Neale, 2002). Children report being wary of third-party involvement in family matters and dislike feeling interrogated rather than consulted (Neale, 2002). Neale recommends a process that "allows for open and independent access for children who need help but respects the privacy and integrity of those who do not" (p. 471). It also is important to take time to build rapport with children who are wary (Smith et al., 2003). Children indicate that being consulted might put them in a difficult situation, reporting that they worry about consequences for their parents or themselves (Cashmore & Parkinson, 2008).

Children coming from abusive or neglectful situations tend to want to be able to actually make decisions about their living arrangements, while children from homes without abuse or neglect desire to participate but let the parents decide (Neale, 2002). This finding was replicated by Cashmore and Parkinson (2008), who also found that children generally reported wanting more time with the nonresidential parent, although a few did not and had even blocked involvement with abusive or neglectful parents. Suggesting that children believe they have little input in court hearings, Block and colleagues (2010) found that the majority of maltreated children in dependency courts felt that they were unable to fully communicate their desires to the judge and about one-third felt (right after their hearing) that they could not communicate with their lawyer and the lawyer did not communicate what they wanted to the judge. Also, 37% of children did not feel that they were believed or listened to when they were in the courtroom.

In a qualitative study, Cashmore (2011) interviewed children about their understanding of, and contribution to, the decision making surrounding their residence. Children who had the opportunity to voice their opinions were not necessarily happier with the final decision, nor did they perceive the final arrangements as fairer, than those who wanted to voice an opinion but did not get to do so. And in a small study in Ireland, children reported having little input into custody decisions, but many appeared to be fine with a minimal role (Hogan, Halpenny & Greene, 2003). Altogether, the mixed findings about children's desire to participate indicate that more research is needed to clarify the conditions in which children want to have a voice in the divorce process.

Research on Children's Capacity to Participate

Do children have the capacity to productively engage with such adult questions? Historically, the legal answer has usually been "no." The legal system has viewed children as lacking adult capacities. While it has presumed competence in adults, it presumes incompetence in children (Halikias, 1994; Woolard, Reppucci, & Redding, 1996). Additionally, the child, embedded within the family unit, has not been treated as an individual by the law (James, 2008).

The question of the capacity of children to participate in legal proceedings has been an issue not only in the realm of family law but also in criminal proceedings (in this volume, see Chapter 3 for discussion of developmental considerations in juvenile delinquency cases and Chapter 4 for discussion of police interrogations of juveniles). Factors that potentially interfere with a child's accurate memory include the child's inattention, prior knowledge (e.g., the child being told that others have confirmed that an event happened), stress, a single (compared to repeated) exposure to an event, developmental maturity, exposure to suggestion (e.g., the interviewer's bias may influence the questions asked, which may suggest to the child what happened), and retrieval cues (Ceci, Kulkofsky, Klemfuss, Sweeney, & Bruck, 2007; Crossman et al., 2002).[2] Additional factors include repeated interviews and the skill level of the interviewer (Ceci et al., 2007; Crossman et al., 2002). When courts determine whether a child witness is competent, the determination generally involves ascertaining the child's understanding of the difference between truth and falsehood and the importance of telling the truth (Bala, Lee, Lindsay, & Talwar, 2000).

The period between ages 5 and 10 years is one of rapid cognitive change that affects how children understand families, divorce, remarriage, and childrearing; for example, 10-year-olds are far more capable of accurately taking

---

[2] Retrieval cues are any stimuli (e.g., objects, scents, sounds) that recall a memory from long-term memory.

the perspective of another person than younger children (Mazur, 1993). Thus, age and maturity levels may be proxies for concerns about accuracy and capacity. Yet a variety of factors can affect accuracy, including mood, understanding of questions, completeness of report, truth telling, weaker memories, the effect of repeated questions, difficulty reporting "don't know," and coaching by a parent (Hynan, 1998). Thus, no matter what the child's age, statements from children should not be accepted uncritically (Warshak, 2003, p. 377). See Chapter 2, this volume, for discussion of developmental theory as applied to legal issues.

In one study, children were assessed for their rationality about custodial decision making (Greenberg-Garrison, 1991). Children ages 9 to 14 years, as well as a comparison group of 18-year-olds, were given two hypothetical vignettes related to custody decisions for divorcing families. They were asked what advice they would give and the reasons for the advice. Children's answers spanned a range of considerations in custody determinations, including stability in relationships, closeness with parents, finances, parenting, and conflict between parents. Domestic relations judges then rated the reasonableness and quality of the responses. Generally, answers from even the youngest children in this study were found to be as competent as those given by the 18-year-olds, although the youngest children gave somewhat less reasonable rationales in response to one vignette. These data provide preliminary evidence that children as young as 9 years are competent to at least be heard in custody decisions, although this study did not measure the performance of children who are actually experiencing the stress of divorce.

Research on Interviewing Children

Research suggests that children are capable of providing reliable information about their experiences and thoughts if interviewed correctly (for a review, see Saywitz, Camparo, & Romanoff, 2010). Carter, Bottoms, and Levine (1996) found that children ages 5 to 7 years were most accurate when they were asked simple questions and when the interviewer created a supportive environment. The researchers manipulated the interview question complexity (simple or complex) as well as the supportiveness of the interviewer (supportive or intimidating). Children gave more accurate responses to simple questions. Creating a supportive environment increased the accuracy of children's answers when they were asked detailed non-abuse-related questions or when the questions were suggestive, but the supportiveness of the interviewer did not matter when the questions were open ended or when they were detailed questions concerning abuse. The researchers also found that it was very rare for children to ask the interviewer to clarify the questions. These findings indicate that how the interviewer behaves affects the accuracy of information children provide.

Collecting inaccurate information from children during an interview that is used to make custody decisions is not the only concern when interviewing children; inadequate interviewing could cause harm to children because it could create false memories. Pezdek and Hodge (1999) found that children often remembered events that had not actually happened to them when the event was suggested to have happened by parents or experimenters.

In a study of children under stress in court, Nathanson and Saywitz (2003) compared the accuracy of responses and stress levels of 8- to 10-year-old children interviewed in a mock court versus a private room. Children who were interviewed in the mock court recalled less information, responded correctly less often, and had more heart rate variability than those interviewed in the private room, suggesting that children interviewed during a court hearing may experience stress that interferes with their performance. These studies demonstrate that the manner in which children are interviewed determines whether they provide accurate information.

Who Talks to the Children During Divorce Proceedings?

The best interest standard includes the child's wishes as a factor and, based on research on the competence of children presented in the previous section, many children appear to be able to provide some level of appropriate input regarding post-divorce parenting arrangements if interviewed correctly. The question then becomes how to best ascertain the wishes of the child in an accurate and reliable manner. As a divorce or separation case traverses the court system, children may talk to one or more adults: judges, guardians *ad litem*, custody evaluators, mediators, and their own parents. The benefits and risks associated with each of these options are reviewed, along with the limited available research on each option.

Judges

One method to hear from children experiencing parental divorce is for a judge to interview them, in what is called an *in camera* (in chambers) interview. This procedure was established in the UMDA (Section 404). Carefully conducted interviews of children by judges are thought, by some, to be a part of the way that the judicial system can "shield the child from...harmful effects" of divorce (Wright, 2002, p. 295). Saywitz and colleagues (2010) encourage judges to interview children out of robes, make the interview voluntary, take into account possible day-to-day variability in children's reports, and obtain the necessary training and skills (e.g., asking simple, open-ended questions) to interview children correctly (Wright, 2002).

Research has revealed how judges conduct child interviews in their courtrooms. In one study, 26 Michigan judges were surveyed about their in camera interviews (Lombard, 1983). Many judges did not make recordings or even take notes regarding the content of their discussions with children, which could lead judges to forget important information. Half of judges indicated that something a child had said changed their ruling, including reports of physical or sexual abuse. These interviews were quite brief; the average length reported was 18 minutes. Similarly, another study found judges spent, on average, only 20 minutes interviewing the child (Crosby-Currie, 1996). Though there are no guidelines on how long a judicial interview of a child should last, custody evaluators generally spend several hours interviewing children, and Pynoos and Eth (1986) suggest that interviews with children who have witnessed violent acts should take 90 minutes. Therefore, an interview lasting only 18–20 minutes may be insufficient. Lacking proper training and sufficient time, judges may not necessarily gather valid or reliable information from children (Ferro & Wilder, 1992; Warshak, 2003).

Indeed, given concerns with the practice of in camera interviews, even promoters say that the process should be approached with caution (Wright, 2002). One concern is due process: When judges interview children without making a record or having others present and then rely on that information to make a decision, it violates the principle of due process by gathering evidence that cannot be rebutted (Ferro & Wilder, 1992). In that regard, an Indiana trial court's ruling decreasing a father's parenting time was reversed on appeal because the appellate court found that the trial had relied improperly on a private in camera interview with the child to the detriment of his father (*McCauley v. McCauley*, 1997). In response to these concerns, most states require some record of the interview (Hirsch, 2003).

Guardians *Ad Litem*

Another potential avenue for listening to children's wishes is through a guardian *ad litem* (GAL). In a case of disputed custody or parenting time, the court may appoint a GAL to represent the children's best interests. GALs may be attorneys or volunteers supervised by attorneys. The GAL role was created under a theoretical framework that presumes a child to be incompetent and in need of representation (Halikias, 1994). Rates of GAL appointments vary by state, with GALs appointed in 23% of contested custody cases in Virginia but only 6% in Michigan (Crosby-Currie, 1996).

GALs serve in a variety of roles, including advocate for the best interest of the child, advocate for the views of the child, and fact finder (Halikias, 1994).[3] In some states, GALs must advocate for the best interest of the child, not necessarily what the child has expressed as his or her wishes (Herman, 2003; Warshak, 2003). The methods used by GALs also vary. In the survey by Crosby-Currie (1996), GALs in Virginia, as compared to Michigan, were

---

[3] In Nebraska, "a GAL has the right to file motions, present evidence and witnesses, cross-examine witness, file petitions on behalf of the child to terminate the parent's parental rights, and to move the court to order treatment and services for the child" (Pitchal, Freundlich, & Kendrick, 2009, p. 12).

more likely to report being at a judge-conducted interview or accessing the record of that interview later. As another example, the GAL may or may not enlist the help of a trained mental health professional, particularly for the child interviews.

In studies, children have expressed some concerns about the role of their GALs. For example, Pitchal, Freundlich, and Kendrick (2009) conducted a focus group with 16 young people who were either currently or previously in foster care. Most felt as if the GAL was not aware of their educational issues and their overall needs. In a study from England, children ages 7 to 16 years with GALs were surveyed (Ruegger, 2001). Overall the children were satisfied and thought GALs were most helpful in listening to them and explaining court procedures. However, children raised concerns; most notably, some children were unclear regarding whether what they said would be confidential and were unpleasantly surprised to find that what they said was shared with their parents. Additionally, some children did not realize that a GAL would not simply be taking the children's point of view and might instead advocate for the GAL's perceived "best interest" even if it deviated from their wishes. Finally, a few children still wanted to be able to speak directly to the court, knowing that the judge was the final decision maker.

One study also raised questions about the adequacy of GAL training. In an evaluation of the GAL system in Nebraska (Pitchal et al., 2009), when asked whether "the training provided to GALs...gave me all the information I needed to perform my responsibilities as a GAL," over half of participating GALs disagreed or strongly disagreed. Overall, issues of training, providing adequate explanations to the children of the GAL's role, and whether the GAL represents the child's wishes or the child's best interest are in need of further clarification.

Importantly, the GAL typically does not serve in an attorney role. Although it is possible in some jurisdictions for children to be represented by an attorney (who serves in a more traditional advocate role distinct from that of the GAL), attorney representation for children is more common in cases in which there has been a threat to the child's wellbeing (neglect or abuse) or the child is facing delinquency charges.[4]

Custody Evaluators

When custody is contested, the judge may order a custody evaluation to assist in making the custody decision. Custody evaluations are "ideally, thorough

---

[4] For more information about attorney representation of children in these cases, see the ABA Model Act Governing the Representation of Children in Abuse, Neglect, and Dependency Proceedings (2011) and the ABA Standards of Practice for Lawyers Who Represent Children in Abuse and Neglect Cases (2007), both available online.

explorations of all facets of the child's relationship with the parents" (p. 308, Crosby-Currie, 1996). In one survey of custody evaluation practices, psychologist evaluators reported spending an average of 2.7 hours interviewing children out of an average total of 21.1 hours spent on the case (Ackerman & Ackerman, 1997). Evaluators engaged in a range of activities, including observing children and parents together, contacting other involved parties, and administering psychological tests. When asked about the decision-making criteria used for making custody recommendations to the court, the wishes of adolescents were ranked fairly high, while the wishes of younger children were regarded as being much less important.

A fundamental problem with evaluating whether children should be heard by custody evaluators is that virtually no studies have addressed the efficacy, effectiveness, reliability, or validity of child custody evaluations (Kelly & Ramsey, 2009; Saini, 2008). In a review by Emery and colleagues (2005), custody evaluations were critiqued as fundamentally unscientific because evaluators used assessment instruments that were not validated properly (e.g., a "Custody Quotient" measure) or used valid and reliable measures that were of dubious value in drawing inferences about future best interest of a child (e.g., measures of IQ). Given a lack of consensus regarding what "the best interest of the child" standard means,[5] guidelines for evaluators may be of questionable utility. Furthermore, there are concerns about adequate training, as many evaluators rely on seminars and self-study to learn about the process without having access to ongoing peer consultation or supervision (Bow, 2006). As reviewed by Saini (2008), judges rule in accordance with custody evaluation recommendations in 90% of cases. The lack of empirical support for custody evaluation practices and the high-stakes nature of custody decisions create a situation in which practitioners should be especially careful when involving children.

Mediators

The Model Standards of Practice for Family and Divorce Mediation define mediation as "a process in which a mediator, an impartial third party, facilitates the resolution of family disputes by promoting the participants' voluntary agreement" (Symposium on Standards of Practice, 2000, p.127). Mediators tend to have a background in law or psychology, and some states allow mediators to interview children as part of the process.

Divorce mediation has generally been viewed as a positive development for family law (e.g., Pearson and Munson's 1984 glowing recommendation), particularly when the baseline for solving custody disputes was litigation. Yet concerns have been raised that moving the field of family law toward mediation (rather than litigation) tends to decrease the role of children (James &

---

[5] This criticism would also apply to judicial and GAL interviews of children.

James, 1999; Timms, 2003). Because mediation is concerned primarily with the process of negotiation between parents, the child's voice is potentially lost in the process (James, 2008). Others are less worried by this development, arguing that the most important function of mediation is to reduce interparental conflict, which will be of greater benefit to children than utilizing a process that hears children but is more adversarial and coercive (Resetar & Emery, 2008). Still others have considered incorporating the voice of the child as a way to improve the positive effects of mediation. For example, Warshak (2003) writes, "the best way to give children a meaningful role...is to involve them in collaborative or conciliatory processes...[and] have children meet with a mental health specialist [who] can bring the child's voice into subsequent collaborative sessions with the parents and attorneys" (p. 376). In attempting to do so, the concerns raised in previous sections (e.g., receiving the proper training to interview children) certainly apply to mediators. The practice of mediators interviewing children also raises the possibility that mediators will step outside their required neutral role to take the position of the child, creating possible role confusion (Simpson, 1989).

An alternative method of mediation that includes children in the mediation process, child-inclusive mediation (CIM), was developed in Australia (McIntosh, 2000). CIM seeks to enhance the ability of parents to consider the perspective of their children during mediation, which ideally leads parents to reduce conflict, make more developmentally appropriate arrangements for children, be more available emotionally, and keep children out of the middle of disagreements (McIntosh, 2007). These goals are accomplished by having a mental health professional, called a child consultant, interview the children. When meeting with the child, the consultant assesses the impact of the divorce, the quality of attachment between each parent and each child, the strengths the child has and the strains he or she is operating under, the developmental needs of the child, and the preferences, if any, of the child. The consultant then formulates this information in a way that the parents can meaningfully use and understand. Rather than simply relaying the child's words to the parents, the consultant works to develop the child's information thematically and present it in a way that minimizes the risk of parents getting angry at the child or rejecting the information. The child consultant then brings the information to the mediation, and the mediator and consultant together work with the parents to create arrangements that meet the needs of their children.

There is some initial evidence that CIM improves outcomes for children compared to another model of mediation developed in Australia (child-focused mediation [CFM]), which also seeks to bring the developmental needs of children to the forefront of mediation but does so by providing psychoeducation to parents and does not involve interviewing the children. At 1 year after mediation, families in the CIM intervention, compared to the CFM intervention, had lower levels of father-reported interparental acrimony, higher levels of child-reported closeness to father, better mother–child relationships, and greater satisfaction and stability of arrangements (McIntosh et al., 2008). Additionally, children in CIM families reported fewer symptoms of anxiety and depression. Four years post intervention, significant differences between the groups remained (McIntosh, Long, & Wells, 2009), including less relitigation of the case and fewer returns to mediation, higher rates of overnights with father, and greater reduction in parental acrimony reported by parents and children for those families that received CIM.[6]

Parents

Last, but certainly not least, the parents themselves may speak with their children about their divorce and hear the children's wishes. There are many reasons parents may keep children out of their discussions during divorce, including wanting to shield children from the process, being unwilling to address difficult issues, or misunderstanding children's needs or capacities (Simpson, 1989). Children may, in turn, not wish to further upset a parent by asking for details or reigniting negative emotions (Butler, Scanlan, Robinson, Douglas, & Murch, 2002).

Parents speak (or do not speak) with their children about their divorce in varying ways. In an English study of 7- to 15-year-olds from recently divorced families, there were discrepancies between what the parent thought the child knew and what the child reported knowing about the divorce (Butler et al., 2002). For example, 29% of children reported not being explicitly told about the separation, while all but one parent reported telling their children. Relative to older children, younger children less frequently recalled being told anything, although it is unknown whether this is an artifact of age (with younger children having difficulty with recall) or older children were actually told more. Over half of the children reported not having received any explanation of what the divorce would mean for them and of not having any input regarding future arrangements. This lack of discussion appeared to leave the children unsure about the future. As one boy replied, when asked what he wanted to know: "Enough to keep me not confused" (p. 92). Interestingly, the children who felt involved with arrangements were the ones most satisfied with those arrangements.

In an early study in England and Wales, parents reported on having children involved during the divorce process (Simpson, 1989). Some parents perceived child involvement as helpful by allowing children the opportunity to express their thoughts. However, some parents thought it had been too upsetting and that the children were given too much power over decisions. Parents also worried about the possibility that their children would be manipulated or influenced by the other parent. This is a realistic possibility, although it is also plausible that parents who hear things they do not like may dismiss what

---

[6] At Indiana University, a pilot study of CIM and CFM was conducted (Holtzworth-Munroe, Applegate, D'Onofrio, & Bates, 2010). Initial findings from this study may be requested from the chapter authors.

they have heard as a product of manipulation or alienation (Timms, 2003); see Chapter 10, this volume, for more on parental alienation.

Ideally, parents would keep children informed through a series of sensitively conducted conversations. A discussion of divorce should be ongoing, as the ability of a child to reason about divorce varies with the child's age and level of understanding (Mazur, 1993).

Discussion and Recommendations

Bringing the voice of the child to discussions of custody and parenting arrangements in divorce and separation cases has become increasingly common over recent decades. However, even enthusiastic proponents agree that the work must be done cautiously and in a manner that is therapeutic to the child (McIntosh et al., 2008). Grimes and McIntosh (2004) warn against adopting an intervention such as child-inclusive mediation in a simplistic way so that hearing children becomes just another item on a checklist.

To include the child's voice, practitioners will need to conduct child interviews. The practical details of how to conduct these interviews are beyond the scope of this chapter, but Saywitz, Camparo, and Romanoff (2010) offer 10 suggestions for interviewing children for custody purposes: (1) use an age-appropriate, private environment; (2) use age-appropriate explanations of the purpose of the interview, the child's role, and the functions of professionals; (3) create an objective, nonjudgmental atmosphere; (4) establish rapport through non-suggestive means; (5) use a supportive, nonthreatening atmosphere; (6) use language appropriate for the child's stage of development; (7) establish ground rules and shared expectations; (8) discuss a wide range of topics germane to the decision-making process; (9) use open-ended, nonleading questions; and (10) avoid suggestive techniques. More extensive guidelines for quality interviews are published elsewhere (e.g., Powell & Lancaster, 2003; Saywitz et al., 2010). For those who are interested in learning how to appropriately interview children, obtaining training and ongoing clinical supervision are highly recommended.

One central question that arises in the discussions of taking children's wishes into account is that of distinguishing between age and maturity. As summarized by Woolard et al. (1996), "the identification of [developmental] trajectories and pathways runs counter to the legal tendency to identify bright line distinctions based on age" (p. 225). In the absence of brief, effective methods for determining maturity, laws need to continue to use the chronological age of the child. However, professionals speaking to children in the context of a divorce should remain alert to the possibility of younger children who are particularly mature as well as older children who may not yet possess the capacity to participate appropriately.

Custody cases in which there are accusations of violence between parents, child abuse, or child neglect are challenging even for experienced professionals (Moloney, 2008). As mentioned in the research findings of Neale (2002) and Cashmore and Parkinson (2008), these are the cases in which children might actually want the most input, perhaps having come to distrust that the adults in their lives can adequately care for them. Practitioners should seek additional training on the dynamics of abuse and violence in order to better serve these children and their families.

Within the process of making arrangements that best serve children, respecting the rights of children means allowing them to have the amount of input they desire. If children wish to be heard from, they should be. If parents themselves are not capable of hearing from their children, then a mutually acceptable or court-appointed neutral third party should step into that role. The third party should be adequately trained, have access to continuing education and consultation or supervision, and be knowledgeable in both psychological research and legal requirements. They should be clear with the children about their role and the fact that their input is one of many factors to be balanced. They must be willing to communicate clearly with the decision makers in the case, with the overall goal of facilitating a process that reduces conflict between the parents.

In conclusion, hearing from children may be an important part of the divorce process. Because "the process of family dissolution and the nature of continuing family relationships are more important to children's mental health than is the structure of any particular custody arrangement" (Emery et al., 2005, p. 2), inviting children to participate may refocus parents and family law professionals on this principle. When done carefully and while respecting the needs and abilities of each unique child, incorporating the child's perspective can enlighten adults and empower children.

References

Ackerman, M. J., & Ackerman, M. C. (1997). Custody evaluation practices: A survey of experienced professionals (revisited). *Professional Psychology: Research and Practice, 28*(2), 137–145. doi: 0735-7028/97.

Amato, P. R. (2010). Research on divorce: Continuing trends and new developments. *Journal of Marriage and Family, 72*(3), 650–666. doi: 10.1111/j.1741-3737.2010.00723.x.

American Bar Association. (1996). ABA standards of practice for lawyers who represent children in abuse and neglect cases. Retrieved July 2013, from http://www.americanbar.org/content/dam/aba/administrative/child_law/repstandwhole.authcheckdam.pdf.

American Bar Association. (2011). ABA model act governing the representation of children in abuse, neglect, and dependency proceedings. Retrieved August 2013, from http://www.americanbar.org/content/dam/aba/publications/child_law_practice/vol30/ChildRepMA.authcheckdam.pdf.

Bala, N., Lee, K., Lindsay, R., & Talwar, V. (2000). A legal and psychological critique of the present approach to the assessment of the competence of child witnesses. *Osgoode Hall Law Journal, 38*(3), 409–451.

Block, S. D., Oran, H., Oran, D., Baumrind, N., & Goodman, G.S. (2010). Abused and neglected children in court: Knowledge and attitudes. *Child Abuse and Neglect, 34,* 659–670. doi:10.1016/j.chiabu.2010.02.003.

Bow, J. N. (2006). Review of empirical research on child custody practice. *Journal of Child Custody, 3*(1), 23–50. doi: 10.1300/J190v03n01_02.

Butler, I., Scanlan, L., Robinson, M., Douglas, G., & Murch, M. (2002). Children's involvement in their parents' divorce: Implications for practice. *Children and Society, 16,* 89–102. doi: 10.1002/CHI.702.

Carter, C., Bottoms, B. L., & Levine, M. (1996). Linguistic and socio-emotional influences on the accuracy of children's reports. *Law and Human Behavior, 20,* 335–358. doi: 10.1007/BF01499027.

Cashmore, J. (2011). Children's participation in family law decision-making: Theoretical approaches to understanding children's views. *Children and Youth Services Review, 33,* 515–520. doi: 10.1016/j.childyouth.2010.05.2008.

Cashmore, J., & Parkinson, P. (2008). Children's and parents' perceptions on children's participation in decision making after parental separation and divorce. *Family Court Review, 46*(1), 91–104. doi: 10.1111/j.1744-1617.2007.00185.x.

Ceci, S. J., Kulkofsky, S., Klemfuss, J. Z., Sweeney, C. D., & Bruck, M. (2007). Unwarranted assumptions about children's testimonial accuracy. *Annual Review of Clinical Psychology, 3,* 311–328. doi: 10.1146/annurev.clinpsy.3.022806.091354.

Crosby-Currie, C. A. (1996). Children's involvement in contested custody cases: Practices and experiences of legal and mental health professionals. *Law and Human Behavior, 20*(3), 289–311. doi: 0147-7307/96/0600-0289.

Crossman, A. M., Powell, M. B., Principe, G. F., & Ceci, S. J. (2002). Child testimony in custody cases: A review. *Journal of Forensic Psychology Practice, 2*(1), 1–31. doi: 10.1300/J158v02n01_01.

Emery, R. E. (2003). Children's voices: Listening—and deciding—is an adult responsibility. *Arizona Law Review, 45,* 621–627.

Emery, R. E., Otto, R. K., & O'Donohue, W. T. (2005). A critical assessment of child custody evaluations. *Psychological Science in the Public Interest, 6*(1), 1–29. doi: 10.1111/j.1529-1006.2005.00020.x.

Ferro, G., & Wilder, J. R. (1992). The in camera interview and the role of counsel in child custody cases: A different view. *Journal of the American Academy of Matrimonial Lawyers, 9,* 107–113.

Greenberg-Garrison, E. (1991). Children's competence to participate in divorce custody decisionmaking. *Journal of Clinical Child and Adolescent Psychology, 20*(1), 78–87. doi: 10.1207/s15374424jccp2001_10.

Grimes, A., & McIntosh, J. (2004). Emerging practice issues in child-inclusive divorce mediation. *Journal of Family Studies, 10*(1), 113–120. doi: 10.5172/jfs.327.10.1.113.

Halikias, W. (1994). The guardian *ad litem* for children in divorce. *Family and Conciliation Courts Review, 32*(4), 490–501. doi: 10.1111/j.174-1617.1994.tb01083.x.

Herman, G. (2003). Who represents your child? *Family Advocate, 26,* 13–15.

Hirsch, J. L. (2003). Does my child get to speak with the judge? How courts "hear" what a child is and isn't saying. *Family Advocate, 26,* 8–11.

Hogan, D. M., Halpenny, A. M., & Greene, S. (2003). Change and continuity after parental separation: Children's experiences of family transitions in Ireland. *Childhood, 10*(2), 163–180. doi: 10.1177/0907568203010002004.

Holtzworth-Munroe, A., Applegate, A.G., D'Onofrio, B., & Bates, J. (2010). Child informed mediation study (CIMS): Incorporating the children's perspective into divorce mediation in an American pilot study. *Journal of Family Studies, 16*(2), 116–129. doi: 10.5172/jfs.16.2.116.

Hynan, D. J. (1998). Interviewing children in custody evaluations. *Family and Conciliation Courts Review, 36*(4), 466–478. doi: 10.1111/j.174-1617.1998.tb01091.x.

James, A. L. (2008). Children, the UNCRC, and family law in England and Wales. *Family Court Review, 46*(1), 53–64. doi: 10.1111/j.1744-1617.2007.00138.x.

James, A. L., & James, A. (1999). Pump up the volume: Listening to children in separation and divorce. *Childhood, 6*(2), 189–206. doi: 10.1177/0907568299006002003.

Kelly, J. B. & Emery, R. E. (2003). Children's adjustment following divorce: Risk and resilience perspectives. *Family Relations, 52*(4), 352–362. doi: 10.1111/j.1741-3729.2003.00352.x.

Kelly, R. F., & Ramsey, S. H. (2009). Child custody evaluations: The need for systems-level outcome assessments. *Family Court Review, 47*(2), 286–303. doi: 10.1111/j.1744-1617.2009.01255.x.

Lombard, F. K. (1983). Judicial interviewing of children in custody cases: An empirical and analytical study. *UC Davis Law Review, 17*, 807–851.

Mazur, E. (1993). Developmental differences in children's understanding of marriage, divorce and remarriage. *Journal of Applied Developmental Psychology, 14*, 191–212. doi: 10.1016/0193-3973(93)90032-Q.

McCauley v. McCauley, 678 N.E.2d 1290 (Ind. App. 1997).

McIntosh, J. E. (2000). Child-inclusive divorce mediation: Report on qualitative research study. *Conflict Resolution Quarterly, 18*(1), 55–69. doi: 10.1002/crq.38901180106.

McIntosh, J. E. (2007). Child inclusion as a principle and as evidence-based practice: Applications to family law services and related sectors. *AFRC Issues, 1*, 1–23.

McIntosh, J. E., Long, C.M., & Wells, Y. D. (2009). *Children beyond dispute: A four year follow up study of outcomes from Child Focused and Child Inclusive post-separation family dispute resolution*. Retrieved July 2013, from http://www.ag.gov.au/Publications/Pages/ChildrenBeyondDisputeApril2009.aspx

McIntosh, J. E., Wells, Y. D., Smyth, B. M., & Long, C. M. (2008). Child-focused and child-inclusive divorce mediation: Comparative outcomes from a prospective study of postseparation adjustment. *Family Court Review, 46*(1), 105–124. doi: 10.1111/j.1744-1617.2007.00186.x.

Moloney, L. (2008). The elusive pursuit of Solomon: Faltering steps toward the rights of the child. *Family Court Review, 46*(1), 39–52. doi: 10.1111/j.1744-1617.2007.00182.x.

Nathanson, R., & Saywitz, K. J. (2003). Effects of the courtroom context on children's memory and anxiety. *Journal of Psychiatry & Law, 31*, 67–98.

Neale, B. (2002). Dialogues with children: Children, divorce and citizenship. *Childhood, 9*(4), 455–475. doi: 10.1177/0907568202009004006.

Nemechek, K. (1998). Child preference in custody decisions: Where we have been, where we are now, where we should go. *Iowa Law Review, 83*, 437–469.

Pearson, J. & Munson, P. (1984). The child's best interest principle: Theory and practice. *Conciliation Courts Review, 22*(1), 1–17. doi: 10.1111/j.174-1617.1984.tb01002.x.

Pezdek, K. & Hodge, D. (1999). Planting false childhood memories in children: The role of event plausibility. *Child Development, 70*(4), 887–895. doi: 10.1111/1467-862.00064.

Pitchal, E. S, Freundlich, M. D., & Kendrick, C. (2009). *Evaluation of the guardian ad litem system in Nebraska: Conducted by the National association of Counsel for Children*. Retrieved July 2013, from http://www.naccchildlaw.org/news/35016/News-NACC-Study---Evaluation-of-the-Guardian-Ad-Litem-System-in-Nebras.htm.

Powell, M. B. & Lancaster, S. (2003). Guidelines for interviewing children during child custody evaluations. *Australian Psychologist, 38*(1), 46–54. doi: 10.1080/00050060310001707017.

Pynoos, R. S., & Eth, S. (1986). Witness to violence: The child interview. *Journal of the American Academy of Child Psychiatry, 25,* 306–319. doi: 10.1016/S0002-7138(09)60252-1.

Resetar, B., & Emery, R. E. (2008). Children's rights in European legal proceedings: Why are family practices so different from legal theories? *Family Court Review, 46*(1), 65–77. doi: 10.1111/j.1744-1617.2007.00193.x.

Ruegger, M. (2001). Seen and heard but how well informed? Children's perceptions of the guardian *ad litem* service. *Children & Society, 15,* 133–145. doi: 10.1002/chi.623.

Saini, M. A. (2008). Evidence base of custody and access evaluations. *Brief Treatment and Crisis Intervention, 8*(1), 111–129. doi: 10.1093/brief-treatment/mhm023.

Saywitz, K., Camparo, L. B., & Romanoff, A. (2010). Interviewing children in custody cases: Implications of research and policy for practice. *Behavioral Sciences and the Law, 28,* 542–562. doi: 10.1002/bsl.945.

Simpson, B. (1989). Giving children a voice in divorce: The role of family conciliations. *Children and Society, 3*(3), 261–274. doi: 10.1111/j.1099-0860.1989.tb00351.x.

Smith, A. B., Taylor, N. J., & Tapp, P. (2003). Rethinking children's involvement in decision-making after parental separation. *Childhood, 10*(2), 201–216. doi: 10.1177/0907568203010002006.

The Symposium on Standards of Practice. (2000). Model standards of practice for family and divorce mediation. *Family Court Review, 39*(1), 121–134. doi: 10.1111/j.174-1617.2001.tb00598.x.

Timms, J. (2003). The silent majority—The position of children involved in the divorce and separation of their parents. *Child Care in Practice, 9*(2), 162–175. doi: 10.1080/1357527032000115738.

Uniform Marriage and Divorce Act, 9A Uniform Laws Annotated, Sec. 402 (1979).

Warshak, R. A. (2003). Payoffs and pitfalls of listening to children. *Family Relations, 52*(4), 373–384. doi: 10.1111/j.1741-3729.2003.00373.x.

Woolard, J. L., Reppucci, N. D., & Redding, R. E. (1996). Theoretical and methodological issues in studying children's capacities in legal contexts. *Law and Human Behavior, 20*(3), 219–227. doi: 0147-7307/96/0600-0219.

Wright, L. (2002). Interviewing children in child custody cases. *Journal of the American Academy of Matrimonial Lawyers, 28,* 295–309.

9

Establishing Child Support and Visitation Enforcement Offices: Promoting Fairness, Compliance, and Children's Wellbeing

Monica K. Miller and Jon Maskaly

When parents divorce, they must establish child support obligations and visitation rights, in part to protect the wellbeing and rights of children. Despite participation from the courts and both parents, many critics believe the family court system still treats individuals in a disparate manner (Parker, 2008); these beliefs are particularly noted by male participants in court proceedings (Hallman, Dienhart, & Beaton, 2007). These critics believe child custody agreements treat parents differently based on custody status. The custodial parent (CP) receives child support from the noncustodial parent (NCP) in accordance with state and federal law. If the NCP fails to pay, there are statutorily prescribed penalties (Miller, 2006). However, should the CP interfere with the NCP's visitation, as defined by the same court order, there are no such well-established consequences (Land, 2000). Although a situation in which a NCP does not want to exercise his or her rights to visitation raises important issues, such situations are beyond the scope of this chapter. In this chapter, "visitation enforcement" means forcing the CP to give the NCP court-ordered visitation; it does not mean forcing the NCP to exercise his or her visitation rights.

There is a need for visitation enforcement, although it is difficult to calculate. Turkat's (1997) literature review indicates that 40% of mothers admit denying visitation and 50% of fathers report being denied visitation; this affects 6 million children. Stolberg and colleague's (2002) review of studies estimates that between 20% and 37% of CPs interfere with visitation. Howe and Covell (Chapter 10, this volume) report that parental alienation (which includes visitation interference *and* extreme attempts to encourage the child to hate the other parent) is as high as 29% of all cases. Less extreme cases of visitation interference are likely even more common. Interference is hard to measure, as only a small percentage of resilient parents will utilize the court system; it is also difficult to know whether interference is legitimate (e.g., denying visitation because of abuse). Further, parents might exaggerate the situation or deny they are interfering (see Stolberg et al., 2002 for review of the child interference research). Despite the lack of definitive and recent statistics on the frequency of visitation interference, it is common enough that there is a federal program that dedicates $10 million a year to promote development of programs addressing visitation enforcement (e.g., parent education; Pearson, Davis, & Thoennes, 2005).

While there are many rationalizations for the disparity created by enforcing the NCP's responsibilities while simultaneously neglecting to enforce his or her visitation rights (see e.g., Pearson et al., 2005), this disparity has negative consequences for both the parents and child, as discussed in this chapter. We argue that the current situation violates principles of justice, has a negative impact on the NCP's perceived legitimacy of the court system, and infringes on the child's and NCP's rights. Furthermore, the effects of unequal enforcement of custody agreements tend to be more detrimental to men than women (Kelly, 1994). Finally, barring certain circumstances (e.g., abuse), children of divorce fare better (e.g., academically, socially, and psychologically) with regular contact with both parents (see generally Hetherington 1999; Nielsen, 2011; Pruett, Williams, Insabella, & Little, 2003). Therefore, the current system has many drawbacks that harm children, parents, and the legal system.

To address these problems, a change in the current system of handling child custody agreements is needed. This chapter suggests the establishment of a Child Support and Visitation Enforcement Office (CSVE Office), which would use mediation to create and enforce all aspects of the child custody agreement. The office would promote equal protection of both parents' rights, increase perceptions of the court's legitimacy, increase compliance with all parts of the custody agreement, and ultimately promote the child's wellbeing.

This chapter begins with a description of child custody agreements (CCAs), followed by a discussion of the legal implications of the current CCA enforcement situation. Next, the justice implications of the current CCA enforcement situation are enumerated, immediately before a summary of the psychological research related to the issue of CCA enforcement. Finally, the chapter offers a description of the proposed CSVE Office.

Child Custody Agreements

To understand why CSVE Offices are needed, it is necessary to understand what a child custody agreement (CCA) is, how the agreements are designed, and the relevant legal standards.

What Is a Child Custody Agreement?

There are four major areas of divorcing parties' lives that must be settled during a divorce: division of property, spousal support, child custody/visitation, and child support (see e.g., Weisz, Beal, & Wingrove, 2013). All states require divorcing parents to have a CCA addressing child support, custody, and visitation (Orakwusi, 2007). In one common custody arrangement,[1] the custodial parent (CP) receives physical custody of minor children, while the noncustodial parent (NCP) typically receives visitation rights and pays child support. The amount of child support the CP receives is typically based on the income of both parents. Although each state makes its own child support laws, the maximum and minimum amounts are based on the Family Support Act of 1988 (42 U.S.C. §§ 654).

Should the NCP fail to pay child support, the court may impose sanctions ranging from a suspended driver's license to garnished wages or a prison sentence (Miller, 2006). Further, if the NCP could pay more in child support (e.g., a salary increase), the state can file a petition to increase child support obligations on behalf of the CP, often at no cost to the CP (Miller, 2006). The rationale for these policies seems sound from the state's perspective. When the legal system compels the NCP to pay child support, the state might have to pay less to support the child (e.g., food assistance programs, Medicaid; Hatcher, 2007). This financial incentive is powerful motivation for the state to enforce child support orders.

On the other hand, the section of the CCA giving visitation rights to the NCP is not enforced with the same zeal as the child support aspects of the CCA. Should the CP interfere with the NCP's visitation as ordered by the CCA, there is relatively little the NCP can do (Feinberg & Loeb, 1994). The NCP must file a petition in family court at his or her own expense. Even then, the judge is unlikely to take action on the first appearance, instead giving the CP time to comply with the order (Mahoney, 2007). All states have some form of a child support enforcement office, while (to our knowledge) visitation enforcement offices do not exist (except temporary offices; Pearson et al., 2005).

The development and enforcement of CCAs have a broad impact. While the majority of divorcing parents are in "traditional families," there is an increasing number of "alternative families" (e.g., gay/lesbian and unmarried couples) who might also need a CCA (Navarro, 2008). One estimate suggests that 50%–60% of children born during the 1990s will live in a single-parent household at some point during childhood; most of these families will have CCAs (Hetherington, Bridges, & Insabella, 1998).

---

[1] Until recent years, only 5%–7% of children nationwide lived with each parent at least a third of the time. Exceptions include Arizona and Washington, states in which 20%–50% of children lived a third of the time with each parent (see Nielsen, 2011 for review)

The "Best Interests" Legal Standard

Modern CCAs stem from antiquated gender roles in which women were seen as more adept at caring for children while fathers earned money (Kelly, 2006). This suggests each parent plays only one role and fails to account for the complex dynamics of the modern family. Historically, judges relied upon the "tender years doctrine," which assumed young children fare better living with the mother and visiting the father (Kelly, 1994). A "mother's love" was seen as crucial to the child's proper development, a claim unsupported by research (Lamb, 1996). The doctrine was also criticized for violating the rights of fathers, who were presumed to be less fit parents (Bennett, 1994). These issues led to the doctrine eventually being abandoned.

The current standard widely used in custody matters is the "best interests of the child" standard (see also Chapters 8, 10, and 12, this volume), which was recommended in the *Uniform Marriage and Divorce Act* during the American Bar Association's 1974 annual meeting (Lowery, 1984). This standard was designed to resolve some of the previous inequities in how CCAs were decided. However, critics (e.g., Kelly, 2006) claim the new standard is also based on antiquated beliefs, as many judges assume the child's best interests are to be with the mother. This leads to custody arrangements favoring the mother and systematically minimizing the father's rights. Interestingly, research (Nielsen, 2011) indicates that young adults whose parents divorced during childhood believe it was in their best interest to live at least a third of their time with *each* parent. This does not happen often, as the vast majority of children live the majority of time with their mother (Nielsen, 2011). Although the best interests of the child standard was meant to put the child's needs first and remove legally endorsed methods of discrimination, it appears that the same discriminatory practices continue (Bennett, 1994; Kelly, 2006).

Legal Implications of the Current Child Custody Agreement Enforcement Situation

Children have the right to contact with *both* parents; this is recognized as being in the "best interests" of children, as most CCAs award visitation to the NCP in order to facilitate the child's contact with both parents. Further, the Supreme Court has repeatedly determined that parents generally have rights to conceive and rear children as they wish (e.g., *Skinner v. Oklahoma*, 1942; *Troxel v. Granville*, 2000). Thus, both parents' and children's rights are threatened by the current CCA enforcement situation.

A Child's Right to Contact With Both Parents

Article 9 of the UN Convention on the Rights of the Child gives children the right to contact with both parents. Chapter 10 in this volume further details the legal foundation that has established that children have a right to contact with both parents. Despite these rights, CPs sometimes interfere with the NCP's visitation (see Chapter 10, this volume). Although many states have adopted strategies to address visitation interference, it still remains a contentious issue requiring legal attention (e.g., *Coker v. Moemeka*, 2011; *Lestenkof v. Lestenkof*, 2012; Stolberg et al., 2002). The current CCA enforcement situation does not protect the child's rights because CPs can deny NCPs visitation, often without legal penalty. By refusing to enforce the visitation aspects of the CCA, the government is failing to protect the child's rights.

The Right to Parent

The Supreme Court has addressed the issue of parents' rights to have children and subsequently raise those children. Together, the cases suggest that individuals have the right to become parents (or not) and parents have the right to raise their children as they see fit (within certain legal limits). *Skinner v. Oklahoma* (1942) establishes that the right to procreate is a fundamental right found in the Constitution, which generally cannot be denied by the state. Further, 90 years ago, the Supreme Court established that parents have the right to raise their children as they see fit (*Myer v. Nebraska*, 1923). More recently, the Court declared that the fundamental right to "care, custody, and control of children" is "perhaps the oldest of the fundamental liberty interests recognized by this Court" (*Troxel v. Granville*, 2000, p. 2060) and choices about the "upbringing of children are among associational rights...sheltered by the Fourteenth Amendment against the State's unwarranted usurpation, disregard, or disrespect" (*M.L.B. v S.L.J.*, 1996, p. 564). In *Wisconsin v. Yoder* (1972), the Court called the right to raise one's children an "enduring American tradition." These cases establish that parents have both a right to procreate and a right to parent their children as they see fit within legal limits.

The current CCA enforcement situation does not protect these rights because CPs can deny NCPs visitation, typically without consequences. If the CP interferes with visitation, the NCP cannot exercise his or her right to raise the children. While it is the CP—not the state—that is restricting the NCP's right to parent, it is an important issue because the state is essentially allowing visitation interference to happen (in violation of a court-ordered CCA) and taking no steps to enforce the court order that would prevent the parent's rights from being violated.

Disparities Within the Parental Roles

While the current system appears to favor the CP over the NCP, this is permissible because NCPs are not a protected class that qualifies for equal protection under the Constitution. However, the situation is very different when gender-neutral language is replaced with the gendered terms suggested by national statistics. The overwhelming majority (80%–90%) of post-divorce children primarily live with their mothers (Nielsen, 2011). By replacing the word "custodial parent" with "mother" and "noncustodial parent" with "father," gender inequities become salient. Specifically, mothers typically receive the benefits of state-sponsored legal support and representation in obtaining compliance with child support payments, while fathers do not receive such legal support to protect their rights to visitation. Additionally, when a mother fails to adhere to the CCA, she faces little or no legal repercussions, but the father potentially faces serious consequences for failing to adhere to the child support portion of the same CCA.

Currently NCPs, most often fathers, have no legal recourse to challenge the differential enforcement of CCAs (Feinberg & Loeb, 1994). This is because the Supreme Court does not acknowledge custody status (i.e., as a NCP) as a class that deserves protection from discrimination. Although NCPs are overrepresented by males and gender discrimination (which *is* prohibited) seems apparent, NCPs are unlikely to make a successful argument that this qualifies as gender discrimination. That is, CCA laws are written to be gender neutral on their face (i.e., the laws are not *intentionally* designed to discriminate against one gender) but are biased in practice. Ultimately, this means the system operates in a seemingly discriminatory fashion, with little hope of a positive legal outcome for the NCP. Currently, the system is designed so the right to parent cannot be fully realized by some NCPs due to limited (or no) access to their children.

Justice Implications of the Current Child Custody Agreement Enforcement Situation

Several principles of justice are violated by the current CCA enforcement situation, the consequences of which could carry over into other areas of the legal system apart from the family court. The two primary justice principles applicable to this discussion are procedural justice and distributive justice. The absence of each could lead to diminished levels of perceived legitimacy of family courts and the legal system in general. Legitimacy is a "psychological property of an authority, institution, or social arrangement that leads those connected to it to believe that it is appropriate, proper and just" (Tyler, 2006b, p. 375). When people believe an authority (e.g., the court) is legitimate, they will adhere to the authority's orders. In essence, individuals internalize the beliefs of the authority (e.g., the courts) and regulate their conduct accordingly with little (if any) legal oversight or sanctions required (Tyler, 2006b). Finally, therapeutic jurisprudence is the notion that legal actors should consider the consequences of their actions and promote therapeutic outcomes that protect the wellbeing of those involved (Sicafuse & Bornstein, 2013; Winick, 1997). These justice principles work independently and in tandem.

Procedural Justice

Procedural justice is a person's perception that he or she was treated fairly and experienced a just process; note that it focuses on the *processes* by which the decisions are made rather than the decisions themselves (Tyler, 2006a). Those coming into contact with the justice system are often just as concerned about how they are treated by the system as they are with the outcome (Johnson, 2004). Perceived fairness can affect a person's future interactions with the legal system. For example, domestic violence suspects perceiving their treatment by police as unfair are likely to respond with anger and defiance during future encounters with police, regardless of the outcome of the initial contact (e.g., getting arrested or not; Sherman & Smith, 1992). In contrast, suspects treated in a more just manner recidivated less frequently (Paternoster, Brame, Bachman, & Sherman, 1997). A victim's sense of fairness is also important; for instance, domestic violence victims who felt they had been heard and had some sense of control over the procedure had more positive sentiments toward the justice system as compared to those with lower sense of voice and control (for review, see Epstein & Goodman, 2013). As these findings indicate—and as procedural justice suggests—people have a desire to have their opinions *heard and considered* in the legal proceedings in which they are involved. If this happens, individuals will be more likely to obey legal orders in the future (Tyler, 2006a).

Distributive Justice

A related principle is distributive justice, which is the notion that all parties involved with the justice system should have responsibility equivalent to their role in the action that brought them to court (Lambert, Hogan, & Barton, 2003). If the distribution of justice is fair, people are more likely to judge the procedures as fair, regardless of the reality (Tyler, Boeckmann, Smith, & Huo, 1997). Taken together, distributive and procedural justice suggest that people are more willing to comply with legal actions and outcomes they perceive as just and reasonable.

When either distributive or procedural justice is perceived as being absent, members of society see the legal system as an unjust source of authority that lacks the right to regulate their behavior. As a result, people may feel the system is not a legitimate authority. When this happens, people are less likely to adhere to the law or court orders (Tyler, 2006b). Bryan (2006) notes that legitimacy is particularly important in the divorce context because outcomes have both personal and societal significance.

Therapeutic Jurisprudence

Finally, the current CCA enforcement situation also violates principles of therapeutic jurisprudence. One of the main principles of therapeutic jurisprudence is the recognition that "substantive rules, legal procedures, and the roles of lawyers and judges produce therapeutic or anti-therapeutic consequences" (Wexler & Winick, 1991, p. 981; see also Chapters 6 and 11 in this volume for discussion of therapeutic jurisprudence applied to other legal situations). Legal actors should strive to achieve therapeutic consequences for the parties involved, while still taking into account other legal issues and concerns (e.g., community safety; Sicafuse & Bornstein, 2013; Winick, 1997). For instance, judges should consider whether a drug-addicted defendant's wellbeing might be enhanced by a sentence of drug treatment and counseling rather than prison.

Justice Principles and the Current Child Custody Agreement Enforcement Situation

These justice principles are relevant to the current discussion; the current CCA enforcement situation does not adhere to the principles of procedural or distributive justice, which likely diminishes many NCPs' perceptions of the law's legitimacy. The current policies and procedures violate the principle of procedural justice by offering differential enforcement of the CCA, which might appear to be an unjust procedure (for an analysis of procedural justice in divorce disputes, see Bryan, 2006). Currently, NCPs have legal consequences for failing to pay child support (Miller, 2006) and receive no state help enforcing their visitation rights, while CPs have few (if any) consequences for not complying with the visitation order and often have the support of the state to protect their rights. The lack of procedural justice has some unintended consequences, including a reduced likelihood the NCP will adhere to the CCA (Pearson & Thoennes, 1990) and reduced perception of legitimacy (Bryan, 2006).

An additional problem emerges from the lack of distributive justice, which suggests that both parents have half of the rights and responsibilities for the child. Generally, the law assumes both parents play equal roles in parenting children both pre-and post-divorce. However, because of the current CCA enforcement situation, the CP can interfere with the NCP's visitation, which would lead to unequal distribution of parenting time. Additionally, NCPs could perceive the current CCA enforcement system as unfair because the government distributes its assistance unfairly; the CP receives help enforcing the child support provisions of the CCA, yet the government does not help the NCP enforce the visitation provisions. Although the parents theoretically have equal rights to their child, the system treats them differently. Thus, according to justice principles, the NCP might be less likely to follow the CCA.

Many of the potential consequences of unequal CCA enforcement are antitherapeutic. The NCP's wellbeing is compromised when he/she feels there is a lack of procedural justice and distributive justice. Similarly, children's wellbeing is compromised when the CP interferes with visitation or the NCP does not comply with the child support order (a topic discussed later).

As a whole, the current CCA enforcement situation can violate principles of procedural and distributive justice. This leads to lowered perceptions of legitimacy of the courts and legal system as a whole. It also leads to antitherapeutic outcomes for parents and children. In order to better protect the wellbeing of children of divorce, therapeutic jurisprudence principles suggest consulting relevant psychological research, which is summarized next.

Psychological Research

After a divorce, the family structure is changed and redefined. Children of divorce are often exposed to a lower standard of living, emotional trauma, and loss of parental relationships (Thompson & Amato, 1999). Children of divorce experience a myriad of problems, including difficulties with social adjustment and subsequent school performance (Hetherington & Kelly, 2002). A primary predictor of a child's post-divorce adjustment is the post-divorce living conditions (Nielsen, 2011; Thompson & Amato, 1999). The more economically disadvantaged the post-divorce condition of the family, the greater the effects on the child. Therefore, the NCP's financial support is essential to the subsequent wellbeing of the child.

Visitation denial compounds these effects. Denial is often coupled with parental conflict and has a variety of negative effects for children, including low self-esteem, anxiety, and self-blame (see Stolberg et al., 2002 for review). The absence of the NCP is strongly correlated with problem behaviors (Amato & Dorius, 2010; Hetherington et al., 1998). Reduced involvement of the father post-divorce has been linked to behavior control problems, especially in boys (Hetherington, 1999). There is also a general relationship between coming from a "broken home" and subsequent criminal involvement (Farrington, 2004). Furthermore, children who have frequent paternal contact after divorce have better socialization, adaptive behavior, and communication skills compared to children with lower levels of paternal contact (Pruett et al., 2003). It is possible to mitigate the negative behavior problems via frequent, positive interaction with both parents (Hetherington, 1999; Nielsen, 2011).

Additional research suggests children perform better in certain aspects of their lives when a relationship with both parents is fostered after the divorce. Specifically, children with a close relationship with their father fare better (e.g., academically) than those whose fathers are not actively engaged in their lives (Amato & Dorius, 2010; Amato & Fowler, 2002). A review of the literature revealed that children who spend at least 35% of their time with each parent fare as well or better than those who only live with their mother (Nielsen, 2011). Additionally, adolescents whose fathers regularly paid child support and were actively engaged in their lives were more likely to finish high school and enroll in college (Menning, 2002). Finally, children of divorce experience a sense of loss after divorce; they frequently indicate that they longed for more contact with their fathers and did not have the quality of father–child relationship they desired (see Nielsen, 2011 for review). As these studies indicate, the current CCA enforcement situation is detrimental to children's wellbeing because the CP can interfere with visitation which can benefit the child.

There are important caveats to these findings: If there is evidence of physical, sexual, or emotional abuse of the child, or if the NCP has no interest in being involved in the child's life, these benefits may not exist. In such cases, contact between the child and parent must be considered individually by a mediator or judge, with help from experts (Amato & Fowler, 2002). In these cases, it might be in the child's best interests to have little or no contact with the NCP to minimize subsequent psychological trauma. Notwithstanding these exceptions, it is in the child's best interests to maintain as much contact as possible with *both* parents (Nielsen, 2011).

Enforcement of visitation is also important because there is a reciprocal relationship between parental involvement and child support. Specifically, children of divorce with more frequent contact with their NCPs are better off financially (Seltzer, 1991; Seltzer, McLanahan, & Hanson, 1998) and a CP receiving more financial support tends to allow more visitation (Sen, 1990). The current CCA enforcement situation potentially creates a cycle in which, when the NCP does not receive visitation, he or she chooses not to pay child support, prompting the CP to restrict visitation rights. This cycle adversely affects the children.

In sum, it is difficult to develop a quality relationship with a child when denied visitation. Research implies a certain frequency of contact is necessary to promote the wellbeing of children; while the number of days necessary is not universally agreed upon, it is likely more than the minimal time allotted by the typical CCA and certainly greater than zero (Kelly, 2006). Some experts recommend at least 35% of a child's time should be with each parent (Nielsen, 2011). Thus, if a CP denies the NCP visitation, the children are harmed. Yet states do not typically enforce visitation orders as strongly as they do child support orders.

Creating a Child Support and Visitation Enforcement Office

A possible solution to the problems associated with the current CCA enforcement situation is to create a Child Support and Visitation Enforcement Office (i.e., the CSVE Office) within the family court. The office would not be drastically different that some existing systems and should be easily adopted and cost-effective. The new office would be located within the family court system. Such an office would be responsible for designing new CCAs and enforcing *all* parts of the CCA. Specifically, the office would be responsible for enforcing child support and visitation disputes in a way that promotes the child's wellbeing.

Costs of a Child Support and Visitation Enforcement Office

Although the cost of establishing the office might seem daunting at first, we argue that, in the end the benefits would outweigh the investment (see also Chapter 6 of this volume for further discussion of weighing up-front costs with long-term benefits). The initial investment in the office could be minimized by expanding existing child support offices to address issues relating to visitation as well as child support. With the use of mediation, additional incurred costs could be offset by reducing the need for as many family court judges as a result of smaller caseloads (e.g., reduction in NCPs suing to enforce the visitation orders). Further, if visitation is enforced, NCPs would have a greater sense that the system is just and might be more likely to pay their child support. This could lead to fewer actions to enforce child support orders the office must process.[2] Assuming that receiving visitation encourages NCPs to pay child support, then enforcement of visitation orders might decrease the amount the state pays to support to the child. This too would lead to long-term savings that will offset the initial expenses of the office. Even if there is ultimately a long-term net increase in expenses, we argue that this is justifiable because the final outcome will ensure that the CP's and NCP's rights are equally protected.

Furthermore, whether the money is spent on the creation of the proposed office or other secondary measures dealing with children of divorce (e.g., counseling, prison), the money *will* be spent. As previously discussed, psychological research indicates children maintaining frequent contact with parents after divorce become better adjusted (e.g., Hetherington, 1999) and perform better academically (Menning, 2002). These benefits (and others discussed earlier) associated with frequent, positive parent–child contact can significantly impact society. Children not finishing high school have higher rates of arrest (Jarjoura, 1996) and children from disrupted and broken families are more frequently involved in criminal activity (Farrington, 2004). Academic success and crime rates affect both society and the state (e.g., costs of imprisoning a criminal). Some of these financial and nonfinancial costs could be partially offset with the creation of the office—if the office can promote positive relationships between children and NCPs and prevent negative outcomes. Of course, this prediction will have to be tested through program assessment of long-term outcomes.

Operations of the Child Support and Visitation Enforcement Office

The CSVE Office would consist of a family court judge or judges (depending on the number of active cases and available funding), at least one attorney

---

[2] There is a positive correlation between visitation and child support payment; however, further research is needed to determine whether receiving visitation *causes* NCPs to pay more child support (see Miller, 2006).

(responsible for representing the best interests of the child), and multiple mediators. Each person in the office would play a different but crucial role in supporting the ultimate goal of promoting equal rights for both parents and the wellbeing and rights of the children. There would be some changes to the current divorce procedures. The first would include the referral of all divorces with children to the office prior to the divorce being finalized. Mediators would help parents establish a CCA (currently a common practice; Weisz, Beal, & Wingrove, 2013). Secondly, a provision would be added to the CCA that states that both parties would be obligated to participate in good faith mediation as a first step to dispute resolution of post-divorce CCA issues. The good faith provision would stipulate that both parties must actually attempt to realistically and equitably settle the dispute through mediation. In cases that cannot be resolved with mediation, a judge would have the ability to force compliance with the CCA (as judges currently do). In the example of the CP interfering with visitation, the judge could force the CP to allow visitation as stated in the CCA; if the CP refuses, the judge can hold the CP in contempt of court and impose sanctions (e.g., fines or jail). This post-CCA enforcement is the primary change from existing procedures.

Mediation would be an essential part of the functioning of the office. Mediation is a common way to resolve legal disputes in general (e.g., Bornstein, Hullman, & Miller, 2013; Stewart & Wood, 2013), including divorce and custody issues (Weisz et al., 2013). There are a variety of strategies for mediation (e.g., Bornstein et al., 2013; Emery, 2012; Pearson et al., 2005; Pickar & Kahn, 2011). Some jurisdictions even offer programs that prepare divorcing parents for mediation so as to help parents through the process (Kitzmann, Parra, & Jobe-Shields, 2012). Studies investigating parental satisfaction with mediation versus the traditional adversarial system report somewhat mixed findings. Mothers were less satisfied than fathers with mediation; this is likely because the traditional adversarial system favored mothers, while mediation treated parents more equitably (Weisz et al., 2013). Other research indicated that parents are more satisfied with mediation and that mediation is correlated with more positive parent–child and parent–parent relationships (Emery, Sbarra, & Grover, 2005). Additionally, parties using mediation to set the terms of their CCA were more likely to adhere to the CCA; these parents also had more functional relationships after the divorce (Pearson & Thoennes, 1990). Such research suggests that mediation is related to some positive outcomes, even though not everyone prefers it over traditional court.

In addition to mediators, the office would employ attorneys representing the best interests of the children. In accordance with principles of therapeutic jurisprudence, attorneys would consult with experts in child wellbeing (e.g., psychologists, social workers) so as to protect the child's interests. Attorneys would also work with the judge and other legal officials to handle disputes arising when an NCP fails to pay child support and/or a CP interferes with visitation. This process would ensure the state is equally protecting the interests of both parents because the state would ultimately be representing the best interest of the child.

A typical divorce would proceed as such: During the divorce, a CCA would be established with the help of a mediator at the office. The CCA would be legally binding. Later, if either party wants the CCA altered (e.g., because the NCP was denied visitation as specified in the CCA), he or she would return to the office. The first stage of the process would involve the CP and the NCP meeting with a mediator to attempt to reach an amicable solution (e.g., changing the visitation to a more convenient time). If a new agreement can be reached in mediation, the amendment would be filed as an addendum to the CCA. In the event an agreement cannot be reached (or if one party continually fails to adhere to the CCA's terms), the next step would be a judicial hearing. In this example, the office's attorney would represent the NCP in the hearing because the CP has violated the CCA. The judge would then address the violation (e.g., holding the CP in contempt of court for violating the CCA). Violators of child support orders and violators of visitation orders should receive similar legal consequences. The majority of cases would likely be resolved satisfactorily in mediation, making judicial decisions rare and reserved for the most extreme cases. This new process would more effectively and efficiently resolve CCA violations.

Evaluation of the Child Support and Visitation Enforcement Office

A final consideration is the evaluation of the new office. After creation of the office, research will be needed to evaluate the legal and financial costs and benefits of the program. Specifically, research should examine CCA compliance rates, comparing compliance before and after the office is established. Additionally, the financial cost of implementing the new program should be evaluated to determine the net costs of such an office. Lastly, research should examine the outcomes for the children (e.g., increased visitation with NCP, psychological wellbeing and adjustment). Funding and cooperation from the offices will be essential for such research.

In sum, the office has the potential to accomplish a great deal with what would likely be only a small investment. The new office would operate in accordance with the principles of justice (e.g., procedural justice, distributive justice, and therapeutic jurisprudence), something that is missing from the current system. Perceptions of justice and legitimacy can encourage parents to adhere to the CCA. Also, if there are violations, there would be a team of people ensuring the best interests of the child are truly represented (according to psychological research indicating that continued contact with and financial support from the NCP promotes positive child outcomes; Miller, 2006). In accordance with therapeutic jurisprudence, the new office would look after both the financial and psychological wellbeing of the child by ensuring that both child support and visitation orders are enforced. The design of the new office would also take into account the legal rights set forth by the Supreme Court in the line of cases (e.g. *Myer v. Nebraska*, 1923; *Skinner v. Oklahoma*, 1942; *Troxel v. Granville*, 2000) that established child rearing as an "enduring American tradition" (*Wisconsin v. Yoder*, 1972), and the United Nations convention, which established that children have a right to contact with both parents.

Conclusion

The purpose of this chapter was to discuss how the current system of establishing and enforcing (or lack of enforcing) CCAs is unfair to both NCPs and children. This violates justice principles and threatens the wellbeing and rights of children. The establishment of a CSVE Office can help protect both parents' rights and the wellbeing and rights of children. The proposed office offers many improvements over the current system.

First, it equally enforces parental rights for both the CP and NCP. The old system has an inherent advantage for the CP (more often women) because the system protected the CPs and their interests but not those of the NCP. The new system holds both parties equally accountable and represents both parties in the same manner when one party fails to adhere to the CCA.

Second, the office's main goal would be to distribute equal parental rights and achieve equal enforcement of all parts of the CCA; this would augment the perceived legitimacy of the family court system. This increase in legitimacy would serve to increase levels of self-regulatory behavior (Tyler, 2006b) such that both parties would be more likely to comply with the CCA. The current system's unequal treatment of CPs and NCPs has the potential to negatively affect perceived legitimacy of the family court system; this is currently a common perception of fathers (Hallman et al., 2007).

Finally, this new office represents a therapeutic solution designed to protect the child's and parents' wellbeing. The current system does not promote the best interests of the child because the CP can interfere with visitation, usually without penalty. According to much psychology research (e.g., Nielsen, 2011), lack of contact with the NCP has negative outcomes for the child. Thus, visitation enforcement would typically be therapeutic for children.

In sum, the new system makes a bad situation (i.e., divorce involving children) into the best possible situation by ensuring the best interests of all parties—especially children—are taken into account. The new system can accomplish this without a substantial cost increase over the current system because of the savings discussed earlier. The new system will protect the rights of parents and the wellbeing and rights of children of divorce and thus should be seriously considered by lawmakers.

References

Amato, P., & Dorius, C. (2010). Fathers, children and divorce. In M. Lamb (Ed.), *Role of the father in child development* (pp. 177–201). New York, NY: Wiley.

Amato, P. R., & Fowler, F. (2002). Parenting practices, child adjustment, and family diversity. *Journal of Marriage and Family, 64*, 703–716. doi: 10.1111/j.1741-3737.2002.00703.x.

Bennett, D. (1994, July 3). I, too, am a good parent. *Newsweek*, p. 18.

Bornstein, B. H., Hullman, G., & Miller, M. K. (2013). Stress, trauma, and wellbeing in the legal system: Where do we go from here? In M. K. Miller & B. H. Bornstein (Eds.), *Stress, trauma, and wellbeing in the legal system* (pp. 293–309). New York, NY: Oxford University Press.

Bryan, P. E. (2006). *Constructive divorce: Procedural justice and sociolegal reform*. Washington, DC: American Psychological Association.

Coker v. Moemeka, 714 S.E.2d 642 (GA. 2011).

Emery, R. E. (2012). *Renegotiating family relationships: Divorce, child custody, and mediation* (2nd ed.). New York, NY: Guilford Press.

Emery, R. E., Sbarra, E., & Grover, T. (2005). Divorce mediation: Research and reflections. *Family Court Review, 43*, 22–37. doi: 10.111/j.1744-1617.2005.00005.x.

Epstein, D., & Goodman, L. A. (2013). Domestic violence victims' experience in the legal system. In M. K. Miller & B. H. Bornstein (Eds.), *Stress, trauma, and wellbeing in the legal system* (pp. 45–61). New York, NY: Oxford University Press.

Family Support Act, 42 U.S.C. § 667 (1998).

Farrington, D. P. (2004). Families and crime. In J. Q. Wilson & J. Petersillia (Eds.), *Crime: Public policies for crime control* (pp. 129–148). Oakland, CA: Institute for Contemporary Studies.

Feinberg, J. M., & Loeb, L. S. (1994). Custody and visitation interference: Alternative remedies. *American Academy of Matrimonial Lawyers Journal, 12*(2), 271–284.

Hallman, M., Dienhart, A., & Beaton, J. (2007). A qualitative analysis of fathers' experiences of parental time after separation and divorce. *Fatherhood, 5*, 4–24.

Hatcher, D. L. (2007). Child support harming children: Subordinating the best interests of the child to the fiscal interests of the state. *Wake Forrest Law Review, 42*, 1029–1086.

Hetherington, E. M. (1999). Should we stay together for the sake of the children? In E. M. Hetherington (Ed.), *Coping with divorce, single parenting, and remarriage* (pp. 93–116). Mahwah, NJ: Erlbaum.

Hetherington, E. M., Bridges, M., & Insabella, G. M. (1998). What matters? What does not? Five perspectives on the association between marital transitions and children's adjustments. *American Psychologist, 53*, 167–184.

Hetherington, E. M., & Kelly, J. (2002). *For better or for worse*. New York, NY: Norton.

Jarjoura, G. R. (1996). The conditional effect of social class on the drop out-delinquency relationship. *Journal of Research in Crime and Delinquency, 33*(2), 232–255. doi: 10.1177/0022427896033002004.

Johnson, R. (2004). Citizen expectations of police traffic stop behavior. *Policing: An International Journal of Police Strategies and Management, 27*, 487–497. doi: 10.1108/13639510410566235.

Kelly, J. B. (1994). The determination of child custody. *The Future of Children: Children and Divorce, 4*(1), 121–242.
Kelly, J. B. (2006). Children's living arrangements following separation and divorce: Insights from empirical and clinical research. *Family Process, 46*(1), 35–52.
Kitzmann, K. M., Parra, G. R., & Jobe-Shields, L. (2012). A review of programs designed to prepare parents for custody and visitation mediation. *Family Court Review, 50*, 128–136. doi: 10.1111/j.1744-1617.2011.01434.x.
Lamb, M. E. (1996). *The role of the father in child development* (3rd ed.). New York, NY: Wiley.
Lambert, E., Hogan, N., & Barton, S. (2003). The impact of work-family conflict on correctional staff job satisfaction. *American Journal of Criminal Justice, 27*, 35–51. doi: 10.1177/1748895806068572.
Land, S. A. (2000). *Child support means more than money: The problem of selective enforcement*. Retrieved July 2013, from http://library.findlaw.com/2000/Aug/1/127286.html.
Lestenkof v. Lestenkof, 2012 WL 205368912 (AK 2012).
Lowery, C. R. (1984). The wisdom of Solomon: Criteria for child custody from the legal and clinical points of view. *Law and Human Behavior, 8*, 371–380.
Mahoney, M. M. (2007). The enforcement of child custody orders by contempt remedies. *University of Pittsburgh Law Review, 68*, 835–877.
Menning, C. L. (2002). Absent parents are more than money: The joint effects of activities and financial support on youths' educational attainment. *Journal of Family Issues, 23*, 648–671. doi: 10.1177/0192513X02023005004.
Myer v. Nebraska, 262 U.S. 390 (1923).
Miller, M. K. (2006). Through the eyes of a father: How PRWORA affects non-resident fathers and their children. *International Journal of Law, Policy and the Family, 20*, 55–73. doi: 10.1093/lawfam/ebi032.
M.L.B. v S.L.J., 117 S.Ct. 555 (1996).
Navarro, M. (September 5, 2008). The bachelor life includes a family. *The New York Times*, p. 1.
Nielsen, L. (2011). Shared parenting after divorce: A review of shared residential parenting research. *Journal of Divorce and Remarriage, 52*, 586–609. doi: 10.1080/10502556.2011.619913.
Orakwusi, A. (2007). Child custody, visitation and termination of parental rights. *Georgetown Journal of Gender and the Law, 8*, 619–655.
Parker, K. (2008). *Save the males: Why men matter why women should care*. New York, NY: Random House.
Paternoster, R., Brame, R., Bachman, R., & Sherman, L. W. (1997). Do fair procedures matter? The effect of procedural justice on spouse assault. *Law and Society Review, 31*, 163–204.
Pearson, J., Davis, L., & Thoennes, N. (2005). A new look at an old issue: An evaluation of the State Access and Visitation Grant Program. *Family Court Review, 43*, 372–385. doi: 10.1111/j.1744-1617.2005.00040.x.
Pearson, J., & Thoennes, N. (1990). Custody after divorce: Demographic and attitudinal patterns. *American Journal of Orthopsychiatry, 60*, 233–249.
Pickar, D. B., & Kahn, J. J. (2011). Settlement-focused parenting plan consultations: An evaluative mediation alternative to child custody evaluations. *Family Court Review, 49*, 59–71. doi: 10.1111/j.1744-1617.2010.01353.x.

Pruett, M. K., Williams, T. Y., Insabella, G., & Little T. D. (2003). Family and legal indicators of child adjustment to divorce among families with young children. *Journal of Family Psychology, 17,* 169–180. doi: 10.1037/0893-3200.17.2.169.

Seltzer, J. A. (1991) Legal custody arrangements and children's economic welfare. *American Journal of Sociology, 96,* 895–929.

Seltzer, J. A., McLanahan, S. S., & Hanson, T. L. (1998) Will child support enforcement increase father-child contact and parental conflict after separation? In I. Garfinkel, S. MacLanahan, D. Meyer J. & J. Seltzer (Eds.), *Fathers under fire: The revolution in child support enforcement* (pp. 157–90). New York, NY: Russell Sage Foundation.

Sen, A. K. (1990) Gender and cooperative conflicts. In I. Tinker (Ed.), *Persistent inequalities* (pp. 123–149). New York, NY: Oxford University Press.

Sherman, L. W., & Smith, D. A. (1992). Crime, punishment, and stake in conformity: Legal and informal control of domestic violence. *American Sociological Review, 57*(5), 680–690.

Sicafuse, L. L., & Bornstein, B. H. (2013). Using the law to enhance wellbeing: Applying therapeutic Jurisprudence in the courtroom. In M. K. Miller & B. H. Bornstein (Eds.), *Stress, trauma, and wellbeing in the legal system* (pp. 15–41). New York, NY: Oxford University Press.

Skinner v. State of Oklahoma ex rel. Williamson, 316 U.S. 535 (1942).

Stewart, M. W., & Wood, S. M. (2013). Civil plaintiffs, trauma, and stress in the legal system. In M. K. Miller & B. H. Bornstein (Eds.), *Stress, trauma, and wellbeing in the legal system* (pp. 123–147). New York, NY: Oxford University Press.

Stolberg, A. L., Volenik, A., Henderson, S. H., Smith, K. C., Van Schaick, K. B., Macie, K. M., ... O'Gara, E. (2002). Denied visitation, its impact on children's psychological adjustment, and a nationwide review of state code. *Journal of Divorce and Remarriage, 36,* 1–19. doi 10.1300/J087v36n03_01.

Thompson, R. A., & Amato, P. R. (1999). *The post divorce family: Children, parenting and society.* Thousand Oaks, CA: Sage.

Troxel v. Granville, 120 S. Ct. 2054 (2000).

Turkat, I. D. (1997). Management of visitation interference. *Judges Journal, 36,* 17–47.

Tyler, T. R. (2006a). Restorative justice and procedural justice; dealing with rule breaking. *Journal of Social Issues, 62,* 307–326. doi: 10.1111/j.1540-4560.2006.00452.x.

Tyler, T. R. (2006b). Psychological perspectives on legitimacy and legitimation. *Annual Review of Psychology, 57,* 375–400. doi: 10.1146/annurev.psych.57.102904.190038.

Tyler, T. R., Boeckmann, R., Smith, H., & Huo, Y. (1997). *Social justice in a diverse society.* Boulder, CO: Westview Press.

Weisz, V., Beal., S. J., & Wingrove, T. (2013). The legal system experiences of children, families, and professionals who work with them. In M. K. Miller & B. H. Bornstein (Eds.), *Stress, trauma, and wellbeing in the legal system* (pp. 63–88). New York, NY: Oxford University Press.

Wexler, D. B., & Winick, B. J. (1991). Therapeutic jurisprudence as a new approach to mental health law policy analysis and research. *University of Miami Law Review, 45,* 979–1004.

Winick, B. J. (1997). The jurisprudence of therapeutic jurisprudence. *Psychology, Public Policy and Law, 3,* 184–206. doi: 10.1037/1076-8971.3.1.184.

Wisconsin v. Yoder, 406 U.S. 205 (1972).

10

Parental Alienation and the Best Interests of the Child

R. Brian Howe and Katherine Covell

> *Hatred is not an emotion that comes naturally to a child. It has to be taught.*
>
> —Judge Gomery of Canada[1]

One of the most harmful possible outcomes of separation and divorce for children is being subjected to parental alienation—being taught to reject, denigrate, or even hate a parent (e.g., Baker, 2005; Clarkson & Clarkson, 2006). Despite widespread evidence of its reality, courts and family law communities have not responded to parental alienation. Denial of its very existence by some, and concerns about its identification or use by others, often have led judges to dismiss claims of parental alienation in custody disputes (Bruch, 2001). Parental alienation violates the best interests of the child, a fundamental principle of family law and the United Nations Convention on the Rights of the Child. This principle is often lost in ideological conflict and intensely political controversy.

In this chapter, we examine the problem of parental alienation from the perspective of the principle of the best interests of the child. We examine the nature of parental alienation, its impact on children, the inadequacy of current legal and policy responses, and reforms that are necessary and in the best interests of the child. Our central argument is that parental alienation is a

---

[1] The above quote is in reference to parental alienation in the case of *PSM v. AJC*, decided by Judge John Gomery on February 15, 1991 (SCM 500-12-184613895).

serious violation of children's fundamental human rights and contrary to their best interests, requiring strong preventive action and early intervention.

Parental Alienation: A General Definition

Since the 1970s, there have been numerous articles written by both researchers and practitioners that describe a child becoming alienated from and hostile toward a parent (see Bernet et al., 2010 for an extensive bibliography). Early observations were similar, but the labels used were different: Among the more common labels were pathological alignment (Wallerstein & Kelly, 1976, 1980) and parental alienation syndrome (Gardner, 1985). These early writings generated a remarkable amount of controversy. As William Bernet and his colleagues (2010) summarized, over the past two decades there has been dissent over the appropriate label (e.g., parental alienation, toxic parent, Medea syndrome, or parental alienation syndrome); the etiology (intentional parent behavior, child avoidance behavior, social worker intrusion, or legal process correlate); and its nature (a diagnosis, disease, disorder, or syndrome).

Rejecting its very existence, the concept of parental alienation has been referred to by critics as "junk science" used to justify custody for fathers (e.g., Faller, 1998; Wilson, 2004). Their overarching concern is the need to protect women and children from abusive fathers who will misuse parental alienation to obtain custody of their children, for instance, by falsely claiming the mother was alienating the child from him (Hoult, 2006; Meier, 2009; Rand, 2011). Meier (2009), for example, expresses her belief that if parental alienation is used in family court disputes, mothers' claims of child sexual abuse or spousal abuse will not be investigated seriously. In fact, she suggests, mothers' claims of abuse will be interpreted simply as evidence of parental alienation. In consequence, protective mothers will be penalized, and documented spouse abusers will be awarded custody or access to children.

It is entirely likely that allegations of parental alienation have been misused by abusive parents to obscure their behavior (Bernet, 2008), and it is possible that abusive fathers have been awarded custody or access inappropriately. But that does not mean that alienation does not exist. What it does mean is that allegations of sexual abuse and allegations of parental alienation should each be thoroughly, and separately, investigated. As Fidler and Bala (2010) pointed out, some children are sexually abused and some are alienated but one does not necessarily include the other.

With the growth of research and clinical observations over the past few years has come more general agreement that parental alienation is a real phenomenon (Bernet et al., 2010). It has become evident that both mothers and fathers engage in parental alienating behaviors (Bernet et al., 2010; Hands & Warshak, 2011; Lavadera, Ferracuti, & Togliatti, 2012). The prevalence of alienating behaviors by either mothers or fathers remains unclear, but estimates indicate it is around 25% to 29% of divorcing parents (Baker, 2010;

Bernet, 2008; Hands & Warshak, 2011). Although parental alienation also occurs in intact families (Gordon, Stoffey, & Bottinelli, 2008), the prevalence is unknown (Fidler & Bala, 2010). It appears to be greatest in high-conflict divorcing families (Bernet, 2008; Johnston, Walters, & Olesen, 2005; Mone & Biringen, 2006), especially when custody and visitation arrangements are court ordered (Spruijt, Eikelenboom, Harmeling, Stokkers, & Kormos, 2005).

In addition to high levels of family conflict, personality characteristics are related to parental alienation. Researchers often report the presence of various personality disorders in the alienating parent (Fidler & Bala, 2010; Gordon et al., 2008). Such parents do not react to the end of a marriage with sadness or a sense of loss; rather, they respond with profound rage, pathological hatred, and desire for revenge (Demby, 2009). In consequence, they use the child as a tool to punish the other parent, have difficulty with empathic responding, and have difficulty appreciating their children's needs. They are unable to see that their child's perspective on the dissolution of the marriage might be quite different from their own (Johnston et al., 2005). Their parenting capacity is vastly impaired. It must be acknowledged that many divorcing parents engage in behaviors that may be seen as alienating, for example, bad-mouthing the other parent. To be considered evidence of parental alienation, however, these behaviors must be intentional, strategic, and involve consistent efforts to create an alliance with the child against the other parent (Baker, 2010). The strategies used are assumed pathological because they reflect the five core manifestations of psychological maltreatment as defined by the American Professional Society on the Abuse of Children: spurning, terrorizing, isolating, corrupting or exploiting, and denying emotional responsiveness (Binggeli, Hart, & Brassard, 2001).

The alienating parent's words and actions convey to the child that the other parent is unworthy of the child's respect, love, and loyalty (Chamberland, Fallon, Black, Trocmé, & Chabot, 2012; Hands & Warshak, 2011). A number of behavioral strategies have been observed among alienating parents. Core among them are vilifying the target parent, limiting communication and contact between the child and the target parent, inducing conflict with the child and the target parent, telling the child the target parent does not love the child, and making unfounded allegations of abuse, neglect, dangerous behavior, or criminal behavior against the target parent (Baker, 2005, 2010; Bow, Gould, & Flens, 2009; Evans, 2006). In addition, the child's emotions are manipulated through becoming angry and eliciting a fear of rejection if the child shows any positive regard for the target parent (Gordon et al., 2008; Teich, 2007). In essence, the child is taught to hate the target parent.

The presence of parental alienation is determined by the resultant child behaviors. The primary behavior that signifies parental alienation is contact or visitation refusal in the absence of legitimate justification (Bernet, 2008). If the child has a history of difficulties with a parent, or if there is a history of maltreatment, then the refusal would be perceived as legitimate. A child who is alienated is one who previously enjoyed a warm relationship with a parent, but after separation refuses to spend time with that parent and cannot provide a logical explanation for that refusal.

Parental alienation is also detected through the child's expressed attitudes and beliefs (Bernet, 2008; Evans, 2006). The child will express a false belief that the target parent is dangerous and must be avoided; in fact, that the parent is "all bad." This extreme and all-encompassing negative response toward a parent is not normally seen in children. Rather, children—even abused children—try to maintain a positive relationship with both parents (Clarkson & Clarkson, 2006). Similarly, children do not lose their love of a parent and come to unambiguously hate that parent simply because of the parent's absence. But pure animosity is characteristic of children who have been subjected to parental alienating behaviors; these children have been taught to hate. Because of such extreme and negative basic beliefs, the child also expresses no remorse about behaving badly to the target parent, behavior that includes imitating the verbal denigration modeled by the alienating parent and derision in response to gifts, support, or any attempt at involvement. The animosity and contact refusal also often generalizes to the extended family of the rejected parent even when the child has had little or no contact with them for some time (Evans, 2006; Fidler & Bala, 2010). They too are seen as "all bad." In fact, the animosity is so all-encompassing that sometimes it even extends to pets of the target parent (Fidler & Bala, 2010).

Effects of Parental Alienation

A child's post-divorce adjustment is affected by parenting behaviors. High-quality parenting by both parents is highly predictive of successful child adaptation (Vélez, Wolchik, Tein, & Sandler, 2011). The key predictor of poor adaptation and emotional and behavior problems is the level and intensity of parental conflict prior to, during, and after the divorce (Jolivet, 2011). Parental conflict, especially in the context of separation and divorce, is a major stressor for children (Kelly & Emery, 2003; Mone & Biringen, 2006). Children who also experience alienation are at risk of a number of psychological difficulties stemming from the loss of the parent, and from the child being taught to deceive, exploit, and denigrate the parent.

The loss of a parent profoundly disrupts the child's attachment relationships, resulting in a loss of trust in others, loss of self-confidence and self-esteem, and difficulties with future relationships (Lowenstein, 2002). Not only is it difficult to trust others but also to trust oneself and one's capacity to perceive others accurately. When children have been alienated from a loving parent with whom they formerly had a good relationship, it is hard for them to reconcile the gap between their memories, experiences, and feelings about that parent with the information they have been given that this parent is worthy only of contempt (Baker, 2005).

Baker (2005) found evidence that children who experienced alienation experience self-hatred, developed in part from learning that they are no longer loved by the target parent and in part from the loss of a previously supportive and loving parent. Children also experience guilt as they mature and come to realize the extent to which they allowed themselves to be exploited and to hurt the target parent. Some attempt to deal with their feelings with drugs and alcohol (Baker, 2005). Most have difficulties with later relationships with their parents and with intimate partners (Gordon et al., 2008).

In addition to these general negative effects of parental alienation, researchers report a range of child outcomes that are associated with psychological maltreatment (Baker & Ben-Ami, 2011). These outcomes include low self-esteem, anxiety, depression, withdrawal, self-destructive or aggressive behaviors, poor impulse control, illogical reasoning, and delayed development (Fidler, Bala, Birnbaum, & Kavassalis, 2008; Lowenstein, 2002).

The Best Interests of the Child

A core principle of modern family law and of international law concerning children is the best interests of the child. According to the United Nations Convention on the Rights of the Child, it is in the best interests of children to have maximum contact and positive healthy relationships with parents. Further, it is not in children's best interests to experience parental alienation. The Convention, approved by the United Nations in 1989 and subsequently ratified by virtually all countries of the world, obligates countries to ensure that their laws, policies, and practices are consistent with the provisions of the Convention, including its general principle of the best interests of the child (Detrick, 1999; Freeman, 2007; Verhellen, 1994). In family law and in child–parent relations, this means that laws and policies must ensure meaningful and maximum contact between children and both parents in postseparation families.

Even in the United States, one of three countries that have yet to ratify the Convention (the others being Somalia and South Sudan), the principles of best interests and parental contact are well established in family law (Kohm, 2008). In most American states, it is expressed in law that after separation, it is in the best interests of children to enjoy maximum contact with both parents unless—for reasons such as past domestic violence or criminality—this is shown to be contrary to their best interests. Moreover, the Convention serves as guide for US policies and practices at some municipal and state levels and for professional practice involving children (Gardinier, 2010; Small & Limber, 2002). In addition, according to Melton (2002), although not yet ratified by the United States, since the Convention has been signed by the American President, the United States is obligated to at least not adopt policies directly contrary to it.

The Convention provides a clear international standard for laws, policies, and practices dealing with child–parent relations after separation and divorce. Under article 3, the Convention states that in all actions concerning children, the best interests of the child shall be a primary consideration. Although the particular content of best interests is not specified in article 3, commentary by the United Nations Committee on the Rights of the Child indicates that "best interests" means not only the general welfare or wellbeing of children but also consistency with the other articles and rights described in the Convention (Freeman, 2007; Hodgkin & Newell, 2007; Howe & Covell, 2013). In particular, best interests require respect for the rights of the child under articles 9, 12, 16, 18, and 19.

Under article 9, children who have been separated from one or both parents have the *right* to maintain personal relationships and contact with both parents on a regular basis. The child's best interests are the only reason to deny contact. A presumption in this article is the importance of contact and of a continuing relationship between children and both parents. Under article 12, children have the right to be heard in all matters that affect them, including custody arrangements and proceedings concerning alienation. Under article 16, children have the right to be protected by the law from any interference with the child's privacy. Such privacy would include the child's private relations with each parent. Interference by an alienating parent would constitute a violation of this right. Under article 19, children are to be protected from all forms of violence, abuse, maltreatment, or exploitation. This would include protection against parental alienation, which is a form of emotional abuse and exploitation by a vengeful parent wanting to alienate the child from the other parent.

Importantly, under article 18, parents have as their basic concern the best interests of the child and both parents have common responsibilities for the upbringing of children. Among other things, this means that a parent has the obligation to respect the rights of the child, including the child's right to have contact with the other parent after separation. The parent is also obliged not to allow ill feelings toward the other parent to interfere with the relations between the children and that parent. It is clear from the Convention that a child's continuing relationship with both parents after separation is in the best interests of the child, and that parental alienation is contrary to the child's best interests. In line with the Convention, in most jurisdictions, the principles of best interests and continuing parental contact are now widely used to guide custody and access decisions (Breen, 2002; Woodhouse, 2006). At the same time, the practice of parental alienation has become widely seen as harmful to children's best interests (Fidler & Bala, 2010; Fidler, Bala, & Saini, 2012). As a result, under family law and in court orders in which one parent is awarded sole custody—still the most common overall outcome—it is usual practice to grant the other parent visitation. In some jurisdictions, to ensure regular contact and continuing parental involvement, there has been the growing use of shared custody and parenting plans and a move toward the principle of equal parental responsibility (Kruk, 2012). There also has been the move in some countries to establish stronger laws in support of contact and against alienation. In the United Kingdom, for example, an initiative was undertaken in 2012 to clarify the law and ensure that children have legal rights to maintain relationships with both parents after a separation (BBC News, 2012). In Brazil, a new law was enacted in 2010 to make parental alienation not only a form of child abuse but also a criminal offense (Library of Congress, 2010).

In summary, to greater or lesser degrees, it has been widely recognized in law that continuing child–parent relationships after separation are in the best interests of the child and that parental alienation is harmful to children's best interests. It is one thing, however, to establish something as a principle and another to put it into effect. There remains a significant gap between the principle of best interests and its implementation. Much of this is due to an approach based on lengthy adversarial proceedings and to the intrusion of gender politics and ideological thinking.

Inadequacy of Current Legal and Policy Responses

Although parental alienation has become recognized as a harmful practice, a problem in many jurisdictions is that legal and policy responses are seriously inadequate. The approach used to deal with alienation tends to be legalistic and reactive rather than proactive, giving little attention to prevention and early intervention (Clarkson & Clarkson, 2006; Fidler & Bala, 2010; Jaffe, Ashbourne, & Mamo, 2010). Responses typically involve lengthy and costly legal procedures. Typically, different judges are involved at different stages of the process, a practice that further adds to delays. Further, procedures are adversarial in nature, featuring competing lawyers who often amplify the conflict and prevent early resolutions of the problem. Contrary to the best interests of children, while cases come to court and drag on through lengthy litigation, parental alienation is allowed to become more entrenched, compromising the healthy development and futures of the children involved.

This does not mean that fair and reasonable decisions are not made in the cases that do go through a lengthy court process (Fidler et al., 2012). In a comprehensive Canadian study, Bala, Hunt, and McCarney (2010), examined 175 cases involving claims of parental alienation between 1989 and 2008. The key challenge for the judges was to determine whether a child's contact refusal was due to genuine parental alienation or some other reason. As found in the study, after considerable deliberation by judges, parental alienation was substantiated in 60% of cases. In the remainder of cases, contact refusal arose from other factors such as previous parental abuse, poor parenting, or the simple disengagement from the parent by a child.

As Bala and colleagues (2010) pointed out, this was a study only of reported legal cases. In the vast majority of cases, target parents of parental alienation have a tendency to give up their effort "to maintain a relationship with a hostile child, either lacking the emotional energy and financial resources to seek to change the situation, or deciding that the child is better off not being 'caught in the middle' of litigation" (p. 165). This clearly is indicative of a flawed legal and policy response to the problem. Target parents are discouraged or prohibited from making a claim of alienation in court due to legal costs. In most jurisdictions, with the high costs of lawyers and with the difficulty of receiving adequate legal aid, many low-income and middle-income parents are unlikely to proceed. Parents are also discouraged by the lengthy litigation and the notorious delays in resolving cases. With multiple meetings and hearings, and with different judges and duelling experts, cases can drift on for years. Finally, target parents are discouraged by an adversarial process that escalates and prolongs conflict, sustaining or increasing emotional difficulties for themselves and the children.

In most jurisdictions, despite calls to improve the process, enforce contact, and ensure the best interests of children, the status quo largely has been maintained (Clarkson & Clarkson, 2006; Jaffe et al., 2010). Much of this has been due to the politics of gender and ideological battles between fathers' rights organizations and women's rights groups. Fathers' rights advocates have claimed that the widespread practice of parental alienation violates the access rights of fathers (Adams, 2006). They call for a reformed system that enforces visitation rights. Women's groups and feminist critics of parental alienation have responded that parental alienation does not exist as a serious problem, and that claims of alienation are a cover for child sexual abuse and domestic violence. In the context of these battles, political and legal authorities have been unwilling to initiate major changes, allowing the costly, reactive, adversarial system to continue. Lost in these battles have been the children, whose rights and best interests have been ignored.

Reforms in the Best Interests of the Child

A major step toward reducing parental alienation would be the replacement of adversarial systems with a parenting plan approach in which parents continue their existing responsibilities and relationships with their children, with the family being restructured rather than disintegrated (Covell, 1999). The articulation of post-divorce parenting plans would facilitate the child's capacity to maintain a meaningful relationship with both parents—one which mirrors the pre-divorce relationship. However, since this approach has yet to be adopted in most jurisdictions, the following discussion is based on current practices. Achieving consistency with the best interests of the child requires the following reforms to optimize the prevention, early intervention, and effective responses to the problem of parental alienation. The key is being proactive rather than reactive.

Parenting Education

A first reform is the requirement of parenting education for all parents considering separation and divorce. Parenting education programs can be designed to reduce conflict after separation, increase parental sensitivity to children's needs, promote more cooperative parenting, educate parents about the rights of the child, and educate parents about the negative effects of family breakdown on children. Parenting education programs exist in many jurisdictions, including 46 states of the United States and all provinces and territories of Canada (Bacon & McKenzie, 2004; Pollett & Lombreglia, 2008). The programs vary in terms of content, duration, and whether they are mandatory or voluntary. Mandatory, lengthy, and comprehensive programs can make a significant contribution to preventing or reducing parental alienation (e.g., Clarkson & Clarkson, 2006).

In a nationwide review of program evaluations of mandatory parent education in the United States, Pollett and Lombregia (2008) reported on the overall effectiveness of programs on reducing conflict, improving parental cooperation, and improving child–parent relations after separation. Their review showed that, although effectiveness varies with factors such as the level of parental conflict and the content of the program, the programs overall have proven to be effective tools for improving conditions for children and parents after separation. Similarly, in a study of programs in Canada, Bacon and McKenzie (2004) concluded that parenting education had overall reduced parental conflict. In their study, although low- to moderate-conflict parents were more influenced by parent education than high-conflict parents, all parents experienced a statistically significant reduction of parental conflict and of conflict in which children were caught in the middle. This indicates that although strong parental education programs may not be the full answer to severe cases of parental alienation in high-conflict families, programs may make a major contribution to reducing alienating behavior. The evidence suggests a need for comprehensive parenting programs early in the separation process, but more interventions are clearly needed for high-conflict parents who cannot be reached through parenting education.

Early Assessment

A second reform, which can take place during parenting education sessions, is the routine and systematic use of assessments in three areas: pre-separation child–parent relationships, parenting capacity, and children's views. Obtaining baseline data on parent–child relationships prior to or at the time of separation would provide an invaluable tool for assessing whether alienation exists if reported later. For example, if a child has a very good relationship with his father—as indicated in joint activities and paternal involvement in schooling, recreation, and child care—but post-separation reports of the father as abusive surface, or the child begins to refuse visitations with the father, this would be strongly suggestive of alienation. Such reports would likely reflect efforts by the mother (in this instance), to break the relationship between the child and his father in the absence of any legitimate justification for so doing.

Parenting capacity assessments can be used to identify the presence of mental illness, which as noted earlier, is often a source of the problem (Jaffe et al., 2010), and the future likelihood of alienation. Some jurisdictions (e.g., Australia, New Zealand) currently use parenting capacity assessments when parents are in a custody dispute, but concerns have been raised that positive self-presentation can compromise the validity of the assessments (e.g., Carr, Moretti, & Cue, 2005). However, as Carr and his colleagues pointed out, you do not disconnect a smoke detector because its sound is annoying. There are means of testing that optimize the validity of the results and those working in child protection have many examples of appropriate procedures that lessen the problem of biased self-presentation (e.g., Harnett, 2007). What would seem most important to the prevention of parental alienation is an assessment that measures the parents' willingness to cooperate with each other to enable continued parenting with the least possible disruption to the child's existing relationship with each parent. This would involve assessing parents' capacity for empathy—understanding and appreciating that the child's perspective is different from their own—and their sensitivity to the child's response to the separation and wishes for the future. Given the high proportion of alienating parents with personality disorders, it would be very useful also to assess parents' flexibility of reflective reasoning and capacity to consider a variety of options, as well as to determine their feelings toward the other parent. Such assessments are less likely tainted by self-presentation bias.

Consistent with the child's participation rights, a concomitant assessment should take place with the children involved. Children do not have a right to choice in custody disputes, but they do have a right to voice their opinions (McIntosh, 2009). This may not be easy. Although children tend to be more honest than adults—they are, for example, less likely to speak in euphemisms, theorize, and filter the truth—it may be difficult to assess their feelings because they may be afraid of hurting a parent or having a parent seek revenge on them. But these difficulties can be overcome. Children's views can accurately be assessed and used as a tool to help determine how well the parent understands the child, as expressed in the parenting capacity assessments. The UK Children and Family Court Advisory Support Service (Cafcass), which includes youth experienced with custody conflicts, provides a good model of child participation. Cafcass is independent of the courts, social services, education authorities, and other agencies. Although critics suggest that Cafcass falls short of the Convention requirements for participation (e.g., Fortin, 2009), the provisions for listening to children are well articulated. The booklets they have developed and used to promote the voices of children allow for a nonthreatening way for them to express their needs, wishes, and feelings directly to the judge. In addition, there needs to be provision for children's ongoing participation through the period of family readjustment. This would allow the early identification of problems and the timely interventions that are essential to prevent severe alienation and its negative developmental outcomes.

Swift Court Action

Whereas taking the proactive measures described earlier may reduce alienation, they are unlikely to eliminate it. It is therefore crucial that there be swift court action when its presence is suspected. This is the third reform. Courts would be well positioned to identify alienation if they had the baseline data on child–parent relationships, parenting capacity, and children's views as described earlier. As noted by Clarkson and Clarkson (2006), courts have remained hesitant to act because of the controversy surrounding the existence of parental alienation, suspicion that abusive parents may use alienation as a cover for child abuse, and a tendency to defer decisions until formal assessments have been made by experts or mental health professionals—which can take much time. Proactive assessments should significantly reduce the delays currently associated with the existing approaches to assessments. Court-appointed assessors such as those used in New Zealand (rather than duelling experts hired by competing lawyers) are also necessary to reduce delays in the identification and response to alienation (Clarkson & Clarkson 2006). Moreover, the common responses of orders for interim contact (Clarkson & Clarkson, 2006), referral to counseling (Fidler & Bala, 2010), and referral to mediation or alternative dispute resolution (Jaffe et al., 2010) need to be accompanied by time limitations to ensure timely resolutions. Interventions are, of course, more swift and effective when there is adequate case management.

Case Management

A fourth reform is the use of single-judge case management. As explained by Martinson (2010), in many jurisdictions and especially in North America, high-conflict cases are often dealt with by several judges at different stages of the process and by judges who are generalists without specialized knowledge of the issues. This contributes significantly to delays because judges who are new to a case must take extra time to become familiar with the parties and issues. This is a particular problem where there is alienation. A family can appear in front of 10 different judges before they even get to trial (Fidler et al., 2012). Thus, parents who are manipulative and alienating their children can prolong the process such that the effect on the children becomes more severe.

A much better approach is a system of single-judge case management. Under such a system, single judges with expertise in family law and in matters of separation and custody would have continuous involvement with a case at its different stages and would be better positioned to understand the context of each stage of a case, to see patterns in a case, and to understand the underlying family dynamics. The length of time for a case would be reduced and specialist judges would be more able to make informed decisions in children's best interests.

Stricter Accountability

Finally, it is crucial that reform takes place to ensure that parents who engage in alienating strategies are held accountable. Currently, it is mostly parents who default on their financial obligations who are held accountable. This sends a message that the most important role played by a noncustodial parent is monetary. The zero-tolerance approach to enforcing child support orders also needs to be applied to enforcement of access orders (see also Chapter 9 of this volume for further discussion on visitation enforcement). The Convention on the Rights of the Child assigns parenting responsibilities to both parents; it does not hold one parent responsible for financial support and the other for all other parenting responsibilities. More important, the Convention explicitly provides the child a fundamental right to a relationship with both parents (with the exception of abusive parents). Thus, parents who deny a relationship through alienation strategies are in contravention of their child's rights and should be held legally accountable. They are also violating their child's right to protection from abuse, as called for by article 19 of the Convention. Parental alienation, then, should be part of child protection legislation and included in all definitions of emotional and psychological maltreatment. As with parents who are found to abuse their children, alienating parents must be held fully accountable through such means as loss of custody or involvement in an intensive treatment program.

Conclusion

Parental alienation is a harmful practice in which one parent makes a purposive effort to undermine a child's previously positive relationship with the other parent and to alienate that child from the other parent. This is contrary to the best interests of the child and the Convention on the Rights of the Child. But in most jurisdictions, current legal responses remain inadequate because of lengthy adversarial proceedings and the intrusion of the politics of gender. Against the practice of parental alienation and in line with the principle of the best interests of the child, what are required are comprehensive parenting education, early assessment and detection, swift court action, single-judge case management, and systems of stricter parental accountability.

References

Adams, M. (2006). Framing contests in child custody disputes: Parental alienation syndrome, child abuse, gender, and fathers' rights. *Family Law Quarterly, 40*(2), 315–338.

Bacon, B., & McKenzie, B. (2004). Parent education after separation/divorce: Impact of the level of parental conflict on outcomes. *Family Court Review, 42*, 85–98. doi:10.1177/1531244504421007.

Baker, A. J. (2005). The long-term effects of parental alienation on adult children: A qualitative research study. *American Journal of Family Therapy, 33*, 289–302. doi:1080/01926180590962129.

Baker, A. J. (2010). Adult recall of parental alienation in a community sample: Prevalence and associations with psychological maltreatment. *Journal of Divorce and Remarriage, 51*, 16–35. doi:10.1080/10502550903423206.

Baker, A. J., & Ben-Ami, N. (2011). To turn a child against a parent is to turn a child against himself; The direct and indirect effects of exposure to parental alienation strategies on self-esteem and well-being. *Journal of Divorce and Remarriage, 52*, 472–489. doi:10.1080/01926180590962129.

Bala, N., Hunt, S., & McCarney, C. (2010). Parental alienation: Canadian court cases 1989-2008. *Family Court Review, 48*, 164–179. doi:10.1111/j.1744-1617.2009.01296.x.

BBC News. (2012, February 3). Children to get access rights to both parents. Retrieved August 2013, from http://www.bbc.co.uk/news/uk-16865916. July 2012.

Bernet, W. (2008). Parental alienation disorder and DSM-V. *The American Journal of Family Therapy, 36*, 349–366. doi:10.1080/01926180802405513.

Bernet, W., von Boch-Galhau, W., Baker, A L., & Morrison, S. L. (2010). Parental alienation, DSM-V, and ICD-11. *American Journal of Family Therapy, 38*, 76–187. doi:10.1080/01926180903586583.

Binggeli, N. J., Hart, S. N. & Brassard, M. R. (2001). *Psychological maltreatment of children: The APSAC Study Guides 4.* Thousand Oaks, CA: Sage

Bow, J. N., Gould, J. W., & Flens, J. R. (2009). Examining parental alienation in child custody cases: A survey of mental health and legal professionals. *American Journal of Family Therapy, 37*, 127–145. doi:10.1080/01926180801960658.

Breen, C. (2002). *The standard of the best interests of the child: A western tradition in international and comparative law.* The Hague, The Netherlands: Martinus Nijhoff.

Bruch, C. (2001). Parental alienation syndrome and parental alienation: Getting it wrong in child custody cases. *Family Law Quarterly, 35*(3), 527–552.

Carr, G. D, Moretti, M. M, & Cue, B. J. H (2005). Evaluating parenting capacity: Validity problems with MMPI-2, PAI, CAPI and ratings of child adjustment. *Professional Psychology: Research and Practice, 36*, 188–196. doi:10.1037/0735-7028.36.2.188.

Chamberland, C., Fallon, B., Black, T., Trocmé, N., & Chabot, M. (2012). Correlates of substantiated emotional maltreatment in the second Canadian Incidence Study. *Journal of Family Violence, 27*, 201–213. doi: 10.1007/s10896-012-9414-8.

Clarkson, D., & Clarkson, H. (2006). The unbreakable chain under pressure: The management of post-separation parental rejection. *Journal of Social Welfare and Family Law, 29*, 251–266. doi:10.1037/0735-7028.36.2.188.

Covell, K. (1999). Promoting parenting plans: A new role for the psychologist in custody disputes. *Expert Evidence, 7* (2), 113–126. doi:10.1023/A:1008959116573.

Demby, S. (2009). Interparent hatred and its impact on parenting: Assessment in forensic custody evaluations. *Psychoanalytic Inquiry, 29,* 477–490. doi: 10.1080/07351690903013959.

Detrick, S. (1999). *A commentary on the United Nations Convention on the Rights of the Child*. The Hague, The Netherlands: Martinus Nijhoff.

Evans, R. A., (2006). Treatment considerations with children diagnosed with PAS. *The Florida Bar Journal, 80,* 69–72.

Faller, K. C. (1998). The parental alienation syndrome: What is it and what data support it? *Child Maltreatment, 3,* 100–115. doi:10.1177/1077559598003002005.

Fidler, B. J., & Bala, N. (2010). Children resisting postseparation contact with a parent: Concepts, controversies, and conundrums. *Family Court Review, 48,* 10–47. doi:10.1111/j.1744-1617.2009.01287.x.

Fidler, B.J., Bala, N., Birnbaum, R., & Kavassalis, K. (2008). *Challenging issues in child custody disputes: A guide for legal and mental health professionals*. Toronto, ON: Carswell.

Fidler, B. J., Bala, N., & Saini, M. A. (2012). *Children who resist postseparation parental conflict: A differential approach for legal and mental health professionals*. New York, NY: Oxford University Press.

Fortin, J. (2009). *Children's rights and the developing law*. Cambridge, UK: Cambridge University Press.

Freeman, M. (2007). The best interests of the child. In A. Alen, J. Lanotte, E. Verhellen, F. Ang, E. Berghmans, M. Verheyde, & B. Abramson (Eds.), *A commentary on the United Nations Convention on the Rights of the Child* (Vol. 3, pp. 1–79. Leiden, The Netherlands: Martinus Nijhoff.

Gardinier, M. (2010). Introduction: Why should the United States ratify the Convention on the Rights of the Child? *Child Welfare: Journal of Policy, Practice, and Program, 89,* 7–13.

Gardner, R. A. (1985). Recent trends in divorce and custody litigation. *Academy Forum, 29,* 3–7.

Gordon, R. M., Stoffey, R., & Bottinelli, J. (2008). MMPI-2 findings of primitive defenses in alienating parents. *American Journal of Family Therapy, 36,* 211–228. doi:10.1080/01926180701643313.

Hands, A. J., & Warshak, R. A. (2011). Parental alienation among college students. *American Journal of Family Therapy, 39,* 431–443. doi:10.1080/01926187.2011.575336.

Harnett, P. H. (2007). A procedure for assessing parents' capacity for change in child protection cases. *Child and Youth Services Review, 29,* 1179–1188. doi:10.1016/j.childyouth.2007.04.005.

Hodgkin, R., & Newell, P. (2007). *Implementation handbook for the Convention on the Rights of the Child*. New York, NY: UNICEF.

Hoult, J. (2006). The evidentiary admissibility of parental alienation syndrome: Science, law and policy. *Children's Legal Rights Journal, 1,* 1–61.

Howe, R. B., & Covell, K. (2013). *Education in the best interests of the child: A children's rights perspective on closing the achievement gap*. Toronto, ON: University of Toronto Press.

Jaffe, P. G., Ashbourne, D., & Mamo, A. A. (2010). Early identification and prevention of parent-child alienation: A framework for balancing risks and benefits of intervention. *Family Court Review, 48*(1), 136–152. doi:10.1111/j.1744-1617.2009.01294.x.

Johnston, J. R., Walters, M. G., & Olesen, N. W. (2005). Is it alienating parenting, role reversal or child abuse? A study of children's rejection of a parent in child custody disputes. *Journal of Emotional Abuse, 5*, 191–218. doi:10.1300/J135v05n0402.

Jolivet, K. R. (2011). The psychological impact of divorce on children: What is a family lawyer to do? *American Journal of Family Law, 25*(4), 175–183.

Kelly, J. B., & Emery, R. E. (2003). Children adjustment following divorce: Risk and resilience perspective. *Family Relations, 52*, 352–362. doi:10.1111/j.1741-3729.2003.00352.x.

Kohm, L. M. (2008). Tracing the foundations of the best interests standard in American jurisprudence. *Journal of Law and Family Studies, 10*, 227–373.

Kruk, E. (2012). Arguments for an equal parental responsibility presumption in contested child custody. *American Journal of Family Therapy, 40*, 33–55. doi:10.1080/01926187.2011.575344.

Lavadera, A. L., Ferracuti, S., & Togliatti, M. M. (2012). Parental alienations syndrome in Italian legal judgments: An exploratory study. *International Journal of Law and Psychiatry, 35*, 334–342. doi:10.1016/j.ijlp.2012.04.005.

Library of Congress. (2010). Brazil: Parental alienation criminalized. Retrieved July 2013, from http://www.loc.gov/lawweb/servlet/lloc_news?disp3_l205402210_text.

Lowenstein, L. F. (2002). Problems suffered by children due to the effects of parental alienation syndrome. *Justice of the Peace, 166*(24), 464–466.

Martinson, D. (2010). One case—one specialized judge: Why courts have an obligation to manage alienation and other high-conflict cases. *Family Court Review, 48*, 180–189. doi:10.1111/j.1744-1617.2009.01297.x.

McIntosh, J. E. (2009). Four young people speak about children's involvement in family court matters. *Journal of Family Studies, 15*, 98–103. doi:10.5172/jfs.327.15.1.98.

Meier, J. S. (2009). Parental alienation syndrome and parental alienation: Research reviews. VAWnet.*org*. Retrieved July 2013, from http://www.vawnet.org/Assoc_Files_VAWnet/AR_PAS.pdf

Melton, G. (2002). Starting a new generation of research. In B. Bottoms, M. Kovera, & B. McAuliff (Eds.), *Children, social science and the law* (pp. 449–453). Cambridge, UK: Cambridge University Press.

Mone, J. G., & Biringen, Z. (2006). Perceived parent-child alienation: Empirical assessment of parent-child relationships within divorced and intact families. *Journal of Divorce and Remarriage, 45*, 131–156. doi:10.1300/J087v45n03-07.

Pollet, S., & Lombreglia, M. (2008). A nationwide survey of mandatory parent education. *Family Court Review, 46*, 375–394. doi:10.1111/j.1744-1617.2008.00207.x.

Rand, D. C. (2011). Parental alienation critics and the politics of science. *American Journal of Family Therapy, 39*, 48–71. doi:10.1080/01926187.2010.533085.

Small, M., & Limber, S. (2002). Advocacy for children's rights. In B. Bottoms, M. Kovera, & B. McAuliff (Eds.), *Children, social science and the law* (pp. 64–72). Cambridge, UK: Cambridge University Press.

Spruijt, E., Eikelenboom, B., Harmeling, J.,Stokkers, R., & Kormos, H. (2005). Parental Alienation Syndrome (PAS) in the Netherlands. *American Journal of Family Therapy, 33*, 303–317. doi:10.1080/01926180590962110.

Teich, M. (2007). A divided house. *Psychology Today, 40*(3), 92–102.

Vélez, C. E., Wolchik, S. A., Tein, J., & Sandler, I. (2011). Protecting children from the consequences of divorce: A longitudinal study of the effects of parenting on children's coping processes. *Child Development, 82*, 244–257. doi: 10.1111/J.1467-8624.2010.01553.

Verhellen, E. (1994). *Convention on the Rights of the Child*. Kessel-Lo, Belgium: Garant.

Wallerstein, J. S., & Kelly, J. B. (1976). The effects of parental divorce: Experiences of the child in later latency. *American Journal of Orthopsychiatry, 46*, 256–269. doi:10.1111/j.1939-0025.1976.tb00926.x.

Wallerstein, J. S., & Kelly, J. B. (1980). *Surviving the breakup*. New York, NY: Basic Books.

Wilson, T. (2004). Discredited junk science justifies custody for fathers. *Off Our Backs, 34*(1/2), 46–48.

Woodhouse, B. (2006). The changing status of the child. In J. Todres, M. Wojcik, & C. Revaz (Eds.), *The UN Convention on the Rights of the Child: An analysis of treaty provisions and implications for U.S. ratification* (pp. 51–63). Ardsley, NY: Transnational.

Part III

LEGAL ACTIONS AFFECTING THE WELLBEING OF CHILDREN

11

The Search for Therapeutic Solutions to Maternal Incarceration: Promoting the Wellbeing of Children

Monica K. Miller and Lacey Miller

There are an increasing number of mothers in prison, affecting as many as 147,000 children (Christian, 2009). This problem is so widespread that 10% of children whose parents are not married and 4% of children whose parents are married will experience their mother's incarceration before they are 5 years old (Fragile Families Research Brief, 2008). This is a legal and social issue because many children do not cope well with losing contact with their incarcerated mothers (e.g., Clarke, 2006). The loss of contact is likely to have significant impact on the children's lives. For example, children of incarcerated parents are six times more likely to be incarcerated as adults than children who have not had incarcerated parents (Finney Hairston, 2007); thus, maternal incarceration is part of a cycle of intergenerational incarceration (DeAngelis, 2001). Further, children of incarcerated mothers are at greater risk of psychological problems such as anxiety, guilt, depression, and low self-esteem (Clarke, 2006).

After their mothers' imprisonment, many children are placed in alternative residences; many go to live with their grandparents, while others move in with family friends or go into the foster care system (Genty, 2007). Conversely, when fathers are incarcerated, more than 90% of children are cared for by their mothers (Acoca & Raeder, 1999; Genty, 2007). Thus, the issue of paternal incarceration is not inconsequential; however, maternal incarceration is unique because of its impact on children, which is why this chapter will focus on maternal incarceration.

Maternal incarceration is an ongoing concern. If left unaddressed, this issue will continue to affect the wellbeing of families and be a burden to society and the criminal justice system. The principles of therapeutic jurisprudence can serve as the basis for policy recommendations that can address this growing issue in a positive way.

Precursors and Consequences of Maternal Incarceration

Prior to the late 1980s, the number of women in prison was so low that problems that women prisoners faced were not considered areas in need of research or policy reform (Acoca & Raeder, 1999). Before the "war on drugs," which gained strength during this time, women accounted for a mere 5% of prison inmates (Acoca & Raeder, 1999). Between 1990 and 1998, the number of women in prison increased by 88% (Katz, 2002) and the number of children with incarcerated mothers rose 131% (Glaze & Maruschak, 2008). This increase is directly related to the war on drugs, because a large proportion of female inmates are convicted of drug-related offenses. Female drug offenders accounted for 34% of state prisoners and 72% of female federal prisoners in the 1990s (Acoca & Raeder, 1999). Prior to the war on drugs, most women were typically considered for alternative sentencing, good time credits, and early parole because their offenses were not considered serious and they were not considered to be at risk of fleeing. Legislation related to the war on drugs, however, established statutes for mandatory minimum sentences, statutory enhancements for repeat offenders, and truth in sentencing (ensuring that inmates serve their full sentences rather than receiving early parole); this legislation increased prison populations dramatically, especially among females (Acoca & Raeder, 1999). The purposes of these laws were to achieve certainty and equality of punishment and to ensure that these punishments were carried out (Gest, 2001). Originally, this legislation was largely enacted to target violent male offenders, yet nonviolent offenders and female offenders also have been impacted by these sentencing guidelines (Clarke, 2006).

One reason the war on drugs had such a profound impact on the growth of female prison populations is because the scope of enforcement was broadened so that people less directly involved with drugs became targets. Women frequently become associated with illegal activities through social contacts, such as boyfriends or husbands who are drug dealers (Acoca & Raeder, 1999). Conspiracy laws adopted during the war on drugs affected many women because the laws assume that they are at least knowledgeable of their significant others' criminal activity and are therefore conspirators. Some women find it hard to leave their relationships because of emotional attachments, economic dependency, or fear of abuse (Clarke, 2006). Thus, they stay in relationships that put them at risk for being charged with conspiracy or other crimes that were more directly committed by their significant others. Of course, there are many women involved with the criminal system who did not have such a history and who were not associated with a male criminal; however, the point here is that the war on drugs increased the number of women who have become entrenched in the criminal justice system.

Unfortunately, legislation and polices resulting in an increase of imprisoned mothers also created "collateral damage" to their children (Clarke, 2006). Many children experience the consequences of these policies. Nearly 70% of female prisoners are mothers (Clarke, 2006), which translates to as many as 147,000 affected children (Christian, 2009). In total, 2% of American children have at least one parent in prison and slightly less than that have both parents incarcerated (Genty, 2007).

The major consequence for children is that they will likely experience a change in their living situation. Sixty percent of women in state prisons were living with their children either at the time of arrest or within a month prior to incarceration and 42% were the primary caregiver and financial supporter of their children (Glaze & Maruschak, 2008). Similar percentages were found for female inmates in federal prisons (Glaze & Maruschak, 2008). Maternal incarceration thus affects many children, who are likely to experience major changes in their lives. Specifically, many will lose contact with their mothers and face new living situations. Only 28% of children whose mothers go to prison are cared for by fathers (Clarke, 2006). For mothers in state prisons, 53% of their children currently live with grandparents, 26% live with other relatives, and 10% live in foster care (Mumola, 2000); these rates are similar for women in federal prisons (Mumola, 2000). When a child's mother is imprisoned, the child will likely be uprooted from home and experience entirely new routines and environments (Dalley, 2000).

There are a variety of consequences that result from the change in living situation. While some children might benefit from being removed from their mothers' care (e.g., if they were abused or neglected), many will experience a great deal of stress related to adjusting to their new homes. Some stressors are financial, as 40% of these new caregivers are unemployed; and for those who do work, the mean annual income is just over $23,000 (Poelmann, 2003). Many of these caregivers are also in poor health and are already taking care of children of their own (Poelmann, 2003). The economic burden of taking on another dependent adds to caregivers' own stress, which is in turn a stressor for the child. These caregivers might have to increase work hours in order to sustain their homes, leaving children without an available parental figure, and thus increasing the child's feelings of abandonment (Murray, 2007). Moreover, children left with relatives or placed in foster care have an increased chance of physical or sexual abuse (DeAngelis, 2001; Look, 2008). While these situations apply primarily to family caregivers, here are other negative effects of living in foster care, such as an increased risk of becoming addicted to substances, dropping out of school, becoming homeless, or being imprisoned (Doyle, 2011).

Thus, the war on drugs included laws and policies that led to increased incarceration of women. Maternal incarceration has consequences for children, including new living arrangements, which threaten the child's wellbeing, as detailed next.

The Wellbeing of Children of Incarcerated Mothers

The problems that children of incarcerated mothers face are multifold and vary depending on factors such as the age of the children, the degree of separation, and the level of mother–child bonding they experienced prior to incarceration (Katz, 2002). Factors such as socioeconomics, family dynamics, and support systems also can moderate the effects of maternal incarceration on children. While a complete examination of the many factors that impact the wellbeing of children of incarcerated mothers is beyond the scope of this chapter, a brief review is needed to understand the reasons why laws, policies, and programs that protect children's wellbeing are needed.

Attachment theorists indicate that separation during infancy can have negative effects on the development of the mother–child relationship (Katz, 2002) and whether a child forms healthy relationships throughout life (Pojman, 2001–2002). Children of incarcerated parents are likely to experience psychological problems such as shame, guilt, and low self-esteem (Clarke, 2006) and antisocial-delinquent outcomes (Murray & Farrington, 2008). For instance, children of prisoners have about twice the risk of anxiety and depression (Murray & Farrington, 2008; see also, Clarke, 2006) and three times the risk of developing antisocial behaviors than children whose parents do not experience incarceration (Murray, 2007). Children whose parents were incarcerated have even more extreme emotional and violence issues than children whose parents were not incarcerated—and this is more pronounced if the incarcerated parent was the mother rather than the father (Novero, Loper, & Warren, 2011). These problems are not reserved for an isolated few, as 76% of children suffer significant emotional problems (Dalley, 2000).

In addition to suffering emotional and behavioral problems, children of incarcerated parents are stigmatized by peers, teachers, and the media. Such societal agents frequently label people who commit crimes as "thugs" and "convicts" in a negative tone (Krupat, 2007). Children of incarcerated parents may feel that, by virtue of their parents' reputation, they will turn out the same way (Bernberg, Krohn, & Rivera, 2006; Krupat, 2007). Often times, the children feel like they are "bad apples, fallen from the tree" (Krupat, 2007). Thus, it is of little surprise that children of incarcerated parents are at increased risk of truancy, drug and alcohol use, and becoming offenders (Clarke, 2006). Thus, maternal incarceration has contributed to intergenerational incarceration (DeAngelis, 2001).

Children with imprisoned mothers also struggle academically (Clarke, 2006; Hagan & Foster, 2012) and are at greatest risk to drop out of school when their mothers are imprisoned (Cho, 2011). This negative effect on educational performance can "spill over" to the entire school; schools with high rates of students with imprisoned mothers have reduced graduation rates as compared to schools with lower rates (Hagan & Foster, 2012), suggesting that maternal incarceration has widespread effects on society in general—not just on the children of incarcerated mothers. Whether children of incarcerated parents are predisposed to develop sociological, psychological, or behavioral problems, or whether such threats to wellbeing are a result of maternal incarceration, the statistics reveal that they are at increased risk of these threats to wellbeing compared to their peers.

Although the wellbeing of mothers is beyond the scope of this chapter on child wellbeing, it is important to note that mothers also experience threats to their own wellbeing related to separation from their children (Foster, 2012); these threats can, in turn, have a negative effect on the children. For instance, mothers are concerned about their children's wellbeing, are saddened and frightened by separation from their children, and are concerned about the inability to bond with their children (Hutchinson, Moore, Propper, & Mariaskin, 2008). In general, "parenting stress" is positively related to violence, aggression, and depression (Loper, Carlson, Levitt, & Scheffel, 2009); indeed, 90% of imprisoned mothers suffer from mental disorders, including depression (Gregoire, Dolan, Birmingham, Mullee, & Coulson, 2010). Mothers express guilt and shame about how their behaviors negatively affect their children and sometimes adopt maladaptive coping strategies (Celinska & Siegel, 2010). Studies such as these indicate that mothers are subject to a variety of threats to their wellbeing because of separation from their children. This can have a secondary effect on the children, for instance, if the mother's stress leads to aggression directed toward the child.

This brief review illustrates the many threats to wellbeing that children face when their mothers are incarcerated. Some prisons have recognized this issue as one that needs to be addressed and have adopted programs to help mothers and their children.

Current Programs for Incarcerated Mothers and Their Children

In some states, programs are available that encourage the bonding and continued relationship between incarcerated mothers and their children. Research has indicated that visitation is essential to maintaining parent–child relationships and increasing the success of reunification upon release (Christian, 2009). Some programs transport children to prisons for visits with their mothers. Other programs teach mothers how to properly communicate with, nurture, and discipline their children. Some programs within correctional facilities provide nurseries to accommodate mothers and infants (Mauskopf, 1998).

Some goals of these programs are to (1) teach incarcerated mothers parenting skills and allow them opportunity to practice parenting in a supportive environment, (2) teach mothers and children coping skills, (3) prevent negative consequences (e.g., depression, recidivism) mothers might experience as a result of being away from their children, and (4) allow children to be motivation for mothers to succeed in their rehabilitation. In order to reach these goals, counseling is sometimes provided by child welfare agencies for children in foster care. Some programs teach mothers parenting skills and encourage them to bond with and nurture their infants, while others teach mothers to take an active role in the development and support of their children by doing the simple things like making photo albums. When regular parent–child interaction does not occur, the basics of parenting can be easily forgotten (DeAngelis, 2001). Thus, it is essential that mothers continue their roles as mothers, even while in prison. Further, many mothers did not learn parenting skills from their own parents—thus, it is essential to break the cycle of poor role modeling and parenting practices.

Some programs are intended to promote mothers' rehabilitation and protect the family (Look, 2008). For example, within the Chicago area, the Residential Treatment and Transition Center provides treatment and focuses on maintaining family structure. In this program, incarcerated women undergo 4 months of intensive substance abuse treatment; they then live in a subsidized apartment with their children while they complete treatment and job training (Look, 2008). The expectation is that women who are able to keep their families intact will view their children as motivation for continued rehabilitation and developing a healthy and crime-free life. Another program for female inmates is the Bayview Correctional Facility in New York (New York Department of Corrections and Community Supervision, 2009). Female inmates within 6 months of release are transferred to this re-entry unit; community service agents help ease reintegration into the community and family life (New York State Department of Corrections and Community Supervision, 2013). Such programs help women with their rehabilitation and help keep families intact while mothers serve their time.

Other prisons have started nurseries or extended visitation programs to address the issues surrounding maternal incarceration. The Nebraska Correctional Center for Women has been addressing problems of incarcerated mothers since 1974 (with the start of the nursery program in 1994) and has successfully decreased risk factors for children (Jordan, 2011). The program consists of parenting classes, extended day and overnight visits with children, and a prison nursery (Nebraska Department of Correctional Services, 2013). Mothers can receive up to five overnight visits per month and extended day visits with their children in the nursery area. In order to qualify for this privilege, mothers must not have committed any recent misconduct. Children are permitted to visit their mothers in this capacity from birth to 16 years of age. The nursery is separate from the general prison area and provides room for up to eight prisoners to live in the nursery with their children for up to 18 months. Mothers who qualify for the nursery program must meet strict eligibility standards; for instance, the mother must have given birth while in prison and is expected to be released within 18 months (Nebraska Department of Correctional Services, 2013). These requirements suggest the program focuses on helping new mothers who will be released soon, rather than mothers who will be in prison for a long time or have older children with whom they may or may not have an established relationship.

Similarly, the Family Service Program at Bedford Hills Facility in New York offers parenting programs for both incarcerated parents and their significant others, counseling services, family support services, mentoring for children, and a nursery. One of the programs at Bedford Hills is a week-long summer camp (Kauffman, 2001). During this week, the children are hosted by a family in the nearby town and visit their mothers daily. The nursery at Bedford is primarily for incarcerated women who are going to give birth while they are in prison and are expected to be released within a short time after giving birth. Mothers are allowed to stay in the nursery with their infants until they are 1 year old; however, extensions can be granted if the mother will be released within the 6 months following (Kauffman, 2001).

Another program, called Girl Scouts Beyond Bars (Girl Scouts of the USA, 2007), serves hundreds of girls and their mothers annually throughout the nation. The Girl Scouts Beyond Bars program provides activities ranging from life skills to the arts; they also help mothers plan for their release. They provide transportation for the girls to visit their mothers in prison, where they have troop meetings and projects. They also provide services and assistance to the caregivers (e.g., foster parents) of the children (Girl Scouts of the USA, 2007). Programs such as these potentially allow women to continue to grow and develop as mothers; they also reduce psychological harm to both mother and child caused by separation.

Although few studies have examined the effectiveness of such programs, the existing research has indicated that a host of benefits are possible. Compared to a control group, mothers who participated in parenting classes had less distress about visitation with their children (Loper & Tuerk, 2011) and lowered recidivism after prison release (see Campbell & Carlson, 2012 for review). Further, participating also reduced participants' stress related to parenting, improved relationships with caregivers, reduced mental distress (Loper & Tuerk, 2011), increased mothers' knowledge about appropriate parenting practices (e.g., age-appropriate experiences), increased appropriate discipline practices, increased mothers' empathetic understanding of their children's emotions, and improved responsible parenting behavior (Sandifer, 2008). Another study indicated that children raised in a prison nursery developed healthy attachment, regardless of their mother's level of attachment; the rate of healthy attachment was higher than a nonincarcerated control group (e.g., mothers with low income, drug use) and was similar to healthy community children (Byrne, Goshin, & Joestl, 2010). Although some programs have not shown significant benefits for children's wellbeing (e.g., Kubiak, Kasiborski, & Schmittel, 2010), many others have revealed that programs do in fact reach their goals. Because there is very little research, and some studies have significant methodological limitations, "success" should be determined with caution. Further, it is possible that evaluations that show no results do not get published in academic journals. As a result, it is not possible at this point to compare programs' outcomes or determine the "best practices" for addressing maternal incarceration.

The programs described earlier are not available on a national level and only reach a small number of children who have incarcerated mothers. It is encouraging, however, that these programs have taken on a more rehabilitative approach rather than a punitive-only approach. As some research has noted, not only does maintaining and supporting the parent–child relationship have potential to ease the stress of incarceration, but it also has potential to increase the likelihood of successful reunification upon release (Finney Hairston, 2007). Such programs can adhere to the principles of therapeutic jurisprudence, which has been defined by one of its creators as the study of the "healing potential" of the law (Winick, 2006).

Therapeutic Jurisprudence

Therapeutic jurisprudence is a way of viewing the law through the "lens" of social science theories (Winick, 2006). For instance, legal actors should consider the psychological and sociological *influences* on crime. Sometimes these influences (e.g., mental health problems or drug addiction) can be addressed, making it less likely that the criminal will recidivate. Legal actors should also consider the psychological and sociological *effects* of legal decisions. Sometimes legal actions can make a person's circumstances more dire (e.g., cause the person to become unemployed), thus increasing the person's chances of recidivism. Legal actors following the principles of therapeutic jurisprudence view legal matters in a sensitive and thoughtful manner yet without ignoring the purpose of exacting justice (Wexler, 1996). Therapeutic jurisprudence does not avoid punitive responses; it merely asks legal actors to consider which legal response will be most therapeutic, and whether nonpunitive responses (e.g., rehabilitation, counseling, anger management classes) might also benefit the individual. Even though the individual might be the primary concern, therapeutic jurisprudence does not require the legal actor to abandon concerns such as the community's safety or judicial efficiency. Therapeutic jurisprudence requires a delicate balancing of many factors, which are unique to each case. This process often necessitates the assistance of professionals such as psychologists who can help legal actors make therapeutic decisions.

The concept of therapeutic jurisprudence was developed by Bruce Winick and David Wexler in the 1980s (Winick, 2006). The idea was originally developed with respect to mental health law but has since expanded to many other areas of law (Wexler & Winick, 1996). Therapeutic jurisprudence can be used to examine existing and proposed legal actions to determine whether they have therapeutic or antitherapeutic effects (Winick, 2006). This multidisciplinary approach can improve outcomes for offenders, victims, and communities. Therapeutic jurisprudence can be used to study the impact of any part of the legal process, including police, courts, and corrections (Winick, 2006; see Chapters 6 and 9, this volume for other applications of therapeutic jurisprudence). For example, therapeutic jurisprudence can be an effective tool to help judges successfully mete out appropriate (i.e., therapeutic) consequences, to help lawmakers design effective legislation, and to help prisons adopt beneficial programming. Unfortunately, the criminal justice system is wrought with legal actions that were well intentioned but resulted in unintended problems. Recognition of such unintended consequences—coupled with the "healing potential" of legal actions based on therapeutic jurisprudence—has led to many reforms in the legal system's response to crime and criminals.

Application of Therapeutic Jurisprudence to Maternal Incarceration

The principles of therapeutic jurisprudence can be applied to the topic of maternal incarceration. Therapeutic jurisprudence principles suggest that it is undesirable that a mother and child are in a worse position when she leaves prison than when the mother was admitted to prison. Incarcerated mothers are often unable to fulfill their roles as mothers, and this has negative consequences for both mothers and children. An approach is needed that holds mothers accountable for their actions but also recognizes the needs of mothers and their children. Taking a therapeutic jurisprudence approach, policymakers and judges must not only consider the misdeed but also possible causes and responses. These legal actors need to consider the therapeutic and antitherapeutic ramifications of law, while still being careful not to forego legal or justice considerations such as deterrence or retribution (Wexler, 1996).

Under the principles of therapeutic jurisprudence, it is essential to consider the outcomes of policies for mothers, children, and society. While sentencing policies that lead to incarceration of mothers meet the goals of retribution, they might have unintended consequences. If so, perhaps a retribution-only approach is not the optimal response. As discussed earlier, women are often involved in crime out of necessity rather than choice, meaning that they experience situations such as abuse, financial problems, and addiction that encourage their involvement in the justice system (Acoca & Raeder, 1999; Clarke, 2006; Katz, 2002).[1] If these circumstances (relationship abuse, inability to find employment to support children, etc.) do not change, it is unlikely that their behaviors will change. If crimes are committed because of an addiction

---

1 This is certainly not to say that women are less responsible for their crimes than men, that men do not commit out of necessity, or that no women choose freely to commit crime. This statement only means that women are more likely to be in situations that put them at risk of committing. For instance, women have more serious employment barriers, are more likely to have children to support, and are more likely to be in an abusive relationship than are men (see generally, Belknap, 2007). These situations put women at risk for being arrested for prostitution, conspiracy, and other crimes. These situations also make it more difficult to seek job training or drug treatment.

to drugs, substance abuse treatment should be considered, not only to help the mother get healthy but to reduce chances of reoffending (Fiorca, 2007). Likewise, if a women is convicted as a conspirator to crimes involving her abusive partner, probation along with mandated counseling and job training could be an effective solution to helping her escape her abusive situation, support herself, and avoid reoffending. Approaches such as this are more likely to be therapeutic than punishment-only approaches.

Incarceration alone is unlikely to address these situations, and thus judges, policymakers, and other legal actors and experts should apply the principles of therapeutic jurisprudence in order to determine how to mitigate these situations. Further, overincarceration can have unintended consequences for more than the mother and child. Some argue that nonviolent drug offenders occupy space in prisons that should be used for violent offenders, thereby creating overcrowding (Boyum & Kleiman, 2004). These effects demonstrate unintended outcomes that may cause additional harms; such harms should also be considered when doing an evaluation of whether a policy is therapeutic or antitherapeutic.

Another concern regarding the (anti)therapeutic nature of criminal sentencing is that those who are affected could come to believe that the legal system and its agents lack legitimacy (Tyler, 2006). Incarcerated mothers and their children may see the legal system as uncaring and unhelpful. Mothers may feel like the system did not recognize the reasons they were involved in the legal system (e.g., involved with their baby's drug-dealing father because of a lack of ability to obtain employment herself). Mothers may feel like they are not treated fairly if the punishment (e.g., incarceration and loss of their children) does not fit the crime, or if the system is unresponsive to their needs regarding children. A sense that the legal system is not a legitimate authority might lead a mother to be less likely to comply with legal orders (Tyler, 2006). A child can also learn this attitude from his mother or develop this attitude on his own if he is old enough to recognize that the legal system has caused him harm by taking him away from his parent. Having a belief that the legal system is not a legitimate authority could increase the child's likelihood of committing crime.

Therapeutic jurisprudence can be used as a tool to determine whether existing or proposed programs have therapeutic or antitherapeutic effects for mothers and children. More specifically, do such programs affect the short-term and long-term wellbeing of mothers and children? In evaluating prison nurseries, there are many aspects to consider when determining whether they are therapeutic or antitherapeutic. The typical goal of prison nurseries is to avoid the trauma of mother–child separation and increase the mother's parenting skills (Pojman, 2001–2002). However, nursery programs are controversial. Opponents argue that no matter how a nursery is decorated, a prison is not a suitable environment for a baby (Mauskopf, 1998; Pojman, 2001–2002). There is also concern that infants' health care, nutritional options, or socialization needs cannot be properly addressed (Pojman, 2001–2002. Often nursery units are not built and staffed so that infants can practice important developmental skills (Acoca & Raeder, 1999). In contrast, proponents suggest that even if living in a prison nursery is difficult, it is better than experiencing separation from one's mother (Pojman, 2001–2002). Nurseries emphasize the importance of mother–child bonding and thus prevent many of the ills that may otherwise result. Thus, nurseries might be a therapeutic option, although it is important to acknowledge the negative aspects that could come with a child living in a prison. Research is clearly needed to determine whether the ultimate outcome is a therapeutic one for children.

Other programs discussed earlier such as visitation, overnight stays, and Girl Scout programming, also can be examined using a therapeutic jurisprudence approach. All of these options are intended to promote contact between incarcerated mothers and their children. Further, mothers might be motivated to exhibit good behavior in order to receive the privilege of visitation. Positive behavior (e.g., attending therapy, not getting into fights) could be therapeutic for both the mother and child if they lead to positive long-term changes in the mother's behavior. Despite these benefits, there are some drawbacks. Obstacles include objections from the child's caretaker and the sometimes substantial distance between the child's home and the prison (Stewart, 2002; Zimmerman, 2005). Children who visit parents in prison are sometimes subjected to invasive body searches and are exposed to loud, sterile, and ominous environments (Stewart, 2002). In addition, the stress of separation will be repeated after each visit. Thus, some of these drawbacks indicate that there are no "perfect" programs that are fully therapeutic—even those that reach the goals of therapeutic jurisprudence by protecting the wellbeing of children can have negative aspects.

These programs attempt to embody the principles of therapeutic jurisprudence by allowing parent–child contact while treating the causes of mothers' crimes. Specifically, they reflect lawmakers' consideration of how legal actions affect the wellbeing of those affected, and they rely on social science research to promote positive outcomes. Holistic approaches not only address the causes and effects of maternal incarceration but possibly also alleviate risks for the children, thus likely leading to a decrease in crime. Thus, effective programs overall promote therapeutic jurisprudence principles, although some aspects (e.g., children being in a prison) detract from the overall promotion of child wellbeing.

Policy Recommendations

Some recommendations can be made using therapeutic jurisprudence principles. First, programming should be developed that takes a holistic approach, drawing from research and theory in various disciplines. Experts in criminal justice, social work, education, psychology, sociology, and related disciplines can all help guide, design, and evaluate programs. Much research is needed if the issue of maternal incarceration is to be addressed in a therapeutic manner. Most generally, program evaluation research is needed to determine whether these programs are successful.[2] Some argue that a pure cost–benefit analysis can determine success; after all, if the savings created by the program are more than the cost of the program, then it is successful. However, some benefits are hard to quantify in dollars.[3] There are many potential outcomes of these programs, including outcomes for the mother (e.g., rehabilitation to a more healthy, crime-free live), the child (e.g., improved mental and social wellbeing, reduced risk for becoming an offender), the justice system (e.g., less overcrowding of prisons and court dockets), and society (e.g., less crime in society). No matter which outcomes are chosen as measures of "success," program evaluation is essential to ensure programs are reaching some or all of their goals.

At a more specific level, research can determine whether changes can be made to protect the wellbeing of mothers and children. For instance, do some programs or practices create harm for children? How frequent are these practices, and are there ways to avoid the harms? As discussed earlier, nurseries are very controversial; they may protect the mother–child bond yet place the child in an environment that is not healthy (Pojman, 2001–2002). Similarly, invasive body searches and the general prison environment can cause children distress. Researchers can help programs implement changes to reduce these harms while still protecting prison security and functioning. Similarly, research can determine whether day visits are more or less beneficial for the children than overnight visits. Specific research can investigate whether such benefits and harms depend on the age, gender, or maturity of the child, the quality of the relationship with the mother, and other factors. More generally, research can determine who should qualify for such programs. For instance, a child may not benefit if he or she has had little quality contact with the mother before incarceration or if the length of the incarceration is quite long. Research could address many of these questions.

The second recommendation is for legislators and courts to reconsider existing laws and penalties in order to prevent oversentencing and antitherapeutic outcomes. Instead of punishment-only legal approaches, legislatures and judges should consider adoption of therapeutic approaches that address the cause of the crime and promote wellbeing. Such a shift is illustrated by the formation of drug courts. Starting in the late 1980s, courts around the country—and the

---

[2] Defining "success" is difficult. Is a program successful if it reduces recidivism, improves child outcomes, improves maternal outcomes, increases family reunification, or achieves some other goal? Measures of "success" are complex and subjective, as is the level of improvement. For instance, if the recidivism rate drops 5%, is that worth the cost of the program?

[3] For instance, how many dollars is it worth if 10% more families are kept intact or if 10% fewer children have social and emotional problems? And, certainly, the benefits are priceless to a mother who is able to get off of drugs, find a job, leave an abusive relationship, and develop a better relationship with her child.

world—began realizing that traditional, punishment-only responses to drug crimes were not addressing the underlying problems of drug use (see, e.g., Nolan, 2001). Instead, such legal responses were creating overcrowded court dockets and prisons; courtrooms were revolving doors for repeat offenders. Some courts initiated innovative "drug courts," which took a more rehabilitative approach to addressing drug addiction and other related ailments (e.g., mental health, unemployment) that were related to crime. Drug courts provide essential services to individuals charged with drug-related crimes. The court supervises the person's treatment and progress, and typically the charges are dismissed if the person successfully "graduates" from drug court. Ultimately, this rehabilitative approach has reduced recidivism and lessened the burden on court dockets in many jurisdictions (Terry, 1999). The drug court model is a viable—and therapeutic—option for dealing with mothers who are not a substantial risk to society and would be better served by receiving treatment, vocational training, and life skills. For women who are a greater risk to society, prison is necessary. However, special reentry courts can help support the mother[4] and child during the transition from prison to the community by providing similar services as the drug courts just described (McGrath, 2012). Rehabilitative responses not only give the mother a chance to improve her life but also might help improve conditions for the child, the court system, prisons, and the community. Thus, legislatures and courts should consider therapeutic solutions to this issue, such as development of specialized courts.

Third, even if a fully established specialized court is not possible, court systems could implement a case-specific, pretrial investigative process for all offenders (and this process could also be part of a specialized court). "One-size-fits-all" remedies such as mandatory sentences would be appropriate for some offenders but would be antitherapeutic for other offenders. Instead of a one-size-fits-all approach, each individual case should warrant its own unique assessment. While such a process would require judicial training and participation from social workers, psychologists, and other experts, it would ultimately produce more therapeutic results. The first step in the process would be to review the circumstances of the crime and the offender to determine the most appropriate sentencing (e.g., incarceration, community-based programming). If the offender has children, then a second step would be to thoroughly investigate placement options for the children to protect them from abusive situations. A third step would be to conduct a comprehensive assessment to determine the needs of the children (Katz, 2002). Programs and therapy sessions should be included for mothers and children, as well as all members of the support system, whether or not the mother is incarcerated. Pretrial

---

[4] As previously noted, this chapter focuses on maternal incarceration so as to focus an otherwise very broad topic of parental incarceration. Thus, recommendations are made with mothers in mind, but the general principles could also be applied for fathers and offenders in general.

investigations for all offenders would help protect wellbeing of offenders (e.g., promote rehabilitation) and any children they might have.

Fourth, changes in existing prison policies and programming can be made to ensure the wellbeing of mothers and children. The Rebecca Project for Human Rights (2010) conducted a state-by-state analysis of policies and conditions for incarcerated women and their children. This report, entitled *Mothers Behind Bars*, graded state and federal facilities based upon prenatal care, shackling of women during labor and delivery, family-based treatment programs as alternatives to incarceration, and prison nurseries. Overall, 21 states received failing grades (Ds or Fs), 22 states received Cs, seven states received Bs, and only one state earned an A-. Such studies highlight the need for prison reforms. The facilities and programs discussed earlier provide an important service to incarcerated mothers and their children. Nevertheless, certain concerns need to be addressed. For instance, prisons could offer the services of a liaison to ensure the planning and execution of visits to coincide with free or low-cost transportation. Additionally, prison security measures are essential, but searches could be refined and less invasive for the children. The resident therapist should be made available for assistance in easing stress before, during, or after visits. Additionally, it is important for prison nursery units to provide trained staff and proper pre- and postnatal care for mothers and children. These units must also meet certain standards for meeting infants' basic developmental and health needs. Finally, programs could be expanded to include many more children. For instance, the Nebraska Correctional Center for Women's nursery only has room for eight children, all of whom must be under 18 months old (Nebraska Department of Correctional Services, 2013), while the Beford Hills facility in New York generally only serves children up to 1 year old (Kauffman, 2001). The Bayview Correctional Facility in New York unit only serves women who are within 6 months of release (Department of Corrections and Community Supervision, 2009). Programs can be expanded to reach more mothers and more children. Such changes in programming can use the principles of therapeutic jurisprudence to help these programs reach their goals.

A final recommendation is to gauge the sentiment toward these programs. Specifically, do mothers, children, caregivers, and prison staff value such programs? Do mothers believe the programs are good motivation for them to participate in rehabilitation? Do they even want to participate in these programs? Family members' sentiment also is important, as they are needed to help hold the mother accountable for rehabilitation (Wexler & Winick, 1996); the sentiment of caregivers is important because they must help with transportation and provide children with support. Thus, it is important to inform and educate these groups about the benefits of the programs. Prison staff must be supportive and helpful. Because negative attitudes can undermine programs, employee selection and training are essential. In sum, researching the sentiment of all these groups is important—as is designing ways to garner greater support for programs.

As an important side note, funding for programs and research is essential. While some of these recommendations require great upfront costs, they might ultimately prove to be cost-savers. Evaluations of drug courts indicate that the up-front costs can be substantial (largely due to the extrajudicial supervision and treatment), but they actually prove to be cost effective because they prevent the costs associated with recidivism (Terry, 1999). Only properly conducted and thorough research and evaluation can determine whether such programs are successful—and how to make changes to increase their success. As such, the ultimate policy recommendation is funding for both programs and the research to design and evaluate such programs and policies.

Conclusion

The response to the increase in crimes associated with drugs in the 1980s led to a great increase in women inmates (Katz, 2002), many of whom are mothers and primary caregivers. Harsh penalties meant to fight the war on drugs have not only led to disproportionate sentencing but also have resulted in additional societal problems. For the children who are born in prison or who are abandoned during the mothers' incarceration, life is filled with difficulties. Ultimately, the war on drugs has unintentionally negatively affected the wellbeing of children of incarcerated mothers. That is not to say that just because a woman is also a mother, she should be absolved of the consequences of her crime. But rather, the totality of the circumstances (including the wellbeing of her child) should be considered when imposing a sentence. By placing mothers in prison for minor offenses, their children are essentially abandoned and, as previously discussed, this can lead to intergenerational incarceration (DeAngelis, 2001) and harm to the wellbeing of both the mother and child.

Programs have been developed to reduce some of the negative consequences of maternal incarceration, such as a break in the mother–child bonding, psychological effects on the child and mother, and criminal recidivism. Although much research is needed, these programs—and alternate sentences—hold promise for reducing such harms to mothers, children, the legal system, and society. Even so, such programs could create harm as well, as children may have negative experiences while visiting or living in prison. Thus, thorough analyses are needed.

While it is important to hold all offenders accountable for their crimes, the principles of therapeutic jurisprudence suggest that a punishment-only approach is not the optimal justice response for all women. Instead, when the legal system seeks out experts in psychology, social work, and other areas, beneficial solutions to this legal and social issue are possible.

References

Acoca, L., & Raeder, M. S. (1999). Severing family ties: The plight of nonviolent female offenders and their children. *Stanford Law and Policy Review, 11,* 133–146.

Belknap, J. (2007). *The invisible woman: Gender, crime, and justice* (3rd ed.). Belmont, CA: Wadsworth.

Bernberg, J. G., Krohn, M. D., & Rivera, C. J. (2006). Official labeling, criminal embededness, and subsequent delinquency: A longitudinal test of labeling theory. *Journal of Research in Crime and Delinquency, 43*(1), 67–83. doi: 10.1177/0022427805280068.

Boyum, D. A., & Kleiman, M. A. (2004). Substance abuse policy from a crime-control perspective. In J. Q. Wilson & J. Petersilia (Eds), *Crime: Public policies for crime control* (pp. 331–382). Oakland, CA: Institue for Contemporary Studies.

Byrne, M. W., Goshin, L. S., & Joestl, S. S. (2010). Intergenerational transmission of attachment for infants raised in a prison nursery. *Attachment and Human Development, 12*(4), 375–393. doi:10.1080/14616730903417011.

Campbell, J., & Carlson, J. R. (2012). Correctional administrators' perceptions of prison nurseries. *Criminal Justice and Behavior, 39*(8), 1063–1074. doi:10.1177/0093854812441161.

Celinska, K., & Siegel, J. A. (2010). Mothers in trouble: Coping with actual or pending separation from children due to incarceration. *The Prison Journal, 90*(4), 447–474. doi:10.1177/0032885510382218.

Cho, R. M. (2011). Understanding the mechanism behind maternal imprisonment and adolescent school dropout. *Family Relations: An Interdisciplinary Journal of Applied Family Studies, 60*(3), 272–289. doi:10.1111/j.1741-3729.2011.00649.x.

Christian, S. (2009). *Children of incarcerated parents.* Washington, DC: National Conference of State Legislatures.

Clarke, C. M. (2006). Maternal justice restored: Redressing the ramifications of mandatory sentencing minimums on women and their children. *Howard Law Journal, 50,* 263–274.

Dalley, L. P. (2000). Imprisoned mothers and their children: The often conflicting legal rights. *Hamline Journal of Public Law and Policy, 22,* 1–16.

DeAngelis, T. (2001, May). *Punishment of innocents: Children of parents behind bars. Monitor On Psychology.* Retrieved July 2013, from http://www.apa.org/monitor/may01/punish.html.

Department of Corrections and Community Supervision. (2009). *Bayview correctional facility opens reentry unit for female offenders returning to New York City, suburbs.* New York, NY: New York State Department of Correctional Services.

Doyle, J. J. (2011, March). Causal effects of foster care: An instrumental-variables approach. *Children and Youth Services Review.* doi: 10.1016/j.childyouth.2011.03.014.

Finney Hairston, C. P. (2007, October). *Focus on children with incarcerated parents: An overview of the research literature.* Retrieved July 2013, from The Annie E. Casey Foundation website, http://www.aecf.org/~/media/PublicationFiles/HAIRSTON.pdf

Fiorca, J. L. (2007). How the Constitution can preserve the strength of existing familial bonds and foster new relationships between female inmates and their children. *Women's Rights Law Reporter, 29*, 49–61.

Foster, H. (2012). The strains of maternal imprisonment: Importation and deprivation stressors for women and children. *Journal of Criminal Justice, 40*(3), 221–229. doi:10.1016/j.jcrimjus.2012.01.005.

Fragile Families Research Brief. (2008). *Parental incarceration and child wellbeing in fragile families*. Princeton, NJ: Center for Research on Child Wellbeing.

Genty, P. M. (2007). Some reflections about three decades of working with incarcerated mothers. *Women's Rights Law Reporter, 29*, 11–13.

Gest, T. (2001). *Crime and politics: Big government's erratic campaign for law and order.* Oxford, UK: Oxford University Press.

Girl Scouts of the USA. (2013). Where girls go, scouting follows. Retrieved from http://www.girlscouts.org/for_adults/leader_magazine/2003_spring/where_girls_go.asp.Glaze, L. E., & Maruschak, L. M. (2008, August). *Parents in prison and their minor children*. Retrieved from Bureau of Justice Statistics website http://bjs.gov/content/pub/pdf/pptmc.pdf.

Gregoire, A., Dolan, R., Birmingham, L., Mullee, M., & Coulson, D. (2010). The mental health and treatment needs of imprisoned mothers of young children. *Journal of Forensic Psychiatry and Psychology, 21*(3), 378–392. doi:10.1080/14789940903294317.

Hagan, J., & Foster, H. (2012). Children of the American prison generation: Student and school spillover effects of incarcerating mothers. *Law and Society Review, 46*(1), 37–69. doi:10.1111/j.1540-5893.2012.00472.x.

Hutchinson, K., Moore, G. A., Propper, C. B., & Mariaskin, A. (2008). Incarcerated women's psychological functioning during pregnancy. *Psychology of Women Quarterly, 32*(4), 440–453. doi:10.1111/j.1471-6402.2008.00457.x.

Jordan, E. (2011). Prison nurseries cut female inmates' risk of reoffending. Retrieved from http://thegazette.com/2011/01/31/prison-nurseries-cut-female-inmates-risk-of-reoffending/.

Katz, L. (2002). Evaluation and services for children of incarcerated mothers with co-occurring disorders. In S. Davidson, & H. Hills (Eds.), *Series on women with mental illness and co-occuring disorders* (pp. xx–xx). Delmar, NY: National GAINS Center. Retrieved from http://gainscenter.samhsa.gov/pdfs/Women/series/ServicesforChildren.pdf

Kauffman, K. (2001, February). Mothers in pison. *Corrections Today*, 62–66.

Krupat, T. (2007, Fall). Invisibility and children's rights: The consequences of parental incarceration. *Women's Rights Law Reporter, 29*, 39–43.

Kubiak, S., Kasiborski, N., & Schmittel, E. (2010). Assessing long-term outcomes of an intervention designed for pregnant incarcerated women. *Research on Social Work Practice, 20*(5), 528–535. doi:10.1177/1049731509358086.

Look, A. (2008). *Alternative sentencing for incarcerated mothers could break the cycle of crime*. Chicago, IL: Medill School.

Loper, A., Carlson, L., Levitt, L., & Scheffel, K. (2009). Parenting stress, alliance, child contact, and adjustment of imprisoned mothers and fathers. *Journal of Offender Rehabilitation, 48*(6), 483–503. doi:10.1080/10509670903081300.

Loper, A., & Tuerk, E. (2011). Improving the emotional adjustment and communication patterns of incarcerated mothers: Effectiveness of a prison parenting intervention. *Journal of Child and Family Studies, 20*(1), 89–101. doi:10.1007/s10826-010-9381-8.

Mauskopf, N. S. (1998). Reaching beyond the bars: An analysis of prison nurseries. *Cardoza Women's Law Journal, 5*, 101–108.

McGrath, E. (2012). Reentry courts: Providing a second chance for incarcerated mothers and their children. *Family Court Review, 50*(1), 113–127. doi:10.1111/j.1744-1617.2011.01433.x.

Mumola, C. J. (2000, August). *Incarcerated parents and their children.* Retrieved from United States Department of Justice website http://www.bjs.gov/content/pub/pdf/iptc.pdf.

Murray, J. (2007). The cycle of punishment: Social exclusion of prisoners and their children. *Criminology and Criminal Justice, 7*, 55–81.

Murray, J., & Farrington, D. P. (2008). The effects of parental imprisonment on children. *Crime and Justice, 37*, 133–194.

Nebraska Department of Correctional Services. (2013). Nebraska Correctional Center for Women. Retrieved from http://www.corrections.state.ne.us/nccw.html.

New York State Department of Correctional Services. (2013). About DOC Retrieved from http://www.nyc.gov/html/doc/html/about/facilities_overview.shtml.

Nolan, J. L. (2001). *Reinventing justice. The American drug court movement.* Princeton, NJ: Princeton University Press.

Novero, C. M., Loper, A., & Warren, J. I. (2011). Second-generation prisoners: Adjustment patterns for inmates with a history of parental incarceration. *Criminal Justice and Behavior, 38*(8), 761–778. doi:10.1177/0093854811406637.

Poelmann, J. (2003). *Children of incarcerated parents.* Retrieved July 2013, from the University of Wisconsin-Madison Center for Excellence in Family Studies website http://www.familyimpactseminars.org/pnl_v03i02_1003.pdf

Pojman, L. M. (2001-2002). Cuffed love: Do prison babies ever smile? *Buffalo Women's Law Journal, 10*, 46–73.

Sandifer, J. L. (2008). Evaluating the efficacy of a parenting program for incarcerated mothers. *The Prison Journal, 88*(3), 423–445. doi:10.1177/0032885508322533.

Stewart, B. G. (2002). When should a court order visitation between a child and an incarcerated parent? *University of Chicago Law School Roundtable, 9*, 165–178.

Terry, W. C. (1999). *The early drug courts: Case studies in judicial innovation.* Thousand Oaks, CA: Sage.

The Rebecca Project for Human Rights. (October, 2010). *Mothers behind bars.* Washington, DC: National Women's Law Center.

Tyler, T. R. (2006). Psychological perspectives on legitamacy and legitimation. *Annual Review of Psychology, 57*, 375–300. doi: 10.1146/annurev.psych.57.102904.190038.

Wexler, D. B. (1996). Some therapeutic jurisprudence implications of the outpatient civil commitment of pregnant substance abusers. In D. B. Wexler & B. J. Winick (Eds), *Law in a therapeutic key: Developments in therapeutic jurisprudence* (pp. 145–148). Durham, NC: Carolina Academic Press.

Wexler, D. B., & Winick, B. J. (1996). *Law in a therapeutic key: Developments in therapeutic jurisprudence.* Durham, NC: Carolina Academic Press.

Winick, B. J. (2006). Therapeutic jurisprudence: Enhancing the relationship between law and psychology. *Law and Psychology: Current Legal Issues, 9,* 30–48.

Zimmerman, A. M. (2005, Fall). Home alone: Children of incarcerated mothers in New York City under the Rockefeller drug laws. *Cordoza Journal of Law and Gender, 12,* 445–469.

12

Immigrant Parents' Perceptions of the "Best Interests of the Child"

Qingwen Xu

In 2010, approximately 3.3 million referrals of child abuse and neglect—involving approximately 5.9 million children—were made to the public child welfare system in the United States (US Department of Health and Human Services Office on Child Abuse and Neglect, 2011). As the population of immigrant children (both foreign-born and US-born children with at least one foreign-born parent) is growing rapidly, the public child welfare system is encountering large and increasing numbers of immigrant children. Approximately one in four US children is an immigrant child (Child Trends, 2010), and there are nearly 1.8 million undocumented children in the United States (Pew Hispanic Center, 2006). According to the National Survey of Child and Adolescent Wellbeing (NSCAW) conducted between 1999 and 2000, 5.2% of all children in the public child welfare system had a parent who was foreign born; among Latino children who came to the attention of public child welfare system, 36.0% had a parent who was foreign born (see Dettlaff, Earner, & Phillips, 2009). The initial national statistics suggest that, even though immigrant children in general are proportionally less likely to be in the public child welfare system than nonimmigrant children, the numbers of immigrant children involved are substantial (Dettlaff et al., 2009).

The primary consideration underlying all decisions regarding children is the "best interests of the child," a principle that guides nearly every dependency court in the United States (Blain & Weiner, 2005). The welfare of the child is the determining factor in establishing child custody, both temporarily and permanently; however, the meaning of the best interests of the child in the context of migration has not been investigated well. Determinations of the best interests of an immigrant child are usually done by social workers, family court advisors, psychologists, and other forensic experts; these tend to be powerful professionals, many of whom do not have substantial specialized knowledge of indigenous culture and/or the US immigration system.

However, parents' and immigrant communities' common understandings and interpretations of the "best interests of the child" remain largely unexplored. In the past, parents were excluded from the decision-making process in the public child welfare system. The effort of gathering parents' perspectives concerning their children's best interests challenges the beliefs of child rights advocates, who typically believe that parents' interests should not take precedence over the child's rights (Eekelaar, 1994). Recent developments in the public child welfare system, particularly concerning innovative practices (e.g., family conferencing, family-to-family initiative, and structured decision making), nonetheless stress the importance of parents, family, and community members, and explicitly seek their input in the decision making for the "best interests of the child" (Burford & Hudson, 2000; Gambrill, 2005). These practices are adopted in response to the criticism raised by minority groups that traditional child welfare practices alienate children from their cultural networks (Connolly, 2006).

Indeed, the perspectives and perceptions of immigrant parents deserve exploration, as they provide valuable views that could serve to inform child welfare professionals, shed light on otherwise valid and useful practices, and ultimately promote the wellbeing of immigrant children. This chapter explores immigrant parents' perceptions. Parents who immigrated from Cambodia, China, Somalia, Mexico, Dominican Republic, and Guatemala offered their descriptions of what they consider to be in the best interests of the child and described their experience with the US child welfare system. Focus groups of immigrant parents reveal what they believe to be in the best interest of their children; such input is the basis for policy suggestions offered at the conclusion of this chapter.

The Best Interests Standard

The best interests standard has many meanings in both legal principle and child welfare practice (Thronson, 2008). At one end of the spectrum, judges and child welfare workers recognize the universal standard of "best interests of the child." The best interests standard is stated clearly in the United Nation's Convention on the Rights of the Child (i.e., "the Convention") as children's rights to survival and development (Article 6), education (Article 28), basic economic welfare (Article 27), and health care (Article 24) and the right to be protected from abuse or neglect (Article 19) and economic and sexual exploitation (Articles 32 and 34). From this universalist perspective, all children, without regard to their own or their parents' citizenship or immigration status, and without regard to whether they are in state custody, should be guaranteed such universal "best interests." This definition has been almost universally ratified (the United States has expressed its intention to ratify but has yet to do so).

At the other end of the spectrum, the best interests standard has not been operationalized with a degree of predictability. In other words, the cultural relativism has led to different criteria for the best interests standard in different cultures. In 1994, the special issue of the *International Journal of Law and the Family* presented a series of studies investigating the variations of the best interests standard in different countries. The journal issue revealed that although the universal definition contained in the Convention received wide acceptance across countries, the best interests of the child should be complied with as if they are strict laws and considered as informal cultural practice that varies across countries.

Therefore, researchers and practitioners tend to allow flexibility in the exercise of this broadly stated standard, given the cultural diversity across the globe and the complex circumstances of each child's situation. Scholars suggest that, in matters pertaining to the best interests of the child, the majority (in Western cultures) should not use their cultural values and practices as the foundation upon which to impose their views on child welfare and child development (Greenfield & Cocking, 1994). In child welfare practices, the best interests of the child may differ within or among cultures, which could lead to dramatically different results but nonetheless benefit the child and the child's wellbeing (Fong, McRoy, & Ortiz-Hendricks, 2006; Fontes, 2005).

In exercising the professional authority to make decisions for children in the public child welfare system, common sense, professional training, education, and personal experience all could play a role in determining the "best interests of the child." As one judge stated, the decision as to the best interests of the child could "draw upon its own common sense and experience in reaching a reasoned judgment" (*Osmanagic v. Osmanagic*, 2005, p. 899). In fact, judgments based on common sense and experience have led to various interpretations of best interests standard, ranging from child's safety and the continuity of the child's relationships with parents, siblings, and significant others, to the child's adjustment to his or her home, school, and community and/or the mental and physical health of the parents. In practice, professionals exercise tremendous latitude in the application of the expansive best interests standard (Clement, 2008), and different groups of professionals sometimes use different criteria when determining what is in the child's best interests. For instance, Britner and Mossler (2002) found that, when making decisions about temporary custody for abused and neglected children, social workers and mental health providers focused on the severity and pattern of abuse, services offered in the past, and parental responses to those services. In contrast, judges relied more heavily on the likelihood of a reoccurrence of abuse and the child's ability to recount the abuse. Further, court-appointed special advocates (CASAs) focused on the stability of the family.

While the discussion about the best interests standard runs squarely into the issues of cultural relativism and universalism, it does not fully account for all the factors that contribute to immigrant children's best interests and/or help the decision making regarding immigrant children in the public child welfare system. When immigrant children are involved, professional interpretations and different priorities might not reflect a cultural understanding of the best interests of the child, as well as the perspectives from immigrant communities and parents.

Migration Psychology Perspective

While best interests of the child is a legal standard, it is also a mental health standard. Psychological studies of migration behavior have identified two fundamental issues that immigrants and society face: maintenance of cultural characteristics and contact between immigrant groups and the majority culture (Berry, 2001). For immigrant groups, pressures to assimilate and give up one's sense of ethnicity are associated with mental health concerns, and failure to assimilate can result in immigrants becoming marginalized. Thus, immigrant children and families demonstrate unique distinctive psychological challenges associated with their adjustment, assimilation, and/or acculturation. For a larger plural society like the United States, certain psychological preconditions such as positive mutual attitudes among ethnocultural groups and acceptance of the value of cultural diversity need to be established in order to pursue a multicultural society (Berry, 2001). Thus, while immigrant groups need to adopt US values, American institutions (e.g., education, health, justice, labor, and child welfare) also need to be adapted to better meet the needs of all groups now living together.

Given the perspective of migration psychology, immigrant children's need to assimilate and their parents' and families' capacity to support the process of assimilation are critical to immigrant children's best interests. Whether cultural assimilation is in the best interests of the child remains controversial among American Indians (e.g., Davis, 2001). Contrary to this specific ethnic group, there is a consensus among scholars that immigrant children's assimilation is a process desirable and inevitable, and a supportive family environment and parent–child cohesion contribute to positive mental health outcomes among immigrant children (e.g., Portes & Zady, 2002; Zhou, 1997). Unfortunately, few studies consider immigrant children's unique psychological needs in the discussion of the best interests standard. Nonetheless, available literature indicates that certain immigrant parents and families might not be ready to meet their children's psychological needs; parents and families often need a variety of psychosocial supports to cope with the migration experience and the resulting pressure (e.g., Perreira, Chapman, & Stein, 2006). For example, experiences such as migration-related family separation, economic hardship due to the lack of English language proficiency, trauma suffered in the country of origin, and family conflicts due to acculturation gap between children and parents could negatively affect the parents' mental health and parenting capacity (e.g., Harker, 2001; Hernandez, 2000; Takeuchi et al., 2007). Family stressors are relevant to the key psychological aspects of the best interests of the child, including the developmental and emotional needs of the child, and the nature of the relationship of the child with each parent, two main factors written into the Uniform Child Custody Jurisdiction and Enforcement Act.

Migration-related factors (e.g., parents' legal status, mixed-legal-status family environment, and the threat of immigration law enforcement) have added to the complexity of child abuse and neglect, and can make the best interests of immigrant children highly controversial (Thronson, 2008; Xu, 2005). Legal research indicates that parents' legal status is irrelevant in determining the best interests of the child in principle (e.g., Thronson, 2006). However, in practice, parents' legal status served the dangerous function of "acting as a repository for the unconscious biases and punitive impulses of judges against immigrant parents" (Abrams, 2006, p. 88). For example, undocumented parents' poor employment prospects and parents' lack of English proficiency are considered in evaluating immigrant parents' ability to meet the physical, developmental, and emotional needs of the child (*Rico v. Rodriguez*, 2005).

Given the immigrant children's situation, the challenges of deciding the best interests of immigrant children are huge from both legal and psychological standpoints. To what extent the US child welfare system and child welfare professionals are willing to adapt existing policies and practice to meet the needs of immigrant children and their families is unknown. Because most professionals in the United States have been trained to see people from the majority group as the norm and people from other groups/countries as deviant, there is still a long way to go. It is not surprising that immigrant children and their families in the child welfare system have unfairly ended up with disparate outcomes; for example, Vericker, Kuehn, and Capps (2007) reported that immigrant children stayed in the child welfare system longer, were more often placed in group homes and institutions, and were less likely to have case goals of family reunification and kin adoption as compared to children from the majority culture. Therefore, when culture and migration experiences profoundly affect the understanding of the best interests of immigrant children, there is a great risk of depending entirely on child welfare professionals' interpretations of the best interests standard, and an even greater danger that the Western-oriented best interests standard could become a source of oppression to immigrant children and parents.

Data Collection

The purpose of this chapter is to explain the culture, values, and beliefs that influence immigrant parents' perceptions and understanding of the "best interests of the child" standard; this chapter also tries to describe child welfare practices from immigrant parents' viewpoints. The focus group methodology was adopted because it is well suited for exploring the complexity of the "best interests" standard within the context of immigration and settlement experiences. Focus groups encourage participants to engage positively in the process of the research and gather perspectives that differ from the researchers' (Krueger & Casey, 2008). Focus groups break down the interviewer–interviewee power relationship and give a greater emphasis to participants' viewpoints and allow participants to set their own agenda. The research protocol and instruments were approved by the Institutional Review Board at Boston College.

Four focus groups were conducted with parents from Cambodia, China, Somalia, and Mexico, and one additional group was conducted with Spanish-speaking immigrant parents from Mexico, Dominican Republic, and Guatemala in hopes of learning more about Latino immigrant parents' experiences. These five groups are the primary immigrant populations in the northeast region of the United States. Participants were recruited through immigrant community organizations that had a working relationship with the researchers. Recruiting participants through the support of immigrant community organizations helped decrease the concern that immigrant parents might not feel comfortable with each other and might hesitate to engage in discussions about their perceptions and experience. As researchers were associated with these community organizations, participants had a certain degree of familiarity and comfort; thus, the focus groups were able to address some sensitive issues, such as child abuse and neglect and their involvement in the public child welfare system. Each participant received a $20 gift card.

The criteria for selecting participants were as follows: (1) at least one child, either US born or foreign born, lived with the parent at the time of focus group interview; and (2) the participant was foreign born. The study included seven Somalis, six Cambodians, eight Chinese, eight Mexicans, and six Spanish-speaking parents with mixed countries of birth, for a total of 35 parents of which 26 (74.3%) were female. Twenty-four parents (68.6%) were between 30 and 50 years old. Twenty parents (57.1%) had lived in the United States for at least 15 years, and seven (20%) had lived in the United States for 5 years or less. Almost all (90.9%) were married; many of them lived in a family with extended family members. Five out of six Chinese parents and six out of seven Somali parents had an education and English proficiency; on the contrary, a majority of parents in the Mexican and Spanish-speaking groups had less than a high school education (approximately 50%) and understood English only "a little" (approximately 64.2%). The majority of parents (62.9%) in the five groups had two to four children, ranging from ages 2 to 17 years old at the time of interview.

Each focus group lasted approximately 2 hours. A standard set of open-ended questions was asked to all five groups. Questions were structured to include the following three major parts: (1) challenges of raising a child in the United States; (2) experience and/or knowledge about the public child welfare system; and (3) understanding and/or interpretation of the best interests standard. Asking probing questions and certain group-specific questions broadened focus group discussions. Participants were also asked to complete a form collecting their demographic information. A social work researcher facilitated all five focus groups with the assistance of bilingual social science graduate students who helped with interpretation and demographic information collection.

Data were first analyzed through the use of narrative analysis in order to better trace parents' stories chronologically and provide insights about life experiences (Chase, 2005). Emphasis was placed on how the parents' experience of raising children in their home countries shaped their perceptions of their present childrearing practices in the United States, how their experiences in the United States have shaped their past perceptions, and how both experiences shaped their perceptions of the "best interests of the child." Thematic coding was then conducted based on the transcripts using the qualitative analysis software HyperResearch 2.6.1. Content was inductively coded for themes emerging from the data. In order to improve the reliability of data coding, the primary researcher and the interpreter/research assistant (who also had a graduate-level social sciences education) coded separately. Categories and subcategories were consequently discussed and developed by the primary researcher and the interpreter/researcher, then meetings were held with community leaders to review preliminary categories/subcategories and findings, do member checks, and explore alternative interpretations of these findings. These meetings helped minimize errors and biases.

Results

Focus group data offered immigrant parents' perceptions and understanding of the "best interests of the child." As professionals in the child welfare system often use such terms as safety, permanency, and stability, which are major outcomes pursed by state child welfare departments (see Children's Bureau, n.d.), ordinary immigrant parents in this study used terms like "good education" and "maintaining tradition and culture" to describe the best interests of their children. Parents' understandings of "best interests" were expressed in their cultural context; group differences were identified. In addition, immigrant parents expressed difficulties and frustration working with the US child welfare system; the feeling of loss of control was conveyed, as parents had difficulties keeping their traditional ways of parenting in the United States.

Education as the Best Interests

Immigrant parents overwhelmingly indicated that education is the number-one element of their children's best interests; they clearly recognized the importance of education for their children's successful development and acculturation in the United States. When asking parents "What do you think are your child's best interests?" a Mexican mother answered, "Education. There is nothing like education. As a parent, there is nothing I want more for my kids than educating them." This sentiment was echoed across all five groups. Parents expressed not just any education, but *quality education*, as being the key to their children's best interests. They said it would give their children opportunities and a bright future in this new society. For example:

> [I]f [children] don't have their education, they don't have anything. Having [an] education, they could have a better life.
>
> What's important for me is [for my child] to go to college. The second is good health, and the third thing is English. You know if [the child] catches up with English more, the more [likely] he will go to college.

Parents across all groups reported that education and a chance for their children to get ahead in life was one of their major motivations for migrating to the United States. For many ethnic groups, pride in education and being able to excel was very important in their communities. Furthermore, immigrant parents had a vested interest in their children's education because, for most, it is through their children that their own hopes and dreams are fulfilled. They believed that education is the only route to prosperity and security in the United States. This sentiment was particularly strong among the Cambodian and Somali parents; both groups were forced to move to the United States as refugees and, in doing so, they saw their children's education as their family's future. One Somali parent said:

> Keep in mind the reason we came here. We know that we have no future here, but [we do] have a future for [our] kids. So we try so hard even though we do not have the financial means; we want our kids to go to school.

Evidently, while parents saw education as their children's first and most important interest, they also had high expectations of their children's schools and children's performance in school. The parents' own educational experience in their home countries left parents disappointed with the US public schools. Specifically, parents were dissatisfied with the curriculum (lack of moral and critical education), homework assignments (homework for average American children is not challenging enough for immigrant children), mandatory standardized testing (testing children's math and reading, which was seen as unfair to immigrant students), and services to assist parents (lack of support services, outreach, and programs).

Cultural Contexts

In the focus groups, children's best interests were discussed in the context of culture (e.g., US education lacked appropriate cultural elements); cultural elements include traditional family values, family roles, morals and religion, preserving the native language, and maintaining an ethnic community identity. The following are comments of two Asian parents discussing the traditional (hierarchical) family structure and family roles, and how these shaped their present practices of childrearing in the United States.

> We respect the people who are senior to us, who are older than us...Like in our family, for example, *GeGe* [meaning older brother] is *GeGe*, *DarJie* [meaning older sister] is *DarJie*, so even it's just that they're older than you, you say *GeGe*, not to just call [them] by [their] first name. Also, we're pretty concerned with family values, or...family bonding...A lot of times, especially with big families...The older ones, a lot of times can teach the younger ones. So, I think it's like the traditional Chinese family...the older ones can set a good example for the younger ones.
>
> The father, he works, he brings the money [home],...the mother stays home. So the mothers have more time to spend [with the children] and to know what's going on with the kids at home,...[at] school, outside...But here, it's completely changed. Everybody has to rush, everybody has to work.

In the two focus groups with Spanish-speaking parents, parents also emphasized the importance of family, morals, religion, and culture to their children's wellbeing and development.

> Our morals, religion, [cultural] traditions, and love [are important to the children]. For me, [having] love in a family [is important]—without it, there is no respect. I don't believe there is anything else. For my family [religion] is very important [to the children] and we can't move forward without it.

Parents stressed that maintaining traditions and culture is in their children's best interests; however, parents reported observing their children's assimilation into their new culture with angst and sadness. What was especially painful for them was seeing their children cast off their culture and traditions, including the demise of their native language skills. Parents worried that their native cultural traditions would soon vanish, as many children had begun to reject their parent's native tongue. As one parent put it:

> He [the child] pretends that he does not understand it in Spanish...it is difficult [to encourage children to speak the native language] because the whole world wants to speak to them in English.

In response to their children's assimilation and gradual loss of their native culture as they assimilate into American culture, some parents faced a dilemma. Some saw this as an advantage—in that it encouraged their children's adaptation in the school setting—and others took the opposite position. Some blamed their children's "Americanization" for some of their "bad" habits such as drug use, gang involvement, and pregnancies at an early age—behaviors that are rare in their native countries. Two mothers described their concerns and said:

> How [children] dress, how they walk, they don't listen to the parents, how easy they accept this [US] culture, they use drugs, and they have drugs in high school.
>
> The way the kids come home and don't listen to you. I know, I see, I smell, I see when they come home. He [the child] is always going out…out…out…and go hang and chill with his friends; it's scary.

Other parents recognized that, without appropriate integration into American society, it was difficult for children to adapt socially.

Loss of Control

Parents expressed "loss of control" when trying to keep their traditional ways of parenting, attempting to support their children's assimilation, or protecting their children from harm. Some excerpts include the following:

> In our country they have to respect their teachers and their neighbors, so everybody were controlling to your kids, everybody were guardians to your kids. Between the school and the house, if [the children] misbehaved, someone who sees they are misbehaving can step in and do something about it.… American culture is damaging the culture because the older they get, the less control you have.
>
> Kids are quite good but it's more of a burden for parents to follow up and constantly check on what kids are doing, to have more control and supervision.… The problem is the kids' friends, who they hang out with, and how their friends are doing at school, and what types of clubs.
>
> I feel [that] myself, my own beliefs, my congregation, is very Chinese-style. They are actually ABCs [American-Born Chinese]. So what comes to us, as very traditional Chinese, [we are] not so compatible [with the children's value system].…[the children are] in between, and then we can't cater to their needs.

Feeling "loss of control" was further compounded by the power and practices of child welfare institutions, mainly the Department of Social Services (DSS; now many states and counties have changed the name to Department of Children and Families). All parents in this study recognized DSS. Parents talked about DSS:

> We don't have the control [over the children]…the agency [DSS] takes the power from the parents. Yeah, because every parent has their own way to raise the kids, that some parents, you know, in some culture, they hit, they don't break bones, they don't hurt, no

blood come out, but, you know, some countries, they raise you to hit sometimes. You know this is not bad.

The [US] system, how it is set up, kids have rights but we came from a culture that we [parents] make all the decisions, no matter what, no one else can interfere between the children and the parent. But here, we are led to believe that DSS is bigger than everybody, so the fear of [DSS or other authorities] undermining how we can raise kids.

I think children here are spoiled a lot. You know why, they are your kids, but finally they are not yours, they are born from the parent but they are not yours, anything happened to them, they belong to the DSS and all those types.

Many parents found themselves losing the ability to discipline or educate their children. In the dialogue pertaining to discipline practices, for some parents, corporal punishment (physical punishment) was an emotional and sensitive issue because most parents had heard that the DSS could be alerted by teachers or neighbors if parents spanked their children or employed other parenting practices considered "abnormal" in the United States. The acronym DSS causes fear in many immigrant communities. For some immigrant parents, DSS is the agency that "comes and takes children away." Parents also described their disappointment and/or distrust of the public child welfare system. They complained that DSS workers lack an understanding of their cultural norms. Due to the lack of knowledge about child welfare systems and laws, many of the parents in the study felt afraid to discipline their children for fear that the school, DSS, or other authorities would get involved. The overall feeling of immigrant parents in this study is that they "lost" their children to American culture after migration, they lost their ability to educate and discipline their children according to their cultural norms, and they could lose their children to DSS due to the "best interests of the child" policy.

Group Differences

While most of these themes were voiced across all focus groups, some groups offered unique aspects of what they believed to be a part of children's best interests. Latino parents focused on family and the importance of "family being together," including family values, maintaining traditional family roles, and ethnic traditions. This finding is probably due to the legal vulnerability that the Latino immigrant population in the United States experiences. Specifically, because Mexican nationals accounted for nearly 89% of those apprehended by US immigration law enforcement agencies, and the majority of immigrants deported by immigration law enforcement agencies were from Latin American countries in 2007 (US Department of Homeland Security Office of Immigration Statistics, 2008), Latino immigrants and their families have been disproportionately affected by this country's immigration law enforcement. In view of deportation-related family disruption and child–parent separation, "family being together" was seen as especially important for Latino children's best interests.

Cambodian parents expressed particular concerns over their children's gang membership and violent behaviors. Youth gangs and juvenile delinquent behaviors have been a major concern in this immigrant community for more than a decade (Arifuku, Peacock, & Glesmann, 2006). Ethnic identity development has been a significant factor associated with juvenile delinquency, particularly among males (Go & Le, 2005). There is evidence that Cambodian American youth experience serious adjustment problems and are often depicted by the mainstream society as low-achieving high school dropouts involved in gangs (McGinnis, 2007). Considering the destructive impact of gang membership on children, it is natural that "staying away from gangs" was considered by Cambodian parents as the best interests of their children.

The Chinese group stressed the value of education and the tradition in producing moral or ethical behavior, which parents said is necessary for their children's wellbeing and development. This finding possibly emerged because parents were recruited through a faith-based Chinese community organization and most parents in the group had obtained college educations; this result should be considered carefully due to its limited generalizability.

The Somali parents focused on the importance of preserving their cultural heritage; considering that Somalis represent an extremely small portion of the US population, they face greater challenges in maintaining Somali cultural traditions and values for their children.

Discussion

Results suggest that immigrant parents have a different perception and/or understanding of the "best interests of the child" than child welfare professionals. Instead of such terms as safety, permanency, stability, and bonding adopted by professionals in the child welfare system, immigrant parents in this study discussed education, culture, and tradition when describing the best interests of their children. They did not perceive that the child welfare system promotes the best interests of immigrant children; rather, the powerful government agency (DSS) and child welfare practices have led immigrant parents to feel powerless and out of control. Clearly, there is a gap between child welfare professionals' and parents' understandings of immigrant children's best interests.

One could argue that child welfare officials might not see education as a concern because of the established K-12 public education and the fact that officials have no power to improve school quality. One could also argue that every parent, particularly those in low-income families, would agree that education is in the best interests of the child. However, these arguments fail to recognize that immigrant children have other educational needs that require additional resources, such as English as Second Language classes, homework assistance, and support to help parents navigate the school system and prepare their children for college. Immigrant children face more pressure than nonimmigrant children to excel in education in order to fit in the new society (Fix & Capps, 2005); this pressure is exacerbated by their need to also satisfy their parents as they are cognizant that their parents sacrificed much for them to have a "chance for a better life" in America (Zhou, 1997). Further, immigrant parents show little sympathy for their children's struggles in developing a new bicultural identity while under pressure to preserve their native traditions and culture. Immigrant parents believe that their children's education should not be limited to academics; bilingual education, cultural education, and programs to reinforce cultural identity and ethical behavior are also critical for their children's development.

Unfortunately, today's public schools often do not have the resources to meet immigrant children's additional educational needs. For instance, schools usually teach cultural education, identity development, and ethical behavior, which was the case in many immigrant home countries. It is clear that some immigrant children's best interests could not be readily served by the public educational systems unless such special programs are in place, which is rare in the majority of US schools (Fix & Capps, 2005). When numerous developmental (both educational and psychological) benefits of biculturalism and bilingualism are nested in immigrant families (Coll & Marks, 2011), decisions about removing an immigrant child or selecting a foster family should be made with great caution. Therefore, the public child welfare system should consider strategies or protocols that could maximize children's educational opportunities in order to meet their special needs in education and acculturation and preserve immigrant children's strengths.

Child welfare decision makers could debate whether the best interests of the child standard requires attending to everything that affects the child or whether certain considerations should be disregarded or prioritized. In addition to the concern over children's safety, both legal and social work professionals have often emphasized the psychological aspects of the best interests of the child, including the bonds developed with caregivers, the stability of ongoing relationships, and the feeling of security (e.g., Mercer, 1998; US Department of Health and Human Services Office on Child Abuse and Neglect, 2003). In general, professionals attempt to assure that "commonly recognized best interests," such as food, shelter, and education for all children, are met. But whether the public systems have met the needs of *immigrant* children in terms of food, shelter, and education, culture, and tradition have not been fairly addressed. For example, is the child receiving culture-based food? Is the child living in a place with private space to practice his or her religion? Is the child being educated at home and in school in a culturally appropriate manner? It should be noted that the psychological best interests of the child depend on these "commonly recognized best interests;" and psychological dysfunction often is a product of unmet daily needs. For immigrant children, these "commonly recognized best interests" might be particularly meaningful to their psychological wellbeing.

It is discouraging, although not surprising, to find out that immigrant parents in this study viewed the child protection system as an "oppressor" instead of an "aid." Different cultures have different definitions of "abuse" and "neglect," as well as different values and attitudes about obedience and parental authority (Fontes, 2002). In many cultures, parents value closeness, dependence, obedience, and family loyalty, which is different from the predominate US culture, which values autonomy and independence (Chiu, 2008). While such cultural values are reflected in child welfare laws and practices, the United States seems to give children more "rights" than in some other countries that are less child centered and more authoritarian, patriarchal, or matriarchal. Thus, discipline, particularly limited use of corporal punishment, probably reflects the traditional way of raising children in immigrants' home countries, and the role of being a parent in their respective cultures. Government interventions into such parent–child relationships were thought as a type of oppression by immigrant parents.

The child protection system (i.e., DSS in this study) has failed to recognize the psychological condition that immigrant parents have been experiencing because of migration. This study indicates that many immigrant parents feel powerless when watching their children assimilate and acculturate; likewise many of them feel powerless in coping with school concerns and disciplinary issues. The powerful institutions of the public child welfare system and the dominant Western norms of childrearing threaten parents' capacity to raise their children in a culturally meaningful way. As a result, many immigrant parents lose their confidence in their parenting capacities; they feel perplexed as to what they *should* do, what they *can* do, and how to nurture, educate, and discipline their children as well as provide the basics of food and shelter. To help parents, the child welfare system is adapting (e.g., new practice models, including family conferencing and family-to-family initiatives) to meet the needs of ethnic minority children and their families. In addition to these positive steps, professionals should be aware that immigrant parents and families may not have the resources and capabilities required to promote their children's healthy growth and development, and might not be well prepared to play an active role in the child welfare system. Professionals can help empower immigrant parents so that they are better able to parent their children.

A final notable discussion point involves the finding that immigrant parents from different ethnic and cultural groups had different concerns regarding their children's best interests. Child welfare professionals should be aware that immigrant communities have varying experiences in their countries of origin, during their migration, and in the United States. Immigrant families also have different cultural traditions and resources for coping with migration-related stressors and acclimating in the new society. When determining the best interests of immigrant children, it should be recognized that there is no "one-size-fits-all" solution. Finally, the system needs to take steps to empower immigrant children and their parents, increase immigrant community capacity, and even nurture a bilingual bicultural child welfare workforce. These efforts could not only help better identify the best interests for immigrant children with specific cultural and migration backgrounds but also address the root causes of child abuse and neglect, related to culture.

In consideration of the immigrant parents' perception of the "best interests of the child," child welfare workers need to have a great amount of patience, make diligent efforts, and solicit systematic supports in order to truly value and understand immigrant parents' input regarding the best interests of the child. They also need to respect parents' culture and tradition, and to communicate and collaborate efficiently. Without programs to assist immigrant parents with navigating the child welfare system and other social systems and integrating into Western culture, these parents will continue to struggle with their parenting responsibilities. And they will continue to live in the fear that they will lose their children either to American culture or to the US child protection institutions—neither outcome would fit the original intention of child welfare laws and practices.

As with all research methods, there are limitations in this study. By its nature, focus group research is open ended and cannot be entirely predetermined and controlled by the researcher. While focus group discussions centered on the best interests of the child standard, some issues remain unexplored. Particularly, as the focus group format discouraged some immigrant parents from trusting others with sensitive or personal information, there was a lack of in-depth discussions regarding parents' psychosocial wellbeing and the extent that psychosocial stressors affected their parenting capacity and parent–child relationships. Additionally, representative samples were not obtained in the focus groups that were assembled. All participants spoke at least a little English—as a result, the study results do not generalize to non-English speakers. Further, immigrant parents were speaking in a specific context, within a specific culture. Thus, results from this study cannot be generalized to different immigrant communities. Further research should consider adopting different research methodologies and holistic approaches to provide a comprehensive understanding of the best interests standard; mental health–oriented quantified studies would greatly help identify the trajectory from immigration psychology to the best interests of the child.

Conclusion

Immigrant parents' understanding of the "best interests of the child"—which varies by immigrant group—suggests the best interests of immigrant children could not be achieved through a "one-size-fits-all" approach. While immigrant parents are learning and adopting American ways of parenting, the US legal and child welfare system should also be adapting. Given the various needs of children with different cultural experiences, the mechanism to define the best interests of an immigrant child must be dynamic. That is, the best interests of immigrant children should not only include those conventional understandings (e.g., what is good for children is based, perhaps, on Western-oriented social sciences and professionals' own beliefs) but also consider factors helping immigrant children to develop into competent adults with rich cultural heritage. Results from this study also suggest that child welfare professionals should continue to discuss and define the best practices in order to build or regain the trust of immigrant communities and establish a reputation for effective interventions and passionate practitioners.

References

Abrams, K. (2006). Immigration status and the best interests of the child standard. *Virginia Journal of Social Policy and the Law, 14*(1), 87–102.

Arifuku, I., Peacock, D. D., & Glesmann, C. (2006). Profiling incarcerated Asian and Pacific Islander youth: Statistics derived from California Youth Authority Administrative Data. *AAPI Nexus, 4*(2), 95–110.

Berry, J. W. (2001). A psychology of immigration. *Journal of Social Issues, 57*(3), 615–631. doi: 10.1111/0022-4537.00231.

Blain, D. M., & Weiner, M. H. (2005). Resolving parental custody disputes—A comparative exploration. *Family Law Quarterly, 39*, 247–266.

Britner, P. A., & Mossler, D. G. (2002). Professionals' decision-making about out-of-home placements following instances of child abuse. *Child Abuse and Neglect, 26*, 317–332. doi: 10.1016/S0145-2134(02)00311-3.

Burford, G., & Hudson, J. (Eds.). (2000). *Family group conferencing: New directions in community-centered child and family practice*. Piscataway, NJ: Aldine Transaction.

Chase, S. E. (2005). Narrative inquiry: Multiple lenses, approaches and voices. In N. K. Denzin & Y. S. Lincoln (Eds.), *The Sage handbook of qualitative research* (3rd ed., pp. 651–679). Thousand Oaks, CA: Sage.

Children's Bureau. (n.d.). *Reports and results of the Child and Family Service Reviews (CFSRs)*. Retrieved July 2013. from http://library.childwelfare.gov/cwig/ws/cwmd/docs/cb_web/SearchForm.

Child Trends. (2010). *Immigrant children*. Retrieved August 6, 2013 from http://www.childtrends.org/?indicators=immigrant-children.

Chiu, E. M. (2008). The cultural differential in parental autonomy. *UC Davis Law Review, 41*, 1773–1828.

Clement, N. (2008). Do "reasonable efforts" require cultural competence? The importance of culturally competent reunification services in the California child welfare system. *Hasting Race and Poverty Law Journal, 5*, 397–440.

Coll, C. G., & Marks, A. K. (Eds.). (2011). *The immigrant paradox in children and adolescents: Is becoming American a developmental risk?* Washington, DC: APA Books.

Connolly, M. (2006). Up front and personal: Confronting dynamics in the family group conference. *Family Process, 45*(3), 345–357. doi: 10.1111/j.1545-5300.2006.00175.x.

Davis, J. (2001). American Indian boarding school experiences: Recent studies from native perspectives. *OAH Magazine of History, 15*(2), 20–22.

Dettlaff, A. J., Earner, I., & Phillips, S. D. (2009). Latino children of immigrants in the child welfare system: Prevalence, characteristics, and risk. *Children and Youth Services Review, 31,* 775–783. doi: 10.1016/j.childyouth.2009.02.004.

Eekelaar, J. (1994). The interests of the child and the child's wishes: The role of dynamic self-determinism. *International Journal of Law and Family, 8,* 42–61.

Fix, M., & Capps, R. (2005). *Immigrant children, urban schools, and the No Child Left Behind Act.* Migration Information Source. Retrieved July 2013, from http://www.migrationinformation.org/Feature/display.cfm?ID=347.

Fong, R., McRoy, R., & Ortiz-Hendricks, C. (Eds.). (2006). *Intersecting child welfare, substance abuse, and family violence: Culturally competent approaches.* Washington, DC: Council on Social Work Education.

Fontes, L. A. (2002). Child discipline and physical abuse in immigrant Latino families: Reducing violence and misunderstandings. *Journal of Counseling and Development, 80,* 31–40.

Fontes, L. A. (2005). *Child abuse and culture: Working with diverse families.* New York, NY: Guilford Press.

Gambrill, E. D. (2005). Decision making in child welfare: Errors and their context. *Children and Youth Services Review, 27*(4), 347–352. doi: 10.1016/j.childyouth.2004.12.005.

Go, C. G., & Le, T. N. (2005). Gender differences in Cambodian delinquency: The role of ethnic identity, parental discipline and peer delinquency. *Crime and Delinquency, 51,* 220–237. doi: 10.1177/0011128704273466.

Greenfield, P. M., & Cocking, R. R. (Eds.). (1994). *Cross-cultural roots of minority child development.* Hillsdale, NJ: Erlbaum.

Harker, K. (2001). Immigrant generation, assimilation, and adolescent psychological well-being. *Social Forces, 79*(3), 969–1004.

Hernandez, D. J. (Ed.). (2000). *Children of immigrants: Health, adjustment, and public assistance.* Washington, DC: National Academy Press.

Krueger, R. A., & Casey, M. A. (2008). *Focus groups: A practical guide for applied research.* Thousand Oaks, CA: Sage.

McGinnis, T. A. (2007). "Khmer pride": Being and becoming Khmer-American in an urban migrant education program. *Journal of Southeast Asian American Education and Advancement, 2,* 1–19.

Mercer, K. L. (1998). A content analysis of judicial decision-making: How judges use the primary caretaker standard to make a custody determination. *William and Mary Journal of Women and Law, 5,* 1–149.

Osmanagic v. Osmanagic, 872 A.2d 897 (2005).

Perreira, K. M., Chapman, M. V., & Stein, G. L. (2006). Becoming an American parent: Overcoming challenges and finding strength in a new immigrant Latino community. *Journal of Family Issues, 27*(10), 1383–1414. doi: 10.1177/0192513X06290041.

Pew Hispanic Center. (2006). *Recently arrived migrants and the congressional debate on immigration.* Retrieved July 2013, from http://www.pewhispanic.org/files/factsheets/15.pdf.

Portes, P., & Zady, M. (2002). Self-esteem in the adaptation of Spanish-speaking adolescents: The role of immigration, family conflict, and depression. *Hispanic Journal of Behavioral Sciences, 24*(3), 296–318.

Rico v. Rodriguez, 120 P.3d 812 (Nev. 2005).

Takeuchi, D. T., Nolan, Z., Hong, S., Chae, D., Gong, F., Gee, G. C., ... Alegria, M. (2007). Immigration-related factors and mental disorders among Asian Americans. *American Journal of Public Health, 97*(1), 84–90. doi: 10.2105/AJPH.2006.088401.

Thronson, D. B. (2006). Choiceless choices: Deportation and the parent-child relationship. *Nevada Law Journal, 6,* 1165–1214.

Thronson, D. B. (2008). Custody and contradictions: Exploring immigration law as federal law in the context of child custody. *Hastings Law Journal, 59,* 453–513.

US Department of Health and Human Services, Office on Child Abuse and Neglect. (2003). *Child protective services: A guide for caseworkers, 2003.* Washington, DC: US Department of Health and Human Services.

US Department of Health and Human Services, Office on Child Abuse and Neglect. (2011). *Child maltreatment 2010.* Washington, DC: US Department of Health and Human Services, Administration on Children, Youth and Families.

US Department of Homeland Security, Office of Immigration Statistics. (2008). *Immigration enforcement actions: 2007.* Retrieved July 2013, from http://www.dhs.gov/xlibrary/assets/statistics/publications/enforcement_ar_07.pdf.

Vericker, T., Kuehn, D., & Capps, R. (2007). *Foster care placement settings and permanency planning: Findings from Texas.* Washington, DC: The Urban Institute.

Xu, Q. (2005). In the "best interest" of immigrant and children: Deliberating on their unique circumstances. *Child Welfare, 84*(5), 747–770.

Zhou, M. (1997). Growing up American: The challenge confronting immigrant children and children of immigrants. *Annual Review of Sociology, 23,* 63–95.

13

Assessment of Mock Jurors' Attributions and Decisions in Child Abuse Cases: Protecting the Wellbeing of Obese Children

Jenny Reichert and Monica K. Miller

The prevalence of overweight and obese children has increased dramatically over the last 30 years; as of 2013, roughly 17% of children (ages 2–18 years) are considered medically obese (Center for Disease Control [CDC], 2013). Obesity in children is a major risk factor for social and psychological issues like discrimination and low self-esteem; children also risk long-term physical ailments like cardiovascular disease, certain types of cancer, and type 2 diabetes (CDC, 2013). As a result, obesity is now considered the single largest health concern among children (Robinson, 2008), and there is also legitimate concern for the psychological wellbeing of obese children. These risks to obese children's wellbeing could have legal ramifications. According to some child abuse laws regarding medical neglect, a minor's physical health is the responsibility of the parent (Myers, 1998), which arguably includes excessive weight gain that could lead to the child's health problems and decreased wellbeing. These potential long-term health consequences might warrant an extension of child abuse laws to specify obesity as a form of medical neglect.

The legal system is currently dealing with an increase of cases involving childhood obesity in both civil and criminal realms (Darwin, 2008). For instance, in 2009, Jerri Gray was arrested in South Carolina and charged with criminal neglect after her 14-year-old son reached a weight of 555 pounds (Cox, 2009).[1] Because

---

[1] Gray also lost custody of the child. Parents can face both criminal and civil consequences resulted to their children's obesity. This chapter focuses primarily on criminal prosecutions.

there was no previous legal precedent, verdicts (measured by community sentiment) in this and related cases will dictate if and when childhood obesity will be treated as a crime in future cases. According to Finkel (2001), community sentiment reflects not the law as enacted by legislators, but rather the ordinary man's notion of what the law "ought to be." Jurors influence policy by bringing with them into the jury box a sense of community sentiment, or how ordinary people think the law *should* work, and why some defendants should be found guilty and others not. In the first two studies in this chapter, the trial summary described a criminal trial and asked participants to act as jurors. In this way, participants acted as community members, whose verdicts reflected a sample of community sentiment regarding these prosecutions and thus may impact the path of child abuse law and policy development.

The first purpose of these studies was to assess support for prosecuting the parents of obese children. The second purpose was to investigate whether *external* factors (e.g., attributions about the cause of the child's obesity related to the case facts) or factors *internal* to the juror (e.g., assignment of responsibility; perceptions of the mother and of the child's suffering; individual differences) influence participants' decisions in criminal child abuse cases involving childhood obesity. The third purpose was to develop a list of factors that influence decisions in these types of cases by asking participants to list their thoughts. To these ends, two experiments manipulated the personal and situational attributions about the cause of the child's obesity, measured participants' attributional complexity, and tested a model of attribution of responsibility; the third study measured general support for and thoughts about child abuse prosecutions for childhood obesity. Results revealed how jurors make decisions about these rare but increasing legal actions that affect children's wellbeing. A brief review of attribution theory lays the foundation for the current research.

Attribution Theory

Jurors often make attributions about defendants in criminal trials; this process influences decisions about guilt and punishment. According to attribution theory, individuals constantly observe the behaviors of others and the behaviors' consequences; individuals then attempt to derive the causes of those actions (Moskowitz, 2005). Generally, individuals are likely to make "situational" attributions when the behavior performed is out of the control of the actor (i.e., the actor did not choose to behave in that way but was compelled to act by external forces). In contrast, if the actor is perceived as in control of the behavior, observers are more likely to make "personal" attributions. Individuals also could make personal attributions to those who have repeated certain behaviors in a variety of settings; the repetition shows a pattern of behavior, which implies that the behavior was not a one-time accident (Moskowitz, 2005). Jurors develop attributions by considering things like case facts, which occur outside or "external" to the juror, and their attitudes and perceptions, which are "internal" to the juror (Moskowitz, 2005). Together, external and internal factors help individuals attribute causality for behavior.

Situational Attributions

Although actors perform behavior, they are not always in direct control of those behaviors. Often actors are exposed to uncontrollable environmental influences that compel them to deviate from their stable personality (Moskowitz, 2005). These environmental influences lead observers to make situational attributions because the consequences of the actor's behaviors are determined to be out of the actor's control. Generally, less offense is taken to unfavorable outcomes if the outcomes are uncontrollable (e.g., caused by an accident or act of nature), and the actor is blamed less for having caused the unfavorable outcome (Gilbert, 1998). The first two studies were constructed to test this idea. An uncontrollable cause (genetic predisposition) for the child's obesity was described in the experimental conditions, whereas no cause was described in the control conditions. When mock jurors perceive that the cause was uncontrollable, they are assumed to be more likely to make situational attributions and should blame the actor less.

Personal Attributions

Observers assume that an actor's personality, thoughts, feelings, and cognitions are displayed by the actor's behaviors, and when behaviors are repeated and consistent, observers often make personal attributions for that behavior. If a consistent pattern of behavior emerges which results in unfavorable outcomes, the actor is blamed more for the outcome as compared to a one-time behavior (Gilbert, 1998). This idea was tested in the first two studies. In Study 1, the mother was described as either normal weight or overweight; mock jurors reading about an overweight mother were expected to infer a pattern of behavior by an overweight mother (who presumably became overweight because of poor lifestyle choices) who passed her poor habits on to her overweight child. In Study 2, the mother had an older child, whose weight was manipulated either as normal weight or overweight; mock jurors reading about the overweight older child were expected to infer a pattern of behavior because the mother had raised two overweight children. When mock jurors believe there is a repeated and consistent pattern of behavior, they should be more likely to make personal attributions and blame the actor more.

Attribution of Responsibility

Controllability and consistency of behavior are external to observers (i.e., participant jurors) and are expected to account for much but not all of the observers' attributions and decisions. There also might be factors internal to the observer, which influence these decisions, like attributions of responsibility. A model of attribution of responsibility (AOR; Gailey & Falk, 2008) was tested to determine which dimensions of AOR contribute to ratings of the parent's responsibility in child obesity cases. The full AOR model includes four dimensions: causality, knowledge, intentionality, and appreciation of moral wrongfulness. More responsibility for a negative outcome (e.g., child's obesity) should be assigned to actors who caused the outcome, knew the outcome would occur, intended to bring about the outcome, and possessed the moral capacity to anticipate the outcome.

To assess the first dimension, causality, jurors determined the degree to which the defendant was the direct cause of her son's overweight. Knowledge, the second dimension, involves the defendant's awareness that her behavior would lead to the negative outcome (obesity) and assumes what a reasonable actor should have known. For the third dimension, intentionality, jurors assess whether the unfavorable outcome was accidental or intentional. The fourth dimension, moral wrongfulness, is less concerned with the specific action and more with the moral capacities of both the actor and the observer (in the first two studies, the defendant and the juror; Gailey & Falk, 2008). The AOR predicts that perceptions of these four dimensions influence attributions of responsibility. In Studies 1 and 2, defendant parents rated by participants as higher on measures of causality, knowledge, intentionality, and moral wrongfulness were expected to be seen as more responsible for their child's condition (according to the AOR model), as compared to parents rated lower on these measures; this was expected to be reflected in verdicts and sentences.

Attributional Complexity

Another factor internal to the observer that could influence attributions is the participant jurors' attributional complexity. When making attributions, individuals often rely on either a simple attribution process or a more complex attribution process (reflecting their attributional complexity), which might influence later decisions (Fletcher, Danilovics, Fernandez, Peterson, & Reeder, 1986). Individuals lower on attributional complexity typically seek simpler explanations for the behaviors in question. For example, they would be less likely to accept an "obesity is caused by many factors" explanation than those who are higher on attributional complexity (Fletcher et al., 1986). Because this would require considering multiple environmental and personal causes of obesity, it would be simpler to accept what the prosecutor has asserted: that the parent caused the child's obesity. In contrast, jurors high in attributional complexity might give the parent the benefit of the doubt because they would likely consider multiple causes, including genetics, the will of the child, availability of food, and exercise options. As a result, respondents lower in attributional complexity were expected to be more likely to render a verdict of guilty and a more punitive sentence than those who scored higher.

Bias Against the Overweight

Participants might also determine verdicts based on their own prejudices against the overweight. Prejudice against the overweight is considered one of the last socially acceptable forms of prejudice (Brochu & Morrison, 2007; Crandall, 1994; Puhl, Moss-Racusin, Schwartz, & Brownell, 2008). Thus, participants might not feel inclined to conceal their prejudice and instead choose a verdict against overweight defendants because of their dislike of overweight people.

This prejudice might even extend to cases in which the defendant is normal weight. Research on ingroup-outgroup bias shows that when social identity is threatened, individuals are more prejudiced against outgroup members and bias is more pronounced for those who highly identify with their ingroup (Fein & Spencer, 1997; Tajfel & Turner, 1986). This is especially highlighted in the psychology of sports fans who display ingroup favoritism and denigrate not only the opposing team, but the *supporters* of opposing teams. This is particularly likely when people highly identify with their own team or when threatened (Wann & Grieve, 2005; Wann, Melnick, Russell, & Pease, 2001). Individuals high in prejudice against the overweight may view the overweight and their supporters as an outgroup; as a result, jurors high in prejudice against the overweight might denigrate an overweight defendant and a normal weight defendant alike, as both "support" an overweight child. As a result, participants who scored higher on measures of bias against the overweight were expected to return more guilty verdicts and more punitive sentences than those who scored lower, regardless of the weight of the defendant.

Overview of Study 1

In Study 1, the factors examined were the mother's weight and the presumed cause of the child's obesity, which manipulated both personal and situational attributions. Mock jurors were expected to infer a pattern of behavior (and thus personal attributions) from the overweight mother and an uncontrollable cause (and thus situational attributions) from the genetic predisposition.

Hypothesis one predicted that, compared to conditions in which the mother was normal weight, participants who read that the mother was overweight would return more guilty verdicts and assign longer sentences. Similarly, hypothesis two predicted that, compared to conditions in which no mention of genetics was made, participants who read that the child's obesity had a genetic link would return fewer guilty verdicts and assign shorter sentences. Remaining hypotheses predicted that participants would be more likely to return verdicts of guilty and a more punitive sentence as scores on the factors of attributions of responsibility (causality, knowledge, and intentionality) increase, as scores on attributional complexity decrease, and as scores on bias against the overweight increase. Although no specific predictions were made, additional analyses tested for (1) an interaction between the two manipulations; (2) relationships between the two manipulations on perceptions of the mother and perceptions of the child's suffering; and (3) relationships between perceptions of the mother and of the child's suffering and verdict/sentence.

Method

Design

The study employed a 2 (presumed cause of obesity: genetic disposition or no mention of genetics) x 2 (mother overweight or normal weight) between-subjects factorial design. Participants were randomly assigned to one condition.[2]

Participants

One hundred and thirty-five student participants were recruited through an online notice and completed the study online for course credit. Of the 135 university student participants, 64.6% were female; they were 49.4% White, 10.2% Hispanic American, 9.1% African American, 7.4% Asian American, and 3.4% other race. Further, 37% considered themselves "not at all overweight," 34.6% considered themselves "average weight," 13.4% "slightly overweight," and 3% "very much overweight." They ranged in age from 18 to 54 years ($M = 20$, $Mdn = 19$).

Procedure and Materials

Participants read a trial summary and completed a questionnaire online. All methods and materials were approved by the university's Institutional Review Board.

Trial Summary. Participants read one of the approximately 600-word summaries, which contained case facts, testimony from witnesses, and a photo of the defendant mother. The trial summary outlined the arrest of the fictional defendant Debra Thompson, described her obese son Matthew's

---

[2] Participants were assigned to conditions as follows: (1) normal weight mother, no mention of genetic link: 36; (2) normal weight, genetic link: 34; (3) overweight mother, no mention of genetic link: 28; (4) overweight; genetic link: 37.

condition, and defined "medical neglect" as a type of child abuse. In all conditions, a pediatrician, Dr. Wright, testified as to the long-term effects of childhood obesity and a neighbor of the defendant testified to Debra's parenting skills and lifestyle choice, describing the effort Debra took to keep her son's weight under control.

In the "genetic" conditions, a second pediatrician testified as an expert witness, explained recent findings showing genetic links to obesity in children, and pointed out that Matthew's father is also obese and suggested that Matthew has the genetics for obesity. In the control condition (i.e., no mention of genetics), this expert did not testify. Maternal weight was manipulated using a photograph of the same woman before (overweight condition) and after (normal weight condition) weight loss.

Questionnaire. Participants completed a survey containing the following sections, in order:

Judge's instructions. Participants read instructions modeled after those given in Florida (adopted in 2002) to prove neglect of a child.

Verdict and sentence. Participants indicated whether the defendant was guilty of medical neglect and recommended sentence using a 9-point scale ranging from 1 ("The least the law will allow") to 9 ("The most the law will allow").

Perceptions. Participants answered 10 questions on a 9-point scale indicating: overall perception of the defendant; how ethical they believe the defendant to be; perceptions of the defendant's parenting skill level; perceptions of Matthew's obesity, including social, emotional, and physical suffering, amount of disability Matthew suffers due to his obesity, and amount of responsibility Matthew has for his own situation. These were combined into two scales: perceptions of the mother ($\alpha = .86$) and perceptions of the child's suffering ($\alpha = .83$).

Manipulation/comprehension check questions. Participants answered multiple-choice questions regarding why the defendant was arrested, and whether an expert testified that there was a genetic link to Matthew's obesity. Participants also rated how overweight the defendant is.

Attribution of responsibility (AOR) survey. Participants answered questions taken from the AOR measure (Gailey & Falk, 2008) measuring causality (4 items, $\alpha = .74$), knowledge (3 items, $\alpha = .76$), and intentionality (4 items, $\alpha = .76$), all rated on a 9-point scale. A factor analysis showed proper loading for individual items; both eigenvalues and visual inspection of the Scree plot were considered in forming factors, which did not include a factor for moral wrongfulness as it did in the original AOR model.

Attributional complexity measure. Participants rated their agreement with 28 statements regarding attributional complexity using a 7-point scale (Fletcher et al., 1986; α = .93). Questions measured the following: level of interest, preference for complex explanations, presence of metacognition, awareness that behavior is a function of interaction with others, tendency to infer complex internal attributions, tendency to infer external causal attributions, and tendency to infer past external causes. Half of the items referred to attributional complexity and half to attributional simplicity.

Anti-Fat Attitudes and Dislike of Fat People scale. Participants completed two 12-item scales measuring perceptions of the overweight (Morrison & O'Connor, 1999; Wrench & Knapp, 2008), which included the Anti-Fat Attitudes Sale (AFA), 12 items phrased negatively in respect to the overweight (α = .82), and the Dislike of Fat People Scale (DFPS), 12 items phrased positively in respect to the overweight (α = .77). Participants rated their agreement with statements such as "Fat people are less sexually attractive than thin people" using a 5-point scale.

Demographic questions. Participants provided demographic information, including age, gender, and racial/ethnic background. They indicated their perceived weight status (overweight, normal weight, etc.).

Results

A total of 5 (2.8%) participants missed the manipulation check question about why the defendant was charged with child abuse, but all participants were included in the analyses, as results were comparable when they were excluded. A t-test for independent samples indicated that the manipulation check for weight was successful, as participants in the "normal weight" ($M = 4.38$, $SD = 1.05$) condition rated the mother as significantly less overweight than participants in the "overweight" condition ($M = 5.69$, $SD = 1.32$) ($t(129) = -6.31$, $p < .01$). The manipulation for a genetic link to obesity was not as successful; 21 participants (15.5%) missed the question about whether an expert testified about a genetic link to obesity and were dropped from the analyses. A total of 135 participants were included in the analyses.

External Factors

This section details several regression models and analyses of variances that demonstrate how the manipulated variables (i.e., "external factors" of interest to this study) affected verdict, sentence, perceptions of the mother, and perceptions of the child's suffering.

Verdict. A binary logistic regression analysis using weight of the mother, presumed cause of obesity, and an interaction between the two as independent variables and verdict as the dependent variable showed no main effect for weight of the mother, no main effect for presumed cause of obesity, and no interaction effect (all $ps > .05$). Overall, only 34.8% of participants found the defendant guilty across all conditions, indicating generally low support for such legal actions.

Sentence. Scores for recommended sentence were compared for all participants, regardless of whether they found the defendant guilty. An analysis of variance (ANOVA) using the weight of the mother, presumed cause of obesity, and an interaction between the two as IVs and recommended sentence as DV indicated no main effects and no interaction effect (all $ps > .05$). Overall, 67.7% responded that the defendant should be punished "the least the law will allow" and 12.1% "the most the law will allow." This indicates low support for punishing mothers of obese children.

Perceptions of Mother. An ANOVA using weight of the mother and presumed cause of obesity as IVs and mean scores for perceptions of the defendant as the DV indicated that there were no main or interaction effects (all $ps > .05$).

Perceptions of Child's Suffering. An ANOVA was conducted using weight of the mother and presumed cause of obesity as IVs and perceptions of the child's suffering as DV. There were no significant main or interaction effects ($ps > .05$).

Internal Factors

Several analyses were performed to determine whether various individual differences (i.e., "internal factors" of interest to the study) affected verdict and sentence. A logistic regression analysis was performed to assess the predictive power of participants' scores on the Anti-Fat Attitudes (AFA) scale and Dislike of Fat People scale (DFPS) on likelihood of returning a guilty verdict. The model was significant ($R^2 = .09$, -2 Log Likelihood $= 142.69$, $\chi^2 = 11.08$, $p < .01$); as scores on the AFA scale increased, the likelihood of returning a verdict of guilty increased as well (WALD $= 5.71$, $p = .01$, Exp(B) $= 1.83$). A separate logistic regression using attributional complexity as IV and likelihood of returning a guilty verdict as DV significantly predicted likelihood of returning a guilty verdict (DV; $R^2 = .06$, -2 Log Likelihood $= 138.65$, $\chi^2 = 6.47$, $p = .01$), such that as attributions became more complex, jurors were less likely to find the mother guilty (WALD $= 5.80$, $p = .016$, Exp(B) $= 1.89$). Further multiple regression analyses revealed no significant effect for AFA, DFPS, or attributional complexity on recommended sentence (all $ps > .05$).

Further analyses were performed to assess how additional "internal factors" like perceptions of the mother and of the child's suffering affected verdict and sentence. Logistic regression using perceptions of both the mother and of the child's suffering as IVs ($R^2 = .36$, −2 Log Likelihood = 103.72, $\chi^2 = 56.93$, $p < .01$) showed that perceptions of suffering (WALD = 3.52, $p = .06$, Exp(B) = 8.24) marginally significantly and perceptions of the mother (WALD = 20.27, $p < .01$, Exp(B) = .72) significantly influenced the likelihood of returning a guilty verdict. Perceptions of the mother also significantly influenced sentence recommendations; as perceptions of the mother became more negative, participants returned more severe sentence recommendations ($R^2 = .19$, $F(4, 125) = 7.20$, $p = .04$; $B = -.84$, $p < .01$).

To test the AOR model, a binary logistic regression analysis using the factors of the AOR model (causal, knowledge, and intent) as IVs and the verdict variable as DV revealed that that the regression model was significant ($R^2 = .26$, −2 Log Likelihood = 118.39, $\chi^2 = 36.12$, $p < .01$). Participants were more likely to return a verdict of guilty as their scores increased on the causal factor (WALD = 17.39, $p < .01$, Exp(B) = 1.83) and as their scores increased on the intent factor (WALD = 8.04, $p < .01$) of the AOR model. There were no significant effects for the knowledge factor ($p > .05$).

Similarly, a multiple regression analysis using the factors of the AOR model as IVs and the sentencing variable as the DV was significant ($R^2 = .17$, $F(3, 116) = 8.03$, $p < .01$); as scores on the intent factor increased, participants recommended a more severe sentence ($B = .51$, $p < .01$). There were no effects for causality or knowledge ($ps > .05$).

Discussion

One purpose of this study was to determine whether jurors would be willing to convict a parent for child abuse for allowing their child to become obese; overall, results from this study indicated that they were generally unwilling, as evidenced by the low conviction rate and light sentence recommendations. The second purpose was to determine whether internal and external factors influenced these decisions. This decision to convict was presumably based on both external and internal factors; however, hypotheses about *external* factors were unsupported. Personal and situational attributions about the cause of the child's obesity (including the weight of the mother and the presumed genetic cause of obesity) did not influence verdict, sentencing recommendations, perceptions of the mother, or perceptions of the child's suffering. Significant effects did emerge, however, concerning *internal* factors and the AOR model. The overall AOR model was significant, indicating that the AOR model is useful in this new context in addition to those previously tested.

Specifically, as participants' scores on the causal or the intent factor of the AOR scale increased, so did their likelihood of returning a guilty verdict. This likelihood also increased as perceptions of the child's suffering became more severe, and as perceptions of the mother became more negative. Higher scores on the intent factor of the AOR model were also related to more severe sentence recommendations, as were perceptions of the mother.

Other internal factors related to decision making were individual differences. Jurors with greater anti-fat attitudes were more likely to find the mother guilty, as were those with simpler attributions. Additionally, the more the jurors felt the child suffered and the more negative their perceptions of the mother, the more likely they were to find the mother guilty.

The number of nonsignificant results based on the manipulations might reflect that the manipulations themselves were not written in a way that properly demonstrated a pattern of the mother's behavior that would lead to personal attributions that increased the likelihood that participants would find her responsible for her child's weight. To address this issue, the second study was structured similarly, but it did not manipulate the weight of the mother to demonstrate a pattern of behavior or poor health choices. Rather, the trial summary described an older child (who is adult age and therefore does not legally qualify as a "child" the mother potentially abused) who was either normal or overweight, with the hopes that this manipulation would better establish a pattern of behavior which indicates that the mother is the cause of the child's obesity.

Overview of Study 2

The factors examined in Study 2 were the weight of the mother's adult child (who is either normal or overweight), as having two overweight children presumably shows a consistent pattern of behavior, and the presumed cause of the child's obesity (genetic predisposition or no mention of a genetic predisposition) to manipulate both personal and situational attributions. The hypotheses and exploratory research questions were identical to those of Study 1.

Method

Design

This study employed a 2 (presumed cause of obesity: genetic disposition or no mention of genetics) x 2 (adult son overweight or normal weight) between-subjects factorial design.[3]

---

[3] Participants were assigned to conditions as follows: (1) normal weight child, no mention of genetic link: 24; (2) normal weight, genetic link: 21; (3) overweight child, no mention of genetic link: 18; (4) overweight; genetic link: 22.

Participants

University student participants ranged in age from 18 to 47 years ($M = 22$, $Mdn = 21$) and 62.4% were female. Ethnic makeup of the 85 participants was 61% White, 14.1% Hispanic American, 7.1% Asian American, 4.7% African American, and 3.5% other race. Of the participants, 37.6% considered themselves "not at all overweight," 23.5% considered themselves "average weight," 15.3% "slightly overweight," and 3% "very much overweight."

Procedure and Materials

As in Study 1, participants read a trial summary and completed a questionnaire online. All materials and procedures were approved by the university's Institutional Review Board.

Trial Summary. The trial summaries were nearly identical to those used in Study 1, with two exceptions: (1) rather than a neighbor testifying on behalf of the defendant mother (as in Study 1), the mother's older child testified as to the mother's efforts to keep her son's weight under control and (2) rather than being shown photographs of the defendant, participants were shown a photo of the mother's adult son who was either overweight or normal weight, depending on the condition.

Questionnaire. Participants completed a survey identical to the one in Study 1. All alpha reliability scores were adequate for all analyses.

Results

Two (2.4%) participants missed the question about why the mother was arrested for child abuse, but all participants were included in the analyses, as results were comparable when they were excluded. Due to an error in the manipulation check question about the weight of the son, it is not possible to tell whether this manipulation was successful. As in Study 1, the manipulation for a genetic link to obesity was not as successful; a total of 11 participants (12.9%) missed the question about whether an expert testified to a genetic link to obesity and were excluded from analyses.

External Factors

This section details how the manipulated variables (i.e., "external factors" of interest to this study) affect verdict, sentence, perceptions of the mother, and perceptions of the child's suffering.

Verdict. A binary logistic regression analysis using weight of the older child, presumed cause of obesity, and an interaction between the two as independent variables (IVs) and verdict as the dependent variable (DV) showed no main effect for weight of the older child, no main effect for presumed cause of obesity, and no interaction effect (all $ps > .05$). Overall, only 27.1% of participants found the defendant guilty, suggesting low support for such prosecutions.

Sentence. An ANOVA including all participants using the weight of the older child, presumed cause of obesity, and an interaction between the two manipulations as IVs with recommended sentence as DV indicated no main effect for weight of the child, no main effect for presumed cause of obesity, and no interaction effect (all $ps > .05$). Overall, 70.6% of all participants indicated that the mother should be punished "the least the law will allow," and no participants indicated that she should be punished "the most the law will allow." This suggests low support for punishing parents of obese children.

Perceptions of the Mother. An ANOVA using the weight of the older child and the presumed cause of obesity as IVs and scores for perceptions of the mother as DV indicated no significant main or interaction effects (all $ps > .05$).

Perceptions of the Child's Suffering. A variable measuring the suffering of the obese child ($M = 5.76$, $SD = 1.62$) was used as a DV in an ANOVA with weight of the mother and presumed cause of obesity as IVs; there were no significant main or interaction effects (all $ps > .05$).

Internal Factors

Several analyses were performed to determine whether various individual differences (i.e., "internal factors" of interest to the study) affected verdict and sentence. A logistic regression analysis was performed to assess the predictive power of participants' scores on the Anti-Fat Attitudes (AFA) scale and Dislike of Fat People Scale (DFPS) on likelihood of returning a guilty verdict. Scores on these measures did not significantly influence likelihood of returning a guilty verdict ($p > .05$). This is contrary to the finding in Study 1.

Separate logistic regression analyses using scores on the AFA, DFPS and attributional complexity measures as IVs (see Study 1), and verdict as the DV revealed no significant effect for attributional complexity on verdict ($p > .05$). However, means for both AFA and attributional complexity scores were trending in the same direction as in Study 1, with increasing AFA scores resulting in a higher likelihood of guilty verdicts and increasing attributional complexity resulting in a lower likelihood of returning a guilty verdict. Additional multiple regression analyses revealed no significant effect on recommended sentence for AFA and DFPS, or attributional complexity (all $ps > .05$).

Further, logistic regression using perceptions of the mother and perception of the child's suffering as IVs and verdict as the DV ($R^2 = .19$, −2 Log Likelihood = 73.03, $\chi^2 = 11.84$, $p <.01$) showed that perceptions of the child's suffering significantly influenced the likelihood of returning a guilty verdict (WALD = 4.41, $p = .03$, Exp(B) = .64); perceptions of the mother did not significantly influence the likelihood of returning a guilty verdict ($p >.05$). However, in a separate linear regression using the same IVs and sentence recommendation as DV, perceptions of the mother did significantly influence sentence recommendations; as perceptions of the mother became more negative, participants returned more severe sentence recommendations ($R^2 = .12$, $F(4, 75) = 2.62$, $p = .04$; $B = −.32$, $p < .01$).

Like Study 1, a logistic regression testing the AOR model revealed that the AOR model was significant ($R^2 = .23$, −2 Log Likelihood = 73.49, $\chi^2 = 20.40$, $p <.01$). Participants who scored higher on the causal factor of the Attribution of Responsibility scale were more likely to return a verdict of guilty (WALD = 10.99, $p <.01$, Exp(B) = 2.27). A multiple regression using scores on the AOR factors as IVs and recommended sentence as DV was significant ($R^2 = .21$, $F(3, 76) = 6.60$, $p <.01$). Participants who scored higher on the causal and intent factors of the Attribution of Responsibility scale recommended a more severe sentence ($\beta = .33$ and .42, respectively; $ps <.05$).

Discussion

Like in Study 1, one purpose of this study was to investigate community sentiment regarding criminal prosecutions of parents of obese children and the second was to determine whether internal and external factors were related to participants' verdicts and sentences. As in Study 1, support for these prosecutions was low, as reflected in the low total number of guilty verdicts and low sentencing recommendations. Also similar to Study 1, external factors (i.e., the manipulated variables) did not influence either verdict or sentence recommendation, but internal factors (e.g., perceptions) did. Jurors were more likely to find the mother guilty as perceptions of the child's suffering became more severe, and jurors recommended more severe sentences for the mother as perceptions of her became more negative. Bias against the overweight did not influence the likelihood of returning a guilty verdict, possibly because there were no photographs of the mother shown and no mention of her weight in the trial summary, whereas in Study 1, the mother in half the conditions was shown as obese. The AOR model predicted the likelihood of returning a guilty verdict and recommended sentence in this study as well as in Study 1, contributing further to the understanding of attributions of responsibility. High scores on the causal factor of the AOR model significantly increased likelihood of returning a guilty verdict, and both the causal and intent factors of the AOR model positively influenced sentencing recommendations.

Study 2 findings reflect a lack of overall support for the prosecutions of parents of obese children, as did Study 1. To address this, a third exploratory study, which allowed participants to freely list their thoughts on the topic, was conducted to assess general support and reasons for one's thoughts about these prosecutions.

Overview of Study 3

In both preceding studies, overall support for the prosecutions was very low. The following study was designed to both assess general support for these prosecutions and develop a typology of factors that influence this support.

Method

Participants

Participants were 112 university students who completed the study online or in person during class time in criminal justice classes. Demographic information was not collected for any participants because of time limitations.

Procedure and Materials

Participants were asked whether they would support legislation prosecuting parents for allowing their children to become obese, and then were asked to list their thoughts on the topic. All procedures and materials were approved by the university's Institutional Review Board.

Support. Participants responded to the following question: "Recently in a number of states, parents have been prosecuted in court for allowing their child to become obese. Using the following scale, how supportive are you of these prosecutions?" using a 7-point scale with responses that ranged from 1 = "Not at all supportive, I do not think parents of obese children should be prosecuted in court" to 7 = "Totally supportive, I think parents of obese children should be prosecuted in court" with a Neutral/No opinion at point 4.

Thought Listing. Participants were given the following prompt: "What factors would influence your support for these prosecutions?" and were instructed to list all thoughts that entered their minds. They were given unlimited space and time to write, and were allowed to write multiple responses.

Results

A total of 112 participants were included in the analysis, including those who did not list any thoughts on the topic presented.

Support

Support for these prosecutions was very nearly normally distributed ($M = 4.19$; $SD = 1.82$). Of the 102 participants who responded, 22.5% responded with "Neutral/No opinion," while similar numbers reported "Not at all supportive" (10.8%) and "Totally supportive" (12.7%). Overall, the distribution of responses favored support for the prosecutions over opposition to the prosecutions: 33.3% responded with less support than the neutral point, while 44% responded with greater support than the neutral point.

Content Analysis

Of the 112 participants, 29 rated their support for the prosecutions but did not list any thoughts in response to the thought-listing prompt. Participants who did not write any thoughts were not more or less likely to support the prosecutions. Open-ended responses were coded into 41 separate themes. Because participants were given space and time to write multiple responses, a total of 156 responses were given.

Of all of the themes that emerged, the four most common themes appeared an equal number of times (19 times, accounting for 16.9% of participants) and were as follows: (1) parents are responsible for their children's health; (2) obesity in general could be caused by numerous factors out of parents' control, like environmental or societal factors; (3) obesity is greatly influenced by factors like socioeconomic status (SES); and (4) obesity is likely caused by genetics. Of the participants who reported their thoughts, 37.2% reported at least one of these themes.

The next most common themes were as follows: determining when it is appropriate to prosecute parents is based on circumstances of the case, including the child's age and severity of the obesity (mentioned 14 times, 12.5%); the importance of parental education on a child's health (mentioned 12 times, 10.7%); and the importance of parental influence on a child's health (mentioned 11 times, or by 9.8% of participants).

Remaining themes were mentioned less often and include the following: parents provide for their children and therefore determine much of their child's health status (mentioned 8 times, 7.1%); children learn from modeling their parents' behavior (mentioned 8 times, 7.1%); consequences of obesity and obesity as an epidemic (6 mentions, 5.3%); the controllability or uncontrollability of weight in general, parental laziness, and the cost of healthy food (5 mentions, 4.4%); and how individual rights to privacy are paramount above the state's rights to interfere (4 mentions, 3.5%).

Finally, participants were concerned with the intentions of the parents (mentioned 3 times, 2.6%), the comparison between obesity and starvation in regard to child neglect (mentioned twice, 1.7%), and how these prosecutions serve to devalue minority groups and women (mentioned twice, 1.7%). Only two participants (1.7%) mentioned how their personal experience with weight-related issues influenced their attitudes.

Discussion

The purposes of Study 3 were to assess community sentiment for the criminal prosecution of parents of overweight and obese children and to develop a typology of factors that influence these decisions. In all, 22.5% marked "Neutral/no opinion" and over a quarter of participants did not list any thoughts about the issue (i.e., reported no thoughts about the factors that would influence their support for prosecuting parents for having obese children). This might indicate that some have not given the issue serious thought or they preferred not to express an opinion/reasoning.

Some participants did have at least somewhat strong attitudes; 26.4% were somewhat or totally supportive of the prosecutions and 19.6% were somewhat or totally opposed. Many mentioned at least one factor that supports *and* at least one that opposes prosecutions. Many participants based their sentiment on the multidimensional nature of obesity, including varying causes of obesity (including genetics and unhealthy family practices); shared responsibility of schools, society, parents, and the children themselves; and the costs of changing lifestyle habits. Most were aware that obesity is caused by numerous factors; notably, three of the four most commonly mentioned comments were related to causes for obesity that are outside parents' control. Nevertheless, participants placed responsibility on parents for their children's health—as one of the most commonly mentioned themes was parental responsibility. Even so, participants did not overwhelmingly feel that this warranted prosecuting parents in court. It may be that individuals require more time and information to develop an informed opinion.

General Discussion

One purpose of this research was to determine whether internal and external factors affect verdicts in the context of childhood obesity cases. *External* (manipulated) factors for both Studies 1 and 2 did not predict verdicts or sentencing; rather, factors *internal* to the jurors, like individual differences in attributions of responsibility and perceptions of the mother and the child's suffering, predicted verdicts and sentencing. Studies 1 and 2 were designed to manipulate attributions that jurors would make by manipulating the case facts. While the manipulation of a genetic cause for obesity was not as successful as intended, the manipulation of the weight of the mother (Study 1) was successful yet still had no impact on verdicts or sentences. Perhaps other manipulations or case facts (e.g., if the child was even more obese than the one in this case) would produce different results in terms of predicting verdicts and the overall level of support for such prosecutions. However, based on these studies, external factors used in these studies do not seem to affect verdicts, sentences, perceptions of the mother, or perceptions of the child's suffering.

In contrast, a variety of internal factors were related to verdict and sentence. In both experiments, mock juror participants were more likely to find the mother guilty of child abuse if they believed that she had caused her son's obesity and intended for him to become obese (as measured by AOR factors). This implies that a mother who is responsible for her son's weight and knows the harms that obesity causes is expected to be careful in making eating and physical activity choices to prevent her child from becoming obese.

Further, the more jurors perceived that the child was suffering, the more likely they were to think that his mother was guilty of medical neglect. This could suggest that a mother is only seen as guilty if she has caused suffering; if there is no suffering, then there was no abuse. Sentencing for her crime, however, was not influenced by the child's suffering. Jurors thought the child had suffered greatly—and thus there was little variability in the suffering scores for the sentencing analysis. On the other hand, it could mean that jurors are not relying on the amount of suffering the child has experienced when making a sentencing decision; instead, they rely on their perceptions of the mother (as perceptions of the mother became more negative, sentencing recommendations became more severe).

Finally, both experiments showed the pattern (though only significant in Study 1) that jurors who are biased against overweight people or who have less complex attributions are more likely to vote guilty than those who are not. All of these findings support the notion that individual differences (e.g., bias, thought processes) can affect a juror's decisions. As such, understanding that participants' decision making is related to individual differences is quite important to understand support for such prosecutions.

The other purpose of the research was to measure sentiment toward prosecutions of parents with obese children. Overall, support for these prosecutions was low. Support in Study 1 (34.8% guilty) and Study 2 (27.1% guilty) was lower than Study 3 (44% of participants indicated at least some support, but only 12% were "totally" supportive). This could mean that Studies 1 and 2 did not provide enough evidence for a conviction; perhaps if there were more evidence, convictions would be higher. Study 3 did not provide specific case facts but instead just asked whether participants supported such prosecutions in general. Perhaps Study 3 participants imagined children who were more obese than the one described in Studies 1 and 2, and thus Study 3 participants were more supportive. In any event, it is not surprising that two different measures of support (verdicts and general support) lead to somewhat different results. Community sentiment research often finds that sentiment changes based on the particular stimuli presented (see Chapter 5 for another example).

The third purpose was to determine what types of thoughts participants had about such prosecutions. Content analysis of the open-ended responses suggests that support for these prosecutions is nuanced and multifaceted. Many participants were not willing or able to list even one thought about the topic, perhaps because they had not thought about the topic much. Those who did list thoughts listed many diverse thoughts. This also lends itself to the contention that support for such a complex issue like prosecuting parents for allowing their child to become obese is determined by factors internal to the juror rather than in the situational factors that would influence support in other cases. Jurors must balance their beliefs about the causes and consequences of obesity to determine who is responsible for obesity in children and how the responsible parties should be dealt with. Overall, community support for criminal legal actions to protect the wellbeing of obese children is low (especially as measured by verdicts), and as a result it is difficult to know whether criminal prosecutions will be successful in the future.

Implications

Results of this study have implications for the legal system, policymaking, social science, and child wellbeing in general. First, the finding that internal factors are related to verdicts and sentences has implications for the legal system—specifically for those involved in trials concerning child obesity as child abuse. Trial consultants can use this information in jury selection. For instance, jurors are more likely to vote guilty if they are biased against overweight people, have low attitudinal complexity, believe that an obese child is suffering, have negative perceptions of a mother whose child has become obese, or score higher on some of the AOR dimensions. Attorneys can select jurors that have the characteristics that would make them prone to a favorable verdict. They can also focus their case accordingly (e.g., highlight or downplay the child's suffering).

Second, results have implications for policymaking. Child abuse laws were enacted to protect the wellbeing of children, which includes guarding children's health. The health consequences of obesity have been deemed so dangerous that they warrant legal intervention, but at the time of this writing, no child abuse laws explicitly list childhood obesity as a punishable offense. If the prevalence of childhood obesity increases, concern for the wellbeing of obese children will grow. Courts are likely to encounter the question in the future and these studies, along with future assessments of community sentiment, could inform those legal decisions. Currently, such legal actions would find low support in the community. If policymakers want to use the legal system as a tool to combat obesity, it first needs to shape community sentiment so that legal prosecutions are normative and expected.

Third, this study has many implications for social science. Studies 1 and 2 both confirm that, as a whole, the AOR model is a success. It had been tested in other settings (e.g., predicting perceptions of sexual assault) and the current studies revealed that the model also predicts support for prosecutions for child obesity. The studies also found either that the manipulations did not manipulate situational/dispositional attributions or that situational/dispositional attributions do not influence verdicts. For instance, perhaps telling jurors that the mother had two children who were obese was not an adequate way to manipulate "repeat behavior." Or perhaps it did communicate to jurors that the mother had repeated the behavior, but that repetition did not lead jurors to attribute more blame to her for the child's obesity. Unfortunately, the studies did not take the measures necessary to test which of these options is correct, but future studies in attribution theory should attempt to clarify this. Further, psychology research in prejudice has found that attitudes toward obese people predict a variety of decisions (e.g., employment and hiring decisions, liability in medical malpractice cases and responsibility for criminal action). This research somewhat expands this line of research. Finally, psychological research on attitude complexity has indicated that attitudinal complexity is related to need for cognition, and this study expands on this body of research in that it also is related to verdicts.

Fourth, the study has implications for children's wellbeing. These prosecutions, while very new, are intended to send a message to parents that they need to protect their children from the harms that are associated with being obese. Yet our participants indicated overall low support for prosecutions. Does this mean that people do not believe that parents are responsible for their child's obesity? Or does it mean that they do not think that the legal system should prosecute parents for their children's obesity? Study 3 suggests the latter only. Clearly there is an obesity problem in the United States, and it needs to be addressed somehow, but prosecutions might not be the best way, because there is only weak support for prosecutions. Perhaps there are other ways to protect child wellbeing associated with the obesity epidemic. For instance, child protective services could intervene when children's health is threatened because of their weight, or the government could focus on providing education for parents, incentivizing healthy food purchases at grocery stores, removing vending machines from schools, restricting the sale of snack foods and sugary sodas and juices in schools, and building playgrounds.

Limitations and Future Directions

This research has several notable limitations. The first limitation is that the task participants were asked to complete was not particularly realistic and thus the responses may not mirror those in the real world. In contrast, real jurors would be exposed to live witnesses and realistic and sometimes graphic or technical evidence. They would also deliberate with other jurors and be aware of the real-life implications of their verdicts and sentences.[4] Although the procedure raises a number of limitations, some studies have indicated that the decisions of mock jurors and actual jurors do not differ greatly, and that mock jurors show signs of taking their task seriously (see e.g., Bornstein, 1999; Bornstein & McCabe, 2005). Further, deliberations can sometimes affect a juror's verdict (e.g., Devine, Clayton, Dunford, Seying, & Pryce, 2000; Miller, Maskaly, Green, & Peoples, 2011), which indicates that results might differ if participants had deliberated. While some research shows these limitations might not be great, these issues are not trivial, and future studies should provide more realistic stimuli or study actual jurors in actual child obesity cases.

A second limitation involves the diversity of the sample. University students were used for all three studies, and thus the findings might not generalize to the population as a whole. Students differ from the general population in many ways, some of which may be relevant to this study. For instance, Reichert et al. (2011) found that, in some cases, community jurors are more sympathetic toward overweight plaintiffs involved in medical malpractice cases than were college student jurors, perhaps because older community members were more likely to have struggled with weight themselves. Because students differ from the population as a whole on these measures, this study might have produced different results if a broader sample was used. Thus, although many studies have indicated that there are few meaningful differences between students and real jurors (e.g., Bornstein, 1999; Hosch, Culhane, Tubb, & Granillo, 2011), it is still important to keep limitations of generalizability in mind.

As mentioned earlier, the manipulations may have been poorly operationalized or too weak to produce intended attributions (which in turn affect verdicts and sentences). Future studies could manipulate other factors to see how such factors affect verdicts (e.g., severity of obesity or suffering related to the obesity, which influenced the likelihood of voting guilty in Studies 1 and 2). A related concern is that Studies 1 and 2 did not ask participants to self-report what factors influenced verdicts. It is possible that, like Study 3 participants, jurors in the first two studies recognized that there are many uncontrollable causes of obesity, and the "controllability" manipulation (i.e., whether the doctor mentioned that genetics might cause the child's obesity) was ineffective because all jurors—regardless of condition—blamed genetics or other uncontrollable causes. Unfortunately, there was no measure to

---

[4] Note, however, that only in a handful of states do jurors make sentencing decisions in non–death penalty cases. In most states, judges make sentencing decisions in non–death penalty cases. In all states that have the death penalty, jurors must make sentencing decisions in death penalty states.

determine what jurors blamed. Perhaps other manipulations would be more successful at manipulating the blame put on the parent.

Despite these limitations, the current studies are useful, as they present the first look into community support and decision making regarding prosecution of parents for their children's obesity. They also helped further what is known in several areas of psychology. Future studies can help advance and clarify these findings.

Conclusion

Obesity is a growing problem in the United States and threatens child wellbeing (CDC, 2013; Robinson, 2008). The legal system has begun addressing the problem through legal prosecutions, raising questions about whether people support such prosecutions. The studies presented here generally indicate that there is low support for such prosecutions. Studies 1 and 2 also found that internal factors, but not external factors, influenced support for the prosecutions (as measured by verdicts and sentences). This indicates that a person's individual characteristics—such as their perception of the mother, bias toward overweight people, and attributional style—impact their support for prosecutions. Further, verdicts were predicted by components of the AOR model, indicating that the attributions people make about the child's obesity affect their verdicts and sentences. The notion that individual beliefs and characteristics are related to support for these prosecutions is bolstered even further by Study 3 findings that there are many different thoughts that individuals rely on when forming their attitudes about prosecutions. Even so, many participants listed no thoughts on the issue, perhaps indicating a lack of previous knowledge of the issue.

Overall, these findings have important implications for law and policy that is designed to protect child wellbeing. There is clearly a problem with childhood obesity, but the low level of community sentiment found in these three studies indicates that criminal prosecutions might not be the best way to address this problem. Perhaps other ways (e.g., educating parents) might be better to address the epidemic. Such measures would protect children's wellbeing in a way that might be more acceptable to the community.

References

Bornstein, B. H. (1999). The ecological validity of jury simulations: Is the jury still out? *Law and Human Behavior, 23*(1), 75–91. doi: 10.1023/A:1022326807441.

Bornstein, B. H., & McCabe, S. G. (2005). Jurors of the absurd? The role of consequentiality in jury simulation research. *Florida State University Law Review, 32*, 443–467.

Brochu, P. M. & Morrison, M. A. (2007). Implicit and explicit prejudice toward overweight and average-weight men and women: Testing their correspondence and relation to behavioral intentions. *Journal of Social Psychology, 147*(6), 681–706. doi: 0.3200/SOCP.147.6.681-706.

Centers for Disease Control and Prevention (CDC). (2013). *U.S. obesity trends (BRFSS)*. Retrieved July 2013, from http://www.cdc.gov/obesity/data/trends.html#State.

Cox, L. (2009). Courts charge mother of 555-pound boy. *ABC News*. Retrieved July 2013, from http://abcnews.go.com/Health/WellnessNews/story?id=7941609.

Crandall, C. S. (1994). Prejudice against fat people: Ideology and self-interest. *Journal of Personality and Social Psychology, 66*, 882–894. doi: 10.1037/0022-3514.66.5.882.

Darwin, A. (2008). *Childhood obesity: Is it abuse? Child Welfare League of America*. Retrieved July 2013, from http://www.cwla.org/voice/0807obesity.htm.

Devine, D. J., Clayton, L. D., Dunford, B. B., Seying, R., & Pryce, J. (2000). Jury decision-making: 45 years of empirical research on deliberating groups. *Psychology, Public Policy and Law, 7*(3), 622–727.doi: 10.1037//1076-8971.7.3.622.

Fein, S., & Spencer, S. J. (1997). Prejudice as self-image maintenance: Affirming the self through derogating others. *Journal of Personality and Social Psychology, 73*, 31–44. doi:10.1037/0022-3514.73.1.31.

Finkel, N. J. (2001). *Commonsense justice: Jurors' notions of the law*. Cambridge, MA: Harvard University Press.

Fletcher, G. J. O., Danilovics, P., Fernandez, G., Peterson, D., & Reeder, G. D. (1986). Attributional complexity: An individual differences measure. *Journal of Personality and Social Psychology, 51*(4), 875–884. doi: 10.1037/0022-3514.51.4.875.

Gailey, J. A. & Falk, R. F. (2008). Attribution of responsibility as a multidimensional concept. *Sociological Spectrum, 28*, 659–680. doi: 10.1037/0022-3514.51.4.875.

Gilbert, D. T. (1998). Ordinary personology. In D. T. Gilbert, S. T. Fiske, & G. Lindzey (Eds.), *The handbook of social psychology* (pp. 89–150). Oxford, UK: Oxford University Press.

Hosch, M. H., Culhane, S. E., Tubb, V. A., & Granillo, E. A. (2011). Town vs. gown: A direct comparison of community residents and student mock jurors. *Behavioral Sciences and the Law, 29*(3), 452–466. doi: 10.1002/bsl.970.

Miller, M. K., Maskaly, J., Green, M., & Peoples, C. D. (2011). The effects of deliberations and religious identity on mock jurors' verdicts. *Group Processes and Intergroup Relations, 14*, 517–532. doi:10.1177/1368430210377458.

Morrison, T. G., & O'Connor, W. E. (1999). Psychometric properties of a scale measuring negative attitudes toward overweight individuals. *Journal of Social Psychology, 139*, 436–445. doi:10.1080/00224549909598403.

Moskowitz, G. B. (2005). *Social cognition: Understanding self and others*. New York, NY: The Guilford Press.

Myers, J. E. B. (1998). *Legal issues in child abuse and neglect practice*. Thousand Oaks, CA: Sage.

Puhl, R. M., Moss-Racusin, C. A., Schwartz, M. B., & Brownell, K. D. (2008). Weight stigmatization and bias reduction: Perspectives of overweight and obese adults. *Health Education Research, 23*(2), 347–358. doi:10.1093/her/cym052.

Reichert, J., Miller, M. K., Bornstein, B. H., & Shelton, D. E. (2011). How reason for surgery and patient weight affect verdicts and perceptions in medical malpractice trials: A comparison of students and jurors. *Behavioral Sciences and the Law*, *29*(3), 395–418. doi: 10.1002/bsl.969.

Robinson, T. N. (2008). Treating pediatric obesity: Generating the evidence. *Archives of Pediatric and Adolescent Medicine*, *16*(2), 1191–1192. doi:10.1001/archpedi.162.12.1191.

Tajfel, H., & Turner, J. C. (1986). The social identity theory of intergroup behavior. In S. Worchel & W. Austing (Eds.), *Psychology of intergroup relations* (pp. 33–47). Chicago, IL: Nelson-Hall.

Wann, D. L., & Grieve, F. G. (2005). Biased evaluations of in-group and out-group spectator behavior at sporting events: The importance of team identification and threats to social identity. *Journal of Social Psychology*, *145*(5), 531–545.

Wann, D. L., Melnick, M. J., Russell, G. W., & Pease, D. G. (2001). *Sport fans: The psychology and social impact of spectators*. New York, NY: Rutledge.

Wrench, J. S., & Knapp, J. L. (2008). The effects of body image perceptions and sociocommunicative orientations on self-esteem, depression, and identification and involvement in the gay community. *Journal of Homosexuality*, *55*(3), 471–503. doi: 10.1080/00918360802345289.

14

A Preliminary Analysis of Public Commentary Supporting and Opposing Mandatory HPV Vaccination: Implications for Policy

Lorie L. Sicafuse and Monica K. Miller

Mandatory human papilloma virus (HPV) vaccination has been the topic of heated public debate recently (National Conference of State Legislatures, 2011). As of 2011, 23 state legislatures are considering bills requiring preteen girls to receive the HPV vaccine before sixth grade. Virginia and Washington, D.C. enacted similar legislation in 2009 (National Conference of State Legislatures, 2011). Policymakers are often influenced by the community's opinions (Finkel, 1995) and will likely consider public sentiment when making decisions regarding mandatory HPV vaccination. Although some researchers argue that incorporating public sentiment into legal decisions increases perceptions of government legitimacy and compliance with the law in general (e.g., Finkel, 1995; Tyler, 2006), other legal professionals assert that laws based on public sentiment can have deleterious legal and social consequences (e.g., Blumenthal, 2003; Justice Scalia, *Planned Parenthood v. Casey*, 1992).

Both public opinions and their underlying *rationale* can help inform lawmakers of the potential for mandatory HPV vaccination to promote or undermine children's wellbeing. Thus, this research provides an initial understanding of public sentiment regarding mandatory HPV vaccination. Specifically, a content analysis examined Internet blogs written by community members supporting and opposing the mandate. Researchers focused on identifying comments that are practical/unemotional, moral, emotional, indicative of cognitive bias, and based on justice principles. Based on this information, policy implications are discussed for lawmakers considering mandatory HPV vaccination.

Mandatory HPV Vaccination: A Controversial Public Health Issue

HPV is the most common sexually transmitted infection (STI) in America (Friedman & Shepeard, 2007). More than 6 million people are newly infected each year (Javitt, Berkowitz, & Gostin, 2008) and approximately 80% of women under age 50 will eventually contract the virus (Self, 2008). Most HPV infections are benign and destroyed by the body's immune system; however, two strains of HPV cause 70% of cervical cancer cases (Javitt et al., 2008). Cervical cancer kills approximately 4,000 women per year (American Cancer Society, 2013), and treatment commonly involves radiation, chemotherapy, and surgery.

In 2006, the FDA approved Gardasil, a vaccine that protects women from these more serious strains of HPV (Javitt et al., 2008). A similar vaccine, Ceravix, met FDA approval in 2009 (US Food and Drug Administration, 2009).[1] Results from multiple clinical trials conducted with large samples of adolescent females and young women (generally ranging from 5,000 to 60,000 participants per trial) indicate that both variants of the vaccine are safe and highly effective in preventing HPV infection and subsequent precancerous cervical lesions (see Lu, Kumar, Castellsagué, & Guiliano, 2011, for a review). Reported adverse reactions to the HPV vaccine are comparable in frequency and severity to those of other routine vaccines (e.g., MMR, Hepatitis variants; see Pomfret, Gagnon, & Gilchrist, 2011, for a review). The HPV vaccine is most effective when administered prior to the onset of sexual activity and potential HPV exposure (Lu et al., 2011). Though these vaccines in general were met with tentative public acceptance (Dempsey, Zimet, Davis, & Koutsky, 2006), proposals to mandate them remain highly controversial (Vamos, McDermott, & Daley, 2008).

Opinions Regarding Mandatory HPV Vaccination

Researchers assessed public attitudes toward the HPV vaccine both before and after its FDA approval. Soon after the development of Gardasil, Hoover, Carfoli, and Moench (2000) conducted a survey that revealed that nearly all

---

[1] Gardasil also was FDA approved for men in 2009. However, there has been little discourse surrounding mandating the HPV vaccine for adolescent males. Thus, though issues concerning mandatory HPV vaccination in males merit further exploration, the current chapter specifically focuses on mandatory HPV vaccination for adolescent girls.

female adolescents and young adults were interested in receiving the vaccine. Interviews and focus groups indicated that parental and public attitudes toward the vaccine were generally positive, but participants had limited knowledge of HPV, cervical cancer risk, and Gardasil (Friedman & Shepeard, 2007; Reiter, Brewer, Gottlieb, McRee, & Smith, 2009). Dempsey and colleagues (2006) found that manipulating parents' exposure to information regarding HPV failed to impact their attitudes toward the vaccine. Yet others reported that a brief educational intervention significantly increased parental acceptance of HPV vaccination (Kennedy, Sapsis, Stokley, Curtis, & Gust, 2011).

Results from such studies may be further informed by prominent opinions about mandatory HPV vaccination expressed by individual professionals and laypersons. Representatives from both groups have advanced practical and unemotional commentary about mandatory HPV vaccination laws. In advocating for these regulations, medical professionals highlight the potential economic benefits of mandatory HPV vaccination (Self, 2008; Tavenner, 2007). Legal professionals as well as community members note that clinical trials demonstrated that the vaccine is nearly 100% effective and has few side effects (e.g., see Teachthefacts.org, 2007; Hannah, 2007). Challenging these regulations, some physicians (2008) have concluded that the HPV vaccine does not meet the criteria for inclusion in mandatory school immunization programs (Opel, Diekema, & Marcuse, 2008). Attorney Sherry Colb (2007) and members of the public (see Self, 2008) argue that the HPV vaccine may have harmful long-term side effects.

Many comments regarding mandatory HPV vaccination, however, are not logic based but instead reflect morals, emotions, and cognitive biases. For example, conservative Christian groups and some parents argue that vaccinations condone premarital sex (see Colb, 2007; Self, 2008), which is contrary to Christian morality. Walker (2007) blogs that arguments against mandating HPV vaccinations are "silly," and an anonymous blogger was "none too happy" about legislative efforts (Telling it Like it is, 2008), demonstrating the presence of emotions in such commentary. More recently, GOP presidential candidate Michelle Bachmann argued that the HPV vaccine could cause mental retardation, though no evidence exists to support this claim (Jaslow, 2011).

Additionally, many community members' comments reflect justice principles. For example, an anonymous blogger invokes the principle of legitimacy by stating, "I don't like or appreciate government officials... telling me what to do with my own children" (Telling it Like it is, 2008), implying that the government is not a legitimate authority in this area. These examples illustrate some of the more subjective arguments regarding mandatory HPV vaccination.

Incorporating Public Sentiment Into Legal Decisions

The notion that laws should reflect public sentiment underlies the concept of democracy. Public sentiment refers to community members' attitudes, beliefs, values, and perceptions of justice (Blumenthal, 2003). Highly complex, variable, and often contradictory, public sentiment can be difficult to assess. Yet "Legislators who routinely ignore their constituents' sentiments are likely to have their terms shortened on election day" (Finkel, 1995, p. 15). Lawmakers' reliance on public sentiment may result in a variety of legal and social consequences.

Benefits and Costs of Incorporating Public Sentiment

Individuals from a variety of disciplines advocate incorporating public sentiment into legal decisions. In *Planned Parenthood v. Casey* (1992), Justices O'Connor, Kennedy, and Souter noted that their decision to uphold the right to abortion was largely based on their perceptions of public sentiment. Academics stress both the value of public sentiment and the dangers associated with discounting community opinions (Finkel, 1995; Tyler, 2006). Perceptions of procedural justice and legitimacy often mediate the relationship between public sentiment and its social and legal consequences (Tyler, 2006). Procedural justice refers to the degree to which legal authorities treat individuals respectfully, uphold the moral values of the perceiver, and utilize fair processes (Blumenthal, 2003). Similarly, legitimacy refers to "the belief that authorities, institutions, and social arrangements are appropriate, proper, and just" (Tyler, 2006, p. 376).

Legal decisions inconsistent with public sentiment may decrease perceptions of government legitimacy directly by undermining public confidence in lawmakers (Finkel, 1995). Additionally, nonadherence to public sentiment may result in laws that many consider unjust and antithetical to their values, impacting perceptions of government legitimacy indirectly by decreasing perceptions of procedural fairness (Finkel, 1995). Because lawmakers are ostensibly elected to represent the community's values, *any* failure to consider public sentiment in policy decisions may be perceived as unfair and undermine government legitimacy. Perceptions of government illegitimacy may result in decreased compliance with not only laws incongruent with public sentiment but also with societal rules in general (Blumenthal, 2003; Tyler, 2006). Conversely, those who view legal authorities as legitimate voluntarily comply with legal regulations and accept legal decisions inconsistent with their preferences (Tyler, 2006).

Despite the benefits of incorporating public sentiment into legal decisions, doing so also may have deleterious consequences. Justice Scalia highlights such potential consequences in *Casey v. Planned Parenthood* (1992). Opposing the majority, Scalia posits that succumbing to public pressure undermines the Court's authority, which may actually *decrease* public perceptions of government legitimacy. Scalia further asserts that past adherence to public sentiment has increased that Court's susceptibility to the "slippery slope" of political pressure, resulting in subjective interpretations of the law.

Blumenthal (2003) also questions incorporating public sentiment into legal decisions. Citing evidence that most individuals are uninformed regarding criminal justice and public policy issues (e.g., see Denno, 2000), Blumenthal argues that basing laws on the opinions of experts, rather than public opinion, would prevent harmful legal decisions resulting from public misconceptions. Blumenthal further suggests that incorporating public sentiment into legal decisions can infringe upon constitutional rights. For example, some legal scholars have argued that policies banning same-sex marriage violate the fundamental right to marry; yet these measures often reflect the sentiments of the community (Tribe & Matz, 2012). "Shaming" punishments and capital punishment also enjoy widespread public support, despite concerns that these measures constitute "cruel and unusual punishment" (in violation of the Eighth Amendment; see Blumenthal, 2003).

Both historic and current legal decisions demonstrate negative societal effects of relying on public sentiment. For example, most community members in the Southern United States supported the historic Supreme Court decision in *Plessy v. Ferguson* (1896), which ultimately legalized racial discrimination (Caldas & Bankston, 2007). More recently, public sentiment has been implicated as a critical factor in the development of three-strikes-and-you're-out laws (Applegate, Cullen, Turner, & Sundt, 1996). Evidence suggests that these laws do not reduce crime (Krovandzic, Sloan, & Vieraitis, 2004) and result in severe prison overcrowding (Chen, 2008). As these examples illustrate, incorporating public sentiment into legal decisions may result in a host of negative outcomes. The dangers associated with adherence to public sentiment may be attributed to the morals, emotions, and cognitive biases that often underlie the opinions and beliefs of community members (Blumenthal, 2003; Finkel, 1995). Thus, lawmakers also must consider the potential consequences of legislation based on these factors.

Effects of Legislation Based on Public Morals, Emotions, and Cognitive Biases

Most legal professionals would agree that laws are intended to protect individuals from harm and infringements upon personal liberty (Abuhoff, 2006). In balancing these two principles, lawmakers must carefully consider the foundations of public sentiment that may influence the development and enactment of laws. In particular, lawmakers must exercise extreme caution when utilizing public sentiment based on morals, emotions, and cognitive biases. Legal professionals and research suggest that laws based on these factors may often be ineffective and fail to maintain individual freedoms or protect the public from harm.

Though conceptualizations of morality vary, it is generally agreed that this term refers to standards or codes of conduct dictating how people "ought to behave" and relate to one another (see Haidt, 2003). Two arguments are frequently utilized to highlight the potential adverse effects of incorporating morality into the legal system. First, morality is an abstract concept and subject to individual interpretation (Cole, 2008; Moffat, 2005). Consequently, legal regulations that reflect the morals of some may actually result in undue harm for others. Cole and Moffat both contend that popular morality was utilized to justify oppressive and inhumane actions in the antebellum South. Cole identifies Jim Crow legislation (mandating public racial segregation in Southern states) as a primary example of moral-based legal regulations that resulted in deleterious social consequences.

Second, legal professionals contend that laws promoting moral principles may infringe upon Constitutional rights, concluding that moral mandates are outside the scope of the US legal system. Upholding women's rights to terminate pregnancy, Justices O'Connor, Kennedy, and Souter stated, "Some of us as individuals find abortion offensive to our most basic principles of morality, but that cannot control our decision. Our obligation is to define the liberty of all, not to mandate our own moral code" (*Planned Parenthood v. Casey*, 1992, p. 850). Similarly, Abuhoff (2006) maintains that a moral-based legal system constrains individuals' basic rights to mandate their own moral code and interferes with free choice.

Despite the negative consequences associated with incorporating morality into law, individuals are often unable to avoid doing so. This may be attributed to the inextricable link between morality and affective response. "Moral emotions" are characterized as any emotional reaction accompanying moral-based judgments or reasoning, though some emotions are more readily associated with morality than others (e.g., anger, compassion, guilt; Haidt, 2003). Experiencing such moral emotions motivates individuals to act according to the moral violation perceived (Haidt, 2003). To illustrate, thinking about legal transgressions that violate one's conception of morality often elicits unpleasant emotions such as contempt, anger, and disgust (Darley & Pittman, 2003). Affective response intensifies as the perceived severity of the moral transgression increases, leading to "moral outrage" that culminates in the desire to punish the offender. Though interdependent, morality and emotion are distinct constructs, and affective response can and often does occur in the absence of any moral judgment or reasoning (Haidt, 2003). Thus, the current study treats moral and emotion-based arguments as separate variables.

Regardless of its origin, affective response often leads to judgment errors (Epstein, Lipson, Holstein, & Huh, 1992; Krauss, Lieberman, & Olson, 2004), furthering the notion that legislatures should be circumspect of emotionally charged public sentiment. Typically, those who process information in an unemotional state carefully scrutinize information, arriving at thoughtful and reasonable judgments (Epstein et al., 1992). Conversely, those experiencing strong emotions tend to process information automatically and rapidly, often relying on heuristics (i.e., cognitive "rules of thumb" people use to make sense of their social world; Kunda, 1999) and arriving at broad and biased conclusions (Krauss et al., 2004). The cognitive biases often reflected in public sentiment may be attributed to this tendency to rely on "cognitive shortcuts" during states of emotional arousal.

Although humans must rely on heuristics to some extent in everyday living (Kunda, 1999), it is extremely difficult to justify the enactment of laws based on erroneous judgments and distortions in reality. Yet many legislators routinely consider public sentiment based on these factors when making legal decisions. Megan's Law and the AMBER Alert system, both developed and enacted in response to public concerns over child abduction and murder (Zgoba, 2004), are two primary examples of legal regulations based on morals, emotions, and cognitive biases. These policies remain popular among lawmakers and the American public, but evidence suggests they are ineffective in protecting children from stranger abductions, molestation, and murder (Griffin, Miller, Hoppe, Rebideaux, & Hammack, 2007; Zgoba, Witt, Dalessandro, & Veysey, 2008). Moreover, these laws may have unintended negative consequences. AMBER Alerts may cause perpetrators to panic and murder their victim to avoid getting caught (Miller, Griffin, Clinkenbeard, & Thomas, 2009). Megan's Law, designed to alert the public to the presence of a convicted sex offender in their community, may actually increase the likelihood of offender recidivism (Levenson & D'Amora, 2007).

Laws based on morality, emotion, and cognitive biases are often well intentioned and motivated by strong personal convictions. Notwithstanding, lawmakers adhering to this type of public sentiment risk enacting ineffective regulations that may have negative social and legal consequences. Thus, an analysis of the factors underlying public sentiment regarding mandatory HPV vaccination may prove highly beneficial to lawmakers considering this legislation.

Overview of Study

Lawmakers considering mandatory HPV vaccination must analyze the costs and benefits of incorporating public sentiment into their decisions. Some legislators may utilize the results of public polls (e.g., "Parents wary," 2007) as an indicator of public support for mandatory HPV vaccination. Yet public polls often yield an inadequate and erroneous description of public sentiment and reveal nothing about the rationale underlying these opinions (Finkel, 1995).

In order to provide a better understanding of public sentiment regarding mandatory HPV vaccination, the current research analyzed blogs written by community members. Specifically, it sought to identify whether commentary is based on practical and unemotional reasoning, morality, emotion, cognitive biases, and justice principles. Although this purposive sample may not be representative of the entire community, individuals who blog about mandatory HPV vaccination are likely highly involved in the issue and may be more inclined to present their arguments to legislators than average community members. Additionally, they may be more likely to vote for politicians who share their views on mandatory HPV vaccination. Thus, lawmakers may be particularly inclined to consider the sentiments of individuals like these.

Research Questions

To determine the nature of public sentiment regarding mandatory HPV vaccination, the current research addressed the following questions:

1. What are the frequencies of comments contained in these blogs that express support for or opposition to the enactment of mandatory HPV legislation?
2. What are the frequencies of entire blogs authored by community members expressing overall support for or opposition to the enactment of mandatory HPV legislation?
3. What is the frequency of comments regarding mandatory HPV vaccination that reflect the following themes: *practical and unemotional reasoning, moral principles, emotional response, cognitive biases, principles of legitimacy,* and *principles of procedural justice*?
4. Do comments supporting and opposing mandatory HPV vaccination differ in the degree to which they reflect the themes cited in question 3?

Method

Sample Selection and Criteria

The purposive sample used for this analysis consisted of 106 Internet blogs authored by community members. Though the researchers intended to analyze 150 blogs, sample size was ultimately constrained by selection criteria. Numerous search terms and search engines were used in initial searches for blogs discussing mandatory HPV vaccination. The final sample was obtained by entering the term "mandatory HPV vaccination blog" (without quotations) into the Google.com search engine, as this phrase produced the greatest number of results. Blogs were selected if they appeared to be authored by community members, were not explicitly identified as an "article" or "editorial," and included any commentary supporting or opposing mandatory HPV vaccination. Such blogs were obtained from individual Web sites, blog Web sites, and online publications. Blogs authored by government officials and legal or medical experts were excluded. This process helped to better approximate the opinions of typical Web-connected community members with strong opinions regarding mandatory HPV vaccination. Due to the anonymous nature of blogs in general, it should be noted that no demographic information regarding the blog authors was recorded.

Theme Operationalization

Because this study aims to describe public sentiment regarding mandatory HPV vaccination by identifying the themes underlying relevant commentary, "comments" served as the primary unit of analysis. In this study, a "comment" was defined as a single sentence or a connected series of phrases or sentences that began by indicating a theme to be discussed and ended with the last sentence or phrase that discussed that theme. A sentence could contain more than one theme or comment, and a comment may be categorized under multiple themes. This analysis specifically focused on the identification and categorization of the following principal themes: degree of support for mandatory HPV vaccination, practical/unemotional, emotion, moral principle, justice principle, and cognitive bias (see Table 14.1 for a portion of the coding scheme). In addition, blogs themselves were categorized according to their overall position on mandatory HPV vaccination.

Comments were often classified under subcategories. For instance, comments expressing "emotion" were classified under "explicit negative emotion," "implicit negative emotion," "explicit positive emotion," or "implicit positive emotion" (see Table 14.1). To assess community members' overall opinions regarding mandatory HPV vaccination, items (entire blogs) were categorized according to their comprehensive position regarding mandatory HPV vaccination (very opposed, opposed, neutral, supportive, and very supportive).

Coding and Intercoder Reliability

The first author and an additional researcher randomly selected 16 blogs (approximately 15% of the overall sample) and coded each blog independently to establish intercoder reliability. Cohen's kappas calculated for each category ranged from .74 to 1, and $\kappa = .80$ for the overall sample, indicating an acceptable rate of intercoder consistency (Stemler, 2001). The remaining cases were split equally between coders and coded independently.

Results

The PASW statistical package was used for all data entry and analysis purposes. Analyses were primarily descriptive. Frequencies for each valence category (unfavorable, favorable, and neutral) were calculated to assess the degree of support for mandatory HPV vaccination expressed in discrete comments and entire blogs. After removing neutral commentary from further analyses (see explanation later), another series of frequencies were conducted for each theme category and subcategory to determine the extent to which they were reflected in valenced (i.e., unfavorable and favorable) commentary. Finally, crosstabs and chi-square tests were used to detect any significant differences

Table 14.1 Variables and Operational Definitions Used to Categorize Community Members' Commentary Regarding Mandatory HPV Vaccination

Variable	Operational Definition and Example
Comment position: supportive	Any comment intended to express support or justification for the enactment of mandatory HPV vaccination legislation.
	For example: "I'm not sure I understand the objections to mandatory vaccination for HPV."
Comment position: neutral	Any comment relevant to mandatory HPV vaccination but that is not intended to express support or justification for the enactment or rejection of mandatory HPV vaccination legislation.
	For example: "Texas governor Rick Perry created an executive order last week that requires all sixth-grade girls in Texas to receive the HPV vaccine."
Comment position: opposed	Any comment intended to express support or justification for the rejection of mandatory HPV vaccination.
	For example: "Mandating this drug would undoubtedly be a mistake."
Overall position: very opposed	Blog contains two or more comments categorized as "opposed" and no comments that are categorized as "supportive."
Overall position: opposed	Blog contains one comment categorized as "opposed" and no comments categorized as "supportive"; or contains three or more comments categorized as "opposed," at least one comment categorized as "supportive," and the number of "opposed" comments exceeds the number of "supportive" comments by two or more.
Overall position: neutral	Blog contains an equal number of comments categorized as "supportive" and "opposed"; or number of "supportive" ("opposed") comments does not exceed number of "opposed" ("supportive") comments by more than one.
Overall position: supportive	Blog contains at least one comment categorized as "supportive" and no comments categorized as "opposed"; or blog contains three or more comments categorized as "supportive," at least one comment categorized as "opposed," and the number of "supportive" comments exceeds the number of "opposed" comments by two or more.
Overall position: very supportive	Blog contains two or more comments categorized as "supportive" and no comments categorized as "opposed."
Practical/ unemotional basis	Comment is based on facts, rational thought, and clear reasoning; may cite accurate statistics or scientific research.
	For example: "A clinical trial involving 20,000 female participants found the HPV vaccine very effective; most of the observed side effects were pain at the injection site, fainting, or dizziness."

(continued)

Table 14.1 Variables and Operational Definitions Used to Categorize Community Members' Commentary Regarding Mandatory HPV Vaccination (continued)

Variable	Operational Definition and Example
Emotional basis: explicit positive/negative	Comment contains a word or series of words conveying an affective response synonymous with the arousal of pleasant (unpleasant) feelings.
	For example: "I was happy to hear about Rick Perry's proposal to mandate the HPV vaccine"; "Gardsil's side effects are horrifying…"
Emotional basis: implicit positive/implicit negative	Comment contains single words, phrases, or sentences that do not explicitly reference emotional states but are intended to convey an affective response associated with the arousal of pleasant (unpleasant) feelings.
	For example: "I think it (the vaccine) is great!!!"; "It's MY child, MY decision Mr. Perry!!!"
Moral basis	Comment reflects the author's conceptualization of a code of conduct held to be authoritative in matters of right or wrong.
	For example: "I do not believe the government should act in a way that basically says you are ignorant to not have preteen unprotected sex."
Cognitive bias	Comment proposes a relationship between two objects, events, or persons in the absence of sufficient evidence substantiating such a relationship or includes errors in probabilistic reasoning; and/or comment makes a statement or assumption that is invalidated by current research or literature.
	For example: "Monogamous women are not at risk for contacting HPV"; "Reported side effects have been written off by the FDA."
Procedural justice: fair/unfair	Comment expresses the perception that any action or intention of government officials or other authority figures who may influence mandatory HPV legislation are fair (unfair).
	For example: "I think the government should be commended for efforts to ensure that every young woman receives this vaccine"; "I think it is unfair that the HPV was tested on predominantly African American, inner-city girls."
Legitimacy: positive/negative	Comment expresses the perception that individuals or organizations should (should not) accept or obey the recommendations or orders of government officials or institutions; or expresses the perception that the government has the authority (does not have the authority) to mandate the behaviors of others.
	For example: "It is the government's job to prevent the spread of HPV"; "The government does not have the right to tell me what to do with my own children!"

in the types of themes expressed in comments opposing and supporting mandatory HPV vaccination.

Comment and Blog Position Regarding Mandatory HPV Vaccination

Frequencies of comments categorized as unfavorable, favorable, and neutral were calculated to address research question (RQ) 1. Analyses revealed that the majority of valenced comments expressed unfavorable opinions regarding mandatory HPV vaccination. Among the 1,316 identified comments, 35% were opposed to mandatory HPV vaccination, 19% were supportive, and 46% were neither opposed nor supportive and subsequently categorized as "neutral." These neutral comments primarily provided background information; they were not used to support a particular position or express ambivalent or uncertain attitudes. Thus, neutral comments were excluded from additional analyses examining themes underlying commentary, yielding a final sample of 711 comments.

The comprehensive positions of blogs (RQ 2) were determined by the proportion of opposing, supportive, and neutral comments included in each individual blog (see Table 14.1). Over half (51%) of the blogs sampled were categorized as "very opposed" to mandatory HPV vaccination. The remaining blogs were categorized as follows: very supportive (29%); supportive (5%); neutral (9%); and opposed (7%).

Underlying Themes

To examine RQ 3, frequencies were calculated for each of the categories and subcategories representing the following themes: practical/unemotional basis, emotional basis, moral basis, cognitive bias, and justice principles. To address RQ 4, chi-square tests were conducted to identify any meaningful differences in the bases of supportive and opposing commentary regarding mandatory HPV vaccination (see Table 14.2 for results).

Practical and Unemotional Commentary. Among the 711 comments included in subsequent analyses, 139 (20%) were based on practical or unemotional arguments. Practical commentary often included statements regarding the incidence of cervical cancer and the efficacy of Gardasil (e.g., "Clinical trials of more than 11,000 females indicated that Gardasil was 100% effective in preventing cervical cancers linked to two types of HPV") that could be supported by current research and scientific evidence (e.g., see Chan & Berek, 2007). Comments supporting mandatory HPV vaccination were significantly more likely to be categorized as practical and unemotional than those opposing mandatory HPV vaccination, χ^2 (1, $N = 711$) = 4.02, $p < .05$.

Table 14.2 Frequencies of Underlying Themes by Comment Valence

Theme	Within Supportive Commentary ($n = 250$)	Within Opposing Commentary ($n = 461$)	Within Total Sample ($n = 711$)
Practical/unemotional	23.6% ($n = 59$)	17.4% ($n = 80$)	19.5% ($n = 139$)
Negative explicit emotion	4.0% ($n = 10$)	1.3% ($n = 6$)	2.3% ($n = 16$)
Negative implicit emotion	4.8% ($n = 12$)	6.1% ($n = 28$)	5.6% ($n = 40$)
Positive explicit emotion	.4% ($n = 1$)	0	.01% ($n = 1$)
Positive implicit emotion	.4% ($n = 1$)	0	.01% ($n = 1$)
Moral principle	5.6% ($n = 14$)	8.7% ($n = 40$)	7.6% ($n = 58$)
Cognitive bias	5.2% ($n = 13$)	19.1% ($n = 88$)	14.2% ($n = 101$)
Procedural justice: unfair	0	9.3% ($n = 43$)	6.0% ($n = 43$)
Procedural justice: fair	1.6% ($n = 4$)	0	.6% ($n = 4$)
Legitimacy: negative	.4% ($n = 1$)	9.8% ($n = 45$)	6.5% ($n = 46$)
Legitimacy: positive	2.4% ($n = 6$)	0	.8% ($n = 6$)

Note. "Within supportive" category represents the percentage of all commentary supporting mandatory HPV vaccination that expressed each theme. "Within opposed" category represents the percentage of all commentary opposing mandatory HPV vaccination that expressed each theme.

Emotional Commentary. Very few comments ($n = 58$) were based on either explicit or implicit emotion. Sixteen comments (2%) explicitly referenced negative emotions (e.g., "Gardasil's side effects are horrifying, and mandating this vaccine would be obscene") and 40 comments (4%) reflected implicit negative emotion (e.g., "A cervical cancer vaccination…are YOU kidding me?"). Only two comments reflected positive affective response. Supportive and opposing comments did not significantly differ in the degree to which they expressed any type of emotion ($p > .05$).

Moral Commentary. Only 8% ($n = 54$) of comments were based on moral principles, and no significant differences were observed between supportive and opposing commentary ($p > .05$). Though these comments were not subcategorized, they generally focused on religious principles, the relationship between HPV infection, mandatory vaccination, premarital sex, and the questionable motives of pharmaceutical corporations. In addition, moral comments often conveyed authors' opinions regarding the ethics surrounding mandatory HPV vaccination or simple authoritative judgments that such legislation was either "right" or "wrong."

Commentary Indicative of Cognitive Bias. Analyses revealed that 14% ($n = 101$) of comments reflected cognitive bias. The majority of these comments were characterized by illusory correlations, attribution errors, or errors in probabilistic reasoning. For example, several bloggers argued that administering Gardasil leads to promiscuity, underestimated the risk of contacting HPV, or overestimated the incidence of cervical cancer in the United States. Other comments did not demonstrate explicit bias but included inaccurate information and were suggestive of cognitive processes resulting in judgment errors (e.g., motivated reasoning, biased memory searches), and thus met the criteria for cognitive bias as defined in the coding scheme. Such comments often discussed unsubstantiated side effects, claimed that the vaccine is ineffective, or denied the link between HPV and cervical cancer. Opposing comments were significantly more likely than supportive comments to reflect cognitive bias and potential cognitive bias, $\chi^2 (1, N = 711) = 25.66, p < .01$.

Justice Principles. Nearly 7% ($n = 47$) of all comments were based on procedural justice principles. Among this group, the 6% ($n = 43$) of comments opposing mandatory HPV vaccination expressed the opinion that the actions or intentions of government officials or other authority figures influencing such legislation were procedurally unfair. Many of these comments questioned the intentions of Texas Governor Rick Perry, who accepted thousands of campaign dollars from Gardasil's manufacturer. The four supportive comments in this subcategory (< 1%) maintained that lawmakers were acting in "the public's best interest" and that mandating Gardasil would ensure equal access to the vaccine. Chi-square analyses revealed that opposing commentary was significantly more likely than supportive commentary to reference procedural justice principles, $\chi^2 (1, N = 711) = 17.49, p < .01$.

Similarly, among the 46 comments (6% of the total sample) reflecting negative perceptions of government legitimacy, 45 expressed opposition to mandatory HPV vaccination. Such commentary frequently challenged the authority of government officials in mandating HPV vaccination and asserted the rights of individuals to make medical decisions for their children. Less than 1% ($n = 6$) of comments, all supporting mandatory HPV vaccination, were based on positive perceptions of government legitimacy. Such comments typically opined that lawmakers were justified in mandating Gardasil, and one blogger supporting mandatory HPV vaccination argued that "The state has a responsibility to maintain public health." As with procedural justice principles, references to legitimacy were more common in opposing commentary than in supportive commentary, $\chi^2 (1, N = 711) = 17.49, p < .01$.

Discussion

The current findings support Finkel's (1995) conceptualization of public sentiment as multifaceted and contradictory; community members used both objective and subjective commentary to express a variety of opinions regarding mandatory HPV vaccination. The present results cannot resolve this controversy, but they may help inform legislative decisions. Accordingly, this section focuses on the potential implications of adhering to public sentiment as assessed in this study. Policy recommendations are proposed that may increase HPV vaccine uptake, regardless of whether it is mandated.

Implications of Public Sentiment Regarding Mandatory HPV Vaccination

Due to small sample size and potential differences between ordinary community members and blog authors, the current results are not representative of overall public support for mandatory HPV vaccination. Though findings suggest that the majority of individuals who share their opinions with the online community oppose mandating the HPV vaccine, more extensive research is needed before any firm policy recommendations are advanced regarding the rejection or implementation of this measure. However, exploring the rationale underlying both opposing and supportive commentary can provide policymakers with a foundation for assessing public sentiment regarding mandatory HPV vaccination, which may lead to more prudent decisions in terms of both public relations and health policy.

A considerable proportion of community members in the current sample used logic or existing research to advance their arguments. These findings suggest that lawmakers should not discount constituents' perspectives on mandatory HPV vaccination based on presumptions of public ignorance. Analyses also indicated that supporters of the mandate were more likely to use practical commentary than opponents. Though use of emotion and morality was infrequent and did not significantly differ among supporters and opponents, commentary reflecting cognitive bias was much more prevalent among opponents of the mandate. Whether it leads to rejection or acceptance of a policy, basing legal decisions on cognitive biases and inaccuracies is generally unwise. If further research using more diverse samples reveals similar patterns of results, policymakers will be faced with a difficult choice. They may incorporate the more rational but less popular perspective into their legal decisions, or they may attempt to satisfy a majority of their constituents by rejecting a logic-based policy aimed at eradicating a potentially deadly virus.

Though lawmakers should be cognizant of bias reflected in commentary opposing mandatory HPV vaccination, they also should consider the possible consequences of nonadherence to these (seemingly) more pervasive sentiments. Few comments overall referenced negative perceptions of procedural fairness and government legitimacy, but the vast majority of those that did opposed mandatory HPV vaccination. Ignoring these sentiments may lead to noncompliance among those questioning the authority and intentions of legislators. Though Virginia and Washington, D.C. have enacted mandatory legislation, parents may refuse to have their children vaccinated for *any* reason by completing a simple "opt out" form (Helderman, 2011). Preliminary figures suggest that most parents in these regions are utilizing this option. At the beginning of the 2010 school year, only 17.3% of eligible girls in Virginia and 23% of eligible girls in Washington, D.C. had received their first "mandatory" HPV vaccination (Helderman, 2011). Substantial rates of noncompliance like these will render this policy significantly less effective in preventing the spread of HPV (Self, 2008). Further, discounting opinions of those opposed to mandatory HPV vaccination may damage relationships between community members and public officials, resulting in decreased compliance with a broad range of legal regulations.

Recommendations for Policymakers

The present results and implications outlined earlier provide only an initial guide for policymakers contemplating mandatory HPV vaccination. Though the foundations of opposing and supportive community sentiment as assessed in this study are important to consider, policymakers should consult future cross-disciplinary research on this topic (e.g., additional assessments of public opinion, further studies of HPV vaccine efficacy and side effects, adherence and reactions to enacted mandatory HPV vaccination policies) prior to making relevant legislative decisions. However, educational interventions may help increase vaccine uptake in the absence of a mandate or help ensure adherence to a mandate already in place.

Parents' limited understanding of HPV and the safety, efficacy, and availability of the HPV vaccine may account for its low uptake among adolescent girls (Etter, Zimet, & Rickert, 2012). Though Gardasil is currently recommended by the Advisory Committee on Immunization (ACIP), it is clear that more proactive measures must be taken to educate parents. Public education campaigns (e.g., television and newsprint ads, mail brochures) may be a more cost-effective means of increasing parental knowledge and subsequent uptake of the HPV vaccine. In addition, lawmakers could implement a policy requiring all public schools to distribute information packets about the HPV and other ACIP recommended vaccines to parents at the beginning of each school year. This information should describe the purpose, efficacy, and risks of these vaccines in simple language. Each information packet should include contact information for the school nurse or a public health official familiar with the risks and benefits of the vaccines to address parental questions and concerns. Public schools could also require students to return a signed statement indicating that the parent has read and understood the information. Such nonpartisan interventions may help minimize public misconceptions about the HPV vaccine without infringing upon individual rights and family privacy.

Efforts also should be made to educate parents about programs providing free or low-cost vaccines to uninsured or underinsured children. Most pediatricians in all states participate in the Vaccines for Children (VCF) program, which provides ACIP recommended vaccines (including HPV vaccines) to uninsured and underinsured children free of charge (Centers for Disease Control and Prevention, 2009). In addition, eight states currently offer free or reduced-cost HPV vaccines for girls who may not qualify for other types of assistance (Henry J. Kaiser Family Foundation, 2008). Yet disparities in vaccine coverage among low-income and high-income children persist, suggesting that many low-income parents may be unaware of such programs (Smith, Jain, Stevenson, Männikkö, & Molinari, 2009), unsure of how to participate, or do not understand the importance of vaccines.

Finally, lawmakers should take a more proactive approach to understanding the issues and sentiments surrounding mandatory HPV vaccination. Public sentiment is dynamic (Finkel, 1995), and mandating the HPV vaccine may eventually prove to be a prudent choice in the future. Educational interventions will likely minimize but not eliminate public sentiment based on cognitive bias, emotions, and morality. Thus, it is imperative that legislators seek out current research and expert opinion regarding cervical cancer, HPV, and Gardasil. Several states offer Family Impact Seminars, which are nonpartisan approaches to providing objective, research-based information regarding policy issues. Legislators choose the topic of each seminar and develop specific policy-relevant questions for organizers, who then assemble a panel of expert researchers and speakers who can address these specific concerns (Wilcox, Weisz, & Miller, 2005). Seminars focusing on mandatory HPV vaccination would provide legislators with high-quality information essential to making conscientious decisions.

Though this study provides a critical foundation in understanding the rationale behind public sentiment regarding mandatory HPV vaccination, its implications are based on the sentiments of a limited and purposive sample. Accordingly, further studies targeting a more representative sample of community members' opinions are needed to solidify the proposed recommendations. Such endeavors will help lawmakers address the public health threat posed by HPV more effectively and minimize negative outcomes that may result from decisions regarding mandatory HPV vaccination.

References

Abuhoff, D. M. (2006). On morality and the law: Truth, justice, and the American way. *Cardozo Public Law, Policy, and Ethics Journal, 4,* 67–77.

American Cancer Society (2013). *What are the key statistics about cervical cancer?* Retrieved August 2013, from http://www.cancer.org/cancer/cervicalcancer/detailedguide/cervical-cancer-key-statistics.

Applegate, B. K., Cullen, F. T., Turner, M. G., & Sundt, J. L. (1996). Assessing public support for three-strikes-and-you're-out laws: Global versus specific attitudes. *Crime & Delinquency, 42*, 517–534. doi: 10.1177/0011128796042004002.

Blumenthal, J. A. (2003). Who decides? Privileging public sentiment about justice and the substantive law. *UMKC Law Review, 72*, 1–21.

Caldas, S. J., & Bankston, C. L. (2007). A re-analysis of the legal, political, and social landscape of desegregation from Plessy v. Ferguson to Parents Involved in Community Schools v. Seattle School District No. 1. *Brigham Young University Education and Law Journal, 2007*(2), 217–256.

Centers for Disease Control and Prevention. (2009). *Vaccines for children program.* Retrieved July 2013, from http://www.cdc.gov/vaccines/programs/vfc/default.htm

Chan, J. K., & Berek, J. S. (2007). Impact of the human papilloma vaccine on cervical cancer. *Journal of Clinical Oncology, 25*, 2975–2982. doi: 10.1200/JCO.2007.10.8662.

Chen, E. Y. (2008). Impacts of "three strikes and you're out" on crime trends in California and throughout the United States. *Journal of Contemporary Criminal Justice, 24*, 345–370. doi: 10.1177/1043986208319456.

Colb, S. (2007, April 4). *Twenty states consider mandating the cervical cancer vaccine: The controversy.* Retrieved July 2013, from the FindLaw website http://writ.news.findlaw.com/colb/20070404.html.

Cole, G. M. (2008). Government promotion of moral issues: What is the government's role in promoting morals…seriously? *Harvard Journal of Law and Public Policy, 31*, 77–84.

Darley, J. M., & Pittman, T. S. (2003). The psychology of compensatory and retributive justice. *Personality and Social Psychology Review, 7*(4), 324–336. doi: 10.1207/S15327957PSPR0704_05.

Dempsey, A. F., Zimet, G. D., Davis, R. L., & Koutsky, L. (2006). Factors that are associated with parental acceptance of human papillomavirus vaccines: A randomized intervention study of written information about HPV. *Pediatrics, 117*, 1486–1493. doi: 10.1542/peds.2005-1381.

Denno, D. W. (2000). The perils of public opinion. *Hofstra Law Review, 741*, 745–751.

Epstein, S., Lipson, A. Holstein, C., & Huh, E. (1992). Irrational reactions to negative outcomes: Evidence for two conceptual systems. *Journal of Personality and Social Psychology, 62*, 328–339. doi: 10.1037/0022-3514.62.2.328.

Etter, D. J., Zimet, G. D., & Rickert, V. I. (2012). Human papillomavirus in adolescent women: a 2012 update. *Current Opinion in Obstetrics and Gynecology, 24*, 305–310. doi: 10.1097/GCO.0b013e3283567005

Finkel, N. J. (1995). *Commonsense justice: Juror's notions of the law.* Cambridge, MA: Harvard University Press.

Friedman, A., & Shepeard, H. (2007). Exploring the knowledge, attitudes, beliefs, and communication preferences of the general public regarding HPV: Findings from the CDC focus group research and implications for practice. *Health Education and Behavior, 34*, 471–485. doi: 10.1177/1090198106292022.

Griffin, T., Miller, M. K., Hoppe, J., Rebideaux, A., & Hammack, R. (2007). A preliminary examination of AMBER Alert's effects. *Criminal Justice Policy Review, 18*, 378–394. doi: 10.1177/0887403407302332.

Haidt, J. (2003). The moral emotions. In R. J. Davidson, K. R. Scherer, & H. H. Goldsmith (Eds.), *Handbook of affective sciences* (pp. 852–870). Oxford, UK: Oxford University Press.

Hannah, J. M. (2007). *HPV vaccine: Mandatory for teenagers or not?* Retrieved July 2013, from the Michigan Family Law website http://jeannehannah.typepad.com/blog_jeanne_hannah_traver/2007/01/hpv_vaccine_man.html.

Helderman, R. S. (2011, February 17). Senate panel kills bill to end Virginia's HPV vaccine mandate. *The Washington Post*. Retrieved July 2013, from http://voices.washingtonpost.com/virginiapolitics/2011/02/a_senate_committee_has_killed.html.

Hoover, D. R., Carfioli, B., & Moench, E. A. (2000). Attitudes of adolescent/young adult women toward human papillomavirus vaccination and clinical trials. *Health Care for Women International, 21*, 375–391.

Jaslow, R. (2011, September 16). Michelle Bachmann's HPV vaccine remarks continue to draw criticism. *CBS News*. Retrieved July 2013, from http://www.cbsnews.com/8301-504763_162-20107489-10391704.html

Javitt, G., Berkowitz, D., & Gostin, L. O. (2008). Assessing mandatory HPV vaccination: Who should call the shots? *Journal of Law, Medicine, and Ethics, 36*, 384–395. doi: 10.1111/j.1748-720X.2008.00282.x.

Kennedy, A., Sapsis, K. F., Stokley, S., Curtis, C. R., & Gust, D. (2011). Parental attitudes toward human pappilomavirus vaccination: Evaluation of an educational intervention, 2008. *Journal of Health Communication, 16*, 300–313. doi: 10.1080/10810730.2010.532296.

Krauss, D. A., Lieberman, J. D., & Olson, J, (2004). The effects of rational and experiential information processing of expert testimony in death penalty cases. *Behavioral Sciences and the Law, 22*, 801–822. doi: 10.1002/bsl.621.

Krovandzic, T., Sloan, J., & Vieraitis, L. (2004). "Striking out" as crime reduction policy: The impact of "three strikes" laws on crime rates in U.S. cities. *Justice Quarterly, 21*, 207–239. doi: 10.1080/07418820400095791.

Kunda, Z. (1999). *Social cognition: making sense of people*. Cambridge, MA: MIT Press.

Levenson, J. S., & D'Amora, D. A. (2007). Social policies designed to prevent sexual violence: The emperor's new clothes? *Criminal Justice Policy Review, 18*(2), 168–199. doi: 10.1177/0887403406295309.

Lu, B., Kumar, A., Castellsagué, X., & Giuliano, A. R. (2011). Efficacy and safety of prophylactic vaccines against cervical HPV infection and diseases among women: A systematic review & meta analysis. *BMC Infectious Diseases, 11*. doi: 10.1186/1471-2334-11-13.

Miller, M. K., Griffin, T., Clinkinbeard, S. S., & Thomas, R, M. (2009). The psychology of AMBER Alert: Unresolved issues and implications. *Social Science Journal, 46*, 111–123. doi: 10.1016/jsoscij.2008.12.004.

Moffat, R. C. L. (2005). Not the law's business: The politics of tolerance and the enforcement of morality. *Florida Law Review, 57*, 1098–1133..

National Conference of State Legislatures. (2011). *HPV vaccine*. Retrieved July 2013, from http://www.ncsl.org/programs/health/HPVvaccine.htm.

Opel, D. J., Diekema, D. S., & Marcuse, E. K. (2008). A critique of evaluation vaccines for inclusion in mandatory school immunization programs. *Pediatrics, 122*, 504–510. doi: 10.1542/peds.2007-3218.

Planned Parenthood v. Casey, 505 U.S. 833 (1992).
Plessy v. Ferguson, 163 U.S. 537 (1896).
Parents wary of HPV vaccine mandate. (2007, May 23). *CBS News*. Retrieved July 2013, from http://www.cbsnews.com/stories/2007/05/23/health/webmd/main2842035.shtml.
Pomfret, T. C., Gagnon, J. M., & Gilchrist, A. T. (2011). Quadrivalent human papillomavirus (HPV) vaccine: A review of safety, efficacy, and pharmacoeconomics. *Journal of Clinical Pharmacy and Therapeutics, 36*, 1–9. doi: 10.1111/j.1365-2710.2009.01150.x.
Reiter, P. L., Brewer, N. T., Gottlieb, S. C., McRee, A., & Smith, J. S. (2009). Parents' health beliefs and HPV vaccination of their adolescent daughters. *Social Science and Medicine, 69*, 475–480. doi: 10.1016/j.socscimed.2009.05.024.
Self, P. (2008). The HPV vaccination: Necessary or evil? *Hastings Women's Law Journal, 19*, 149–158.
Smith, P. J., Jain, N., Stevenson, J., Männikkö, N., & Molinari, N. (2009). Progress in timely vaccination coverage among children living in low-income households. *Archives of Pediatric and Adolescent Medicine, 163*, 462–468. doi: 10.1001/archpediatrics.2009.25.
Stemler, S. (2001). An overview of content analysis. *Practical Assessment, Research, and Evaluation, 7*(17). Retrieved July 2013, from http://pareonline.net/getvn.asp?v=7&n=17.
Tavenner, M. (2007). *Should the HPV vaccine become mandatory for girls? Point: Yes, it will help prevent diseases* [Web log post]. Retrieved July 2013, from the PROTO website http://protomag.com/assets/should-the-hpv-vaccine-become-mandatory-for-girls?page=1.
Teachthefacts.org. (2007, April 7). *The HPV vaccine: A tough issue* [Web log post]. Retrieved July 2013, from http://www.teachthefacts.org/2007/04/hpv-vaccine-tough-issue.html.
Telling it Like it is. (2008, January 14). *HPV vaccine: My child- my decision* [Web log post]. Retrieved July 2013, from http://www.tellinitlikeitis.net/2008/01/hpv-vaccine-my-child-my-decision.html.
Tribe, L. H., & Matz, J. (2012). The constitutional inevitability of same-sex marriage. *Maryland Law Review, 71*, 471–489.
Tyler, T. R. (2006). Psychological perspectives on legitimacy and legitimation. *Annual Review of Psychology, 57*, 375–400. doi: 10.1146/annurev.psych.57.102904.190038.
US Food and Drug Administration. (2009). *FDA approves new vaccine for prevention of cervical cancer* [Press release]. Retrieved July 2013, from http://www.fda.gov/newsevents/newsroom/pressannouncements/ucm187048.htm.
Vamos, C. A., McDermott, R. J., & Daley, E. M. (2008). The HPV vaccine: Framing the arguments FOR and AGAINST mandatory vaccination for all middle school girls. *Journal of School Health, 78*, 302–309. doi: 10.1111/j.1746-1561.2008.00306.x.
Walker, J. (2007, February 20). Injecting speed: Why the rush to require the HPV vaccine? *Reason*. Retrieved July 2013, from http://www.reason.com/news/show/118758.html.
Wilcox, B. L., Weisz, P. V., & Miller, M. K. (2005). Practical guidelines for educating policymakers: The Family Impact Seminar as an approach to advancing the interests of children and families in the policy arena. *Journal of Clinical Child and Adolescent Psychology, 34*, 638–645.

Zgoba, K. (2004). Spin doctors and moral crusaders: The moral panic behind child safety legislation. *Criminal Justice Studies, 17*, 385–404. doi: 10.1080/1478601042000314892.

Zgoba, K., Witt, P., Dalessandro, M., & Veysey, B. (2008). *Megan's Law: Assessing the practical and monetary efficacy*. Washington, DC: National Institute of Justice.

15

The Law and Child Wellbeing: Where Are We and Where Do We Go From Here?

Twila Wingrove and Jennifer L. Jarrett

This book's chapter authors have identified a number of areas in which the law has a direct impact on the wellbeing of children, either by promoting it (e.g., gender-specific juvenile delinquency programs) or, arguably, by hindering it (e.g., the potential downsides of juvenile sex offender laws). This concluding chapter is devoted to three goals. First, we identify common themes involving the intersection between psychology, the legal system, and the wellbeing of children. Second, we identify potential solutions for improving communication between psychologists, lawyers, and policymakers through research and education. Third, we look ahead to a topic that will certainly be debated in the future: youth and technology.

Themes

The first section of this chapter addresses underlying themes that are relevant to shaping child-related public policy and affecting child-related legal decisions. The first two themes have to do with better defining what child and adolescent wellbeing is—acknowledging developmental abilities and limitations and better defining the best interests of the child standard. The final two themes are relevant to public policy more generally—defining "justice" and outlining the role of community sentiment in shaping new laws and practices.

Developmental Abilities and Limitations

Children are a vulnerable population because of their cognitive and psychosocial immaturity. Civil and criminal courts are forced to balance promotion of a minor's wellbeing against the rights of others involved in the legal proceeding, while also finding a resolution to the matter at hand. In several chapters of this book, authors have persuasively recommended programs that serve just that purpose (e.g., child custody offices in Chapter 9), but some concluding points are worth making.

In the delinquency and criminal context, recognition of minors' developmental abilities is especially important for two reasons. First, any individual juvenile's developmental trajectory will directly affect his or her ability to engage in all aspects of the legal system, from understanding *Miranda* rights (Chapter 4) to making plea decisions and participating in the defense at adjudication or trial (Chapter 3). Fortunately, the Supreme Court seems to be increasingly recognizing the need for developmental sensitivity when processing juveniles in criminal court (see Chapter 3). For example, age is now relevant to *Miranda* practice; however, judgments of age and understanding are subjective. Time and research will tell whether law enforcement officers will be accurate when assessing a juvenile's understanding of *Miranda* rights. Despite the court's willingness to consider juveniles' development in these circumstances, it is not clear that the court is equally concerned about juveniles who are processed in juvenile court.

Second, after a juvenile has been adjudicated or prosecuted, the court should mandate a developmentally appropriate mode of rehabilitation for that child. If the state's determined rehabilitation program is developmentally suitable and tailored individually to the juvenile, the juvenile's chance of rehabilitation is greatly improved. Legislations are slowly acknowledging and addressing children's developmental deficits, but they have not capitalized on the developmental abilities of children to be rehabilitated (Chapters 3 and 6 discuss the need for improved rehabilitation programs).

As noted in several chapters (e.g., Chapters 3 and 4), the juvenile justice system's response to delinquency has shifted away from rehabilitation and toward punishment and retribution. When done properly, juvenile offenders might respond more positively to rehabilitation than adult offenders. By focusing on goals other than rehabilitation, children's wellbeing is directly undermined. Furthermore, failing to improve rehabilitation programs serves only to increase the likelihood that these juveniles will remain in the system for longer, creating significant costs for society and government.

Developmental abilities and limitations must also be considered in the civil context in proceedings in which children are involved or indirectly affected. For example, a parental divorce always affects a child's wellbeing, and courts are required to consider the best interests of the child in all the decisions involving that child. Those involved in the divorce process often try to ascertain the developmental needs of children in these situations and craft outcomes that will promote these needs. However, truly developmentally based decision making in this context involves balancing the child's needs against a child's interests and abilities regarding self-determination. For example, depending on the children's maturity and preferences, their wellbeing might be promoted by being granted an opportunity to weigh in, either formally or informally, on the custody decision-making process. Furthermore, when issues of parental alienation have been raised, a court's instinct might be to ignore the child's wishes on the basis that the child has been effectively brainwashed by one of the parents. However, in even those cases, there might be ways to support children both by protecting their needs and allowing them some opportunity to engage in the process, whether their involvement is through conversations with a clinician, in mediation, or by speaking to the judge (see Chapters 8 and 10).

Ultimately, it is in the best interest of *all parties* when policies are developmentally appropriate and recognize that a child's wellbeing might be promoted in different ways at different life points. Developmentally appropriate policies need to balance the goals of nurturance (i.e., protecting young children's welfare) against the goals of self-determination (i.e., providing minors with their own set of rights). Since at least the 1970s, legal and psychological scholars have noted the inherent tension between those who favor one policy perspective over the other (i.e., the "child savers" versus the "kiddie libbers"; see Mnookin, 1978). However, these goals need not be seen as conflicting—recognition of developmental needs and capabilities ought to determine the balance.

As a final note, all of this discussion presumes that legal actors—law enforcement officers, lawyers, and judges—are knowledgeable about child and adolescent development. That is not a realistic presumption. Efforts must be made to increase legal actors' developmental knowledge. Continuing education sessions organized by developmentalists would be appropriate ways to train actors locally. In addition, researchers should begin to prioritize translating their knowledge into context-specific practice points. Such information could be published in trade journals or self-published and made publicly available. Finally, perhaps the best way to learn from each other is by building more active partnerships between legal actors and local psychologists or mental health professionals. By becoming available when questions arise, psychologists could provide education on topics in a more fluid, directly relevant way.

What Is "the Best Interests of the Child" Standard? Is it Useful?

In the American court system, many legal decisions in which children are involved are governed by "the best interests of the child" standard, including custody decisions in both the divorce and child protection context. The best interests standard is straightforward on its face, but it has been the subject of considerable criticism (e.g., Emery, 2007; Frolik & Whitton, 2012; Kohm, 2007; Riggs, 2005; Ritenhouse, 2011). Most of the criticism is targeted at the fuzzy nature of the standard; there are few guiding principles and judges have a lot of subjective freedom to insert their individual ideas of a child's best interests into a case. As discussed in Chapter 12, this may be especially problematic when the decision crosses cultural lines.

Of course, one could argue that the benefit of such a flexible standard is that it does allow courts the freedom to create outcomes that are nuanced and developmentally appropriate. While this interpretation is certainly possible, it is unlikely given judges' limitations in understanding of child development, as discussed earlier, not to mention the lack of time and resources that a judge has to dedicate to every case.

In the context of this book, the real question is: Does the best interests of the child standard promote or hinder children's wellbeing? From a research perspective, the answer to this question is unclear. There is certainly psychological and legal commentary arguing that the best interests standard, at best, is a poor way of promoting wellbeing (Cohen, 2012; Freeman, 2007). And there is some research establishing that there is wide variability in how judges interpret the best interests standard. For example, Crosby-Currie (1996) demonstrated that judges' practices with regard to hearing children's wishes in custody cases were different both within and between states. Similarly, Artis (2004) found that judges use the parent's gender as a determinant of custody in cases involving the custody of a young child or infant, which might be contrary to the child's best interests. Specifically, judges were more likely to give custody to the mother when the child was young, consistent with doctrine that predates the best interests standard (i.e., the "tender years" doctrine). However, there is little, if any, research that makes the final leap between judicial interpretations of the standard and children's outcomes.

This is a gap that needs to be filled, but filling the gap is an understandably intimidating task to tackle. For one thing, operationalizing interpretations of the best interests standard in a measurable way is a challenge. Second, there may be few courts that are willing to support research of this nature. Even if they did, it is difficult for parents to return for follow-up sessions due to their busy schedules. Researchers have developed programs of research in other areas of child wellbeing in the face of similar challenges. It is our hope that some researchers will take up this call as well.

Despite the criticisms of the best interests standard, it is important to remember that the standard currently dominates legal decision making regarding child wellbeing. Therefore, the best interests standard is expected to be fully comprehended and applied to all decisions made by legal professionals and professionals working with the courts: researchers, police officers, clinicians, judges, juries, and attorneys. The implication of this might be that, at the local level, legal actors must be aware of their courts' particular interpretations of best interests—what factors do they consider especially weighty?

The Role of Justice

Multiple chapters in this book have highlighted the significance of referring to justice goals when shaping child- and family-related policies (Chapters 4, 6, 9, 10, 11, and 14). Importantly, several authors have demonstrated that justice principles can be served without necessarily interfering with other goals of the system, like retribution and punishment or promoting the welfare of children and juveniles. For example, Salerno and colleagues (Chapter 5) demonstrated that refusal to extend sex offender registration laws to juveniles might simultaneously promote juveniles' wellbeing while not actually interfering with public safety in a measurable way.

In addition, promoting justice is consistent with the theme discussed earlier in this chapter: recognizing developmental abilities and limitations. A policy that accurately applies developmental principles and knowledge to the law inherently promotes wellbeing, which is the central tenet of therapeutic jurisprudence. For example, Miller, Miller, and Broadus (Chapter 6) demonstrated that developmental and clinical science has established a number of ways in which male and female juvenile offenders differ. This knowledge, applied to the treatment context, implies that crafting gender-specific treatment programs within juvenile facilities will likely be more effective and lead to therapeutic outcomes for youth. Their preliminary research supports this notion.

It is important to note, however, that justice might not always be promoted by emphasizing protection of children, especially if that means repressing self-determination rights. This may be especially true for adolescents, who might have a heightened expectation for and ability to engage in self-determination. For example, rights to self-determination could be granted in the child custody context by allowing certain minors a more active role in the custody placement decision, as some states already do (see Chapter 8). However, it is important to note that when increased rights to self-determination are granted in this kind of civil domain, one consequence is the implication that juveniles should be held to equivalent standards and levels of culpability in criminal contexts. It is this tension that can only be appropriately balanced by relying on developmental science. Developmentalists must seek the answers to the question of children's differing abilities and needs through research, and they must be engaged in conversations with legal scholars and policymakers about how to frame these research questions and research findings in legally relevant ways. The importance of communication is taken up in a later section of this chapter.

The Role of Community Sentiment

A final theme in this book revolves around the role of community sentiment in shaping public policy. Studies reported in various chapters addressed community sentiment regarding a variety of child- and adolescent-relevant issues, including HPV vaccinations, juvenile sex offenders, and childhood obesity cases (Chapters 14, 5, and 13, respectively). The role of community sentiment is a controversial one for researchers and policymakers. If the goal of public policies is promoting child wellbeing above all else, then one might question whether community sentiment is relevant, especially in cases in which developmental and clinical science provides clear indications of what is in the best interests of children. However, the reality is that what is best for children often involves a value judgment. For example, is it better for obese children to be separated from their parents when their parents appear to be doing little to help these children lose weight? Or is it better for these children to remain in their parents' homes, while service providers address underlying problems with the entire family unit? Science certainly can provide information about the separation of children from their families, but public viewpoints are relevant, too. After all, aren't policies supposed to reflect the values of the community at large?

Two particular challenges are ascertaining how to measure community sentiment and exactly what level of influence community sentiment should have on shaping policies. When it comes to measurement, researchers have established that sentiments shift based on the contexts in which they occur (e.g., Chamberlain, 2009; Miller, Blumenthal, & Chamberlain, forthcoming). For example, when sentiments shift from supporting an issue to opposing it over time, this information is highly relevant to deciding whether the policy should evolve. There should always be some concern when policymakers begin to develop laws that fly in the face of community sentiment in this regard, especially when anticipating potential problems with enforcement. If communities do not support laws mandating HPV vaccines, for example, then parents may opt to ignore those laws, despite the apparent protective effects of vaccinating their children (see Chapter 14). There are also occasions when one might expect the opposite: Legislatures could adopt policies that reflect community sentiment, but are, in fact, contrary to the wellbeing of children. These policies might be popular but misguided, in that they do not adequately promote the wellbeing of children.

One solution to resolving potential conflicts between community sentiment and proposed policies might be better communication between policymakers, researchers, and local communities. Whenever there is a mismatch between community sentiment and the state of the science, the question becomes whether the community is misunderstanding the science or whether the scientists are misunderstanding or ignoring the role of community values. The reality is that, in many cases, policies reflect a balancing of values and knowledge; clearly these two constructs inform each other, but one cannot always entirely replace the other. While improved communication and education among stakeholders is key (and taken up in the next section of this chapter), it may not always be a complete solution. Furthermore, scientists run into the danger of losing their credibility if they begin to be seen as advocates for particular policies rather than advocates for knowledge in general. Finally, scientists must also be cautious in not presuming that everyone will agree with the prioritized rank of knowledge over other pieces of information that policymakers may see as relevant, like the support of their constituents.

While community sentiment shifts over time, it also appears to change as a function of the nature and context of measurement. The authors of this book have taken multiple approaches to measuring sentiment, from content analysis of comments made by community members to attitude surveys. There are dangers to any singular approach to measuring community sentiment because it will inevitably be inadequate. As with much of science, sampling, convergence, and replication are integral. If we find that multiple adequate community samples reflect the same kind of attitude about a particular policy, even after trying different methodology and defining the terms in different ways, then we can become confident that we have a true measure of community sentiment. For readers who are interested in exploring the methodological issues surrounding measurement of community sentiment, they are encouraged to seek out other work by Finkel (e.g., 2001), Blumenthal (2003), and Miller, Blumenthal, and Chamberlain (forthcoming).

How to Move Forward: Improving Communication and Education

One idea that the contributors of this book have illustrated successfully is that there are important gains to be made by pooling the knowledge of all those involved and invested in improving children's outcomes associated with legal system involvement. This book has chapters written by legal scholars, mental health care professionals, and psychological researchers, each of whom has a unique perspective on the interaction of children and the legal system. One clear avenue for promoting children's wellbeing in this domain is creating as many opportunities as possible for these professionals to share their knowledge with each other and with policymakers.

A few models for these kinds of conversations have promise. For instance, Family Impact Seminars have been used to educate lawmakers as to the likely impacts their laws will have on children and families. In such seminars, researchers speak to lawmakers as neutral scientists, rather than lobbyists, in order to promote general wellbeing in families (Wilcox, Weisz, & Miller, 2005; for more information, see the Policy Institute for Family Impact Seminars' website at http://familyimpactseminars.org). Joint conferences or symposia between different professional institutions also show some promise, as they provide an opportunity for a more interdisciplinary conversation. For example, the American Bar Association Section of Family Law and the American Psychological Association regularly hold a joint continuing education conference on a special topic related to children in the legal system.

Similar approaches can be taken to educate other groups as well. Researchers can share information with judges and lawyers during continuing education seminars and through relevant publications. In particular, researchers could seek to publish their findings and recommendations in more brief, straightforward formats and in outlets that are aimed directly at relevant communities, like legal practitioners or mental health professionals (e.g., *Court Review*, a journal sponsored by the American Judges Association).

Improved educational efforts can also be made to train professionals before they even embark on their careers. For example, professors can do their part by educating future legal actors who are in courses in criminal justice, social work, public health, and other social sciences. These are the individuals who will be making decisions that will impact families in the future.

As a final note, while it is clearly important to increase interdisciplinary communication and educational efforts, scholars should not forget that it would be equally impactful to create materials that can educate parents and children themselves. For example, a great deal of research exists on effective ways to aid children in the transition through their parents' divorce (Bagshaw, 2007; McConnell & Sim, 1999; Oliphant, Brown, Cambron, & Yankeelov, 2002). Efforts to make evidence-based and simply-written brochures widely available to parents, mediators, and family law courts could directly assist those parents in choosing what is in their children's best interests. Similar efforts could be made to explain the dependency or delinquency court processes to children using developmentally appropriate language. Many organizations have created some of these materials at the local levels, but availability and topics of these materials are inconsistent. One model that could remedy this problem is an approach taken up by the National Association of School Psychologists (NASP). NASP has published multiple editions of a collection of reproducible handouts designed for teachers and families on a wide variety of school-related issues (Canter, Paige, & Shaw, 2010). It is available in CD format, so that people can easily print selected handouts and make them available.

A Look Ahead

While the chapters in this book touched on many of the topics related to developmental policy that dominate current debate, the law and the field of psychology both continue to evolve. As such, we thought it best to end this book with a look to one topic that is likely to get a lot of media, research, and policy attention in the future: youth and technology. Technological innovations seem to continuously impact lifestyle, not only for adults but also for youth. Children in the millennial generation have increased access to and immersion in social technologies that earlier generations were not even exposed to during childhood. The effect of the use of these technological advances has been the subject of a lot of speculation from the news media. In this section, we briefly discuss three specific areas related to the interaction between minors and technology. In so doing, we will refer to recent media reports, the current state of the research, and the policy implications involved.

Violent Video Games

The question of the impact of violent video games is not new, but it has been raised again after recent episodes of mass violence, including a school shooting in Connecticut and a movie theater shooting in Colorado. For example,

Brown (2013) suggests that video gaming may play a role in aggression, but it is hard to be certain given the wide use of these games by most adolescents.

Research on the effects of video game violence has been ongoing for decades, with split views on how strong the relationship is between playing video games and aggression (Anderson & Bushman, 2001; Ferguson, 2007). A meta-analysis of video gaming research and aggression conducted by Anderson et al. (2010) suggested that violent video games should be considered a causal risk factor for aggressive behavior. However, Ferguson (2007) claimed that these results occurred as a consequence of a publication bias favoring finding a significant relationship between video games and aggression. After correcting for the publication bias, Ferguson (2007) did not find evidence confirming the relationship. Regardless of these differing opinions, all psychologists agree that immersion in violent video games alone does not produce an adolescent likely to engage in acts of extreme violence. Generally speaking, other risk factors must also be accounted for, like an unhealthy home life and biological markers, to truly understand youth violence.

From a policy perspective, this debate has sometimes led to propositions to limit access to violent video games. In fact, video games are now subject to a rating system, requiring packages to indicate whether substantial violence is involved. Attempts to restrict actual sales of video games have failed. In 2010, the US Supreme Court struck down a California law that prevented minors from buying violent video games as a violation of free speech protections (*Brown v. Entertainment Merchants Association*, 2010). Ultimately, parents are the ones who govern which activities their children participate in, so there may be only a limited role for legislation to play.

Cyber Bullying

Cyber bullying is a new phenomenon for adolescent development. It is defined by Hinduja and Patchin (2010) as the willful and repeated harm of a target by a bully using cell phones, computers, or any other electronic device, and it is considered a new form of aggressive behavior. The news often paints a grim picture when teen suicide stories arise, claiming that cyber bullying is the main cause for the teen's death. Some journalists have claimed that mental health problems are the main cause for teenage suicide, and that cyber bullying is not a major causal link. Others maintain that cyber bullying is an agitator without which teens might not have taken their lives (Grenoble, 2012).

As a form of aggression, cyber bullying is currently a burgeoning area of research. Presently, researchers have mainly gathered data about the prevalence of cyber bullying and its role in teenage suicides. However, some researchers have begun investigating the consequences of cyber bullying. Hinduja and Patchin (2010) found that adolescents who participate in cyber bullying are at a higher risk for suicidal thoughts or actions; "participants" includes both victims and perpetrators. These results are alarming given that most attention is focused on the victims in these types of incidents.

As cyber bullying becomes more common, research investigating its effect on normative adolescent development will become necessary, especially to inform policies and practices related to school violence and aggression. Just as policy definitions of aggression evolved to include nonphysical, relational components a couple of decades ago, definitions will need to continue to evolve to include bullying that occurs over the Internet or telephone, rather than in person. Similarly, researchers who have devoted their careers to designing bullying prevention programs will need to test whether elements of these programs are equally effective at preventing cyber bullying or whether the programs need to be modified.

Social Networking

While cyber bulling and violent video games are widely acknowledged as at least thematically related to aggression, social networking is more ubiquitous and likely less harmful. Nonetheless, American teenagers are widely involved in social networking sites and online chat programs. Immersion in these programs, along with the escalating preference for texting and tweeting over telephone calls and letters as a form of communication, has effectively changed the way that teenagers communicate. This new way of communicating has implications for social development, especially relationship building, as well as cognitive development.

Media sources have certainly recognized this possibility. For example, a *BBC News Magazine* article (2013) recently published a piece in which three British teenagers provided their perspectives on social media. They acknowledged that they tend to stay up late communicating with friends, and that frequent immersion in social media has replaced other activities like reading or participating in athletics. Multiple American news outlets have raised these questions and others about youth and social media, sometimes drawing different conclusions about how social media impacts children's development (see, e.g., Etheridge, 2012; Parker-Pope, 2012). Social media is often portrayed as the culprit responsible for stripping children of their childhood, but some have suggested that this technology provides a way for introverted youth to become more extroverted (Youth Resources, 2011).

Researchers have only just begun studying the impact of newer technologies, especially social networking sites, on development. Some of these early studies can shed some light on what future research might reveal. For example, Blais, Craig, Pepler, and Connolly (2008) conducted a longitudinal study of 884 adolescents and found that youths' satisfaction with their friendships and romantic relationships was impacted by the kinds of experiences they had online. Those who reported chatting more with strangers or using the Internet for general entertainment reported lower relationship quality than those who used the Internet to communicate with people they already knew. These and other findings suggest that Internet activity might not always hinder relationship building, but it depends entirely on the kinds of Internet activity that youth are involved in (Blais et al., 2008; Valkenburg & Peter, 2007).

From a policy perspective, research on both cyber bullying and social networking raises questions of how much contact youth should be allowed to have with these technologies and who should regulate their contact. In terms of regulation, there are limits to what the government can do, constitutionally and logistically, to regulate youths' access to social media. Clearly, parents are in the best position to monitor their children's Internet activity. Software developers are continuously creating new products that can help monitor what sites youth visit and what they type. But will the surmounting ability for parental monitoring promote child wellbeing?

Research on the impact of parental monitoring in other contexts has suggested that healthy parental monitoring allows increasing freedoms concurrent with the child's developmental maturity. Offline, studies have linked more parental monitoring with lower amounts of early sexual activity, substance abuse, criminal activity (Huang, Murphy, & Hser, 2011), delinquent friend selection, and the impact of delinquent peers on decisions (Tilton-Weaver, Burk, Kerr, & Stattin, 2013). When participants rated higher levels of parental monitoring, they tended to rate higher quality in their relationship with their parents than when there were low levels of parental monitoring. However, when a child perceived the parent to be excessively controlling, the effect of parental monitoring was reversed and the children were more likely to select delinquent peers and those delinquent peers had a stronger influence over the child (Tilton-Weaver et al., 2013). Studies on parental monitoring and Internet usage have found that higher reported levels of parental monitoring were linked to lower levels of Internet addiction (Lin, Lin, & Wu, 2009). Further research needs to be conducted in the Internet context to fully explore whether parental monitoring can be an effective intervention tool for unhealthy Internet behaviors.

Conclusion

The purpose of this book was to identify the multiple areas of the law in which issues of child wellbeing are directly implicated. In so doing, it was the editors' goal not only to provide a source of information but to contribute to the dialogue between mental health practitioners, researchers, legal actors, and policymakers. We sought to identify common ground between these groups and to clarify the points of disagreement. Ultimately, all of those invested in this topic want the same thing: to craft policies and practices that maintain and promote the wellbeing of children. And the best way to achieve that goal is to communicate with each other: Policymakers need to understand the state of the science, and researchers and mental health practitioners must understand the state of current policy. In respecting each other's roles and contributions to the ultimate goal, that goal can be furthered. These efforts are an essential step in protecting the wellbeing of children who are involved in the legal system.

References

Anderson, C. A., & Bushman, B. J. (2001). Effects of violent video games on aggressive behavior, aggressive cognition, aggressive affect, physiological arousal, and prosocial behavior: A meta-analytic review of the scientific literature. *Psychological Science, 12*, 353–359.

Anderson, C. A., Shibuya, A., Ihori, N., Swing, E. L., Bushman, B. J., Sakamoto, A.,...Saleem, M. (2010). Violent video game effects on aggression, empathy, and prosocial behavior in Eastern and Western countries: A meta-analytic review. *Psychological Bulletin, 136*, 151–173. doi:10.1037/a0018251.

Artis, J. E. (2004). Judging the best interests of the child: Judges accounts of the tender years doctrine. *Law and Society Review, 38*, doi: 10.1111/j.0023-9216.2004.00066.x.

Bagshaw, D. (2007). Reshaping responses to children when parents are separating: Hearing children's voices in the transition. *Australian Social Work, 60*, 450–465. doi:10.1080/03124070701671164.

BBC School Report. (2013, March 21). Teenagers and their sleepless lives. *BBC News Magazine*. Retrieved July 2013, from http://www.bbc.co.uk/news/magazine-21876118.

Blais J. J., Craig, W. M., Pepler, D., & Connolly, J. (2008). Adolescents online: The importance of internet activity choices to salient relationships. *Journal of Youth and Adolescence, 37*, 522–536. doi: 10.1007/s10964-007-9262-7.

Blumenthal, J. A. (2003). Who decides? Privileging public sentiment about justice and the substantive law. *UMKC Law Review, 72*, 1–21.

Brown, J. (2013, February 15). Video games: Violent, yes. But do they make us violent? *PBS NewsHour*. Retrieved July 2013, from http://www.pbs.org/newshour/rundown/2013/02/how-parents-and-policymakers-handle-violent-video-games.html.

Brown v. Entertainment Merchants Association, 559 S. Ct. 1448 (2010).

Canter, A. S., Piage, L. Z., & Shaw, S. (Eds.). (2010). *Helping children at home and school III: Handouts for families and educators*. Besthesda, MD: NASP.

Chamberlain, J. (2009). *The malleability of community sentiment: Contextual explanations for shifts in attitudes toward gay rights* (Ph.D. dissertation). University of Nevada, Reno.

Cohen, G. (2012). Beyond best interests. *Minnesota Law Review, 96*, 1187–1274.

Crosby-Currie, C. A. (1996). Children's involvement in contested custody cases: Practices and experiences of legal and mental health professionals. *Law and Human Behavior, 20*, 289–311.

Emery, R. E. (2007). Rule or Rorschach? Approximating children's best interests. *Child Development Perspectives. 1*, 132–134. doi:10.1111/j.1750-8606.2007.00029.x.

Etheridge, P. (2012, November 27). Young people and social media: Docs examine pitfalls. *CNN*. Retrieved July 2013, from http://www.cnn.com/2012/11/23/health/youth-social-media/index.html

Ferguson, C. J. (2007). The good, the bad and the ugly: A meta-analytic review of positive and negative effects of violent video games. *Psychiatric Quarterly, 78*, 309–316. doi:10.1007/s11126-007-9056-9.

Finkel, N. J. (2001). *Commonsense justice: Jurors' notions of the law*. Cambridge, MA: Harvard University Press.

Freeman, M. (2007). The best interests of the child. In A. Alen, J. Vande Lanotte, E. Verhellen, F. Ang, E. Berghmans, and M. Verhyde (Eds.), *A commentary on the United Nations Convention on the Rights of the Child* (Vol. 3, pp. 25–75). Leiden, The Netherlands: Martinus Nijhoff.

Frolik, L. A., & Whitton, L. S. (2012). The UPC substituted judgment/best interest standard for guardian decisions: A proposal for reform. *University Of Michigan Journal of Law Reform, 45*, 739–760.

Grenoble, R. (2012, October 11). Amanda Todd: Bullied Canadian teen commits suicide after prolonged battle online and in school. *Huffington Post.* Retrieved July 2013, from http://www.huffingtonpost.com/2012/10/11/amanda-todd-suicide-bullying_n_1959909.html.

Hinduja, S., & Patchin, J. W. (2010). Bullying, cyberbullying, and suicide. *Archives of Suicide Research, 14*, 206–221. doi:10.1080/13811118.2010.494133.

Huang, D. C., Murphy, D. A., & Hser, Y. (2011). Parental monitoring during early adolescence deters adolescent sexual initiation: Discrete-time survival mixture analysis. *Journal of Child and Family Studies, 20*, 511–520. doi:10.1007/s10826-010-9418-z.

Kohm, L. M. (2007). Tracing the foundations of the best interests of the child standard in American jurisprudence. *Journal of Law and Family Studies, 10*, 337.

Lin, C., Lin, S., & Wu, C. (2009). The effects of parental monitoring and leisure boredom on adolescents' internet addiction. *Adolescence, 44*, 993–1004.

McConnell, R., & Sim, A. J. (1999). Adjustment to parental divorce: An examination of the differences between counselled and non-counselled children. *British Journal of Guidance and Counselling, 27*, 243–257.

Miller, M. K., Blumenthal, J. A., & Chamberlain, J. (Eds.). (forthcoming). *Handbook of community sentiment*. New York, NY: Springer.

Mnookin, R. (1978). Beyond kiddie libbers and child savers. *Journal of Clinical Child and Adolescent Psychology, 7*, 163–167.

Oliphant, E., Brown, J. H., Cambron, M., & Yankeelov, P. (2002). Measuring children's perceptions of the Families in Transition program (FIT): A qualitative evaluation. *Journal of Divorce and Remarriage, 37*, 157–163. doi:10.1300/J087v37n03_09.

Parker-Pope, T. (2012, January 9). Worrying less about teens, texting and social media. *New York Times.* Retrieved July 2013, from http://well.blogs.nytimes.com/2012/01/09/worrying-less-about-teens-texting-and-social-media/.

Riggs, S. A. (2005). Is the approximation rule in the child's best interests? *Family Court Review, 43*, 481–493. doi:10.1111/j.1744-1617.2005.00048.x.

Ritenhouse, D. (2011). What's orientation got to do with it? The best interest of the child standard and legal bias against gay and lesbian parents. *Journal of Poverty, 15*, 309–329. doi:10.1080/10875549.2011.589260.

Tilton-Weaver, L. C., Burk, W. J., Kerr, M., & Stattin, H. (2013). Can parental monitoring and peer management reduce the selection or influence of delinquent peers? Testing the question using a dynamic social network approach. *Developmental Psychology, 49*, 1–14 doi:10.1037/a0031854.

Valkenburg, P. M., & Peter, J. (2007). Online communication and adolescent wellbeing: Testing the stimulation versus the displacement hypothesis. *Journal of Computer-Mediated Communication, 12*, 1169–1182. doi:10.1111/j.1083-6101.2007.00368.x.

Wilcox, B. L., Weisz, P., & Miller, M. K. (2005). Practical guidelines for educating policymakers: The family impact seminar as an approach to advancing the interests of children and families in the policy arena. *Journal of Clinical Child and Adolescent Psychology, 34,* 638–645. doi:10.1207/s15374424jccp3404_6.

Youth Resources. (2011, August 15). Research confirms social media's impact on adolescent development. *Evansville Courier and Press.* Retrieved July 2013, from http://www.courierpress.com/news/2011/aug/15/research-confirms-social-medias-impact-on/.

Index

A
abuse
    child abuse, 5, 24, 35, 73–75, 83, 84–87, 100, 124, 126, 128–129, 133, 139, 156, 160–161, 165, 166, 174, 175, 192–194, 196, 197, 205, 206, 210, 211, 216, 218, 220, 227–229, 206, 210–233
    domestic violence, 20, 144, 159, 162
    sexual abuse, 8, 67, 71, 83, 85, 128, 162
    substance abuse, 84, 85, 87, 97, 98, 106, 117, 124, 176, 178, 181–182, 265
Adam Walsh Act, 67–68, 78
adolescents/adolescence, 13–14, 16–18, 20, 21, 23, 24, 25, 26, 33, 42, 46, 50–63, 68, 73, 74, 77, 87, 103, 104, 106, 122, 124, 130, 146, 235, 235, 249, 255, 257, 259, 263, 264
aggression, 44–45, 83, 87, 90, 93, 94, 98, 158, 177, 263, 264
A. H. v. State of Florida, 72, 77
amenability to treatment. *See* rehabilitation
American Psychological Association's Ethical Principles of Psychologists and Code of Conduct, 110, 115
AMBER Alert, 240
attachment, 22–23, 158, 176, 179
attorneys, 20, 35, 38, 39, 40, 41, 53, 56, 59, 61, 63, 72, 125, 128, 129, 131, 145, 148, 150, 161, 162, 165, 228, 250, 255, 258, 261
attribution theory, 74, 211–214, 217–220, 222, 225, 227, 230, 231, 247

B
Bayview Correctional Facility, 178, 186
Bellah v. Greenson, 108, 109
best interests of the child, 6, 50, 53, 61, 98, 122, 124, 127, 128, 129, 130, 141, 147, 149, 150, 151, 155, 159–166, 192–196, 198–200, 202, 203–207, 255, 256, 257–259, 262
    legal standard, 141, 193–196
Bram v. US, 52

Breed v. Jones, 36
Brown v. Mississippi, 52
bullying, 45, 264–265
Brown v. Entertainment Merchants Association, 263

C
Civil Commitment Statutes, 113
Charles McGee Center, 87, 88, 89, 94, 96, 98
child custody. *See* divorce
child custody agreements, 138, 139–140, 141, 142, 143, 145, 147, 149–150
child-focused mediation, 131
child-inclusive mediation, 131
child maltreatment. *See* abuse
child protection, 17, 23, 164, 166, 201, 202, 205, 206, 230, 257
Child Support and Visitation Enforcement Office, 139, 147–151
  costs and benefits of, 148
  evaluation of, 150–151
  operations, 148–150
child visitation. *See* visitation
clinical guidelines, 104
Coker v. Moemeka, 142
community sentiment. *See* sentiment
confessions, 50–53, 54, 59, 61, 62, 63
conflict, parental, 123, 130, 131, 146, 157
confidentiality, 109, 110, 114
Constitution, 4, 36, 37, 39, 40, 83, 105, 142, 160, 238, 239
coping skills, 33, 28, 83, 84, 85, 92, 96, 99, 173, 177, 195, 205
counseling, 87, 91, 93–95, 98, 99, 100, 145, 165, 177, 179, 180, 182
court-appointed special advocates, 194
court case management, 165–166
culpability, 36, 39
culture, 6, 192–194, 195, 199–201, 202, 203, 204–205, 206, 257
custody evaluators, 129–130
cycle of offending. *See* intergenerational offending

D
Data Safety and Monitoring Boards, 107, 113
Delinquency, 16, 21, 22, 23, 24, 33–34, 67, 70, 83–100, 103–116, 125, 129, 176, 203, 255
Department of Social Services. *See* Child protection
deterrence, 70, 98
developmental maturity, 41, 45
development, 6, 13–29, 52, 123–126, 255–6, 257, 265
  biological influences, 14–15
  cognitive development, 19–21
  environmental influences, 15
  physical development, 17–19, 210
  social and emotional development, 21–26, 146
distributive justice, 143, 144, 145, 150
diversion programs, 38
divorce, 20, 22, 24, 25, 121–134, 146, 149, 155–170, 262
domestic violence. *See* abuse
drug courts, 85, 185
Dusky v. US, 40

E
Ecological Systems Theory, 15
education, 84, 87, 92, 98, 99, 100, 176, 198–199, 202, 203–204, 236, 261, 262
election, 237
emotional development/trauma, 13, 14, 16, 18, 19, 20, 21, 26, 33, 42, 44, 45, 52, 63, 84, 85, 92, 99, 106, 109, 112, 131, 132, 146, 147, 157, 158, 160, 162, 174, 176, 179, 184, 196
empowerment rationale, 122, 123
enlightenment rationale, 122, 123, 124
environment, 99
ethics, 6, 53, 103, 104, 105, 109–110, 111–113, 115, 203, 204, 216, 247
ethical guidelines, 104
evaluations
  psychological, 87
  substance abuse, 87

F
false convictions, 50–51
family, 84, 85, 87, 91, 121, 202
family court system, 138
Family Impact Seminars, 261
Family Service Program, 179
Family Support Act, 140
fathers' rights, 141, 143, 156, 162
focus groups, 197, 206
Food and Drug Administration, 235
foster care, 173, 175, 178

G
gender, 25, 43–45, 83–100, 106, 174
    bias, 44, 138, 139, 142–143
    differences, 149, 173, 176
    roles, 86, 141
Girls' Program, 86–87, 92, 93, 96, 97
Girl Scouts Beyond Bars, 94, 179
Graham v. Florida, 33, 50
guardian ad litem, 127, 128–129

H
health, 87, 89, 92, 100, 234–240
history
    divorce, 121, 122, 139
    juvenile courts, 5
    juvenile justice, 5, 83
    psychological development, 5, 125
human papilloma virus (HPV). *See* vaccines

I
identity, 24–26, 86, 158
immigrants. *See* immigration
immigration, 192–196, 203–206
incarceration, parental 84, 173–187
    consequences of, 174
    precursors of, 174
    programs for, 177–178
infants/infancy, 17, 19, 22, 23, 24–25
In re Gault, 6, 36
In re Winship, 36
intergenerational offending, 84, 176
interrogation, 50–63
    length, 62
    parents, 59, 61
    race, 60, 61
    recordings, 62, 63
    stress, 62
interview, 121, 122, 124–127, 130, 133
Institutional Review Boards, 107, 113, 115
    adverse events, 107
    human subjects/participants, 107

J
Jacob Wetterling Crimes Against Children and Sexually Violent Offender Registration Act, 67
Jackson v. Hobbs, 50
J.D.B. v. North Carolina, 6, 21, 33, 50
judges, 77, 124–125, 126, 127–128, 130, 161, 236–237, 239, 258, 258, 261
judgment and decision-making, 20, 21, 24, 72–76
Juvenile Court Act, 34–35, 75
juvenile competency, 40–41
juvenile justice system, 34–37, 71
    punitive approaches, 35–36, 184–185
    processing, 37–40
    rehabilitative approaches, 36–37, 177–178, 180, 185
juvenile offenders, 33–34, 203 (*see also* delinquency)
    sex offenders, 66–82

K
Kent v. US, 35, 39

L
law, defined 2–3
lawyer. *See* attorney
legal abilities, 21
legitimacy, 4, 98, 139, 143, 144, 150, 151, 182, 234, 237
Lestenkof v. Lestenkof, 142

M
maternal incarceration. *See* parental incarceration
McGee Center. *See* Charles McGee Center
McKeiver v. PA, 36
measurements, 3
media, 16, 50, 59, 77, 176, 262, 264, 265

mediation, 85, 123, 130–131, 139, 148, 149, 150, 262
Megan's law, 67, 240
memory, 125
Meier v. Ross General Hospital, 108
mental health, 42–43, 84, 105–106, 111, 114, 173, 176, 177, 179, 195
mental illness. *See* Mental Health
migration psychology, 195–196, 205
Miller v. Alabama, 6, 33, 36, 39, 50
Miranda rights, 21, 50, 51, 52, 53, 54, 59, 256
M.L.B v. S.L.J, 142
Model Standards of Practice for Family and Divorce Mediation, 130
morality, 21, 67, 76, 199, 200, 203, 213, 216, 234, 236, 237, 238–240, 242, 245, 246, 248, 250
morality based law, 238–239
moral outrage, 239
Multidisciplinary Assessment Model, 35
Myer v. Nebraska, 142

N
Nally v. Grace Community Church of the Valley, 109
National Association of School Psychologists, 262
National Survey of Child and Adolescent Wellbeing, 192
National Youth Screening & Assessment Project, 41
Nebraska Correctional Center for Women, 178, 186
norms, 86, 98

O
obesity, 18, 210–233
Office of Human Research Protections, 115
Office of Sex Offender Sentencing, Monitoring, Apprehending, Registering, and Tracking (SMART), 68
O'Sullivan v. Presbyterian Hospital in City of New York at Columbia Medical Center, 108
Osmanagic v. Osmanagic, 194

P
parens patriae, 34
parent-child relationships, 22–23, 176
parental alienation, 138–139, 155–170
parenting assessments, 163–164
parental monitoring, 23, 265
parental stress, 177, 179
parenting styles, 23
parenting education, 163, 177, 178
parenting plans, 162–163
peers, 20, 23–24, 265
personality disorders, 157
Piaget, 19–20
Planned Parenthood, 90, 93, 95
Planned Parenthood v Casey, 234, 237, 239
Plessy v. Ferguson, 238
prejudice, 72–76, 176, 214
prison nurseries, 182–183
procedural justice, 143–144, 145, 150, 237
psychological problems. *See* mental health
psychology, defined 1–2

R
race/ethnicity, 25, 73–74, 106, 195, 199–200, 202–205
Rebecca Project for Human Rights, 186
recidivism, 24, 69–70, 100, 144, 177–178, 179, 180, 184, 187
rehabilitation, 24, 42–43, 69, 84, 86, 97, 98, 99, 100, 178, 180, 184, 185, 186, 256
relationships, 85, 87, 91, 93, 96, 121, 126
religion, 86, 236
    research ethics, 109, 110–111
Code of Ethics of the National Association of Social Workers, 109
Residential Treatment and Transition Center, 178
restorative justice, 84–85, 97–99, 100
retribution, 76, 181
Roper v. Simmons, 6, 33, 36, 50
Rule of Sevens, 5, 34
run-away. *See* status offenses,

S

self-destructive behavior, 83, 159. *See also* suicide
sentiment, 6, 71–76, 121–134, 144, 186, 193, 211, 224–226, 234–240, 259–260
sexual activity, 66, 67, 235, 265
sex offender registries, 67
   state policies, 68
   consequences of registering, 70
   public support, 71–77
Sex Offender Registration and Notification Act (SORNA), 66, 67, 77
Department of Justice Supplemental Guidelines, 77–78
sexting, 70, 75, 77
sexual orientation, 75
shaming, 238
Skinner v. Oklahoma, 141, 142
social context theory, 86, 99–100
social networking, 264
social science, 53, 85, 86, 229
Society for the Reformation of Delinquents, 34
socioeconomic status, 74, 146, 175, 203
status offenses, 37, 83, 84, 85
stigma. *See* prejudice
substance abuse. *See* abuse
suicide, 4, 39, 43, 46, 70, 103–110, 263
   intent, 111, 114
   protective factors, 106
   suicidality, 103–104, 107, 111, 112, 113, 115
   suicide risk, 105–106, 108, 113–114
stress, 16, 18–19, 22, 158, 175, 176, 196
Sullivan report, 63
Supreme Court, 4, 33, 35, 36, 39, 40, 45, 50, 51, 52, 141, 142, 143, 151, 237, 238, 239, 256
Swisher v. Brady, 36

T

Tarasoff v. Regents of University of California, 108
Technology, 262, 263, 264
tender years doctrine, 122, 141, 258
testimony, 6, 127
therapeutic jurisprudence, 4, 84–85, 97–9, 100, 143, 144–146, 149, 150, 151, 180–184, 187, 259
therapy. *See* counseling
therapeutic interventions, 42–43, 45
transfers to criminal court, 35, 38–40
Troxel v. Granville, 141

U

Uniform Crime Reports, 60
Uniform Marriage and Divorce Act, 122, 127, 141
United Nations Convention on the Rights of the Child, 141, 155, 159–161, 193
Utilitarianism, 76

V

Vaccines, 18 234–240, 260
video games, 262
visitation, 138–151, 157, 160, 162, 164–166, 177, 178, 179, 183
   enforcement, 138, 145, 148, 166
   interference, 138–139, 142
Vistica v. Presbyterian Hospital, 108

W

Waiver. *See* transfers to criminal court
War on Drugs, 174–175, 187
Wisconsin v. Yoder, 142
wishes of the child, 20–21, 160, 164–165

Y

Yarborough v. Alvarado, 50, 51

CPSIA information can be obtained
at www.ICGtesting.com
Printed in the USA
BVHW040506031219
565453BV00008B/124/P